2025–2026 TOWN BRANCH
WRITING COLLECTION

ELEVENTH EDITION | UNIVERSITY OF KENTUCKY DEPARTMENT OF WRITING, RHETORIC, AND DIGITAL STUDIES

Town Branch Writing Collection

Eleventh Edition
University of Kentucky Department of Writing, Rhetoric, and Digital Studies
2025–2026

Copyright © by University of Kentucky Department of Writing, Rhetoric, and Digital Studies
Copyright © by Van-Griner, LLC

Cover Image: © Taiga/Bigstock
Photos and other illustrations are owned by Van-Griner Learning or used under license.

All rights reserved. No part of this book may be reproduced or transmitted in any form or by any means, electronic or mechanical, including photocopying, recording or by any information storage and retrieval system, without written permission from the author and publisher.

Printed in the United States of America
10 9 8 7 6 5 4 3 2 1
ISBN: 978-1-64565-653-1

Van-Griner Learning
Cincinnati, Ohio
www.van-griner.com

President: Dreis Van Landuyt
Senior Project Manager: Maria Walterbusch
Customer Care Lead: Lauren Wendel

Ridolfo 65-653-1 Su25
338388
Copyright © 2026

Brief Table of Contents

Chapter 1 Rhetoric 1

Chapter 2 Rhetorical Situation 29

Chapter 3 Audience 45

Chapter 4 The Process of Composition 83

Chapter 5 Reading and Responding 119

Chapter 6 Rhetorical Analysis 135

Chapter 7 Argument 149

Chapter 8 Using Evidence 177

Chapter 9 Research 201

Chapter 10 Citation 229

Chapter 11 Writing with Style 253

Chapter 12 Public Speaking 283

Chapter 13 Visual Rhetoric and Design 311

Chapter 14 Understanding Genres 349

Chapter 15 How to Make Your Own Documentary 371

Chapter 16 Making an Informative Podcast 391

Chapter 17 Considering Accessibility and Disability 401

Chapter 18 ChatGPT and LLMs and Their Place in Writing Classes 421

Chapter 19 Navigating Team Dynamics in the Writing Classroom 427

Index 439

Table of Contents

Acknowledgments ... xix
Changes in the Eleventh Edition ... xix
To the Student ... xx
Major in Writing, Rhetoric, and Digital Studies ... xxi
Minor in Writing, Rhetoric, and Digital Studies ... xxii
Minor in Professional and Technical Writing ... xxiii
Pre-Law ... xxiv

Chapter 1 Rhetoric — 1

- **A Brief History of Rhetoric** ... 2
- **What Kinds of Rhetoric Are There?** ... 4
  - Types of Evidence ... 7
    - Ethos ... 7
    - Pathos ... 8
    - Logos ... 11
      - Inductive Reasoning ... 11
      - Deductive Reasoning ... 13
  - Stasis ... 16
    - Discovering Stasis Claims ... 17
      - Question of Fact: Did I Actually Take Your Umbrella? ... 18
      - Question of Definition: Was the Act One of Theft, or Was It Something Else? ... 18
      - Questions of Quality: Was My Act a Terrible Act? ... 18
      - Question of Cause/Effect: What Caused This Act? What Effects Did It Have? ... 19
      - Question of Proposal: What Should We Do? ... 19
    - How Can You Use Stasis Questions to Understand Others' Arguments? ... 19
    - Using Stasis for Inventing Arguments ... 20
- **Sophistic Appeals** ... 22
  - The Sophists ... 22
    - Mythos ... 23

       Logos 23
       Nomos 24
   Video Resources 27
       Former Mayor Jim Gray on the Rhetorical Force of Words 27
       Mayor Jim Gray on Using Pathos and Emotional
       Persuasion to Change Perceptions of Place 27
       Kevin Patterson on the Everyday Importance of Rhetoric 27
       Kevin Patterson on the Importance of Storytelling and Perception 27
   Notes 28
   Works Cited 28

Chapter 2 Rhetorical Situation   29

   Elements of a Rhetorical Situation 30
       Exigence 31
           How Can Thinking about Exigence Improve
           Your Ability to Persuade Others? 32
               From the Very Beginning, Explain Your Message 33
               Explain Why Your Message Is Needed 33
               Help Your Audience to Visualize What Should
               Be Accomplished in Response to the Exigence 34
       Audience 34
           Types of Audiences 34
               General Public Audience 35
               Target Audience 35
               The Power of an Audience 37
       Constraints 39
           Types of Constraints 40
               Genre Constraints 40
               Material Constraints 41
               Cultural Constraints 41
           Purposely Breaking Convention—When Constraints Are Undermined 41
   Rhetorical Situations and the WRD Classroom 42
   Notes 43

Chapter 3 Audience — 45

- Appeal to Conventions, Genres, Expectations ... 47
- Appeal to Interests ... 50
- Appeal to Stickiness ... 52
- Appeal to Knowledge ... 54
  - Allusions in Politics ... 56
  - Allusions in Popular Culture ... 58
- Appeal to Provocation ... 60
- Appeal to Language ... 64
  - Using Gender Neutral Pronouns ... 67
    - Review ... 69
- Appeal to Clarity ... 70
  - Student Writing Example: "Writing on the Wall" by Catherine A. Brereton ... 72
- Video Resources ... 79
  - Stella Parks on Writing and Audiences ... 79
  - Griffin VanMeter Describes How Social Media and Audiences Can Help Spread a Media Campaign ... 80
- Notes ... 80
- Works Cited ... 81

Chapter 4 The Process of Composition — 83

- Invention: Starting from Scratch ... 85
  - Finding an Argument (or *Stasis*) ... 86
    - Brainstorming ... 87
  - Reading and Making Notes ... 89
  - Responding ... 89
    - Pointed Conversations ... 90
    - Reader Response ... 90
  - Moving ... 91
  - Cubing ... 92
- Arrangement: Planning for an Argument ... 93
  - Outlining ... 93
- Following a Classical Template ... 94

- Organizing Your Thoughts 96
- Assembly: Constructing Your Claims 98
    - Drafting 99
    - Binge Writing 99
    - Scheduled Writing 100
    - Sprint Writing 100
    - Spartan Writing 101
  - Framing Your Argument 102
    - Introductions 102
    - Conclusions 107
- Revision: Improving Your Approach 109
  - Revising 110
    - The Argument's Structure 110
    - The Auditor's Understanding 111
    - The Writer's Style 111
  - Editing 112
    - Using Lanham's Paramedic Method 112
    - Using AI-Assisted Writing Apps 115
- The Recursive Composition Process 116
- Video Resources 117
    - Mayor Jim Gray on Using Writing to Solve Problems 117
    - Stella Parks on Her Writing Process 117
    - Stella Parks on Writing Proposals 117
    - Griffin VanMeter on Using Writing as a Creative Process 118
- Notes 118
- Works Cited 118

Chapter 5 Reading and Responding — 119

- Can You Think in Questions? 120
- Reading Reports and Editorials 121
- The "So What?" Question 125
  - How Do Emotions Fit In? 126
- Preparing Questions for Peer Review 128
- Responding to Peers' Work 129
  - Peer Review Checklist 131
    - Global 131
    - Local 132
- Notes 134

Chapter 6 Rhetorical Analysis — 135

- Analyzing Texts 136
- Analyzing Arguments 139
- Rhetorical Analysis Exercises (The Progymnasmata) 140
  - Fable 141
  - Narrative 141
  - Chreia 142
  - Maxim 142
  - Common Topic 142
  - Refutation 142
  - Confirmation 143
  - Encomium 143
  - Invective 143
  - Comparison 143
  - Characterization 143
  - Description 144
  - Thesis 144
  - Law 144
- Rhetorical Analysis of Spaces 145
- A Quick User's Guide to Rhetorical Analysis of Texts 145
- Notes 147

Chapter 7 Argument — 149

- Argument Begins in Agreement 150
- Argument Requires a Claim 153
- Evidence 154
- Warrants 157
- Logical Argumentation 159
- Fallacies 163
  - Deductive Fallacies 164
    - Of Relevance 164
    - Of Presumption 164
    - Of Grammar 165
  - Inductive Fallacies 165
    - Of Weak Induction 165
    - Of False Analogy 166
- Stakeholders 167
  - How Do You Find Stakeholders? 168
- Stakeholder Analysis 169
- Dealing with Opposing Arguments[5] 169
  - Identifying Opposing Arguments 171
  - Acknowledging Opposing Arguments 172
  - Critiquing Opposing Arguments 173
  - Proposing Your Own Solutions 175
- Notes 176

Chapter 8 Using Evidence — 177

- Step One—Review: What Do I Have? 179
  - Case Study 1: Judith Miller's Reporting on Weapons of Mass Destruction ... 183
- Step Two—Reflect: What Does It Mean? 184
  - Case Study 2: Media Misunderstands Supreme Court's Obamacare Vote 187
- Step Three—Respond: What Do I Do with It? 189
  - Case Study 3: CaroMont Regional Medical Center's Rebranding Campaign .. 191
  - Case Study 4: The Fabrications of Stephen Glass 196

Step Four—Revise: How Do I Make It Better? 198
Notes 199

Chapter 9 Research   201

How Do You Start Research? 204
Different Kinds of Research: Primary versus Secondary 206
   Doing Primary Research 207
      Using Observations 209
      Creating Surveys 209
      Conducting Interviews 210
         Does My Topic Really Call for an Interview? 210
         How Can I Find the Right Expert? 211
         How Do I Ask for an Interview? 211
         How Do I Interview Well? 212
      Using Archives 214
      A Word about Ethical Primary Research 216
      Student Writing Example: "The Men Behind the Dust" by Sheldon Parrott 216
   Doing Secondary Research 217
      Sites for Secondary Research 218
         Libraries 218
         Electronic Archives 220
         Here's a Sampling of E-Archives Beyond the UK Library's Links 223
Doing Online Research: Why *Wikipedia* Is Not Bad for You 224
Wikipedia *224*
Evaluating Online Sources for Credibility 226
Video Resources 226
   Kevin Patterson on Doing "Research" 226
Notes 227

Chapter 10 Citation — 229

- What Is Citation, Anyway? — 230
- Using Sources — 231
- Roles of Citation — 233
- Weaving — 238
- Citation Styles — 239
  - Some Style Resources — 240
- How to Create a Works Cited Page and Cite Common Sources Using MLA — 243
  - Works Cited — 243
    - Author — 243
    - Title of Source — 244
    - Title of Container — 244
    - Other Contributors — 245
    - Version — 245
    - Number — 245
    - Publisher — 245
    - Publication Date — 246
    - Location — 246
    - For More Than One Work by an Author — 247
    - For Work with No Known Author — 247
    - For More Than One Author — 247
    - Citing Electronic Sources — 248
      - Citing an Entire Website — 248
      - A Page on a Website — 248
      - An Image (including a painting, sculpture, or photograph) — 248
      - An Article in a Web Magazine — 249
      - An Article in an Online Scholarly Journal — 249
      - Article in an Online-Only Scholarly Journal — 249
      - Article in an Online Scholarly Journal That Also Appears in Print — 249
      - An Article from an Online Database (or other electronic subscription service) — 250
      - E-mail (including e-mail interviews) — 250
      - A Listserv, Discussion Group, or Blog Posting — 250

      A Post on X (formerly Twitter) 250
      A *YouTube* Video 251
    Other Common Sources 251
      Interviews 251
Notes 252

Chapter 11 Writing with Style   253

The Appeal of Style 254
Voice 255
    Perspective 256
    Tone and Diction 257
    Figurative and Descriptive Language 258
    Breaking the Rules 260
    Writing with Dialect 261
Syntax 264
    Choosing Effective Subjects 265
    Choosing Impactful Verbs 267
      Passive Voice 268
      Nominalizations 269
    Building an Effective Sentence 270
      Simple Sentences 271
      Compound Sentences 272
      Compound Subjects and Verbs 272
      Subordination 273
Rhythm and Elegance 275
    Emphasis 275
      Strategies for Shifting Emphasis 276
    Punctuation 277
    Coordination and Balance 279
Conclusion 281
Notes 282

Chapter 12 Public Speaking — 283

- Organization — 285
  - Beginnings — 285
  - Middles — 287
  - Endings — 288
  - Organizing a Group Presentation — 289
- Audience Analysis — 291
- Working with Visuals and Presentation Aids — 292
  - Audience First — 292
  - Constraints — 293
  - Presentation Aids: Media and Design — 294
    - Simplicity — 294
    - Continuity — 296
    - Variety — 296
  - Visuals — 297
    - Informative Visuals — 299
    - Other Props — 299
    - Verbal Citations — 300
      - Captioning Images — 301
      - Citing Sources — 301
      - Finishing Up with Sources — 301
- Delivery — 302
- Practicing and Preparation — 304
- Self and Peer Evaluations — 306
  - Self-Evaluation — 306
  - Peer Evaluation — 307
    - Feedback on Content — 308
    - Feedback on Organization and Structure — 308
    - Feedback on Delivery — 308
- Notes — 309

Chapter 13 Visual Rhetoric and Design — 311
- Close Looking — 314
- Learning to See — 318
  - ... and How to Talk about It — 319
- Content and Context — 319
- Form — 321
  - Reading: Formal Elements of Visual Design — 323
    - Form and Content Activities — 324
- Visual Arrangement — 327
- Unity — 328
- Emphasis — 330
- More Arrangement Techniques — 331
  - Juxtaposition — 332
  - Grids — 334
  - Two Kinds of Balance — 334
  - Visual Hierarchy — 336
- Media Literacy and Visual Rhetoric — 340
  - Goals of Media Literacy — 341
  - How to Practice Media Literacy—Ask Questions — 341
  - Media Manipulation and Disinformation — 343
- Notes — 348

Chapter 14 Understanding Genres — 349
- Genres as Form, Function, and Action — 350
  - Genres Are about Categorizing — 350
  - Genres Are about Negotiation — 351
  - Genres Are Malleable — 351
  - Genres Are Tied to Social Actions — 352
- Naming, Categories, Knowledge, and Existence — 354
- Argument, Negotiation, and the Malleability of Genres — 355
- Genres and Social Action — 358

    Strategies for Understanding Genres 360
        Names, Categories, and Forms 361
        Histories of Negotiation 362
        Development and Change 362
        Actions and Impact 363
    Genre and Audience 363
    Wikipedia as a Genre 364
    Notes 368

Chapter 15 How to Make Your Own Documentary   371

    One: Pre-Production 372
    Two: The Shoot 377
    Three: Post Production 379
    Bibliography 384
    Nuts and Bolts 384
    Slightly More Aesthetic/Philosophical
    (for students who want to dig a little deeper) 385
    Even More Philosophical (but essential if you really want to keep doing this) .. 386
    A Fistful of Documentaries 386
        Somewhat Experimental 386
        Cinéma Vérité 387
        Engaged History and Activism 388
    Autobiography 388
    Kentucky 389

Chapter 16 Making an Informative Podcast   391

    Script 395
    Practice 397
    Recording 398
    Notes 399

Chapter 17 Considering Accessibility and Disability — 401

- Introduction to Accessibility and Disability 402
  - A Short History of ADA and the Disability Rights Movement 402
- Person-First vs. Identity-First Language: Listening to Disabled Activists and Using their Language — 403
  - The Difference of Opinions Between PFL and IFL 404
  - Crip Theory 406
  - Identifying Support Groups Versus Hate Groups 406
- Terms to Avoid 408
  - Terms to Avoid 409
  - Terms to Use With Caution 411
- Activity 413
- Creating Inclusive Digital Texts 416
  - Photographs, Charts, and Illustrations 416
  - Hyperlinks 417
  - Making PDFs and Digital Files Accessible 417
  - Video and Audio Files 418
  - Organizing Accessible Content 419
  - Additional Notes on Accessibility 419
  - Works Cited 419

Chapter 18 ChatGPT and LLMs and Their Place in Writing Classes — 421

- Academic Integrity 422
- Privacy Concerns 423
- Additional GPT and LLM Concerns 424
- Responsible Use 425
- Notes 426

Chapter 19 Navigating Team Dynamics in the Writing Classroom — 427

- Teamwork in WRD 110 and WRD 111 428
  - Team Contracts 428
  - Coordinating Time to Meet Outside the Classroom 429
  - Communication and Communication Modalities 430

- Strategies for Smooth(er) Sailing 431
  - Back Scheduling 431
  - Delegating Tasks 431
  - Notetaking During Team Meetings 432
  - Using Collaborative Applications 432
  - Setting Meeting Agendas and Goals 432
  - Routine Check-Ins 433
- Additional Teamwork Challenges and How to Work Through Them 433
  - Procrastination 433
  - Unproductive Feedback 434
- Team and Self Evaluations 436
- Notes 437

Index — 439

ACKNOWLEDGMENTS

On behalf of the Department of Writing, Rhetoric, and Digital Studies (WRD), we thank the following people for their contributions to this book: Joshua Abboud, B Bailey, John Barbour, Phil Barnett, Beth Connors-Manke, Craig Crowder, Megan Pillow Davis, Rachel Elliott, Roslyn Fleming, Margaret Frymire, Steven Gerencser, David Gifford, Ashleigh Hardin, Drew Heverin, Jordan Honeyblue, Rachel Hoy, Jennifer L. Hudgens, Deborah Kirkman, Leslie Malland, Tom Marksbury, Brian McNely, Emily Naser-Hall, Brandy Scalise, Jeff Rice, Jenny Rice, Jim Ridolfo, Justin Roberts, Katherine Rogers-Carpenter, Krystin Santos, Lisa Schroot, Nathan Shank, Jamie Stoike, Brittany Sulzener, Andrew Thibaudeau, Brandon West, Elizabeth Wright, and Aubrey Keller. We also thank our editor Maria Walterbusch at Van-Griner Publishing for her work on editing and layout design. We especially thank Dr. Tom Shown for his generous donation to WRD. Without his support and encouragement, this textbook would not be possible.

CHANGES IN THE ELEVENTH EDITION

The 11th edition includes updates to out of date content including web links, and images. Some chapters have been reorganized or combined for clarity. **Web links** for the current edition are available by chapter at http://wrd.as.uky.edu/townbranch. If you have feedback on the 11th edition that you would like to share, please e-mail j.abboud@uky.edu.

TO THE STUDENT

I am excited to welcome you to the University of Kentucky and this Composition and Communication course (WRD 110, 111, or 112). While this WRD course(s) satisfy the first-year general education requirement for Composition and Communication in the UK Core, the Department of Writing, Rhetoric, and Digital Studies (WRD) also offers a B.A. or B.S. in professional writing, digital design, and rhetorical theory. If you are interested in these subjects but are worried about the time commitment of a major, the Department also offers a less intensive WRD Minor or a minor in Professional and Technical Communication.

If any of these areas of study interest you, contact WRD Director of Undergraduate Studies Dr. Craig Crowder. His office is on the 13th floor of Patterson Office Tower and his e-mail cacr223@uky.edu. In the pages that follow, you will find descriptions of all three degree programs and additional information at http://wrd.as.uky.edu.

On behalf of all WRD faculty, we wish you success in your studies at the University of Kentucky.

Sincerely,

Jim Ridolfo
Chair, Department of Writing, Rhetoric, and Digital Studies

WRITING, RHETORIC, AND DIGITAL STUDIES

WHAT CAN A WRD MAJOR DO FOR YOU?

A Bachelor of Arts or Bachelor of Science degree in Writing, Rhetoric, and Digital Studies (WRD) will make you more competitive and successful in *any* career, especially the increasing number of professions that demand high-level writing abilities. Grounded in the traditions and art of rhetoric, WRD majors learn writing and persuasion for technological landscapes built on change. An excellent primary major for careers that require strong critical thinking and written communication across various media (print, digital, visual), WRD is also the perfect double major for students who want to couple writing with another course of study.

The World Moves Fast. Don't Major in Slow. Choose WRD.

WRD MAJORS CAN AND WILL:

- Analyze public arguments in all media
- Receive intensive instruction in writing
- Understand cultural traditions in language, writing, and visual expression
- Produce written, aural, and visual texts that address public concerns
- Study with nationally recognized, locally respected, award-winning faculty

WRD MAJORS GO ON TO WORK IN:

- Freelance writing
- Technical writing
- Public relations
- Business & entrepreneurship
- Product management
- Strategic marketing
- Social media marketing
- Community advocacy
- Literacy Education
- Higher Education
- Grant writing
- Publishing
- Editing
- Medicine and the health care industry
- Politics
- Law

Minor in WRD.

Nearly every profession values strong skills in writing, visual communication, and persuasion. You can develop these skills with a Minor in Writing, Rhetoric, and Digital Studies, and add real value to your résumé.

3 Easy Steps.

1. Declare the Minor by visiting the A&S Advisors in POT 202
2. Take WRD 300 — Introduction to Writing, Rhetoric, and Digital Studies
3. Take 5 more courses: 3 at the 300 or 400 level, and 2 more at *any* level (200 and above)

Have you already taken a WRD course or two, beyond the 100 level? **They count**. Questions? Ask! — Dr. Kishonna Gray - unicorn@uky.edu | @UKWRD | wrd.as.uky.edu

You're filled with bright ideas about how to change the world. Make sure that employers and colleagues hear them, understand them, and *act* on them.

Minor in Professional and Technical Writing.

The most important skills that employers want universities to emphasize are (a) critical thinking and analytical reasoning, (b) the ability to analyze and solve complex problems, and (c) the ability to communicate effectively in writing (Hart Research, 2015). These are *exactly* the skills you'll develop and practice with a Minor in PTW.

3 Easy Steps.

1. Declare the Minor by visiting the A&S Advisors in POT 202
2. Take WRD 204, WRD 300, WRD 306, & WRD 406
3. Choose 2 more courses from WRD 203, WRD 208, WRD 301, WRD 304, WRD 305, WRD 310, WRD 322, WRD 405, or WRD 408

Have you already taken WRD 203 or WRD 204? **They count**. Questions? Ask! — Dr. Kishonna Gray - unicorn@uky.edu | @UKWRD | wrd.as.uky.edu

Are you Pre-Law?
Welcome to WRD.

The study of law is the study of **rhetoric**—argumentation, persuasion, and advocacy.

The Department of Writing, Rhetoric, and Digital Studies (**WRD**) offers pre-law students intensive instruction in these areas, and in written communication and research, through courses such as

WRD 301: Style for Writers
WRD 322: Rhetoric and Argument
WRD 422: Public Advocacy
WRD 320: Rhetorical Theory and History
WRD 420: Rhetorical Traditions
WRD 418: Legal Writing

WRD is an **ideal major or minor** for pre-law students, and a complementary **double major** for pre-law students in Political Science, History, Philosophy, or English.

Have you taken WRD 304? **You're already on your way to a major or minor in WRD**.

Questions? Ask! — Dr. Kishonna Gray - unicorn@uky.edu | @UKWRD | wrd.as.uky.edu

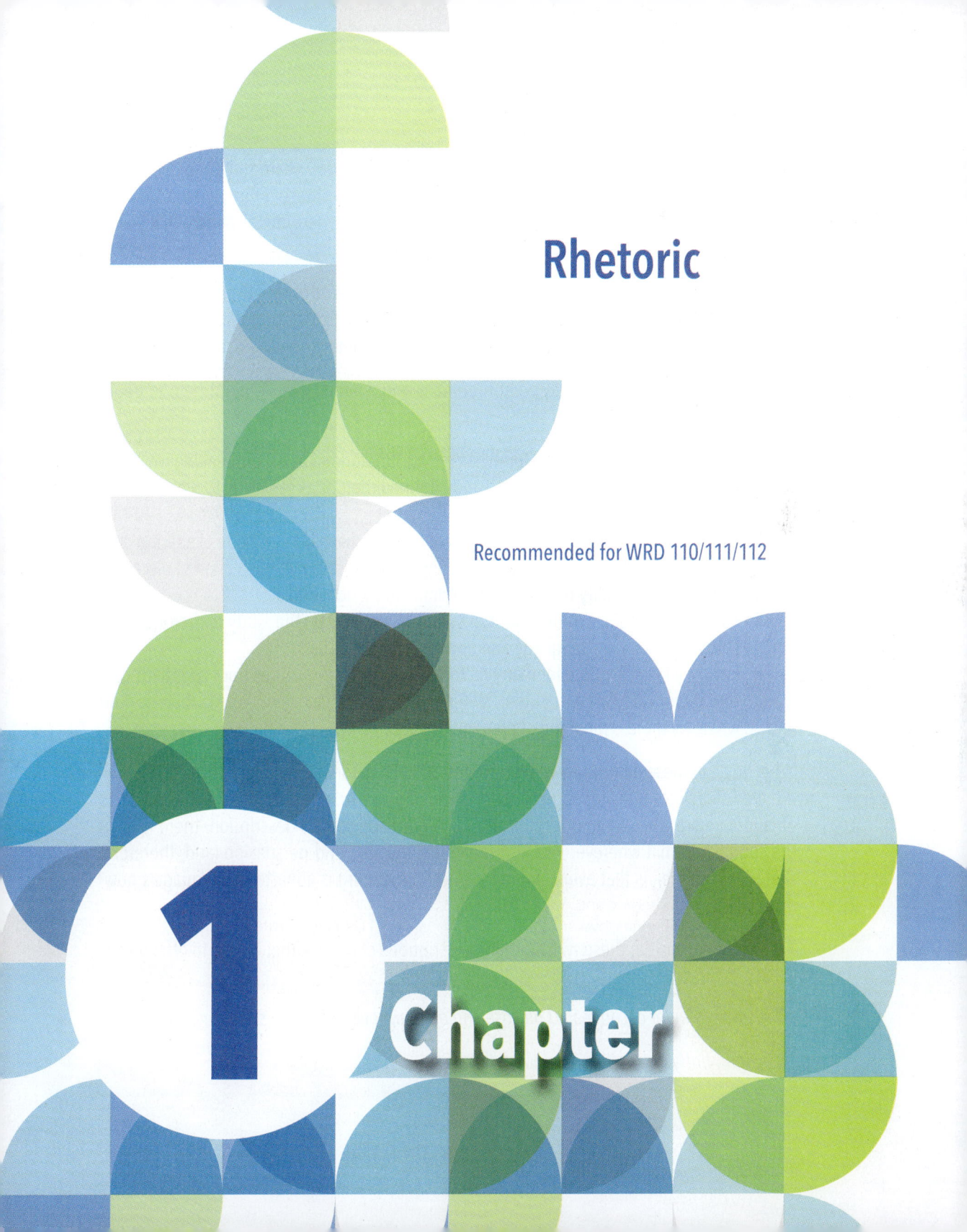

Rhetoric

Recommended for WRD 110/111/112

Chapter 1

Chapter 1   Rhetoric

A BRIEF HISTORY OF RHETORIC

The word rhetoric has a bad reputation. How many times have you heard someone say, "That's just a bunch of rhetoric?" Sometimes people will even use the phrase "empty rhetoric," which is really just another way of saying that rhetoric is all fluff. So, when you tell people that you're studying rhetoric, they might ask you one single question: why?

If rhetoric were really just empty speech, then it might be a waste of time to study it in college. However, rhetoric is not the opposite of meaningful content. In fact, rhetorical scholars often explain that rhetoric is what gives content its meaning. Rhetoric makes meaning.

To better understand just exactly what rhetoric is and what it does, it might help to begin with a few definitions.

- First-century Roman orator Quintillian wrote, "Rhetoric is the art of speaking well."[1]
- Fourth-century BCE rhetorician Aristotle defined rhetoric as seeing all available means of persuasion.[2]
- Twentieth-century rhetorician Lloyd Bitzer defined rhetoric as "a mode of altering reality, not by the direct application of energy to objects, but by the creation of discourse which changes reality through the mediation of thought and action."[3]
- Twenty-first-century rhetorician Krista Ratcliffe says that "the study of rhetoric is the study of how we use language and how language uses us."[4]
- Finally, a favorite quote for many rhetorical scholars today comes from twentieth-century rhetorician Kenneth Burke: "Wherever there is persuasion, there is rhetoric. And wherever there is meaning, there is persuasion."[5]

What do all of these definitions have in common? Each theorist defines **rhetoric** differently, but they all believe that *language* has some kind of powerful effect in the world. The effects of language are what we might call rhetoric. In Kenneth Burke's description, there is even the suggestion that wherever you find meaning, you also find persuasion (and, therefore, rhetoric). That means that every single instance of meaning is a matter of language's powerful effect.

For example, consider these two different descriptions of a snack that I'd like to offer you:

> *A small cylinder of congealed glucose and gelatin, covered in corn starch.*
>
> *A light, fluffy treat with a sweet vanilla taste.*

Which one would you prefer to eat? Unless you love congealed glucose, you might find yourself more interested in the second version. Both of these descriptions actually refer to the same treat: marshmallows! But the first description definitely would not help to sell many marshmallows. Words like "cylinder" and "congealed" are not usually what we associate with tasty treats. At the same time "light, fluffy" and "sweet vanilla" are quite often words we might connect with deliciousness. Even though the two descriptions are focusing on the same thing—marshmallows—the words we choose can actually create different perceptions for the audience.

In a more serious example, consider how a simple word like "Ms." had powerful effects for many women. Before the contemporary revival of the word "Ms." in the 20th century, women were either identified as "Miss" or "Mrs." The distinction between these two terms marked women as being either unmarried ("Miss") or married ("Mrs."). However, the title "Mr." did not reveal men's marital status. During the 20th century, many women objected to being defined by their husband (or lack of one) in everyday life. Therefore, when the neutral title "Ms." was suggested, many women and men welcomed this transformation. With this new title, a person did not need to ask about a woman's marital status before properly addressing her. This tiny word changed the lives of millions of women, and it also helped to create a different perception of women.

This is why rhetorical theorists like to say that rhetoric helps to change reality.

Rhetoric is also sometimes referred to as a form of deliberation. The term deliberation implies careful thought about a complex problem. Juries deliberate during trials, but we also deliberate about a range of issues. Maybe you and your family engaged in deliberation when you tried to decide where to attend college. Did you discuss different school options? Did you find yourself discussing the merits and drawbacks of certain ideas?

In public life, we are regularly involved in deliberations over serious issues. Just take a look at the current news for some indication of what problems, crises, and needs we are now discussing in the public sphere. Some of these deliberations have been going on for years: How should we address environmental problems? How can we end school violence? Should people with terminal illnesses be allowed to have physician-assisted suicide?

We deliberate about these questions because they do not have clear answers. If you and a friend disagreed about the year that Churchill Downs first opened, we would not call this a deliberation. Why not? Because you can do a little research and find that Churchill Downs officially opened in 1875. The disagreement can be settled with factual information that is accessible by everyone. However, not all questions are so easily settled. For those questions that do not have clear answers, we must discuss the merits and drawbacks of different possibilities.

One famous Greek rhetorician named Isocrates (436–338 BC) saw the need for rhetorical deliberation long ago. In his famous text called *Antidosis,* Isocrates writes:

> *For since it is not in the nature of man to attain a science by the possession of which we can know positively what we should do or what we should say, in the next resort I hold that man to be wise who is able by his powers of conjecture to arrive generally at the best course, and I hold that man to be a philosopher who occupies himself with the studies from which he will most quickly gain that kind of insight.*[6]

Isocrates notices that human nature does not contain the power to know everything. Some questions we face do not have definitive answers. But, continues Isocrates, we are not hopeless. Wise people will use their "powers of conjecture" to arrive at the best course. Notice that Isocrates does not say that we will necessarily arrive at the *right answer,* but he does believe we can deliberate with one another to reach the best possible answer.

Recall Aristotle's definition of rhetoric as *seeing all available means of persuasion.*[7] He did not mean that rhetoric is the same thing as persuasion. Rather, he meant that rhetoric is the process of discussing with others in order to see all possibilities in a situation. We use reason, discussion, debate, and persuasion in order to collectively arrive at a response that is fitting. Deliberation, therefore, relies upon powerful usage of language, or what we call *rhetoric.*

WHAT KINDS OF RHETORIC ARE THERE?

A great deal of our contemporary rhetorical theory has very ancient roots. In the fifth century in Athens, the Greek people were trying a new experiment, a form of democracy that required all citizens to participate. As you can imagine, such a widespread participation required citizens to speak in public about legal matters and political matters, regardless of whether they had any type of professional training. For this reason, new schools began to pop up all across Athens. These schools taught rhetoric and oratory, including the art of persuasion. Some of the schools were taught by teachers, known as Sophists. They taught people how to be persuasive when they stood in front of a large group. They later came to have a bad reputation from rival schools, including Plato's philosophical school.

It is Aristotle, however, that we usually turn to for a formal definition of rhetoric. Aristotle was certainly not the first to teach about rhetoric, but he was the first to really systematize it and to write it down. Aristotle also believed, much like Isocrates, that rhetoric was necessary because so many of our social and political questions do not have clear answers; rather, they are questions that we must deliberate with others about. Many of Aristotle's teachings on rhetoric were about how to be persuasive on matters that did not have a right or wrong answer.

Aristotle believed that rhetoricians typically find themselves in one of three situations where rhetorical oratory (or writing) is necessary. These three different situations ask very different kinds of questions, and they require different kinds of discourse and language:

- **Deliberative:** This is the rhetorical occasion that looks toward the *future* in order to ask, *"What should we do about_____?"* Lawmakers very often engage in deliberative rhetoric when they debate about laws that should or shouldn't be passed.
- **Judicial or forensic:** This is the rhetorical occasion that looks toward the *past* in order to ask, *"What happened?"* Courts of law are great examples of judicial rhetoric since they are often trying to determine details that have already occurred.
- **Epideictic:** This is the rhetorical occasion that looks to the *praiseworthiness or blameworthiness of someone or something*. Think about giving an award or making a eulogy. Epideictic comes from the Greek word *epideixis:* to shine, to show forth. Award speeches are good examples of epideitic discourse since they are praising the award receiver.

There are two basic elemental properties of any persuasive discourse: **claim** and **evidence.** Aristotle taught that argument could very broadly be divided into two categories based on how they use evidence. Following Aristotle, we call these two categories **artistic** and **non-artistic** arguments.

- **Non-artistic argument** is when the evidence supporting the claim is not somehow *invented* by the rhetor. For example, the evidence supporting the claim may be based on eyewitness testimony, the legal language of contracts, and so forth.

  > **Example:** *"You owe me $10,000 (claim) because you signed a contract saying you would pay me $10,000 if I built you this doghouse (evidence)."*

- **Artistic argument** is when the rhetor *invents* the evidence used to support the claims. By "invent," we don't mean that the rhetor falsely creates facts and other evidence. Rather, the rhetor is responsible for deciding how to make the argument persuasive to her audience.

  > **Example:** *"You should let me borrow your car (claim) because I am very responsible (evidence)."*

Most of the arguments we hear and make every day are examples of *artistic arguments*. We may have a claim, but we must consider our audience and decide the best possible evidence that will persuade this particular audience at this particular time.

In the examples above, I do not need to consider what is likely to persuade an audience if I have a contract specifying that you will pay me for services I rendered. On the other hand, if I am about to ask you for a big favor, then I need to consider what is most likely to persuade you. I will choose from a number of possible arguments (the process of rhetorical invention).

This chapter examines types of evidence that are used in *artistic* arguments. We will look at the different qualities of evidence that are used to support claims.

Types of Evidence

Aristotle taught that artistic rhetoric could have three main types of evidence, called **"appeals."** We now commonly call these the appeals of **ethos, logos,** and **pathos.** Any argument uses all three of these appeals, though they each have different effects. Try not to think about these as separate elements that are either present or absent in arguments. They are present in every argument, though they may be emphasized to a greater or lesser degree.

Ethos

Sometimes **ethos** is defined as the character of the speaker or writer. Think about how a writer might seek to support a claim based on her own reputation, background, qualifications, and credentials.

A writer or speaker always creates some kind of ethos. He may draw explicitly upon his personal or professional credentials in order to support his claim. On the other hand, he may fail to establish a very sound or stable reputation. The writer may come across as unprofessional or unreliable. In this case, you might say that his ethos was very unpersuasive.

When you read a writer's text or hear a speaker talk, consider that rhetor's ethos. How does he appear before you? Does he carry weight with you based on how he looks, sounds, or presents himself? Does his language or speech make you feel closely connected to him, or does his speech make him seem distant from you?

Exercise: Thinking about Ethos

Think of how someone's story or background changes how you listen to them. Imagine yourself listening to or reading about international military actions.

Would you weigh the ethos of an author differently if she or he had recently served a tour of duty in the military? Why or why not?

Find an example (TV commercial, magazine advertisement, online advertisement, etc.) of a celebrity or well-known individual selling a product based, at least partially, on his or her ethos. For example, an NFL player selling his shoes is partly using his ethos to help support the claim that these are good shoes. Does the celebrity's ethos convince you to buy the product? Why or why not?

Ethos is something we are always generating, even if we are not aware of it. Another way of thinking about ethos is as a kind of persona. Think about how some entertainers create personas to seem more flashy, exciting, bad, or smooth. Even when you don't create entirely new personas for yourself, you are always crafting some kind of public version of yourself for others to consider. Your words, style, sources, quotes, flourishes—these are all part of your ethos.

> ### Exercise: Ethos and Persona
>
> Come up with a new (stage) persona for yourself. Give yourself a new name and style. *How would this persona dress, move, speak?*
>
> Write an introduction that captures this persona in his/her own words and style. Read these introductory pieces aloud (preferably in the verbal style of your new persona)! Discuss whether or not you have put this much thought into your own real persona/ethos in texts that you write.

Ethos is like a set of directions that tell other people how to read you. Your ethos is always sending out these messages, saying quite a lot about who you are, what kinds of things you stand for, how you think, and so forth.

These messages happen even when you don't consciously plan for them! For example, if I wear sweatpants to an interview (just because they're my most comfy clothes, and I want to be relaxed for the interview), I'm saying a lot about myself: *I don't take this job seriously. I don't understand professional behavior. I am probably not attentive to details. I won't be a great employee.* Of course, I'm not trying to send these messages! But, nevertheless, that's my ethos doing the talking.

> **Ethos and students:** What's one easy way for students to establish a strong ethos with professors?

Pathos

In addition to relying on ethos in making a persuasive argument, rhetors also rely upon the powerful work of emotion and feeling. With each choice of word, tone, or picture, we create a kind of sensation within our audiences. These may be good feelings, sad feelings, confident feelings, proud feelings, fearful feelings, or many other kinds of feelings. Borrowing from the Greek term for *"experience,"* we call this rhetorical power the work of **pathos.**

Although pathos is sometimes translated as emotion, we should probably broaden our understanding of pathos to mean something more like *feeling* and *felt experience*. For example, the experience of boredom might not exactly be an emotion like happiness or sadness, but we have all had the experience of being intensely bored. We have also probably all had an experience of personal shock. Some people describe that experience in terms of embodied feelings: *My heart was racing. It felt like my stomach dropped into my knees. I suddenly felt numb.* These kinds of experiences are not easily encapsulated in familiar terms like "sadness" or "anger." But we can talk about them as felt experiences, or pathos.

The same might be said for the degree and intensity of emotions you feel at different times. A particular argument might make you feel mildly irritated, while the person sitting beside you may feel intense anger. When we talk about pathos, we should therefore consider the *range* of felt experience (including the intensities, emotions, and embodied experiences) that come with those rhetorical choices.

Pathos is a powerful rhetorical tool for persuasion because an audience's emotional state can help move it to certain kinds of action. Think about the old cliché that a speech should always open with a joke. Even though opening with a joke is not always the best advice, the idea is that laughter puts people in a relaxed mood and might ultimately make them feel friendlier toward the speaker. You can also probably think of many examples where authors have used heartbreaking images of sickness, disease, and even death in order to get their audience to donate money or time. A television advertisement for the American Humane Society may use images of abused and lonely animals, all played over melancholy music. The idea is that these images, along with the music and words, may move you to some kind of action (like donating a few dollars to the Humane Society).

Even the most plain, ordinary text is meant to produce *some* kind of responses. Do you remember the feeling that you had when reading your acceptance letter into college? Did the words convey a sense of pride and positivity? If you received any rejection letters, do you remember if they were worded in such a way to convey rejection with a sense of regret on the part of the school?

Exercise: Writing to Convey Feeling

In a group, decide how you will create emails that fit the following scenarios:

1. You are a small business owner who is hiring someone to work at the front desk. You had many good applicants, but you were only able to hire one person. You want to craft an email to those people who you could not hire, and you need to tell them that they will not be getting the job. However, you thought these people were very good, and you don't want to discourage them. In fact, you may want to be able to hire them in the future, so think carefully about how to use pathos as a tool for delivering bad news.
2. Imagine that you want to make an argument for giving UK students a full week's vacation leading up to Thanksgiving. You would need to make an argument to the University administration. How might you make your claim and evidence? What kinds of *feelings* would you aim to create for your audience? Would you want to assure them that UK students are *responsible* and *serious,* perhaps as a way of persuading them that you need this time to get important projects done? Would you try to avoid creating feelings of *anger* by insulting past decisions not to cancel classes for the whole week?

Pathos: Always Working

Our words and images always create some kind of experiential feeling, even if we do not intend for those feelings to be felt by our audience.

For example, think about the last time you sat through a lecture that was intensely boring. The speaker probably did not find the material boring, and she most certainly did not want to bore her audience. However, authors do not always have complete control over the way his or her words are experienced by audiences.

Watch a recent speech that your instructor assigns, or one that you find online (TED talks, for example). As you watch the speech, try to determine how pathos is used by the speaker in both her choice of words, her voice, her tone, and even her movements.

Are they effective? Why or why not?

Would they be more or less effective for different audiences or for different occasions?

> ### Feelings versus Logic?
>
> Sometimes people mistakenly claim that pathos should be secondary to other forms of rhetorical appeals. This claim comes partly from the post-Enlightenment philosophers who argued that humans are completely rational, and emotions are only a cheap imitation of real thinking. In fact, some philosophers even went so far as to suggest that logic is associated with men, and emotions are associated with women. Because logic was "good" and emotion was "bad," students have historically been encouraged to only rarely (if ever) use pathos in their writing and speaking.
>
> Now, however, we know more about how the brain and nervous system process thoughts and emotions. We have learned that emotions and thought are not mutually exclusive. Neuroscientist Antonio Damasio has written extensively about how thinking and cognition are deeply enmeshed with feeling.

Logos

The third type of rhetorical appeal that Aristotle discussed is one that we now call **logos.** This term sounds like our modern term "logic," but logos is not exactly the same as logic. The Greek word **logos** can also be translated as "word" and "order." You might think about logos as the logic of how claims and their arguments are arranged. Logos is the structure of our arguments.

Rhetorical theorists have argued that we can either structure our arguments using **inductive reasoning** or **deductive reasoning.**

Inductive Reasoning

Inductive reasoning generalizes conclusions from facts or details. You might be familiar with inductive reasoning through your experience with the scientific method. Whenever we practice the scientific method, we make many observations to lead up to a conclusion.

As an example of how rhetoricians might use inductive reasoning, consider UK sophomore Emily Markanich's opinion column in the *Kentucky Kernel*, "Today's Dating Is Outdated":

> Welcome to the age where casual dating has turned into casually hooking up. If you're dating, it's serious, but if you're "friends with benefits" then it's no big deal. "Talking" is the equivalent of dating and the mere concept of dating is a frightening, outdated notion in which only our parents willingly participated.

Let's be honest, the times have changed, and not in the most beneficial of ways. We give ourselves away without even considering the consequences of what we are doing to our hearts.

We're either getting our hopes up just to have them dashed by the harsh reality that "he was only into me for my breasts" or "she was only into me for my abs." Or we're hardening our hearts and becoming so callous toward the thought of love that we don't even register the feeling when it presents itself.

This new-age concept of casually "hooking up" isn't casual. It's detrimental. How many of us can say that we know of someone, or have been the person, who's been hurt by casually hooking up?

All of us have, regardless of gender. Sure, it starts out innocent. Just one night to not feel alone, but then that one night turns into a week of nights and only then does the prospect of a date occur.

Some run for the hills; others get their hopes up about a casual fling actually turning into something real for once, only to have those hopes dashed once again. Can't we go back to the social norms to which high school restricted us?

Remember the times when if a guy wanted to "get with" a girl then he would have to ask her out on a date and actually "date" her? Where, "Hey, do you want to come over tonight and watch a movie?" wasn't code for, "Hey, want to hook up?"

What I want to know is where the lines became blurred and who is to blame for this. Do we blame the booze, our exes, our parents' marriage, or do we blame ourselves?

And if we only have ourselves to blame, why can't we be the ones to fix it? We teach people how to treat us by how we treat ourselves. I'm not suggesting to turn to abstinence or avoid the bars at all cost. What I am advising is that you show yourself a little respect and treat others with that same respect.

I think you'll be surprised by how far it gets you.[8]

Look at how Markanich constructs her argument. Her main claim—that a culture of more meaningful relationships may also create a more respectful culture—is not explicitly stated at the very beginning. She saves these claims until the very end. "We teach people how to treat us by how we treat ourselves," Markanich writes. The majority of her opinion piece shares small examples of miserable situations that are created by the "hooking up" culture. She describes "dashed hopes," hurt feelings, and misplaced blame. Markanich uses these many examples to build up to her larger claim: we should rekindle older dating practices. By sharing small examples, illustrations, and observations in support of a larger point, Markanich arranges her argument via inductive reasoning.

Deductive Reasoning

Deductive reasoning draws its conclusion from larger principles. Think of deduction as a form of reasoning, or a structure to the argument. One popular rhetorical form of deductive reasoning is called an **enthymeme.** An enthymeme is what we call a **syllogism** that has a missing premise.

Syllogisms are forms of arguments that have two premises and a conclusion.

> *All men are mortal.* (Premise 1)
>
> *Socrates is a man.* (Premise 2)
>
> *Socrates is a mortal.* (Conclusion)

In a syllogism, the conclusion is drawn from the previous premises. However, just because a syllogism is constructed properly does not mean that it is true! Consider this logically sound syllogism:

> *Winter days in Kentucky are perfect for sunbathing.*
>
> *Today is a winter day in Kentucky.*
>
> *Today is perfect for sunbathing.*

In terms of structure, this syllogism is internally consistent. However, if you know anything about Kentucky winter days, you might doubt the validity of this conclusion! So, be careful of assuming the logically consistent arguments are always true.

You probably don't hear people using full syllogisms in their arguments very often. This is because spelling out all the premises and the conclusion might sound a bit boring or unnecessary. However, imagine what might happen if someone said this to you:

> *There's a blizzard warning for our area tomorrow, so school might be cancelled.*

Did you understand the link between these two statements? If you wrote it out as a syllogism, it might look like this:

> *There's a blizzard warning for our area tomorrow.* (Premise 1)
>
> *Blizzards often cause schools to be cancelled.* (Premise 2)
>
> *School might be cancelled tomorrow.* (Conclusion)

It would have been a little strange to actually state Premise 2 aloud since you can presumably already figure this part out on your own. Would it have been odd to hear someone say the following?

> *There's a blizzard warning for our area tomorrow, and blizzards often cause schools to be cancelled, so school might be cancelled.*

That unstated premise makes this syllogism an enthymeme. The Greek word enthymeme comes from the words *en*—meaning "to see"—and *thumos*—meaning "the mind." An enthymeme is an argument that literally causes audiences to fill in the missing premise themselves. They "see" it in their minds!

Consider this enthymeme, for example:

> *Congressional candidate Rhonda Weller is not a politician; she's a businesswoman.*
>
> *You should vote for Rhonda Weller.*

Chapter 1   Rhetoric

What is the missing premise here? The missing premise seems to be that businesswomen (and businessmen) make good congressional candidates, while politicians are not desirable. The author who made this argument did not supply this missing premise, of course. The readers could easily fill in the gaps.

In the example of Rhonda Weller for Congressional candidate, do you think having the reader "fill in the gaps" made this argument stronger or weaker? Is there any kind of strategy to withholding the premise rather than stating the whole syllogism? Aristotle believed that having audience members fill in the missing premise helped rhetoricians make their case even more persuasive. Why? Because by supplying the missing premise themselves, the audience is actually making the argument for you.

Exercise: Enthymemes

Figure 1. When You Ride Alone, You Ride with Hitler![9]

Arguments are often made through forms other than printed and spoken words. Arguments can also rely upon images to make their case. Enthymemes can also be created through images. Consider the WWII-era advertisement above.

What is the stated premise and conclusion?

What is the unstated premise of this conclusion?

Remember that logos is the structure of various arguments and messages. All texts use some kind of logos, just like every building uses some kind of design. As a rhetorical analyst or author, your job is to pay close attention to the details of that design.

Exercise: Using Ethos, Pathos, and Logos

Imagine that you will be making the argument that all professors at UK must keep assigned textbook costs to $100 or less per course. You will need to make this argument to three different audiences:

- Fellow UK students
- Professors
- University administration

What kinds of ethos would you need to convey to these different audiences? How would you use the powers of pathos in each different situation?

Write a brief outline of your arguments to each of these audiences. Would it be better to use an inductive structure to build your argument? Or, would it be better to use deductive reasoning? What are your stated and unstated premises?

Stasis

Imagine that you and your roommate are having a disagreement about whether you think you should leave the lights and TV on when nobody is home. Maybe you think it is a waste of electricity, but your roommate thinks having the TV and lights on will deter possible robbers. You can imagine yourself standing face to face while arguing about this issue. You are on one side of the issue (it's a waste), and your roommate is on the *other side* of the issue (it's not a waste). Both of you are arguing about the same question—*Is it a waste to leave the TV and lights on when nobody is home?*—but you answer this question differently. You are both in **stasis,** standing face to face on the same issue.

Although it might sound paradoxical, an argument must begin in agreement. That is, people who are participating in a debate must make sure that they are debating the same questions. They will not agree to answer those questions in the same way, of course. People participating in debates and deliberations often have strongly and passionately different answers to the same questions. For example, people who weigh in on the question of how to reduce teenage pregnancy answer in radically different ways:

- Provide better sex education
- Teach abstinence only
- Give teenagers better access to birth control
- Reduce teenage access to birth control
- Teach boys more respect for women
- Have girls play sports when they are young

Even though these answers are very different, even contradictory, they all respond to the same question: *How can we reduce teen pregnancy?*

What happens if you find yourself not in stasis with another person? You have probably had the experience of "arguing past" someone. It can seem like you are arguing two different questions. In fact, chances are good that you probably were arguing two different questions. You were not standing face to face with your interlocutor. Instead, you were each responding to two different questions. Trying to argue with someone when you are not in stasis is a trying activity. For example, some deliberations and arguments about gun control can be quite difficult if Person A wants to extend background checks while Person B does not see a lack of gun control as a problem. In this situation, they are both arguing *about* guns, but they are not trying to resolve or respond to the *same question* about guns.

Stasis theory refers to the place where two disputants "stand"—i.e., the place where they agree to disagree, where both agree something is an issue.

Discovering Stasis Claims

Ancient rhetorical scholars found that most claims could be divided into several different types of questions:

Questions of fact: Is it real? Does it exist? Did it happen?

Questions of definition: What is its definition? What is it called?

Questions of quality: Is it good/bad, just/unjust, greater/lesser, etc.? Is it serious?

Questions of cause/effect: What caused it? What effects does it have?

Questions of proposal: What should we do?

These stasis questions were used prominently in ancient Roman law courts, and their form is still used to think through legal cases today. To proceed with a court case, both the prosecution and the defense must agree to the main question, or claim, being debated. Imagine that I took your umbrella last week without your knowledge, and I suddenly found myself appearing before a judge. Before I am charged with anything, the court may want to first run through the stasis claims to decide what argument to make:

Question of Fact: Did I Actually Take Your Umbrella?

If I did not actually take it, then we would stop here. I would argue that I was framed or wrongfully accused, and you would argue that I did indeed take the umbrella.

However, let's say that I admit to taking your umbrella. Then, we would move on to the next stasis question.

Question of Definition: Was the Act One of Theft, or Was It Something Else?

I may admit to taking the umbrella, but I do not want to define it as theft. I want to say that it was simply "borrowing." I was going to return it in perfect shape. However, you might argue that taking without permission is always considered theft.

But, let's say that I admitted to actually stealing the umbrella. It was theft. We can agree on that question, so we'll move to the next stasis question.

Questions of Quality: Was My Act a Terrible Act?

Let's say that I agree to have stolen your umbrella in a moment of sheer thoughtlessness. I was feeling mean or rotten on that day. But I might also argue that taking an umbrella is not a terribly awful act. It did not impact your life in serious ways (beyond having to buy another umbrella), and you were not physically or emotionally harmed. You might not share this opinion, however, and you want to see me spend the rest of my life in prison for theft. In this instance, we would be arguing over questions of quality: How bad was this act?

On the other hand, maybe you agree that the act was mean but was not terribly horrible. We might want to still ask one more question before moving on to the bigger question of what to do.

Question of Cause/Effect: What Caused This Act? What Effects Did It Have?

You might argue that the monetary price of your umbrella was very insignificant, but the umbrella had been a present from your favorite grandmother. The sentimental attachment to your umbrella is priceless, and you have found yourself depressed for weeks as a result of the theft. Furthermore, even after you got it back, you now find yourself unable to trust people around your umbrellas ever again. In this case, you would be arguing about effects. If I try to argue that such effects are highly improbable from a simple case of umbrella theft, we would be arguing the stasis of cause/effect.

Finally, if we could resolve all of these other questions, we might still find ourselves arguing the question of proposal.

Question of Proposal: What Should We Do?

You may wish to see me pay a fine or even serve some community service as a result of my theft. However, I may argue that an apology (and the returned umbrella) should be sufficient. If we had disagreements about the appropriateness of various proposals, we would be arguing the stasis of proposal.

How Can You Use Stasis Questions to Understand Others' Arguments?

The stasis questions are incredibly helpful for understanding the arguments and claims that others are making. When you read or hear an argument being made, you might ask yourself the following questions:

- Is the author making a **claim of fact:** Is s/he arguing whether something exists or whether it happened?
- Is the author making a **claim of definition:** Is s/he arguing what something should be called or how it should be classified?
- Is the author making a **claim of quality:** Is s/he arguing whether something is good or bad, just or unjust, greater or lesser, etc.? Is s/he evaluating something?
- Is the author making a **claim of cause/effect:** Is s/he arguing about the cause that led to something? Is s/he arguing about the effects that something will have?
- Is the author making a **claim of proposal:** Is s/he arguing about the best course of action in a certain situation?

Once you understand what kinds of claims and questions are being deliberated, you can formulate a more appropriate response to your interlocutor. You can also use this list of stasis questions to reflect and better understand your own claims. Are you in stasis with your interlocutors? Are you all arguing about the same questions? If not, how can you first agree to what your argument will be about?

Exercise: Shifting Stasis

Find a recent opinion piece in your campus newspaper. Use the above questions to try and determine what kinds of stasis claims the author is making. Now try to imagine how the author's argument might change if the main stasis were shifted to another kind of stasis claim.

For example, if the author's main claim is one of definition, how might it change if he or she were to make an argument of quality?

Using Stasis for Inventing Arguments

Not only are the stasis questions useful for analyzing other people's arguments, but you can also use the stasis claims to help formulate your own arguments. This is why we say that the stasis questions are a form of invention or **heuristics.** If you know that you will need to make an argument about a certain issue, but you are not quite sure what you want to say about it, use the stasis questions as a way to generate ideas.

The following is an inventional writing exercise that might help to get your thoughts flowing:

Exercise: Invention

1. Sit down with a piece of paper and a timer. Write down your main issue or topic focus in a few words (for example, "veterans returning to school").
2. Spend five minutes generating as many questions as possible under each of the stasis headings. (Use the list below as a guide.) You should come up with questions about your topic—not answers—relating to that particular stasis area. For example, under the "fact" stasis, you will try to come with as many questions about your topic that relate to its "facts" or existence.
3. When you are finished, look back over your questions and circle the ones that seem the most interesting to you. If you would like, you can do another timed writing exercise for each of the circled questions. Go through the whole list again.

Exercise: Invention (continued)

Questions based on stasis areas:

Existence or Facts

- Did _____ happen?
- How did it happen?
- What are the facts of _____?
- How did _____ begin?

Definition

- To what kind of larger class of things or events does _____ belong?
- What parts of this story need more definition, or do this person's words suggest a new kind of definition?
- How is _____ different from other things?
- Is the meaning of _____ misunderstood?

Quality

- How serious of a problem is _____?
- Is _____ a good thing? A dangerous/helpful/beautiful/etc. thing?
- How do different people/stakeholders think about _____? The stakeholders involved may include: _____.

Cause/Effect

- What are the causes of _____?
- What are the consequences of _____?
- What kinds of effects does _____ have?

Proposal

- What should be done with _____?
- Should we reconsider how _____ works?
- What kind of future should _____ have?
- Does _____ need any kind of change?

SOPHISTIC APPEALS

If you've ever taken a writing class before, chances are you've heard of rhetorical appeals. They're those fancy Greek words that a guy named Aristotle thought up: *ethos, pathos, logos.* (If you're new to the appeals, or if you need a refresher, go to Page 2 in this book.) These three appeals are a staple in writing classes because they're intuitive, they're easy to learn, and, most importantly, they work. Credibility (*ethos*), emotion (*pathos*), and argument (*logos*) are crucial to effective writing, and the appeals give writers of all levels useful tools to elevate their own work. In other words, the rhetorical appeals are pretty important.

There's another set of appeals that's less well-known than the rhetorical appeals, but just as useful: the sophistic appeals. We call them "sophistic" because they're associated with the Sophists, a group of teachers who traveled Greece giving out speaking advice to anyone able to pay their fees. The Sophists were active even before Aristotle gave us his rhetorical appeals, which are in some ways a response to the teachings of the Sophists. Aristotle thought the Sophists peddled in cheap oratorical tricks, whereas he wanted to turn rhetoric into an orderly system. The rhetorical appeals were part of his attempt to do just that.

But as useful as Aristotle's appeals are, they have some limitations. They're very good at telling us *how* someone is arguing their case, but not very good at telling us *why. Ethos, pathos,* and *logos* represent different persuasive techniques, but they don't explain why someone might be making their argument in the first place, or what they might be trying to achieve by doing so. That's where the sophistic appeals come in. The sophistic appeals—*mythos, logos,* and *nomos*—can help us analyze and construct arguments by focusing on an argument's purpose and outcomes.

The Sophists

The Sophists were active before Aristotle came along, but once he introduced his version of the rhetorical appeals in his treatise *Rhetoric,* the Sophists took a back seat. In fact, the Sophists were hardly even mentioned in discussions of rhetoric until the nineteenth century, when some philosophers started to pay more attention to them. But one of the first people to really examine what the Sophists had to say about rhetoric was Susan C. Jarratt. In her book *Rereading the Sophists: Classical Rhetoric Refigured* (1991), Jarratt shows us the differences between the Sophists' and Aristotle's versions of rhetoric by giving us sophistic counterparts to Aristotle's appeals: *mythos, logos,* and *nomos.*

Mythos

When you first look at the term *mythos,* what's the first thing you see? You may have recognized how close it is to the English words *myth* or *mythology.* In fact, those words actually come from *mythos,* and they give us a pretty good idea of what the word means in its original Greek sense. According to the scholar Robert L. Fowler, *mythos* means "significant speech," a "pronouncement, not just utterance" (53). Fowler says that *mythos* represents a specific kind of speech: just saying something doesn't make it *mythos.* Instead, as Fowler says, "*Mythos* denotes the whole package ... when *mythos* is in play, something is at stake" (53).

What Fowler is getting at is that *mythos* is a kind of speech that has authority, much like the old myths about the Olympian gods had authority for the ancient Greeks. For Jarratt, grappling with authority was an important part of the Sophists' rhetoric. She says that "the mythic world is based on an uncritical acceptance of a tradition warranted by nature" (42). To the Sophists, *mythos* meant ideas, narratives, or traditions that held cultural authority and, because of that authority, were difficult to challenge. I like writing teacher John Edlund's definition here: *mythos* is a "story that nearly everyone in a community knows that serves as a reference point for community values and behavior" ("Sophistic Appeals").

Every culture has a *mythos,* of course. Our culture may not believe in the myth of twelve gods living on Mount Olympus, but there are ideas and beliefs that we take for granted. They may even make us uncomfortable when someone challenges them. Think of the ideal of the American Dream, the notion that anyone in America can make it big if they work hard enough. Whether or not that's true, it's an idea that holds powerful sway in American culture.

It's worth pointing out that *mythos* is not necessarily a good thing. This is different from Aristotle's appeals, which are all things we want to see in a good persuasive argument. Instead, *mythos* is our starting point. In sophistic rhetoric, our first step is to identify a *mythos* that we think is wrong, some kind of assumption or narrative that we think needs to be challenged. From there, we can challenge that *mythos* by using the next two appeals: *logos* and *nomos.*

Logos

If you know about Aristotle's appeals, you should already be familiar with the term *logos.* For Aristotle, *logos* is just one way of persuading our audience. *Ethos* means persuasion through credibility and personal character, *pathos* means persuasion through emotion, and *logos* means persuasion through rational discourse. The sophistic use of *logos* means more or less the same thing. The main difference, though, is in how we use *logos* in our argument.

At its most basic level, the Greek word *logos* simply refers to the act of speech. But it also has a lot of connotations and overtones that make it difficult to translate. For Aristotle, *logos* means rationale discourse or argument. One way to persuade an audience is to present it with things that appeal to the rational side of our minds, like logic, evidence, or demonstrations. In sophistic rhetoric, *logos* means something similar, but there are a few differences. Instead of limiting itself to rational discourse, the sophistic *logos* incorporates all kinds of persuasion that we can use through language. This includes logic, of course, but also things like stories or anecdotes. To quote John Edlund again, sophistic *logos* includes "any kind of persuasion that uses words including logical arguments, but also stories, images, poetic language, incantations, etc." ("Sophistic Appeals").

The purpose of *logos* is tied directly to *mythos*. *Mythos*, as we just saw, means some kind of narrative or idea that is unquestioningly assumed in a culture. *Logos*, on the other hand, is meant to challenge *mythos*, to show that, actually, the thing we assumed to be true may not actually be correct. We do this through logical arguments, demonstrations, and counternarratives, all of which fall under the umbrella of *logos*. In other words, the purpose of *logos* is to challenge the assumptions of *mythos*. Once we've done that, we can move on to the final step in this process: *nomos*.

Nomos

Nomos is another of those Greek words that's difficult to translate. According to Jyotirmaya Sharma, its original and most literal meaning had to do with the appropriation of land, but it eventually came to mean a social norm (17–18). Another word for *nomos* might be "custom," the things that people in a culture do naturally and that are accepted as normal.

Right away, we can see how *mythos* and *nomos* line up. If *mythos* means the ideas that a culture has accepted as normal, it's easy to see how those ideas would influence *nomos*, the practices that a culture considers normal. After all, our social norms and customs are a reflection of the ideas that shaped them. This is an important point: *nomos* is determined by *mythos*.

Nomos is our goal. The goal of sophistic rhetoric is to change social norms, to change the way we do things, by addressing the underlying assumptions that make those norms possible. We do this by using *logos*, or persuasive discourse, to make others see how, actually, the myths and narratives we took for granted are actually wrong. Once we see the errors in our thinking, we can start to change our social norms, too. To sum up: **We use *logos* to challenge *mythos* and change *nomos*.**

Example: What does sophistic rhetoric look like in action? Let's look at an example. On December 6th, 2016, then-President Barack Obama delivered a speech about counterterrorism at MacDill Air Force Base in Tampa, Florida. Let's look at parts of his speech and tease out how President Obama uses *mythos, logos,* and *nomos* to convey his message.

The first thing we have to ask is, who is the President's audience? *Mythos* and *nomos* are each concerned with the ideas and customs of a specific culture, so to use or analyze them properly, we first need to see what culture is being addressed. The President is, of course, addressing American culture, but that's probably too broad to be useful. Because the speech was given on an Air Force base to members of the Air Force, it's more likely that the culture he's targeting is military culture. If that's the case, the President's speech will probably try to convince his audience about certain policies (*nomos*) that he thinks are important for that culture.

Now that we understand the President's audience, what mythos is his speech trying to challenge? I think we can find it in this paragraph:

> *I came to this office with a set of core convictions that have guided me as Commander-in-Chief. I believe that the United States military can achieve any mission; that we are, and must remain, the strongest fighting force the world has ever known. (Applause.) I believe that we must never hesitate to act when necessary, including unilaterally when necessary, against any imminent threats to our people. But I have also insisted that it is unwise and unsustainable to ask our military to build nations on the other side of the world, or resolve their internal conflicts, particularly in places where our forces become a magnet for terrorists and insurgencies. Instead, it has been my conviction that even as we focus relentlessly on dismantling terrorist networks like al Qaeda and ISIL, we should ask allies to do their share in the fight, and we should strengthen local partners who can provide lasting security.* ("Remarks")

The President begins this paragraph by identifying himself with his audience and showing them he shares similar values, such as maintaining "the strongest fighting force the world has ever known." But then he shifts and tries to challenge certain ideas about foreign policy:

> *But I have also insisted that it is unwise and unsustainable to ask our military to build nations on the other side of the world, or resolve their internal conflicts, particularly in places where our forces become a magnet for terrorists and insurgencies.*

This is the *mythos* the President is challenging: the idea that it is America's job to "build nations" or police the world's conflicts. Right after this, the President also gives us a glimpse into the *nomos* that he has tried to change during his Presidency:

> *Instead, it has been my conviction that even as we focus relentlessly on dismantling terrorist networks like al Qaeda and ISIL, we should ask allies to do their share in the fight, and we should strengthen local partners who can provide lasting security.*

The *mythos* of American policing says that it's America's job to make sure the world is safe. But here, the President says he has tried a different approach, one that shares the responsibility for safety between nations.

What about *logos?* How does the President use language to challenge *mythos?* His speech is long and has many examples of *logos,* but here's one. After summarizing America's and its allies' progress against the terrorist organization ISIL, the President says this:

> *So the campaign against ISIL has been relentless. It has been sustainable. It has been multilateral. And it demonstrates a shift in how we've taken the fight to terrorists everywhere from South Asia to the Sahel. Instead of pushing all of the burden onto American ground troops, instead of trying to mount invasions wherever terrorists appear, we've built a network of partners.*

This a direct challenge to the *mythos* the President is confronting. The old way of thinking says that it's America's job to police the world, but the recent success of multilateral efforts shows that they work better. The President uses *logos* (the success of multilateral efforts at global safety) to challenge *mythos* (the idea that America should police the world) and change *nomos* (policy changes that reflect and encourage multilateral solutions).

VIDEO RESOURCES

Former Mayor Jim Gray on the Rhetorical Force of Words

Jim Gray was elected Mayor of Lexington in 2010 and re-elected for another four year term in 2014. In 2016 he ran for the United States Senate against Rand Paul. Mayor Gray is also the former CEO of Gray Construction, which is a successful international construction firm. As part of his daily work in the Mayor's office, Mayor Gray uses writing in a number of ways. In this interview clip, he talks about how he chooses particular words for their rhetorical effect.

(https://vimeo.com/103941623)

Mayor Jim Gray on Using Pathos and Emotional Persuasion to Change Perceptions of Place

In this clip, Mayor Gray describes how he uses pathos (emotional appeals) in order to affect how people see a place like Lexington.

(https://vimeo.com/103941621)

Kevin Patterson on the Everyday Importance of Rhetoric

Kevin Patterson manages the Beer Trappe, a craft beer specialty shop in Lexington. Kevin is a native to eastern Kentucky, and he is an active participant in social media discussions of craft beer. As part of his job, Kevin uses rhetorical theory and writing in a number of ways. In this interview clip, he describes the role rhetoric plays in his everyday work life.

(https://vimeo.com/103940588)

Kevin Patterson on the Importance of Storytelling and Perception

In this clip, Kevin Patterson talks about the importance of storytelling and narrative on how people perceive different products.

(https://vimeo.com/103939686)

NOTES

[1] Quintilian. *The Institutio Oratoria of Quintilian.* Translated by H. E. Butler, Harvard University Press, 1996.

[2] Aristotle. *Rhetoric.* Translated by W. Rhys Roberts, University of Pennsylvania, 2013, I:4:1359.

[3] Lloyd Bitzer. "The Rhetorical Situation." *Philosophy and Rhetoric 1,* 1968, p. 4.

[4] Krista Ratcliffe. "The Current State of Composition Scholar/Teachers: Is Rhetoric Gone or Just Hiding Out?" *Enculturation, 5,* no. 1, 2003.

[5] Kenneth Burke. *Rhetoric of Motives.* University of California Press, 1969, p. 172.

[6] Isocrates. *The Antidosis.* Harvard University Press, 1929.

[7] Aristotle. *Rhetoric.* I:4:1359.

[8] Emily Markanich. "Today's Dating Is Outdated." *Kentucky Kernel* (Lexington, KY), January 29, 2014.

[9] Weimar Pursell. *When You Ride Alone, You Ride with Hitler!,* 1943, http://www.archives.gov/exhibits/powers_of_persuasion/use_it_up/images_html/ride_with_hitler.html.

WORKS CITED

Edlund, John R. "Sophistic Appeals: *Mythos, Logos,* and *Nomos.*" *Teaching Text Rhetorically,* 9 Jan. 2020, https://textrhet.com/2020/01/09/sophistic-appeals-mythos-logos-nomos/.

Fowler, Robert L. "*Mythos* and *Logos.*" *Journal of Hellenic Studies,* vol. 131, 2011, pp. 45–66, doi:10.1017/S0075426911000048.

Jarratt, Susan C. *Rereading the Sophists: Classical Rhetoric Refigured.* Southern Illinois UP, 1991.

Obama, Barack. "Remarks by the President on the Administration's Approach to Counterterrorism." *The White House: President Barack Obama,* 6 Dec. 2016, https://obamawhitehouse.archives.gov/the-press-office/2016/12/06/remarks-president-administrations-approach-counterterrorism.

Sharma, Jyotirmaya. "Understanding Nomos." *Studies in Humanities and Social Sciences,* vol. 5, no. 1, 1998, pp. 17-37.

Rhetorical Situation

Recommended for WRD 110/111/112

Chapter 2

When we get ready to leave our house and go out into the public, we often do a certain amount of preparation and take into account the nature of the task we are setting out to do. If going for a job interview, we may try to anticipate what questions we will be asked, and we do our best to sound confident and well-informed during the interview itself. If we know we are going to a doctor's appointment, we make sure we have a method of payment and insurance info, mentally run down what we need to ask or bring a written a list, and try to arrive to the office right on time. When we do these things, we prepare ourselves to encounter a particular situation—one that hasn't happened yet, but we still know how to plan for—and then navigate that situation to the best of our ability. In doing so, we increase the likelihood that our "mission," whether it be landing a job or picking up a carton of milk, will succeed.

The **Rhetorical situation** may be defined as a combination of certain people, events, objects, and relationships that seem to be related to some problem that can potentially be solved by someone persuading the right people to change the problem; it is the phrase rhetoricians use to describe the circumstances in which a rhetorician finds him- or herself whenever there is some need to speak out about some issue or problem.

> Lloyd Bitzer, a twentieth-century rhetorical scholar first introduced the concept of rhetorical situations in his well-known essay "The Rhetorical Situation." In that essay, Bitzer offered the following definition:
>
> *Rhetorical situation may be defined as a complex of persons, events, objects, and relations presenting an actual or potential exigence which can be completely or partially removed if discourse, introduced into the situation, can so constrain human decision or action as to bring about the significant modification of the exigence.*[1]

In this unit, we will discuss the elements of the rhetorical situation and how you might use this model as a way to both analyze and produce public arguments.

ELEMENTS OF A RHETORICAL SITUATION

While each rhetorical situation will have its own specific context, there are some common features or elements that will be present in every rhetorical situation. Just as the various shirts in your closet contain different patterns, styles, and textiles—yet all have neck and arm holes—each rhetorical situation will possess the following common features but remain unique due to the particular context surrounding it. These main elements common to all rhetorical situations are **exigence, audience,** and **constraints.**

In other words, every rhetorical situation has an **exigence** (a problem), a **rhetor** (the person speaking out), an **audience** (the people hearing the rhetor, though the rhetor can choose to target a more precise audience), and **constraints** (things that might limit the rhetor, exigence, or the audience). In order for an exigence to exist, there must be potential for a solution. Something without potential for change is not an exigence in a rhetorical situation. For a rhetor to have an audience, she must have a platform from which to speak. This doesn't always mean a podium on a literal platform, but any opportunity for public expression.

Exigence

A rhetorical situation comes into existence the minute we perceive the need for a problem to be solved. **Exigence** is the term used to describe the impetus that provides such a need. Exigence may take the form of a problem, obstacle, or some other defect or deficiency that the rhetor identifies, wishes to overcome or alter, and that can be ameliorated through discourse.

This last criterion is particularly important because for a rhetor's message to be successful, it must be delivered to an audience that could potentially be persuaded by it, on one hand, and it must address a problem or conundrum that is potentially fixable through rhetorical appeal, on the other. The exigence may not always be fixable, but it certainly must be changeable.

Thus, while one could argue rain is a nuisance best confined only to agricultural areas that need it for crop health, such a line of reasoning doesn't qualify as exigence because it would receive little support; endorsing this belief will not actually prevent rain from falling in cities.

Instead, an example of exigence might arise when a spectator attends a tennis match where a participant is injured playing on a wet court. The spectator might recognize that the situation could have been prevented and begin lobbying for a change in rain-delay protocol. Since rain-delay procedures could, feasibly, be altered or amended due to such advocacy, we would consider this motivation for speaking out an example of exigence.

In addition to furnishing the motivation to deliver a message, a rhetorical situation's exigence can have a profound effect on a rhetor's discourse by helping, in part, to determine the appropriate audience to persuade. If we stick with the rain example mentioned above, we could see how the nature of the problem (loose rain regulations can lead to athletes being injured) could influence whomever a rhetor chooses for his or her target audience (members of tennis associations, umpires, tennis fans, professional players, etc.).

> ### No Exigence? No Argument.
>
> If there is no exigence, no perceived problem, then a rhetorical situation seems to not exist. Consider how odd it might be to try and persuade an audience that they should breathe with their lungs.
>
> Of course, there is no real need to make such a persuasive case on this subject since we breathe with our lungs whether we like it or not. Most of us do not have any options. You could indeed make such a speech, but it's more likely to be an empty exercise than a real rhetorical situation.

Furthermore, when rhetors think critically about their situation's exigence and why it is important, they often discover deeper, underlying issues or problems that add to the urgency and ethos of their proposed course of action. The argument is no longer about a system's failure to protect a particular athlete, on a particular day, playing on a particular court. Instead, the event becomes symbolic of a cultural proclivity to put fans' wishes ahead of competitors' safety or the tendency to be reactive rather than proactive about athletes' health during competitions.

By including the implications behind a rhetorical situation's exigence, you can actually create a stronger message because the various people who encounter that message will often relate more strongly to issues of public concern (in which they feel they have a stake) rather than one isolated incident (which they may feel does not pertain to them). In this way, exigence is important because it not only provides the catalyst for a rhetorical situation to develop, but it also shapes and contributes to the exchanges between rhetor and audience that comprise rhetorical discourse as a whole.

How Can Thinking about Exigence Improve Your Ability to Persuade Others?

When you want to persuade an audience, your first job is to convince them that there is a problem that needs solving or a situation that needs changing. Your audience needs to believe that there is an exigence for which they can do something. If you can accomplish the following goals before moving into your main argument, you will gain your audience's attention from the very beginning.

From the Very Beginning, Explain Your Message

As a rhetor, clearly identifying your topic and goal can lead to a more focused message that comes across as polished, refined, and cohesive. It can also help ensure you stay on track during the research and composing processes. In other words, you are trying to provide an anchor for your audience. From the beginning, your audience should have a sense of the general topic you will address. Also keep in mind the abilities of your audience members to enact change. Keep your audience's contribution abilities in mind as you assess your topic and goals.

Explain Why Your Message Is Needed

After anchoring your audience by introducing the general topic, you will need to establish the exigence. By telling them why your message is needed, you are trying to persuade your audience that they have something to lose by not listening to you. They also have something to gain by continuing to give you their undivided attention. It is not enough for you, the rhetor, to feel that there is a problem to be solved. Your audience must also share that feeling. You are responsible for helping to create that shared feeling with your audience.

For example, say we are writing a piece arguing against the proposed natural gas pipeline that, if approved, would span our state and run through eighteen Kentucky counties on its way to the Gulf of Mexico. We may say that our message needs to be heard because the pipeline has not yet been approved and so there is still time to prevent it from being built, or that we need to wait and assess the environmental impact the pipeline's construction could have on our state's historical sites (some of which lie in the pipeline's proposed route).

Though such answers are important to our message, we could go a step further and broaden the reason why we should pursue this course of action by mentioning concerns and issues relevant to beyond our state's boarders—such as land rights and usage, the potential problems of imminent domain and property rights, and the impact of such projects on the environment we all share. By expanding our message, we have supplied even more ways for audience members to connect with a topic and feel strongly about it—important steps toward persuading people to adopt a specific course of action toward or proposed solution to a problem.

Help Your Audience to Visualize What Should Be Accomplished in Response to the Exigence

As you help your audience to understand the exigence they face, you should also help them to understand the goals that can address the problems. Think about what you want to accomplish. Are you proposing a solution that is truly cause for celebration, or will the solution necessitate a certain amount of sacrifice for the greater good or require short-term hardship for long-term benefits? When you specifically frame your proposed course of action, your audience will know that you've thoughtfully considered the situation's exigence and the merits and drawbacks of potential solutions. It will help you come across as realistic and well-versed in the topic chosen, thus enhancing your ethos.

Audience

Discourse is a two-way street. A speaker or writer may feel moved to create written or spoken messages, but unless someone later interprets these messages (even if that person is the rhetor, like in a private journal), the messages dead end and communication breaks down before it has begun. If communication is stifled and information does not pass from rhetor to listener/reader/viewer, a rhetorical situation does not develop because no discourse is able to occur. For this reason, **audience** is a key element of rhetorical situations.

Types of Audiences

There may be several different types of audiences involved in one rhetorical situation. Think, for example, of the wide variety of people who may read an editorial article in a newspaper. There will be those who read the article because they are interested in the topic and also hold a strong opinion about it; these readers may either agree with the author's point of view or be actively opposed to it.

Additional readers will be undecided on the issue and in search of more information before they draw their own conclusions. Other readers will simply "find" the article in the paper and decide to read it on a whim. These readers will live in different areas, be of different ages, and possess different needs (desire for information, entertainment, etc.). For these reasons, it is important to think about who could potentially encounter your message and which methods might serve best when appealing to those you, as the rhetor, hope to persuade.

General Public Audience

As the name suggests, this term refers to an audience comprised of various individuals from all walks of life. It could also be thought of as a generic, "every man/woman" sort of audience base.

Yet what might seem to be a rather straightforward and simple concept on the surface can become more complex when considering the people a particular rhetor might imagine comprise the "general population." No one composes in a vacuum. Instead, all rhetors are influenced, whether consciously or not, by the societal norms characterizing their own specific communities and culture. As a result, some rhetors may assume that the general population is made up of people whose world views, beliefs, and personal background are similar to their own.

While this may sometimes be the case, often the diversity found in an audience of the general public is much greater due to the non-specific nature of the audience pool (one need only read the comments section of any online article to see an example of this). While this large coverage can result in a message receiving more "air play," many who encounter a message made for a general audience may fail to heed its importance because they feel the message doesn't apply to them, find it off-putting because the message assumes too much, or find that the message simply does not "stand out" from the myriad other messages vying for the general population's attention. There are many factors that make up each individual, which means the idea of a general audience is ideal, not realistic. You must take into account the audience's education level, political affiliations, religious affiliations, community involvement, favorite sports teams, and other potentially deal-breaking characteristics that would cause an audience member to tune out your message. For these reasons, many rhetors find that narrowing their audience base can enhance the actual productive power of their messages.

Target Audience

Instead of beginning from a general public *audience,* rhetors are more successful when they develop a more narrowly focused target audience. The term "target audience" refers to individuals the rhetor *intends* to persuade and desires to speak with. They are the rhetor's target.

> ### Generally, There Is No Such Thing
>
> Look around the room right now (or next time you're in a crowded room). You might well have some things in common with these people. You might all be college students, or you might all be under forty years old. Now think of how much you probably don't share in common with everyone in this room. Some of you might be extremely liberal, while others are extremely conservative. Some of you might have experience with terminal illnesses, while others of you have never experienced a loved one's death. Some of you might love watching reality TV, while others of you absolutely hate TV altogether. Some of you might be very religious and others not religious at all. The point is that even an audience who seems to have a lot in common can actually be extremely different. This is what makes the "general public audience" a pretty unhelpful concept. There is no general public audience. Publics (even just small crowds, like the one you're in) are filled with people of different backgrounds, opinions, and beliefs.

Often, rhetors will formulate their idea of target audience during the early composing and researching stages because anticipating the needs, preferences, and expectations of a target audience can help a message's appeal. For example, if a blog writer wanted to target women aged 24–35 with disposable income, the writer might include cultural references thought to appeal more to women, use traditionally "feminine" colors when setting up the site, and utilize a vocabulary familiar to college-educated individuals. Though certainly not an exhaustive list, rhetors will often formulate their target audience with the following criteria in mind:

- What level of familiarity does my target audience have with this subject?
- What age is my target audience (approximately)?
- What type of vocabulary would my target audience be most familiar with (keeping in mind field-specific jargon, "buzz" words, etc.)?
- Are there any cultural preconceptions my target audience might have that I need to consider?
- Is this target audience hostile or open to my message?
- What tone and style is my target audience used to?
- How might my target audience respond to my examples/research/reasoning? What could they object to or be persuaded by?
- What do I *want* my audience to do about my exigence?
- What *can* my audience do about my exigence?

The Power of an Audience

Initially, we may think an audience has limited power in a rhetorical situation since the rhetor composes and delivers his or her message to a "passive" group of listeners. Audience members, however, can actually exert quite a bit of influence over a rhetorical situation. Because an audience is made up of dynamic human beings who will use their own intellects, opinions, and communications to respond to a message or its features, an audience has the potential to radically alter a rhetorical situation.

Anyone who has ever witnessed a political speaker shift from opinionated comments to rapidly apologetic back-pedaling has seen a prime example of how an audience's reaction to a message can determine the future course of that message. Because an audience is able to respond to messages with emotion and intellect, they often force a successful rhetor to adapt his or her message by clarifying, elaborating, or otherwise revising the information presented—sometimes even to the point where the initial context of a rhetorical situation is changed (such as when an informational meeting morphs into a debate, or a casual conversation becomes a profession of love).

Exercise: Case Study

Identifying Elements in a Rhetorical Situation

Sometimes it can be a little tricky to identify elements of a rhetorical situation. Take, for example, the controversy surrounding Colin Kaepernick's 2016 protests. Beginning in the NFL preseason and throughout the 2016 season, Kaepernick knelt during the pregame singing of the National Anthem. He argues, "People don't realize what's really going on in this country. There are a lot of things that are going on that are unjust. People aren't being held accountable for. And that's something that needs to change. That's something that this country stands for freedom, liberty and justice for all. And that's not happening for all right now. [sic]"[2] The protests received mixed reactions. Fans, sportscasters, and fellow players were outraged that Kaepernick would kneel in front of the American flag in a protest against social injustice and racial inequality in America. While some burned #7 jerseys, others demanded action from the NFL organization. The next season, Kaepernick found himself unsigned, hated by many, and revered by even more. He won multiple honors, including the 2017 *Sports Illustrated* Muhammad Ali Legacy Award, and donated more than one million dollars to charities. So why are some people still confused? Well, during heated debates where we allow ourselves to get offended and not use our rhetorical analysis skills, no one really talks about the actual exigence.

Chapter 2   Rhetorical Situation

Exercise: Case Study (continued)

For some, Kaepernick's kneeling appeared as an exigence. However, an American citizen peacefully exercising his 1st Amendment right is not an exigence. Remember, a proper exigence must allot for change. Since forcing citizens to stand for the National Anthem is constitutionally illegal, Kaepernick's kneeling is not the exigence.

Others believed the NFL was the exigence for allowing such behavior. But again, do we really want to see an organization or country forcing people to stand for an anthem? Still others believed that public figures, such as Donald Trump, calling attention to the protest by openly threatening Kaepernick were the exigence for giving Kaepernick any attention at all. But again, an exigence must allot for change, and we can't outlaw free speech.

So, what is our exigence? As Michael Rosenburg clarifies, the protest "was never supposed to be about him [Kaepernick]. It is about Tamir Rice and the world's highest incarceration rate and a country that devalues education and slides too easily into violence."[3] This, put simply, is the exigence Kaepernick is addressing. By analyzing the situation, we see that Kaepernick is not the exigence, but rather, he is the rhetor. He's speaking out in protest by using his body, what we call bodily rhetoric.

So, if Kaepernick is the rhetor, that makes his platform (something every rhetor needs) the football field. The audience is anyone watching football, sports-related news, or national news outlets. His constraints, or limits to his argument, include people who do not watch football, the generalization of his argument, and the fact that filming his protest on live TV is completely out of his control since he has no authority over broadcasters or TV crew. During the 2017 season, most coverage of NFL games failed to televise the pre-game protests (still regularly occurring throughout the NFL and many other sports). By analyzing the situation instead of reacting immediately, audience members can realize what the true rhetorical situation really is. In this case, Kaepernick is the messenger of a larger, ongoing exigence occurring across America.

The relationship between a rhetor and the audience is give-and-take in nature. For this reason, it is wise for any rhetor to try to anticipate the expectations, needs, and possible reactions an audience might have when composing and refining the rhetorical moves employed in his/her message. The rhetor's power stops once the words have been delivered. You may have heard the phrase "you can't take back your words." This is true, and once you've projected those words out to your audience, you've lost your control over those words. Now, it's up to the audience to interpret and respond to those words. This is why it is important for the rhetor to choose her words carefully.

To best communicate with your audience, the **impact** of your words should match their **intent.** By using the words that best match your meaning, you can do a better job of making sure the impact that your words have upon your audience is what you intended. If we do not choose our words wisely, then we can cause offense and/or misunderstandings.

Constraints

Anticipating how an audience could interpret your message is one important way to acknowledge and work through **constraints.** Constraints are any external factors, aside from the rhetor and audience, which could impact a message's success. Often, constraints refer to the parameters the rhetor must compose in and the context within which the audience will receive and interpret a message. Constraints are not bad things that ruin a rhetor's argument, but the walls in which to house an argument. For example, rhetors often operate under constraints that arise due to genre (a press release cannot be as long as a novel), occasion/social convention (it's best not to curse during a eulogy), or culture (it's important to write in a language the majority of readers know). Likewise, the social and historical context surrounding an audience and rhetor during a rhetorical situation can place additional constraints on the table. We can see the power of such constraints in current debates surrounding the inclusion of rape jokes in stand-up comedy or the resonance of Congressman Bobby Rush wearing a hoodie on the House floor shortly after the death of Trayvon Martin in 2012.

What is going on in the world "outside" of a rhetorical situation matters because, in reality, it is impossible to not bring the "outside world" into rhetorical situations through the various associations, symbols, and preferences we all carry with us every day. It is this inclusiveness that gives rhetorical discourse its potentially persuasive power and creativity, but it also means that we as rhetors and audience members should be aware of constraints and the possible impact they could have on our messages and our interpretation of the messages of others. Doing so means not only being a responsible rhetor or audience member, but also being a more active participant in the exchanges of information that formulate our lives.

Types of Constraints

Genre Constraints

Genre constraints arise as a result of the particular medium in which a rhetor works. The different types of communication (written, spoken, and visual) have various qualities not shared with other types, and the multiple forms available within these larger categories will also have their specific traits (think rock music versus opera music). If a rhetor wishes to create a message that accords a genre, he/she must be familiar with the distinctive elements that comprise that genre. Genres may also be blurred or combined to create new forms of communication, but it is still important to know the constraints that help place a message into a specific genre so that such blurring/blending can be successfully recognized and appreciated. Genre-based constraints often center upon one of the following:

- Tone
- Visual presence
- Style
- Duration
- Text presence
- Design
- Delivery method
- Purpose/use
- Artistic precedent
- Platform

Exercise: Genre Constraints

Together with a partner, come up with short speeches that fit both of the following occasions. You might choose one person to be the speechmaker, or you might want to switch off.
- Write a "wedding toast" for your partner. This should be done in the style of a wedding reception toast, in order to praise and celebrate him or her. (Have fun with this speech! Feel free to make up details that might make this speech appropriate for the occasion.)
- Write a short eulogy for your partner (who happily lived to a ripe age of 100 years). This should be done in the style most appropriate to a memorial service or funeral.

How did the different *genres*—wedding toasts and eulogies—constrain what you were able to write? Even though both speeches were praising or honoring your partner, did you notice that the occasions changed such details as tone, delivery, style, and even word choices? Now try summing up each of those speeches in a post on X (formerly Twitter). How did your word choice change? How did the platform and genre constraints of X affect your writing and message?

Material Constraints

Material constraints are those constraints that occur due to the materials or equipment needed to compose and deliver a message successfully. They can range from making sure you have enough pens and paper, computer access, or a working microphone, to ensuring that you have clear images, a venue that can accommodate your visual aids, or the appropriate amount of alloted space.

Cultural Constraints

Cultural constraints refer to those factors that can influence a message's efficacy and are socially constructed. Cultural constraints may take the form of proprietary "rules," those unspoken guidelines that determine what proper etiquette is during a particular rhetorical situation. They may influence a rhetor's word choice, balance of pathos/logos/ethos, or even a rhetor's choice of dress. An example of a cultural constraint is the unspoken rule that no one wears white to a wedding except the bride. Now this "rule" might not be written anywhere, but imagine trying to perform the wedding toast you wrote earlier while standing next to the bride or groom when you're both wearing white. Would your white dress or suit affect your message of happiness for the couple? How would your attire affect your message and ethos? Socially accepted norms can play a significant role in a rhetor's ability to reach the target audience.

Purposely Breaking Convention—When Constraints Are Undermined

Occasionally, rhetors will intentionally thwart constraints to produce a reaction from the audience, create a larger potential audience, enhance their abilities to promote change, or break the boundaries of what a traditional genre is thought to encompass or do.

For example, look at Oprah Winfrey's 2018 acceptance speech for winning the Cecil B. DeMille Award for lifetime achievement. Compare that to Sally Field's 1985 Oscars acceptance speech in which she famously says, "you like me."[4] Like every genre, acceptance speeches have their conventions and constraints. Typically, the conventions of an acceptance speech are what Field gives us: thank-you, some version of "I'm honored," and heartfelt messages to loved ones. Time, television censorship, recognition for studios, and the diversity of audience members might be constraints to the speech. While Field's speech was under two minutes per Oscars outline, Winfrey's was nearly ten minutes. Here we see the different variations on speech conventions in different awards ceremonies and for different levels of recognition. This is not the only way Winfrey's speech is not a typical award acceptance speech. While Winfrey begins her speech traditionally with telling us what inspired her and thanking those who support her, she diverges from the traditional genre conventions of an acceptance speech when she begins to talk about the #MeToo Movement. Consider her closing sentiments:

> So I want all the girls watching here, now, to know that a new day is on the horizon! And when that new day finally dawns, it will be because of a lot of magnificent women, many of whom are right here in this room tonight, and some pretty phenomenal men, fighting hard to make sure that they become the leaders who take us to the time when nobody ever has to say 'Me too' again.[5]

Here, Winfrey's speech has completely broken genre conventions. It is no longer about her humility and thankfulness; it is about advocating for victims of sexual harassment. In breaking the typical genre conventions of an acceptance speech, Winfrey expands her intended audience, uses her platform for advocacy rather than humility, and establishes herself as a pillar of support for victims.

Other times rhetors may choose to eschew some of the conventions of a particular genre or to mix and match across several genres. Many multimedia presentations do this by mixing elements of written text, visuals of various types, and other sound components. They may sample various pieces from "well-known" works of art or music (such as Eminem's use of Cheech and Chong's "Earache My Eye" in his refrain to "Untouchable"),[6] or mesh together genres to create a hybrid (such as a graphic novel). Often this synthesis of styles and genres produces innovative and interesting messages that appeal to audiences. However, adopting such a path also carries risks. If a synthesis is too extreme, an audience may find it jarring or incomprehensible.

Ultimately, it is the job of the rhetor to deduce the constraints most important to him or her, figure out how to accommodate those constraints effectively, and decide whether the risk of breaking some of the constraints outweighs the possible consequences that could arise from such a choice.

RHETORICAL SITUATIONS AND THE WRD CLASSROOM

As you complete the WRD curriculum here at UK, you will have the opportunity to compose in a variety of mediums and genres. Since WRD assignments often include aspects of written, oral, and visual composition, you will become well versed in many of the conventions characterizing these mediums. A keen sense of the rhetorical situation surrounding these assignments, from the parameters the instructor requests for each assignment to the nuances of your own target audience, will help the efficacy and overall impact of your message.

In addition, some assignments you receive in WRD may require you to conduct a rhetorical analysis of someone else's work. Thinking about the context and factors that comprised the rhetorical situation surrounding this person's work may help to facilitate this task. Remember the Kaepernick case study and that the elements of a rhetorical situation can often be tricky to identify. You must examine each situation closely and take time to define your terms. It will require you to use your powers of critical thinking; but if you examine the ways in which a rhetor's work upholds or plays with genre conventions, social expectations, and cultural norms, you may find some interesting information to include in your analysis.

NOTES

[1] Lloyd Bitzer. "The Rhetorical Situation." *Philosophy and Rhetoric 1,* 1968, p. 6.

[2] 49ers Staff. "Key Quotes from Colin Kaepernick, 49ers Teammates on Aug. 28." *49ers.com,* Aug. 28 2016, http://www.49ers.com/news/article-2/Key-Quotes-from-Colin-Kaepernick-49ers-Teammates-on-Aug-28/bf85743d-3b62-4b29-bfd1-c733f743e708.

[3] Rosenberg, Michael. "Colin Kaepernick Is Recipient of 2017 Sports Illustrated Muhammad Ali Legacy Award." *Sports Illustrated,* Nov. 30, 2017. https://www.si.com/sportsperson/2017/11/30/colin-kaepernick-muhammad-ali-legacy-award.

[4] "Sally Field Wins Best Actress in 1985." *Oscars.go.com,* http://oscar.go.com/video/tear-jerking-oscar-speeches/sally-field-wins-best-actress-in-1985.

[5] Jester, Julia. "Full Transcript to Oprah Winfrey's Golden Globe Acceptance Speech." *NBC News,* Jan. 10, 2018. https://www.nbcnews.com/pop-culture/tv/read-oprah-winfrey-s-full-golden-globes-speech-n835626.

[6] Aswad, Jern. "Tommy Chong Talks Eminem's Cheech & Chong Sampling 'Untouchable': 'Racism is Ignorant and He's a Warrior.'" *Variety.com,* Dec. 8, 2017. http://variety.com/2017/music/news/tommy-chong-talks-eminems-cheech-chong-sampling-untouchable-racism-is-ignorance-and-hes-a-warrior-1202634514/.

Audience

Recommended for WRD 111/112
and as needed

Chapter 3

When you write, you always write for someone else. Even if that someone else is your teacher, you still are writing for *someone*.

Writers sometimes forget about audience. In school, writers produce quickly written work and forget about the people who will eventually read that work. As a result of this oversight, our work can sometimes get weighed down with clichés, grammar errors, a lack of organization, a lack of research, and other problems. When these problems appear in our writing, it is usually because we have forgotten to consider our audience. And, unfortunately, if too many of these problems exist, we can assume that the reader will most likely stop reading at some point.

Unless you are writing something private, like a journal or a diary, you can be sure that at some point someone will be reading your writing. Maybe it will be your instructor and your class peers. But, for the rest of your life, your writing will probably also be read by many other kinds of audiences: your coworkers, your family and friends, your clients, your fans, and many other kinds of readers. This chapter will give you some tips and advice for how to take audience into account during your writing process.

Audience is a generic term. We don't always know the make-up of the audience receiving our work. And even when we think a specific group will read our work (like certain professional groups, ethnic groups, religious groups, or peer groups), the members of that group won't all receive the work in the same way. No audience is so homogenous that one message will mean one thing to all its members. For instance, think about yourself as a member of the group "college students." Not all college students think in the same way or share the same opinions. Just because something is written for an audience of "college students" doesn't mean every member of that group will agree, like, or even care about that message.

Still, recognizing the potential audience is important. Even if audiences aren't homogenous, we can still make some assumptions about audiences when we write. There are tools and strategies you can use so that an audience, whoever it is, will be interested, angered, encouraged, provoked, saddened, helped, or moved in some way. Your goal as a writer should always be to create a reaction in your audience. If your audience experiences no reaction to your work, then there was no reason for them to read or watch what you created.

What follows are some strategies for thinking about how to reach your audience. These are not the only strategies writers can engage, but you can use these as starting points for your work.

APPEAL TO CONVENTIONS, GENRES, EXPECTATIONS

Each profession has its own demands and interests. In the citation chapter, we noted that citation style is a professional interest. Using MLA for your citations, for instance, is an appeal to the professions that recognize MLA as the appropriate style. Other professions use different citations styles, such as APA. If you use APA style when writing for audiences of social science professionals, for instance, you are recognizing that readers who study Psychology will understand your citations.

In that sense, citation style shows recognition of your audience.

There are other professional recognitions to consider as well. Some of these recognitions are formatting based: headings, subheadings, salutations, and closings. Some of these recognitions are content specific, such as using the right terminology (people who work in real estate use one set of terms; people who work in medicine use another).

In the business world, a list of my professional qualifications and experience would be commonly called a "resumé." However, in universities and colleges, the resumé is referred to as a "curriculum vitae" (or CV for short). If I apply for a job as a professor at a university, my letter will use the phrase "curriculum vitae" and *not* "resumé." This is because my audience—other academics, in this case—does not use the term "resumé" on a regular basis.

Another way of saying this is that all writing is part of a specific **genre.** A genre is an audience-directed form of writing. The writing associated with a genre is carefully constructed so that the reader or viewer will recognize these conventions. Imagine yourself watching a movie where the main character finds herself all alone in a dark, creepy, old house filled with cobwebs. She moves slowly down the creaky floor toward a spooky closet door that is shut. She puts her hand on the old doorknob. The audience might instinctively shout,

"Don't open the door!" Why not? Because in the genre of horror movies, opening a closet door in a dark, creepy house often means trouble! The filmmakers know how to construct the conventions—darkness, old houses, cobwebs, the lone character, creaky floors—so that the audience recognizes the genre: **horror!** We expect something spooky to happen next because we know the genre's conventions.

So, too, does the romantic comedy have audience expectations. Think of a movie like *When Harry Met Sally* or *Pretty Woman*. The romantic comedy is a professional genre as well; it is a movie industry genre. An audience watching a romantic comedy typically has expectations:

> Boy meets girl. → Boy gets girl. → Boy loses girl. → Boy gets girl again.

Again, there is variety to this organizational scheme, but it typically is the basis for a romantic comedy because *audiences* expect this structure.

All genres work with audience expectation. A school essay is also a genre: your teacher expects you to fulfill its conventional requirements. To do well on an essay, you need to know the teacher's (the audience's) expectations. In school, those conventions might include proper headings, numbered pages, works cited or bibliography, typewritten pages, and so on. Here are a few other examples of genres and audience expectation.

White papers can look very different, depending on the context in which they appear. Some white papers are very long, while some may be fairly short. Nevertheless, because the white paper is a professional writing genre, it does need to address some basic audience expectations. An audience reading a white paper typically expects the following:

- An introduction
- Background information
- Solution or solutions
- Conclusion

There can be variety to this organization, but overall, this is what the audience expects. Just like horror film audiences have certain expectations, professional writing genres like white papers also have audience expectations.

A **white paper** is a good example of a **professional document,** one that comes with certain audience expectations. A white paper is a type of report that defines an issue, outlines a problem, or markets a product for a business or organization.

Figure 1. An example of white paper.[1]

The white paper is just one example of a professional writing genre. There are many, many genres and conventions associated with different kinds of writing. You will find it helpful to ask yourself, *"What are the audience expectations for the genre in which I am writing?"* What do typical readers of this genre expect you to do? Do they expect a certain kind of introduction? Do they expect anecdotes and personal stories? Do they expect the pages to be formatted in a certain way? Do they expect certain kinds of evidence and citations? Every type of writing fits in some type of professional genre scheme. Your task is to consider the expectations of that genre before you begin writing.

Appealing to your audience's expectations is one way to start thinking seriously about your audience. There are other types of appeals to consider as well.

APPEAL TO INTERESTS

Appealing to an audience's interests is another way to get your audience's attention. We can't always positively know what our audience is interested in, but we can make informed assumptions. By "informed assumptions," we mean that writers should go beyond stereotypes or common beliefs about groups.

Sometimes writers make the mistake of lumping whole categories of people together, just because they share demographic features: gender, age, ethnic background, political affiliation, birthplace, religion, etc. Not all women love shopping for shoes. Not all teenagers love playing video games. Not all Kentuckians love horses. Instead of relying on stereotypes, therefore, we can consider some other ideas for how to make informed assumptions about our audience's interests.

Consider this article in the *Dallas Observer*, **"Shock Top Sent Me $100 Worth of Swag and Two Awful Beers. That Sums Them Up Perfectly"** *(https://www.dallasobserver.com/restaurants/shock-top-sent-me-100-worth-of-swag-and-two-awful-beers-that-sums-them-up-perfectly-7023176).*

The author received a box of campfire swag (free merchandise) and two Shock Top beers because InBev (the brewery conglomerate who sent the products) hoped the author would write a positive review on his website. That review, in turn, would help sales. But there was just one problem. The author feels that the box of campfire-related products (Sterno can, stowaway pot, and items to make s'mores) is targeted not to a craft beer drinker (as the brewer intends) but to a stereotype. A craft beer drinker is someone who drinks beer from smaller breweries, which do not use artificial ingredients. Unfortunately, Anheuser-Busch, the brewery who makes Shock Top, uses artificial ingredients that craft beer drinkers find objectionable:

> Craft beer is booming, taking a bigger slice of the beer market every year, and the foreign-owned corporations are scared shitless. But rather than improve their products by not using trash ingredients, they're spending money to play craft-beer dress-up, buying out breweries or creating their own pseudo-craft companies. This package of swag is such a brazen insult it almost seems like satire. It's more than $100 worth of marketing swag that reduces its badly missed target audience to a stereotype, and, almost an afterthought, a grand total of two beers. You couldn't ask for a more literal illustration of their priorities.[2]

In this case, targeting didn't work. Shock Top made an assumption about its audience's interest: *Craft beer drinkers will want these camping products and, thus, our beer.* In this case, though, this assumption was a misinformed one. As the author makes clear, the targeted audience of craft beer drinkers does not want cheap swag; they are more interested in improved products and better ingredients.

Facebook and other social media are great places to think about appeals to interest. Many people post to social media what they believe, what their political views are, which sports teams they follow, and what they do for fun. Users do so because they often believe they are appealing to their friends' interests: *"If I like X and Y, my friends probably do, too."* In this way, appeals to interest are based on an assumed commonality (the way Amazon will show you what it thinks you are interested in buying because of what other people, like you, bought).

Assuming others share your interests, though, can be risky. When you appeal to a supposed common belief, you can just as easily be appealing to what someone does not believe in. Sharing your interest so easily can backfire. Media consultant Arik Hanson once had a Facebook status update about this issue.

Arik Hanson
7 hours ago ·

Really surprised at how many people who work in the professional services industry share their political viewpoints here on FB. After all, you never know when a client is listening (and what their political views are). Am I in the minority in thinking that's a pretty risky move?

Figure 2. Advice from a social media expert about posting political opinions on Facebook.[3]

Merely sharing, then, is not without risks. Just because you believe in X or Y, doesn't mean someone else does as well. Consider the YouTube sensation PewDiePie whose 2017 fall-from-grace began when he misjudged his audience. Known for his vulgarity and gaming, PewDiePie took jokes too far when he published Anti-Semitic videos and memes. Though his audience might have been OK with vulgar language and crude jokes, they were not OK with hateful racial and religious slurs. PewDiePie was quickly dropped from Disney and YouTube for sharing his racist views. His fans abandoned him, and his subscriptions plummeted. This shows that just because an audience likes one thing, they might not stand for another.[4] A client, as in Hanson's case, may abandon you if he or she discovers your public sharing and disagrees with you. Or it may cause the client to enter into a different relationship with you. Reactions are not entirely predictable. On the other hand, figuring out others' beliefs can help you later appeal to interest. Just make sure you know what the possibilities are when you share interests.

Because people are eager to express their interests, Facebook can target users with advertisements based on those expressed interests. On Facebook, we recognize that not only are we addressing an audience (the friends who read our updates), but that we are an audience for someone else (advertisers paying Facebook to be connected to you via your updates).

Beyond the question of what is or is not ethical about directing ads to Facebook users, this practice of targeting is a matter of audience identification. In the example of Facebook's targeting, advertisers are trying to make a connection between our status updates (our writing) and what interests us (as well as those people who are friends with us).

APPEAL TO STICKINESS

In their book *Made to Stick,* Chip Heath and Dan Heath describe this process of targeting ideas toward a specific audience. The sticky nature of a message, they write, is based on a few things:

- **Simplicity:** Keep things simple.
- **Unexpectedness:** Generate interest and curiosity.
- **Concreteness:** Use specific imagery.
- **Credibility:** Demonstrate credentials.
- **Emotions:** Make people feel something.
- **Stories:** Perform a story.[5]

For the Heaths, these six principles are often found in sticky ideas. Using six principles when targeting an audience may sound simple, but it's actually quite complex.

Advertisements recognize their potential audience (those who will buy the company's products) by often appealing to that audience's interests.

Apple's "Think Different" campaign is one such example.

This ad appeals to its audience (young, creative, technology users) by saying

> *Albert Einstein was the type of person who could think differently.*
>
> *Apple sells products to help you think differently.*
>
> *If you want to "think different," buy something by Apple.*

Does the "Think Different" advertisement follow the Heaths' idea of being sticky?

Figure 3. According to Apple, Albert Einstein "think[s] different."[6] *(Image Courtesy of the Advertising Archives.)*

- **Simplicity:** It uses one image.
- **Unexpectedness:** One doesn't usually associate Einstein or the other figures featured in the ads in the series with computers (in fact, Einstein precedes the personal computer).
- **Concreteness:** Einstein and the other featured figures are recognizable (the person who lives next to you, for instance, would not work in this ad).
- **Credibility:** Einstein is a highly credible figure for his work in physics.
- **Emotion:** The figures tap into our emotional connections; we think these are smart or creative people.
- **Stories:** If Einstein was so creative and innovative without a Mac, can I be like him with a Mac?

> **Discussion Questions**
>
> 1. What's the audience interest being appealed to in the "Think Different" advertisement?
> 2. **Levi's® "Go Forth" commercial** *(https://www.youtube.com/watch?v=FdW1CjbCNxw)* also appeals to its audience (young jeans-wearers) by appealing to a series of tropes and ideas that might interest them. While the narrator of the video is the nineteenth-century poet Walt Whitman, the audience for this video does not need to know that fact. Instead, the keywords of the poem,
>
>   - Grow
>   - Freedom
>   - Enduring
>   - Strong
>   - Ample
>   - Equal
>   - Fair
>
>   are meant to be appealing by telling a story young people will relate to and identify with. These terms are meant to create the feeling of having spirit, conviction, the desire to "go forth" and do good. Levi's wants its audience to make a connection between the idea and the jeans. Can you apply the Heaths' principles to this video as well? How?

APPEAL TO KNOWLEDGE

Specific audiences bring specific knowledge to their reading experiences. Audiences' backgrounds can greatly affect what they read and what they understand. One benefit of considering your audience's knowledge is that doing so increases the likelihood that your writing will be comprehensible to your audience. Consider whether or not your audience would know the definition of a term or catch a cultural reference. Pausing to define terms or explain references can help your audience understand you clearly.

Awareness of an audience's knowledge also empowers you to make your work more compelling to that audience. Different readers will draw upon different kinds of *cultural knowledge* to understand what a text means. Knowing your audience often means knowing the kinds of cultural knowledge your audience has.

Tapping into an audience's cultural knowledge can be powerful. It can grant you the opportunity to share a message in a specific way or to make an argument more persuasive than if you used generic ideas or references as evidence.

One way to appeal to your audience's background or cultural knowledge is to use **allusions.** Allusions are references to what the writer believes will be understood as shared knowledge. We allude to people, time periods, historical moments, popular culture, famous sayings, and other information we expect the audience to already know.

On January 18, 2013, National Public Radio ran a piece on the usage of allusions or references in popular culture (Found here: **In a Fragmented Cultureverse, Can Pop References Still Pop?** *http://www.npr.org/2013/04/14/177204413/in-a-fragmented-cultureverse-can-pop-references-still-pop*).

The hosts of the show point out that, many times, TV shows or performances reference texts that they don't expect their entire audiences to be familiar with. But the mere act of referencing, the NPR story shows, can still speak to larger issues the writers want to express.

How does a simple allusion help an audience to understand complex or large issues? It works by "anchoring" meaning in the text. Imagine for a moment that some complex issue under discussion is a boat floating on rough waters. Without any kind of anchor, that boat may well get carried away by the waves and wind. If there is an anchor, however, that boat will likely not get lost in the chaos. The same might be said about complex issues being debated. If there is an "anchor" to an outside reference, then your audience may better understand why this issue is relevant or interesting. By anchoring difficult topics to something closer to home, writers can help their readers better understand their meaning.

Let's take a look at a few examples of how allusions appeal to a common background or cultural knowledge.

Allusions in Politics

Political campaigns, protests, and other acts involved with political issues often appeal to audiences by making allusions.

A popular **political allusion** that tapped into its audience's cultural knowledge involved signs carried by African American sanitation workers striking in Memphis in 1968. The signs were addressed to an audience of white employers, but also a larger American viewership watching the protests from home on their TVs.

Figure 4. Sanitation workers strike in Memphis in 1968.[7] (© by Richard L Copley with permission)

"I am a man" is an allusion to the U.S. Declaration of Independence: All men are created equal. By saying "I am a man," the striking workers are saying: Our Declaration of Independence says all men are created equal. You, our audience, know this. You also know that we are men. Then, treat us equally.

We also can call this type of allusion an **enthymeme.** An enthymeme is a type of reasoning in which a major or minor premise is hinted at, but not explicitly stated. Without all of the premises presented, the reader still is able to reach a conclusion.

For instance,

- **Major premise:** We hold these truths to be self evident, that all men are created equal.

- **Minor premise:** African American garbage workers are men.
- **Conclusion** (implied on sign): Treat me equally.

This allusion is enthymemic.

Another example is more recent. During Barack Obama's first campaign to be president, the Hope poster created by Shepard Fairey was widely disseminated at political rallies, in cities, online, and elsewhere.

Figure 5. The Hope poster, created by Shepard Fairey.[8]

Since the Hope poster's creation, many other visual editors have alluded back to this image to make a point. If you go to Google Images, for instance, and search for "Obama Hope Poster," you will find thousands of similar images, from R2D2 to Bob Hope to Steve Jobs to Alfred E. Newman to Big Bird. The creators of these images expect that you, the reader, will make the connection between the original poster and the newer image. You won't connect Obama's policies per se, but you will, it seems, connect the election's spirit of hope and renewal that many of Obama's supporters initially felt.

This connection may be satire (Alfred E. Newman, Big Bird), or this connection may be about applying hope elsewhere (Steve Jobs).

Like the previous example, the usage of the Hope image as allusion depends on an audience reaching an implied conclusion based on the image's familiarity and previous association with Obama.

Chapter 3   Audience

Allusions in Popular Culture

In **popular culture,** we often encounter allusions to other popular culture items. The writer or creator of the popular culture work (song, video, TV show, movie, tweet, meme) will make an allusion with the expectation that the audience will recognize the reference and understand the overall meaning. In turn, the text itself, the author believes, will be stronger because of the allusion.

Because most of us listen to music and watch movies and TV shows, popular culture is an appropriate example regarding how to use allusions.

Some make pop culture allusions in their everyday lives. Take for instance, President Barack Obama's 2013 Tweet alluding to *Mean Girls:*

Figure 6.   White House tweet, 2013.[9]

Making "fetch" happen is something *Mean Girls'* character Gretchen tries to accomplish throughout the movie. The scene where antagonist Regina George tells Gretchen that fetch is "not going to happen," is well-known and regularly referenced by various genres of social media. Here, Obama uses a pop culture item (the Tweet) to reference another (*Mean Girls*).

Allusions can also take place across genres. Television series such as *Gilmore Girls, Arrested Development,* and *South Park* base entire scripts, scenes, and themes upon pop culture references. Consider this brief clip of Jason Sudeikis trying to use what he thinks is "hip" lingo when talking to a teenage girl pretending to be his daughter: *https://youtu.be/k9M_i8s_fnk.*

The avid UK Wildcats fan, Drake, gave us *YOLO* in his 2011 song, "The Motto." For Drake and his fans, life's motto should be "You Only Live Once (YOLO)." By 2013, *YOLO* was trendy with tweens and young teens. While *YOLO* had great popularity, it quickly became associated with a certain age group. Sudeikis' use of the phrase in 2013 alludes to Drake's song and franchise, but it also complicates the joke in this scene. By alluding to teenage lingo, Sudeikis' character proves to be an out-of-touch father figure failing to successfully communicate with the next generation. We can all laugh at this joke because, I'm sure, we've all had to roll our eyes through a tragic "dad joke." In this way, pop culture allusions can add elements of depth and humor.

Film director Quentin Tarantino also uses allusions for similar purposes. He expects his audience to understand his movies' references to popular culture trivia, Kung Fu films of the 1960s and 1970s, and Blaxploitation movies. He also likes to name drop popular culture references. By doing so, he creates a relationship with his audience so that the films feel a part of everyday discourse.

Take a look at **this collage of Tarantino popular culture references** *(http://www.collegehumor.com/video/6860507/every-pop-culture-reference-from-tarantino-movies)* set up on a timeline from the 1900s to the present.

See how many references and allusions you recognize. By drawing on over a century of culture references, Tarantino shows us that we can always find a way to anchor a text for our audiences. A fight scene in *Kill Bill* is transformed, for instance, when O-Ren and Beatrix Kiddo exchange the parts of **"Silly Rabbit, Trix Are for Kids"** *(https://www.youtube.com/watch?v=VIOmYThtLWg);* the reference anchors the scene. The reference to a 1970s cereal commercial appeals to audiences who grew up seeing it on television. The reference, in turn, transforms the tension of the scene into something slightly playful and funny.

If the scenes in question did not use all of these references, would the films still be as meaningful? If, in *Pulp Fiction,* Jules didn't try and calm Yolanda down near the film's end by saying **"Be like Fonzi,"** would the scene be as powerful? Would it have the same meaning? Why not? What does the allusion to Fonzi do for the scene? How does it transform the robbery of the restaurant?

APPEAL TO PROVOCATION

While we sometimes feel that we have to appeal to our audience's needs, knowledge, or interests by being accommodating, we can also use the same knowledge to provoke. We don't always have to try to win over an audience. We don't always have to appeal to an audience. In fact, there are times where a writer needs to provoke her audience in order to:

- Get a point across.
- Engage in a debate.
- Push a reader's buttons.
- Start a conversation about a hot topic.
- Attract attention.
- Place the idea at the center of a conversation.
- Get the idea noticed.

In 2013, a high school senior named Suzy Lee Weis wrote an Op-Ed for the *Wall Street Journal* entitled **"To (All) the Colleges That Rejected Me"** *(http://www.wsj.com/articles/SB10001424127887324000704578390340064578654)*. In the short essay, Weiss complains about not getting into college because she was "just being herself."[10] Instead of engaging in a number of extra-curricular activities, as many other classmates did in high school, Weis felt that she followed the popular advice to be herself. Being herself, it turned out, did not get her into college; her classmates did get into college. Once rejected, Weis felt that she had been treated unfairly for not doing what other classmates did in order to be accepted to college.

Whether an actual complaint or a joke, Weis's piece provoked enough people that it was covered in a number of other publications including the ***Washington Post*** *(http://www.washingtonpost.com/local/education/pittsburgh-teen-bitterly-lashes-out-at-colleges-that-rejected-her/2013/04/02/dc60ce5e-9b9d-11e2-9bda-edd1a7fb557d_story.html)*, **the *Today* show's website,** and elsewhere. A Google search for the Op-Ed brings up over 200,000 hits. The response to Weis's essay was very intense. By pushing the right buttons, she found her audience. In the comments sections of many of these online publications, readers complain that Weis is selfish, spoiled, privileged, and lacking any sense of what it takes to get into college.

Whether these critiques are true is not evident. But if we look at some of the topics Weis discusses—the things she feels she didn't do—we can see what provoked her audience so strongly:

- She mocks the SAT.
- She mocks charity.
- She mocks diversity.
- She mocks high school students who work part-time.
- She mocks tiger parents who encourage their children to have hobbies.
- She mocks high school students who have internships.

In other words, she finds the buttons to push. Weis mocks the categories typically used to determine whether or not someone should be admitted to college: high SAT scores, extracurricular activities, and highly respected hobbies. By mocking these categories, Weis made her audience uncomfortable. She made her audience angry. And the result was highly effective. She reached a very large audience by being provocative. Instead of only being read in the *Wall Street Journal* (a major feat by itself), she was read in many other online spaces.

This example doesn't mean a writer should always provoke. After all, your audience may find your provocations completely objectionable. You risk angering the very people you want to reach. If one goes too far (using racist, sexist, discriminatory, or insulting language, for example) one's ideas might reach a large audience, but the response could be detrimental (losing one's job, being ostracized, being accused of hate speech, etc.).

However, Weis's example does show that provocation can sometimes be productive, particularly when the goal is to reach a larger number of people. In Weis's case, she did not engage in hateful speech but pushed many people to consider her ideas in a dramatic way. We might make the argument that Weis was successful in her provocation.

Here is another example of how writers sometimes appeal to provocation in their attempts to reach an audience. Roger Baylor is the owner of New Albanian Brewery in New Albany, Indiana, right outside of Louisville. Baylor runs a blog called **The Potable Curmudgeon** *(http://potablecurmudgeon.blogspot.com)*. Baylor, who is passionate about local food and local beer, can be quite provocative in his online writings.

In one blog post, **"Second Hand News Usually Is Mistaken"** *(http://potable curmudgeon.blogspot.com/2013/03/second-hand-news-usually-is-mistaken.html)*, Baylor recognizes the effects his writing may have on his audience.

Chapter 3   Audience

> Words I write are published alongside my name, because to me, anonymity is tantamount to cowardice. For those like me with strong views, there is an inescapable element of living and dying by the rhetorical sword, and I accept this condition of the engagement.
>
> Give and take is common, but every now and then, a complaint will be registered to the effect that someone, somewhere, has taken offense at words I've written. Actually I'm delighted with such feedback, and quite willing to discuss particulars, so long as we're reasonably clear about parameters.[11]

Over a series of posts, for instance, Baylor has expressed anger at an Indiana liquor chain named Big Red Liquors. Accusing the chain of being a monopoly and of ejecting his brewery from a **Big Red sponsored event in 2003** *(http://potablecurmudgeon.blogspot.com/2012/04/nine-years-later-and-absolute-power.html)*, Baylor has critiqued Big Red several times and argued against the chain stocking beers from his brewery. **This post** *(http://potablecurmudgeon.blogspot.com/2013/03/big-red-liquors-pursues-its-monopoly-in.html)* begins with a specific provocation.

By posting a picture of the middle finger, Baylor is trying to:

- Provoke Big Red Liquors as potential audience.
- Let his other readers know how angry he is by featuring a provocative image.

In his recounting of the event *(http://potablecurmudgeon.blogspot.com/2012/04/nine-years-later-and-absolute-power.html)* that led to his conflict with Big Red, Baylor describes the liquor chain's representatives in a provocative manner:

> Our walking papers were verbally delivered to us by two members of the Big Red Liquors management team, John Glumb and Wade Shanower, a pair of wholly corporate, well-fed and utterly plain men who differed from the other polo shirts in attendance by the shared habit of spluttering ominously, brilliant white teeth clinched, blue neck veins bulging in a most unhealthy way and misshapen, contorted faces as red as their Big Red Liquors knits.[12]

Notice Baylor's usage of language:

- "Corporate, well-fed and utterly plain men"
- "Polo shirts"
- "Brilliant white teeth clenched"
- Contorted, red faces

The descriptions, entirely unflattering, are meant to have a provocative effect.

Figure 7. The label featured on one of Baylor's beers (and his blog). Image by Roger Baylor.

In addition, if you look at the figure above, you will see Baylor's own version of the Obama poster. Hope, in this case, is replaced with Hops and an image from one of the brewery's beer labels.

By openly critiquing a major Indiana retail outlet, Baylor is specifically using provocation as a way to address his audience. This provocation might:

- Position him and his brewery as independents in a market dominated by conglomerates and chains.
- Establish for his audience (those who visit his restaurant/brewery and buy his beers) an ethos as fiercely independent.

Whereas provocation helps Weis get her ideas to a large audience, provocation helps Baylor create a specific ethos. Both are productive usages of provocation.

APPEAL TO LANGUAGE

The chapter thus far has discussed many ways that you can connect with your audience to communicate effectively, whether that be use of MLA for an essay or use of a reaction image or meme to create a particular type of humor online. These discussions have focused mainly on how to bend the structure and content of your writing to your audience, but we can also keep the *language* of the audience in mind.

The way you talk—and, by extension, the way that you write—is closely tied with your **identity.** The words that you say and the way that you say them always mark you as *something;* what that something is depends on how you craft your language, and who your audience is.

This *something* can be the identity of an individual (e.g., you, a family member, an actor or actress, a politician) or a group (e.g., ethnic groups, such as white or African American; social groups, such as Greek life or a sports team; political groups such as democrats and republicans; religious groups such as Christianity, Islam, or Judaism; communities such as TikTok or Reddit users, etc.). Any individual, group, or organization can mark their identity with the way that they use language, and you as a writer can often create a shared ethos (See Chapter 6: "Rhetorical Analysis.") by acknowledging that.

Let's consider the example of accents. Those who speak with a southern dialect mark themselves as from the south. If you are somewhere like Cincinnati, Ohio, these people are often identified as *other,* in this case meaning from somewhere else, out-of-state, and further south. Therefore, they can use their language and the way that they speak to mark a *southern, non-local identity.* In the same sense, they could accommodate their speech and try to be less southern, actively choosing to not mark a southern identity. For example, they could not use the word *y'all,* as this word is associated strongly with southerness.

However, language can be manipulated—amplified or muffled—depending on what kind of identity is important given the goal of your writing or speech. Continuing the example of southerness, imagine you are a northern politician campaigning in Alabama. You might try to connect with your audience (i.e., southerners) by using their language, which is part of their identity as southern. Many politicians do this by incorporating lexical items such as *y'all* into their language, trying to make themselves, and thus their message, less distant and more appealing to their audience. Such an appeal may fail or succeed, depending on a variety of complex factors related to the rhetorical situation.

Because language is so closely connected to identity, it is important to consider the **language of the audience** when writing or speaking. Any given audience has a *language profile:* how they use language collectively, and what kind of language varieties they use. Some audiences have a uniform language variety. For example, consider your friend group in high school; you and your friends likely are from the same region, and likely talk the same way. Other audiences have a more varied language profile. For example, consider the state of Kentucky; there are many different groups of people that make up Kentuckians. There are rural and urban areas, different ethnic groups, different incomes brackets, northern Kentuckians versus central, eastern, and western Kentuckians, and so on. All of these groups of people may use language differently, and yet make up the whole of Kentucky.

If you wanted to text both your friends and your parents about having won a free pizza, would both texts look the same? Consider the availability of vocabulary and the formality that shape your message.

- Will your parents understand terms like *lmao* and *bro?* Will they understand emojis?
- Can you swear to your parents, or do you have to keep your language clean?

Here are some aspects of your audience's language that you can pay attention to:

- **Vocabulary:** Different audiences have access to and use different words. For example, the term OP (original poster) is familiar to those who use social media, but you should not assume that a general audience would understand this term.
- **Dialect:** This term refers to a regional or social variety of speech. For example, California or Louisiana dialects are spoken by people from those regions. Cockney English is spoken by the working-class Londoners, and thus is both regional and social.
- **Register:** This term refers here to the variety of language determined by social setting and often speaks to the level of *formality.* If you do not match the register of your audience, you often don't appear as credible. For example, answering a professionally formatted email without parroting the formatting in your response (e.g., not including a greeting and conclusion) may make you seem too informal and possibly even flippant. In the same sense, dressing in a tuxedo for an in-class speech makes you seem unaware of the necessary formality of the situation, and thus less credible.

Just as you subconsciously modify your use of language depending on audiences, it is important to be able to transfer this skill to **academic writing.** Sometimes called scholarly writing, academic writing takes on specific genre conventions to share knowledge with a critical and informed audience. In this situation, the audience and the writer belong to a scholarly community, and because of this, the audience expects that the writer adhere to certain conventions. Do you remember when this chapter discussed identity? In this situation, the writer needs to mark themselves as members of an academic community by sharing the language conventions of this community. This is not meant to devalue different registers and dialects, but instead to add a new register to whichever dialect and registers you already have.

There are many misconceptions when it comes to academic writing. For example, many think of academic writing as complicated and therefore feel the need to unnecessarily complicate their writing style. These writers may be confusing the need for formality with complicated style. While academic writing does need to be kept formal, it should also be kept as clear and concise as possible. This can be done by carefully considering your choice of words. Choosing words with precise meanings improves your communication and lets you better explain your ideas to your audience. For example, many phrasal verbs (such as *stand up, stand by, take back, turn down, look up*) have very vague meanings. The verb *turn up* has a variety of meanings *(increase, arrive, to be found, appear)*, any of which could be a better substitute for this word in an academic situation.

It is also important to be aware of different genres within academic writing. There can be rather large differences between how you write within these different subjects. For example, a grant application would probably use emotional appeals, but a research article would probably be devoid of these. Despite both of these types of writing falling under the umbrella of academic writing, they have different genre conventions. Other forms academic writing may take are annotated bibliographies, essays, and conference papers.

An important convention for some of these forms of academic writing is **objectivity.** Objectivity is the quality of examining an issue or proving a point without the interference perception or emotion caused by bias. In some forms of academic writing, you are seeking to prove your thesis to your reader by the strength of your arguments, not your opinions; therefore, you must be cautious of stating your personal opinions too blatantly. This could sabotage your writing because it may undermine your ethos as a non-biased researcher. Another component of objectivity is using language sensitively. There are representatives of different religious, ethnic, and gender groups that will read your writing, so you should consider your language so as not to offend your readers.

As with all forms of writing and speaking, understanding your audience and their expectations is a key aspect of proving your thesis. By adhering to the conventions of academic writing, you become more credible in the eyes of the academic community. A large part of WRD is to familiarize you with these conventions, so if at first you don't recognize them, don't panic.

Chapter 3   Audience

Exercise: How Audience Changes a Text

Figure 8. University of Kentucky. (Photo by Daderot (Own work) [CC0 or CC0], via Wikimedia Commons from Wikimedia Commons. https://commons.wikimedia.org/wiki/File%3AJames_F._Hardymon_Building_-_University_of_Kentucky_-_DSC09128.JPG.)

Consider you are posting the above image with a caption about the weather on Instagram under the following personas: a personal, private account, a famous person's account (e.g., Kim Kardashian), and a professional business account (e.g., The Wyatt).

1. Who are the audiences of each account, and how do they differ between these three accounts? Is there any overlap?

2. What are the goals of each account, and how do they differ?

3. Write a possible caption for each account. How could you cater to both the audiences and the goals of each account in the caption of the Instagram post? What kind of language can each account use?

Using Gender Neutral Pronouns

Pronouns are used to refer to nouns in your writing. They can limit repetition and make your writing more streamlined.

Personal pronouns include I, you, he, she, ze, xe, it, they.

Possessive pronouns include my/mine, our/ours, your/yours, his, her/hers, zir, xem, its, their/theirs.

A preferred pronoun is the pronoun a person chooses to represent themselves. Some people prefer *he* or *she,* while others prefer *they,* and still others prefer *ze* or *xe.*

Devin-Norell's article, **"Gender-Neutral Pronouns 101: Everything You've Always Wanted to Know,"** is an excellent reference. They explain why using the correct pronouns is both respectful and necessary. They write, "It's an acknowledgement and recognition of our existence. The usage of these pronouns and names validates both our identities and experiences, and helps us to continue feeling connected to others, as the culture surrounding us continues to shift and evolve."

Link: *https://www.them.us/story/gender-neutral-pronouns-101-they-them-xe-xem*

In conversation and in writing, it is not a good idea to guess someone's preferred pronoun. Oftentimes, people think they know someone's pronouns based upon their name. However, many names are gender neutral—like Blake, Evan, Jordan, Ryan, and Tyler. Therefore, it is always best to default to gender neutral pronouns, like generic *they.*

Gender neutral pronouns are pronouns that are not gender specific. They have been handled in different ways over the years. Dennis Baron's book, *What's Your Pronoun?: Beyond He and She,* includes an historical overview of the use of pronouns in the English language.

- Generic *he:* Generic *he* used to be the standard. But this method ignores everyone who doesn't identify as male. We don't use generic *he* anymore.
- *He or she:* This method ignores people who are gender fluid or gender nonbinary. It can also be cumbersome in your writing. In addition, neither MLA nor APA styles support the use of *he or she* as a gender neutral pronoun.
- Generic *they:* Generic *they* is grammatically correct and inclusive of everyone. It also makes your writing more streamlined. Generic *they* is the new standard for writing.

Using generic *they* might seem a little weird at first because we're taught that *they* refers to multiple people. However, both MLA and APA styles now encourage the use of generic *they* to refer to singular or plural subjects when their gender pronouns are unknown or inconsequential. As Baron states in an interview with National Public Radio (NPR), "Singular they is here to stay."

Here are some examples of singular generic *they*:

- They — Alex is my new roommate. They seem really nice.
- Them — Every student gets an email address assigned to them.
- Their — Jordan parked their car illegally and got towed.
- Theirs — This desk is theirs.
- Themselves — That person needs to stop taking themselves so seriously.

There are also tactics for avoiding the use of gender specific language. When possible, choose language that is inclusive of everyone.

Instead of this:	Use this:
Chairman	Chairperson
Congressman	Congressperson
Fireman	Fire fighter
Mailman	Postal worker
Policeman	Police officer

The titles of professions do not need gender markers. Some examples include professors, teachers, doctors, nurses, scientists, and so on. There is no need to specify that a doctor is female or a teacher is male.

You can also revise your writing to avoid the use of pronouns.

Some examples include:

- Each student needs to submit a final project.
- Every resident is responsible for washing dishes.
- Every driver needs to use turn signals.
- Each employee must fill out a timecard.
- Every voter should submit the registration before the deadline.

Review

- Use generic *they* to refer to singular or plural subjects in your writing. Generic *they* is grammatically correct and all inclusive.
- Avoid the use of gender specific language, especially if it is potentially inaccurate.
- Do not put gender markers on the titles of professions.
- Revise your writing to avoid the use of unnecessary pronouns.

APPEAL TO CLARITY

Most of what we've discussed so far deals with issues of content or structure. We are figuring out how to reach an audience by writing specific content or organizing material in familiar ways. Sometimes forgotten in discussions of audience is the importance of **proofreading.** Proofreading means going over your work so that you discover any typos, spelling errors, grammatical errors, or wrong information before an audience receives the work.

Why is that important? And what does proofreading have to do with audience?

Think about it this way. An audience reads your work. You don't want to lose credibility (ethos) over spelling or grammatical errors. Often, errors are the result of forgetting about audience. A typo not caught in proofreading can indicate that the writer is not paying enough attention to his or her own work.

Figure 9. Sometimes a simple misspelling can cost you customers.[13] (Photo courtesy of Rob Brink.)

Once your audience sees your error, they may think less of you as a source of information. Your readers may believe that a writer who is unable to fix a simple grammar error, or who misspells a major word in the first sentence, is not a writer capable of forming an important idea.

Let's imagine I'm applying for a job. I write a letter, but I do not proofread it before sending it off. The letter misspells the addressee's name, has a run-on sentence in the first paragraph, has two more misspelled words in the first few sentences, and gets the company's name wrong. The audience for this letter—the person deciding on interviews—is not only likely to reject my application, but is also likely to stop reading early on.

Unfortunately, proofreading is more than just reading over your work. Because our eyes may not catch simple errors (we *think* we wrote the word or sentence correctly, but our eyes don't see what we really wrote), we often need someone else to read our work.

Always ask a roommate, friend, classmate, or someone else at the University to look over your work before you turn in it. At the very least, you will get an audience's impression. You can use that impression to catch errors or refocus certain parts of your work.

Ask your readers to mark any places that are confusing or difficult to understand. They may also be able to tell you whether they found themselves easily following your line of reasoning, or whether the organization needs some help. Asking for help with proofreading and feedback is not just something beginning writers do. In fact, professional writers often ask many people to read over their work.

Exercise: Advertisements for Yourself

When we say writers "should know their audience," we mean that writers need to consider who may be reading or watching their works. But we also mean that writers need to understand how the words they use, the images they create, and the stories they tell will forge connections with the audience in question.

Another guideline for reaching your audience might simply be to *forge a connection*. Much of what is discussed in this chapter is how to forge connections in different ways.

Practice some of the rhetorical tools described in this chapter by making an advertisement for yourself.

Using Chip and Dan Heath's principles of stickiness, as well as the other tools described in this chapter, turn yourself into an advertisement:
1. Think of the kind of story you wish to tell about yourself. (**Examples:** You as a great runner. You as a world-class sandwich maker. You as a wonderful roommate.)
2. Target it to a certain audience (perhaps your dorm, class, neighborhood, or friends).
3. Use a dominant image and/or some shared cultural allusions.
4. Consider what kind of *genre* your advertisement will be and what expectations your audience might have for that genre.
5. Consider whether or not you will use provocation in any way.

Student Writing Example: "Writing on the Wall" by Catherine A. Brereton

In the following award-winning essay, University of Kentucky undergraduate Catherine A. Brereton tells a personal and emotional story about violence against women. She draws on a number of different types of research to help make her point. As you read Brereton's essay, try to identify the techniques she uses to reach her readers. How did you react to her words and the stories she shares? What makes her writing so effective?

Nikki Burdine wants to be my Facebook friend. Nikki Burdine is something of a minor celebrity; she's an occasional news anchor and frequent reporter for one of our local television channels. Just this morning she popped up on the morning news show, covering for an absent colleague; I watched her on the small screen hooked up to the elliptical machine at the gym as I struggled through half an ungodly-early-hour of going nowhere.

I don't know why she wants to be my Facebook friend. I'm in Starbucks when the request pings in on my phone screen; I managed to grab one of the few comfortable chairs and I'm alternating between research, writing, and knitting. Mostly the knitting wins; it's late spring and my motivation for research died along with the end of the semester.

⊱✦⊰✦⊱✦

Amongst other things, I'm researching violence against women, and Hanna Rosin, the author of the hard-backed book currently stuffed down the side of my chair and gathering crumbs from other people's cookies, chirpily tells me that crimes against women are lessening. She places, amongst the neatly cherry-picked statistics, a quote from a noted criminologist who firmly believes that women "might as well be living in Sweden, they're so safe."[1] So safe that one of the girls in one of my classes was raped less than a year ago by some guy she met in a bar. She wrote about it in a reflection piece for the class; our instructor—with the girl's permission—read out loud her description about being pinned down and penetrated while her housemates sat just yards away, on the other side of her closed bedroom door.

⊱✦⊰✦⊱✦

I accept Nikki Burdine's friend request. A few minutes later, a message flashes onto the screen. She's researching for a news report and thinks I might be able to help her. Is there some way she can meet me, that day, if possible? I type back that I'm in Starbucks, is that any use? She tells me that she can be there in half an hour, if I don't mind waiting. I ask her what the news report is about; I'm sure she's contacted me by mistake.

"I'd like to talk to you about Leigh Anne Kinder."

෬ৎ৩෬ৎ৩෬ৎ৩

Kelsey isn't feeling good. She has 926 Facebook friends, and in her profile picture she's smiling out at them from beneath a black and white beanie hat. She's dyed her red hair black since I last saw her, and it looks like she's had her lip pierced, but the picture is grainy and I can't quite tell. She looks pale, though, and her smile is shallow, barely turned up at the corners. Last Saturday, she posted a status about the trial. It's seven weeks and one day away, and she's terrified.

Kelsey regularly goes to counseling. Sometimes, she posts about it, but usually it just remains unsaid, the only clue being her weekly headaches, near-constant insomnia, and a vague, general feeling of malaise which she communicates to her absent friends via the news feeds of Facebook. I often think of posting some kind of reassuring comment on her Facebook wall, but always hesitate to the point of cowardice. I belong to a different time in Kelsey's life, and watch now from the sidelines as she tries to put the pieces back together.

෬ৎ৩෬ৎ৩෬ৎ৩

We learned about Leigh Anne via Facebook. It's confusing, at first; Facebook's new security settings toss up all kinds of things in my news feed and it seems I'm getting notifications of people who have been posting on Leigh Anne's wall. I haven't spoken to Leigh Anne in person for maybe two years, not since she moved back to West Virginia to be with her not-quite husband and his family. He had struggled to find decently paying work here, and was going back, I was told, to the mines. They were going to live in a trailer up the road from his family; Leigh Anne would have more support and her not-quite husband would have a job. Things would calm down.

But she and her not-quite-husband split up not long after. They shared custody of their young daughter; Leigh Anne kept her eldest daughter from a different father. She emailed once or twice to tell me how she was doing. Her ex-not-quite-husband had turned into quite a different man, given to temper and loud voice. She couldn't bear it, and they parted. She met someone new, new to her

Chapter 3   Audience

friends at least, an old high-school sweetheart, and she was infatuated. They were married within the month.

☙❧☙❧☙❧

The girl in my class was raped by a man she met in a bar. She complains in class, with as much bravado as she can muster, of the police response. She'd been drinking; that alone should constitute what happened as non-consensual, but they question her relentlessly as if maybe she'd said yes in some kind of drunken haze and had simply forgotten about it. They ask her about other sexual encounters; did she make a habit of picking up men in bars and taking them back to her apartment? She tells them that he had offered to walk her home; he seemed like a nice guy. No, she didn't know his full name. She has bruises on the inside of her thighs. They ignore the bruises and ask her again about her last boyfriend.

☙❧☙❧☙❧

It's almost 10 p.m. when the text alert sounds. A female colleague of my partner has been arrested. The woman has been accused of slashing another woman's face to ribbons on a Tuesday afternoon outside a dress shop in our local mall. It's been all over the nightly news, which we never watch, but tonight we turn it on to find out more. The victim's face was criss-crossed with what police believe was some kind of razor blade, and she's lucky to be alive—one centimeter lower and her jugular would have been severed. The news report tells us that the victim half-knew her attacker, that she had dated her attacker's ex-boyfriend. The attacker apparently took a friend with her to pin down her victim and hold her still while she carved up her face.

☙❧☙❧☙❧

Nikki Burdine arrives. She's petite, well-dressed, and incredibly perky, with a bright smile and perfectly white, perfectly straight teeth. Despite the humidity, her hair is immaculately coiffed and falls in rich waves onto her tiny shoulders. She's wearing stiletto heels and a short skirt, and she has a healthy, perpetual tan. As she clicks across the tiled floor, the men huddled in the comfy chairs next to mine stop their conversation to look at her. She scans the coffee shop and settles on me as the most likely person to be me, before introducing herself with a confidently outstretched hand, and a light, made-for-television voice that matches her appearance.

When she asks me about Leigh Anne, her voice slips into a practiced, pacifying tone, the same tone I adopt when I'm soothing an upset child. My voice lowers in unconscious mimicry.

"Did you know Leigh Anne's husband?" she says. "Did you ever meet him?"

I answer in the negative. The only thing I knew about Leigh Anne's new husband—and now, I suppose, technically her ex-husband, is that they once were high school sweethearts. She said on her Facebook wall—or maybe it was in an email—that he made her smile. There's a photo of the two of them on her Facebook page. It was taken the October they met, not terribly long after she moved away. He's sat on a dirt bike, and is pulling her in close, with his arm around her waist. The sun is shining directly at them; they're both squinting slightly, and one of his eyes is closed, as if he's winking at the camera. She has her hand protectively on his thigh, and her dark blonde hair is pinned back from her face by a pair of sunglasses. The first comment on the photo calls them an "adorable cute couple." The second comment says: "Its fuckin sad to see how he fuckin killed her."

⊱✿⊰

Hanna Rosin believes that feminists are "irritated" by the latest statistics from the White House, statistics which claim that "women today are far less likely to get murdered, raped, assaulted, or robbed."[2] She writes of women-turned-poisoners, women who plan and plot and scheme "unprovoked, premeditated"[3] attacks on their husbands and boyfriends, and girls who shatter the windows of drive-through fast food restaurants because they can't get their preferred junk food fix exactly when they want it. Nicole Bewley, who has been accused of slashing Nicole Kyaw's face in a busy mall, purportedly planned her attack to such a degree that she took a friend with her. There is nothing opportunistic about having a friend hold down your intended victim so that you can disfigure her for life. Hannah Rosin states that "what looks like warped logic in one context can look like empowerment in another."[4] I look at Nicole Bewley's mugshot on our local news-station's webpage and wonder if this is the face of the empowered woman.

⊱✿⊰

Kelsey has been enrolled at five different schools in three different states in the last eight months. She's lived—or so I gather from a careful perusal of her Facebook—in five different houses with five different families, and she's been in foster care just the once. The couple that she lives with now has permanent guardianship, and Kelsey seems happy; she calls Laura her second mom and wonders what she would do without her. But Kelsey's half-sister, possibly her nearest blood relative, no longer lives in the same state. Her Facebook wall hints that she's only seen her sister for maybe three or four days in the last eight months.

Kelsey has 58 profile pictures. After three of her in the black and white beanie is one of her new tattoo. It's on the outside of her calf, and takes up most of her lower leg. She has a large anchor, wrapped around a rope-edged heart. In the center of the heart, there's a lighthouse, and waves crashing onto a beach. Below the rope-edged heart, the words "the sun embraces the darkest shadow" wind their way around the base of the anchor. There's a date tattooed at the very bottom, and at the very top, above the anchor, the words "In Loving Memory Mom & Mawmaw" are indelibly marked on Kelsey's skin. She says it gives her a little more closure.

৩৮০৩৮০৩৮০

Leigh Anne's mom, Gloria Sue, had been staying with her for a while. Leigh Anne's dad was terminally ill, and Leigh Anne needed both the emotional support and practical help of her mom. Gloria Sue was in the house when Leigh Anne's new husband slit his new wife's throat. News reports say that Gloria Sue hadn't seen her daughter for two days; Leigh Anne's new husband told her she was sick with the flu and didn't want to be disturbed. Gloria Sue checked on her anyway, only to find her daughter's lifeless body lying in an upstairs room. Leigh Anne's new husband slit Gloria Sue's throat too, and left both the bodies bleeding out onto the upstairs carpet while he (allegedly) raped Leigh Anne's oldest daughter, his step-daughter. His trial is in seven weeks and one day.

৩৮০৩৮০৩৮০

Nikki Burdine wants to film an interview with me. We go outside to the parking lot where her cameraman is waiting, and in front of the coffee shop and a chi-chi cupcake store she asks me the same questions she has already asked me. I try to be articulate, but the sun is in my eyes and I'm squinting. The cameraman stops the interview and asks me to turn in a different direction, but then the cupcake shop is in full view and somehow that doesn't seem appropriate. Eventually, we settle on a position where, over Nikki Burdine's shoulder, I'm watching people pop in and out of the shop to buy their chi-chi cupcakes, but only the traffic whizzing past on the busy road behind me can be seen by the audience who will watch my interview on the six o'clock news.

⊗☙⊗☙⊗☙

My partner calls me from work the day after her colleague was arrested. She tells me that Nicole Bewley no longer works for the company and that her electronic access card—the one that grants access to the private offices—has been revoked. She doesn't know if she is in custody or out on bail, but the offices are filled with quiet whispers about the colleague who slashed a woman's face; everyone wonders if they saw signs of inherent violence, or if maybe they said or did something untoward that might have justified some kind of violent attack. I believe Nikki Burdine was the reporter that first broke the story.

⊗☙⊗☙⊗☙

Timothy Parsons (allegedly) showed Kelsey the dead bodies of her mother and grandmother before he (allegedly) raped her. (Allegedly), he told her he would kill her too if she didn't have sex with him. After he (allegedly) raped Kelsey, he left the house leaving behind two dead bodies and an (allegedly) raped teenage girl. It was 24 hours before Kelsey was able to free herself from the ties that had been used to restrain her during her (alleged) rape. Timothy Parsons was found the following day and arraigned without bail.

⊗☙⊗☙⊗☙

Kelsey doesn't talk about the rape, at least not on Facebook. Those details only came out in the subsequent news reports. When she talks about the events of last year, she talks of how much she misses her mom and her mawmaw, how much she wishes they were still here to help her, and how she'll make them proud of her. When she talks about the upcoming trial, she talks about justice for them, and "even" for herself, as if she's decided that being tied up and raped is somehow less noteworthy than death. She has an album on her Facebook page of photographs from the funerals, filled with pictures of the shiny white coffins containing the bodies of her mom and mawmaw, and close-ups of the pink and purple floral displays, elaborate sprays of roses and carnations that dripped from the top of the coffins to the ground. The funerals took place on a sunny, green day. The trees in the background were heavy with foliage and the grass still retained the neon verdancy of spring, unmarked as yet by *the brutal summer sun. The photos show family members dressed in bright colors, smiling at the camera, squinting when the sun hit their eyes. It looks like almost any other happy family event, apart from the two shiny white coffins in the background.*

☙☕☙☕☙

After we've finished the interview, Nikki Burdine hangs around for a little while; her cameraman needs a cigarette and she needs a cold drink. She orders some kind of iced tea from Starbucks, which they mess up, so she waits with me while they make her another. Curious about my British accent, she asks what brought me to Kentucky, and we talk for a little while about immigration rights. Neither of us mention Leigh Anne. Her iced tea is finally ready, the cameraman has finished his cigarette, and she has to head back to the studio to edit the piece for that evening's news. When I watch the report that night all I can focus on is my large, pink face, like a disembodied head floating above Richmond Road as the traffic flies past and the people I know I can see over Nikki Burdine's shoulder buying their expensive cupcakes. My 16 year old daughter, once a good friend of Kelsey's, makes fun of my voice, which sounds plummy and pretentious alongside Nikki Burdine's soft Kentucky drawl. We don't talk about what happened to Leigh Anne and Gloria Sue. We don't talk about what happened to Kelsey.

That summer, I sit in Starbucks every morning. Instead of studying I knit Kelsey a shawl. It's a gesture that brings only me comfort. It's pink, and soft, but pink, I now realize, isn't really her color, and a shawl isn't really her thing. I knit it anyway, and send it the mail with a note telling her how sorry we all are, and that the shawl is the closest thing I can manage to a hug. I wonder if she ever got the shawl; she never mentions it and I don't want to ask.

☙☕☙☕☙

Nikki Burdine moves on to new stories: such is the nature of her job. Her news station picks up the story of woman with the slashed face, and then, doubtless, the story of someone else. There's always a new story, always another woman who has been murdered, raped, assaulted, or robbed, and the stories of Leigh Anne and Gloria Sue, of Kelsey, the girl in my class, and the woman with the slashed face, are quickly subsumed beneath more stories of more women, quickly forgotten, quickly reduced to statistics.

Those statistics report "plummeting rates of completed rape, assaults, attempts, and threats."[5] Criminologists report that women are "a lot harder to victimize," claiming that "people don't admit these trends because there is a lot of discomfort ... about girls succeeding so well ... while boys are on a destructive decline."[6] I think of the women I know who, in the last year, have been murdered, raped, and assaulted, and ponder the meaninglessness of this statistical decline.

☙❧☙❧☙❧

Leigh Anne's Facebook page is still active. Every so often, my news feed will show that she has received a horoscope or inspirational quote. Her wall is peppered with daily Bible verses and images of her with "R.I.P" photo-shopped in alongside clip-art red roses and hearts. Sometimes, Facebook suggests that I accept Gloria Sue's friend request and tells me that we already have two mutual friends; one of these is Leigh Anne, the other is Kelsey. All three of them defy the statistics.

NOTES

[1] Hanna Rosin. *The End of Men and the Rise of Women.* 2012. Riverhead Books. Pg 17.

[2] Ibid. Pg 182.

[3] Ibid. Pg 178.

[4] Ibid. Pg 182.

[5] Ibid.

[6] Ibid. Pg 183.

VIDEO RESOURCES

Stella Parks on Writing and Audiences

Stella Parks is a pastry chef (formerly the head pastry chef at Table 310 in Lexington), a blogger, and a cookbook author. Stella is a native of Louisville, but she has lived all over the world. As part of her daily work as a pastry chef and blogger, Stella uses rhetorical theory and writing in a number of ways. In this interview clip, she describes how she thinks about audience in her writing.

Chapter 3 Audience

(https://vimeo.com/103938664)

Griffin VanMeter Describes How Social Media and Audiences Can Help Spread a Media Campaign

Griffin VanMeter is co-owner of the branding firm **Bullhorn Creative** *(http://bullhorncreative.com)*, as well as the creative director of Kentucky for Kentucky *(www.kentuckyforkentucky.com)*. Griffin grew up in Lexington, though he has also lived and worked around the country. As part of his creative work, Griffin uses writing and rhetorical theory in many ways. In this interview clip, he describes how audiences and social media helped spread the wildly popular "Kentucky Kicks Ass" video.

(https://vimeo.com/104015857)

You can also watch the **"Kentucky Kicks Ass"** video:

(https://vimeo.com/55873402)

NOTES

[1] *Planet Argon,* last modified 2014, http://planetargon.com.

[2] Jess Hughey. "Shock Top Sent Me $100 Worth of Swag and Two Awful Beers. That Sums Them Up Perfectly." *Dallas Observer,* April 4, 2013.

[3] Arik Hanson. "Should PR Folks be Sharing Their Political Viewpoints on Facebook?" *Communication Conversations,* last modified 2014, http://www.arikhanson.com/2012/11/06/should-pr-folks-be-sharing-their-political-viewpoints-on-facebook/.

[4] Chokshi, Niraj. "Disney Drops PewDiePie and YouTube Distances Itself After Reports of Anti-Semitic Videos." *New York Times,* Feb. 14, 2017. https://www.nytimes.com/2017/02/14/business/pewdiepie-youtube-disney.html.

[5] Chip Heath and Dan Heath. *Made to Stick: Why Some Ideas Survive and Others Die.* Random House, 2007, pp. 16–17.

[6] "Albert Einstein Think Different Apple Advertising." *Tomorrow Started,* last modified October 4, 2011, http://www.tomorrowstarted.com/2011/10/dumbing-down-a-nation-when-did-being-stupid-become-cool/.html/albert-einstein-think-different-apple-advertising-2.

[7] *Campus Circle,* last modified 2014, http://www.campuscircle.com.

[8] "Barack Obama 'Hope' poster." *Wikipedia,* last modified May 9, 2014, http://en.wikipedia.org/wiki/Barack_Obama_%22Hope%22_poster.

9. "The White House Just Made A *Mean Girls* Joke on Twitter That Involved Bo and Ahhh Amazingness!" *Alloy,* Aug. 13, 2013, file:///C:/Users/lrmal/Downloads/White%20House%20Makes%20Amazing%20Mean%20Girls%20Reference%20on%20Twitter.html.

10. Suzy Lee Weis. "To (All) the Colleges That Rejected Me." *Wall Street Journal,* March 29, 2013.

11. Roger Baylor. "Second Hand News Usually Is Mistaken." *The Potable Curmudgeon* (blog), March 25, 2013, http://potablecurmudgeon.blogspot.com/2013/03/second-hand-news-usually-is-mistaken.html.

12. Baylor. "Nine years later, and absolute power still corrupts Big Red Liquors absolutely." *The Potable Curmudgeon* (blog), April 20, 2012, http://potablecurmudgeon.blogspot.com/2012/04/nine-years-later-and-absolute-power.html.

13. Robert Brink, *RobBrink,* accessed June 27, 2014, http://www.robbrink.com.

Works Cited

American Psychological Association. "Singular 'They.'" *American Psychological Association,* American Psychological Association, Sept. 2019, https://apastyle.apa.org/style-grammar-guidelines/grammar/singular-they.

Baron, Dennis. *What's Your Pronoun?: Beyond He and She.* Liveright/Norton, 2020.

Devin-Norelle. "Gender-Neutral Pronouns 101: Everything You've Always Wanted to Know." *Them.,* Condé Nast, 22 May 2020, https://www.them.us/story/gender-neutral-pronouns-101-they-them-xe-xem.

Garcia-Navarro, Lulu. "Author Interview: Dennis Baron On 'What's Your Pronoun?'." *NPR,* NPR, 26 Jan. 2020, https://www.npr.org/2020/01/26/799629318/author-interview-dennis-baron-on-what-s-your-pronoun.

Modern Language Association of America. "How Do I Use Singular They?" *MLA Style Center,* Modern Language Association of America, 4 Mar. 2020, https://style.mla.org/using-singular-they/.

Purdue Online Writing Lab. "Gendered Pronouns & Singular 'They.'" *Purdue Online Writing Lab,* Purdue University, https://owl.purdue.edu/owl/general_writing/grammar/pronouns/gendered_pronouns_and_singular_they.html.

The Process of Composition

Recommended for WRD 110/112

Chapter 4

Let's say you've just been handed an assignment to make an argument of your own—an essay, speech, etc. You are eager to get started on your project and jump right in! But, occasionally, students like you find this a little intimidating. How exactly should you start? How do you know if you're making an effective argument? How do you know when you're done?

All of these questions are about the **Process of Composition.** We call it a process because good writing does not simply pour out of writers already neat, perfect, and ideal. Professional writers hardly ever sit down and craft a finished piece of writing in one attempt. They begin with ideas, sketches, notes, and flashes of arguments. Then they work on putting their case together, steadily, over a period of time—on composing what they want to say. During this time, they might move around paragraphs or sentences they wrote the day before. They might expand on some ideas and make notes to revisit other ideas later. Depending on how complex their ideas are and who they are hoping to reach, this process can take anywhere from five minutes to five years. That is the nature of composition—a systematic and purposeful development of an argument to meet the needs of a given rhetorical situation.

Once writers have composed their thoughts and made an (initial) draft, the work of revision begins. Every writer revises a little differently. Some people like to read what they've written and revise as they re-read. Some people like to read their drafts without planning to revise right away. They simply get a sense of what they've done. Other writers like to get feedback from other readers before beginning to revise.

This chapter offers some suggestions for making your own composition process stronger, more intuitive, and more rewarding. The suggestions that follow are real tips that are taken directly from professional writers. Try them out next time you are faced with a new project—whether that is an academic assignment, a personal argument, or a professional document.

> **Exercise: Discuss Your Writing Process**
>
> When you are asked to compose an argument, how do you typically go about it? Take a moment to reflect on your own **Process of Composition**—on how you typically write—and consider the following:
> - What do you normally do after you get a writing assignment?
> - Do you begin right away, or do you wait a few days (maybe too many)?
> - Do you usually write entire essays in one sitting, or do you give yourself some time to revise and rethink?
> - Which of these habits do you want to keep, and which do you want to change? Why?
> - Do you prefer to gather your thoughts or develop an argument as you write?
> - How often do you revise or reorganize your essays, or do you just check for errors before submitting an assignment?

INVENTION: STARTING FROM SCRATCH

Whether talking with a friend, writing a novel, or putting together an essay for your WRD course, composition always begins with an act of **Invention.** In the public imagination, this creative act of discovery is often tied to the work of ambitious entrepreneurs or kooky characters with Eureka moments. But in composition studies, *Inventio* is the act of finding a rhetorical claim and expanding on it. In other words, this initial step in the Composition Process asks, "How did you figure out what you wanted to say?"

Invention, an Aristotelean concept, has deep roots in rhetorical theory (See Chapter 1), but it is still seen as a mysterious, almost magical process. Can you identify when and where *your* last essay topic came from? Do you know exactly *how* a thesis statement is determined? Don't worry; you are not alone. This is a struggle that many writers and speakers have tried to grapple with, attributing this creative act to everything from a team of idolized Muses, a stroke of insight, or even the random firing of neuronal synapses. The truth is, we still don't have a definitive answer for this.

Even if we do not understand it completely, "starting from scratch" is still a skill that can be honed. This section offers some suggestions to help you craft a specific argument or, more generally, develop this *heuristic* ability.

Finding an Argument (or *Stasis*)

One of the first things that professional writers do when facing a new project is to get a lay of the land: to attempt to understand who they are talking to (Chapter 3), what the problem is (Chapter 2), and why they might care (Chapter 1). This rhetorical awareness is something that most of take for granted—until we are confronted with a "graded assignment" or another high stakes essay, speech, or interview. But even with the simplest communication, most people will take the time to understand what is at *issue,* before making a definitive claim.

Take a simple recommendation. If my friend asks me what movie I would recommend, I can come up with a number of suggestions that *might* work—movies that I have enjoyed in the past—but if I want to offer an effective suggestion, I will first consider the reason they're asking (*exigence*), the movies they've enjoyed in the past (*context*), etc. If they want a quick, light film for a relaxing Sunday afternoon, for instance, then I am not going to suggest Hitchcock's *Psycho*—for instance. This is something that we usually have little trouble navigating—as we evaluate the rhetorical situation that underscores the arguments that we make. I doubt you struggle to make an effective recommendation of your own—one that accounts for the rhetorical situation and the needs of your audience (or friend).

Rhetorical theorists call this *stasis,* but most people simply think of this as picking an appropriate topic that will (a) address the problem/opportunity at the heart of an argument (exigence) and (b) appeal to an intended audience. Usually, simply choosing a relevant issue that you have some familiarity with (or expertise in) is enough to jumpstart a project. And, whether responding to a friend's text or writing a long research paper, this narrowing in on a critical topic is the first step toward an effective response. *Plus,* if all else fails, read the assignment prompt for inspiration.

Brainstorming

One of the most common ways of finding something to write/speak about is the well-worn practice of brainstorming. This practice helps writers of all kinds develop an argument or identify an issue that they could contribute to meaningfully. Professional communicators and students alike will turn to these activities to generate potential topics or elaborate on claims as they go. You have probably tried out some of these brainstorming activities in high school. The following activities are pretty typical ways of getting some ideas down on paper:

- **Webbing/Mind-Mapping:** Whatever you might call it, this is an invention activity that asks writers to track the development of an idea by charting the free association of ideas in your own head (or your team's). To do this, you would *web* ideas (or map your thoughts) into clusters of related thoughts/topics. This tactic has a way of helping you find issues that you are interested in or have more familiarity with. Wherever your mind tends to focus your attention, there is usually room for an argument/idea to develop.
- **Free Writing:** Similar to *Webbing*, free writing is a brainstorming activity that relies on the continuous, unfiltered stream of ideas and allowing yourself space (five to ten minutes) to develop an initial stance on a topic/issue. In other words, free writing allows a writer to chase down a topic by forming the argument first, then figure out if their idea will work for the given rhetorical situation. This tactic has been very influential, even inspiring an influential approach to composition as a whole.[1]
- **Journalistic Inquiry:** If you need a little more structure than free association allows, then you might benefit from a simple series of open questions about a given topic/issue. Asking who, what, where, why, when, and how may seem too simple, but this journalistic starting point offers a better sense of a given rhetorical situation, an assignment prompt, or even just how much you know about a topic. Simply asking the question(s) can help you focus your attention on relevant and critical issues that need more attention. This is an effective brainstorming activity—especially if you are not sure about why you should be writing or speaking up in the first place.

Try out some of these invention exercises to see if they end up helping form ideas of your own.

Exercise: Brainstorming

1. With a pen and paper in hand, open the prompt for your next assignment in this class—a discussion post, an essay, etc.—and consider what you are being asked to do to complete this activity/task.
2. Choose one of the brainstorming exercises listed above (Webbing, Free Writing, or Journalistic Inquiry) and spend five minutes doing this *first activity*.
3. Choose a different brainstorming exercise and repeat #2 while thinking through the *same* prompt/assignment.
4. When you are finished, compare your chart, paragraph, etc. and reflect on the assignment.
   - Which exercise proved more useful in generating ideas for your response?
   - Did the exercises help you think about the assignment in different ways? How so?
   - Did a combination of *inventive* exercises offer a greater sense of how to approach this assignment? Or was it more distracting?
   - Do you feel ready to write or do you need more time to prepare/generate ideas?

Free writing, for example, is a very easy and quite productive brainstorming exercise—an invention activity anyone can do. Give yourself a certain period of time, like five minutes to ten minutes. Don't make it too much longer because you can easily find yourself getting exhausted or tired of this activity. Sometimes, shorter periods of time are the best for getting some creativity going. Take out a pen and paper (or sit at your computer) and start writing for that set period of time. Don't stop at any time until your timer goes off. Keep writing. You can start by simply making the first sentence about your topic. Then write whatever comes to mind. It might seem to be directly related or it might not. This brainstorming activity is all about free association, so do not worry about remaining "on topic." Don't edit yourself at this point. Whatever comes to mind, simply write it down. Once you've reached the time limit, *then* you can go back and reread what you've already written.

Are there any ideas that came out of this free writing session (or another brainstorming activity)? Sometimes, what might seem like a crazy or unrelated idea is actually some part of your brain trying to tell you something. Invention, after all, is focused on generating your own rhetorical perspective on a topic—on fostering awareness of your stance on an issue, no matter how unrelated it may seem to the original topic. This is why you don't want to edit yourself during brainstorming sessions. If you found an idea that you really like, then you might start another short brainstorming session that more directly focuses on that new idea. Whether through free association or critical inquiry, brainstorming is a skill that rewards continual refinement and practice.

Reading and Making Notes

One of the first things that most professional writers do when facing a writing project is to *read*. They might read books and articles about the subject that they're studying, or they might read primary research that relates to their topic. No matter what they read, most professional writers find that they have to be familiar and invested in the conversations that are taking place about this subject. This is because it is really difficult, if not impossible, to simply come up with a brilliant idea off the top of your head. This is just not how our brains work. Everyone, even professional writers, have to listen to the voices around them in order to come up with something that is interesting and worthwhile to write.

When reading these things, these same writers will also make notes. It might be something as simple as a summary or a direct quotation with a page number of whatever they've read. But it might also be some ideas that were sparked during the reading. For example, I usually have a notepad with me, and I will write down page numbers and ideas that come to me as I read things that I want to respond to.

The advantage of reading and making notes is that you can go back to these notes during the "real" writing stage, and you can remember whatever it is that you want to respond to. Ultimately, it will make your life so much easier when you begin by taking notes and reading.

Responding

While brainstorming can be a solitary and deliberate attempt to generate ideas, it is not the only exercise that writers and speakers use to develop an argument. Invention can be pursued successfully both individually and in coordination with other voices. Some writers prefer to compose claims on their own, but others prefer to talk it out and reach an argument alongside other rhetors. Either way, the simple act of *replying* can work wonders and help you focus your argument and/or develop a more effective case.

Whether crafting a new argument or simply elaborating on an existing one, try out the exercises below to take a "conversational" approach to Invention.

Pointed Conversations

Often, writers will get ideas about what they want to write by simply talking to other people. This might mean corresponding with other writers (both in your course and with professionals), but it might also just mean talking to friends or family. Sometimes you can get perspective on a subject by asking your friends or family what they think about an issue or topic. Whether intentional or accidental, the connections that you make in talking through your argument can prove very productive in the long run.

Talking out loud actually uses a different part of your brain than reflecting on an idea internally. Some writers find it helpful to simply talk to themselves out loud, working through the idea and debating the issue(s) in order to activate that part of the brain. It might sound a little nuts, and maybe more than a little embarrassing—to talk out loud to yourself. For this reason, you might want to find a quiet place to try this out. But once you feel safe and private, this awkward activity might jumpstart some ideas that simply were not flowing when you were thinking about the subject internally or quietly.

Reader Response

While talking about a topic might prove productive, it is not the only way to generate ideas "in conversation" with others. Many professional writers will begin a new project by simply studying up on the topic. They might read books and articles on the subject that they're interested in writing about, or they might look into primary research that relates to their topic. No matter what they read, most writers find that they want to be familiar with and invested in the conversations that are taking place about this subject before they add their own perspective.

Reading and responding to other arguments about a topic is beneficial in two ways. First, it helps you get a better sense of the topic and find where your perspective fits in. It is really difficult, if not impossible, to simply come up with a brilliant idea off the top of your head. This is just not how our brains work. Everyone, even professional writers, have to listen to the voices around them in order to come up with something that is interesting and worth writing about.

But this also helps invent new arguments and perspectives—especially when brainstorming alone is not doing the trick. When reading other arguments/texts on a subject, most writers will take notes about the topic ***and*** how they feel about it. This might be something as simple as a summary or a direct quotation with a page number of whatever they've read. But it might also be an idea or two that were sparked by the reading. You could use a notepad, a dedicated document on your laptop/iPad, or a series of Post-Its, but whenever you are reading/researching a subject, try writing down page numbers and ideas that come to you or claims that you want to respond to.

The advantage of reading and making notes is that you can go back to these annotations during the "real" writing stage, and hopefully, they will remind you of whatever it was that you wanted to say about this text (and the arguments within it). Ultimately, it will make your life so much easier when you begin by taking notes and reading.

Moving

Just as talking out loud activates different parts of your brain and highlights different aspects of an argument, some writers will actually get up and move in order to achieve the same results. Many professionals have talked about going for walks or runs while thinking about their subject. This is no accident.

Physical movement also requires us to draw upon different brain functions. With something else to focus on, your mind is allowed to process your claims, organize your thoughts, and critically appraise your stance—even if all you are "thinking" about is putting one foot in front of the other. For this reason you may find yourself thinking about your subject in new and creative ways when doing something as simple as going for a walk, a run, or even a bike ride. Even simply taking a break to catch up with a friend—whether you talk about your topic (see above) or not—can have a profound impact on the development of an argument. You should try taking a movement break, and when you get home, open up your laptop and write down any ideas that may have occurred to you in the last thirty to forty-five minutes.

Cubing

As noted above, Invention is as much about figuring out how to develop a nuanced argument as it is about brainstorming a topic/stance. We've all had those moments where we need to explain our claim(s) a little more, develop examples, or simply find support. Not to mention the ever-present college issue of meeting a word count. And while you could do any of these invention exercises to deepen or elaborate on your argument, many writers turn toward a more focused practice called "cubing." This series of imaginative exercises forces writers to literally consider their topic from multiple perspectives, and as a result, it can prove helpful in the development of more effective and nuanced arguments.

Imagine that you're looking at a six-sided cube, each side with a different activity on it (see the table below). As you "cube," you will respond to each of the six prompts while thinking about your topic/argument. Get some paper and a pen (or sit at your computer) and set a timer for three to five minutes. During this allotted time, write as much as you can in response to the first suggested activity. When you reach your time limit, start the timer over and do the second prompt. Keep repeating until you've finished responding to all six.

- Describe your topic
- Associate your topic
- Apply your topic
- Compare your topic
- Analyze your topic
- Argue for and against your topic

ARRANGEMENT: PLANNING FOR AN ARGUMENT

After writers generate ideas for an essay, response, etc., the next thing they usually do is make some kind of a plan. This **Arrangement** of claims, subclaims, evidence, and/or appeals is the second step in the Composition Process—the organizing of your thoughts into a coherent and compelling case. Depending on the nature of the response/argument, these plans can look like formal outlines, rough notes, or even just an internal logic inside the mind of a writer/speaker. When writing a high stakes report for a class or trying to convince a friend to go get some coffee, effective arguments tend to be more successful when you take the time to unfurl your case in a logical and considerate order.

A lot of thought has been put into the *proper* arrangement of ideas, as rhetoricians from Greek Antiquity to the Modern Era have debated the best way to organize a speech, but a consensus has not been reached. Rhetorical experts have generally focused on formal oration and political speeches, but the organization of an engaging Insta caption is far less formal than a 2,000 word report. And, as a result, the order of information is harder to nail down. An effective argument, whether explicitly planned or not, does not follow a particular formula, despite what the experts (and most students) might prefer.

As noted in Chapter 2, effective arguments are responsive to the needs of a given rhetorical situation, so in terms of organization, the simple answer is *"It depends."* But no one really likes that answer, so the following section offers some advice on how to arrange your arguments—both in this course and elsewhere. The next time you start planning an argument, you might try a number of these different planning approaches and see which one works best for you.

Outlining

You're probably very familiar with formal outlines, this classic arrangement technique has been used by professional writers for as long as writing has existed, and it has persisted because it works. Outlining can be helpful because they help you to visually organize your ideas and arrange the argument so that as you write, you can see how your ideas link together. Whether using a structured outline, bullet points, or just a series of notes, an outline helps writers (and speakers) do the following:

- (Re)Structure a given argument to fit the needs of an audience;
- Utilize evidence effectively;
- Identify gaps in a developing claim; and
- Track the development of a draft over multiple writing sessions.

Outlines can be divided into major sections and subsections, making an argument easier to visualize and manage as it is developed. But these nested sections are up to the individual preferences of a given writer. You might choose to write an intricate outline that reflects a highly nuanced and complex argument, or you might prefer a simpler approach that only lists major claims, leaving the rest implied. Some writers prefer a "working outline" that reflects the intended rhetoric. While other writers like to annotate their outline so that they can see exactly where they plan to go. Whatever outline style you choose to use, this arrangement exercise is an easy way to force yourself to pay attention to the organization of your argument.

It can be easy to feel bound by an outline, but in reality, professional writers often review and update their planned order and argument as they write. You might think of an outline as a kind of guide that changes as you write and think about your topic. Use your outline as an organizing principle and not something that you must follow to the letter of the law. I often use plans when I'm writing, and I love to use headings and subheadings so that I can imagine how my argument might look when I finish. But, once again, a plan can also change and be updated as you write.

FOLLOWING A CLASSICAL TEMPLATE

For centuries, speeches were organized around a very traditional progression. By studying the evocative speeches of Roman senators, ruling monarchs, and other influential leaders throughout history, students would have been taught a formulaic approach to *oration*. It may not have been the most effective argument for a given situation, but if it worked for Caesar, it should work for you—or so the thinking went. This arrangement included the following distinct movements (or sections):[2]

- **Exordium:** An introduction that catches the attention of the audience and establishes the argument (*thesis*).
- **Narratio:** Background information that establishes a shared understanding of the topic (*stasis*).
- **Partitio:** A section that previews the major points of contention that the speaker planned to defend (*a road map*).
- **Confirmatio:** The longest section in which the argument is set forth and (hopefully) confirmed.
- **Refutatio:** A section that refutes potential counterclaims that might undermine the speaker's case.
- **Peroratio:** A conclusion that sums up the case.

This classical arrangement is still used to organize a great many speeches (see Chapter 12), but it is not practical in the modern essay. A predictable and rigid format does not allow for the flexible and nuanced organization that most writers prefer—professional or not. Further, this arrangement imparts a distinct antagonistic relationship with the audience—a relic of its political (and judicial) origins that can be seen in a mandated refutation, etc. And yet, despite falling out of favor, the classical argument has remained influential.

When you start planning a new writing project, you are not alone if you immediately divide it into three distinct parts. Writers will typically start with an introductory section that establishes an intriguing thesis (*Exordium*) and provides any necessary context (*Narratio*). And if you can help the reader understand how the essay will proceed, then all the better (*Partitio*). This is typically followed by a deliberate and careful defense of the central argument (*Confirmatio*) that accounts for a skeptical audience (*Refutatio*). And to conclude, most writers recap their argument as a way to reinforce the essay's thesis (*Peroratio*).

This three-part *arrangement*—intro, argument, conclusion—might be an overly simplistic approach to organize an essay, but as a *template,* this is not a bad starting point. This classic approach allows writers a chance to (a) address the concerns of their audience(s), (b) focus attention on making a compelling and effective argument, and (c) refine the purpose (thesis) of their text. In short, this *template* works if you use it for a clear rhetorical purpose.

Exercise: A Classical Recommendation

While this traditional arrangement works in more formal speeches, the progression from *Exordium* to *Narratio* can be too rigid for most arguments. But in thinking through this order, it can still prove helpful in developing a nuanced and productive argument, in thinking through how to organize an effective claim(s). And that is what you should do here:

1. Choose a movie, TV Show, or song that you have recently enjoyed and write a quick (200 word) recommendation for your roommate (or friend). This "argument" should include, at a minimum, a *Narratio, Confirmatio,* and *Refutatio* section and should be ordered as noted above.
2. Once you are done, reflect on the process.
   - Does this argument *feel* like you? Is this how you would typically *arrange* a recommendation? For your roommate/friend?
   - Did this organization strengthen your recommendation? Why/Why not?
   - If you were to "revise" this, what would you add? What would you take out?
3. If you have the time, try out this recommendation. Was it effective? Did it convince your roommate/friend to give this movie/show/song a try?

Organizing Your Thoughts

Although there's not one "correct" way of structuring an argument/essay, there are some organizational strategies that writers can use to help them organize their ideas. The following are some very popular organizational patterns that are useful for arranging essays, speeches, or any kind of project that needs to have a coherent structure:

- **Chronological Order:** This pattern of organization is useful for describing events that happened along a certain timeline. For example, if you're talking about the history of desegregation on the University of Kentucky's campus, you might want to organize your essay by year. You might also think about chronological patterns for describing any kind of events that happen in a series.
- **Spatial Arrangement:** This pattern of organization is most useful for describing the locations and comparable distances of various artifacts. For example, people who argue that Rupp Arena needs to be improved often begin by describing the current structure of Rupp—from parking lot to entry points to bathrooms to the court itself.
- **Comparison/Contrast:** This pattern of organization is useful when you are comparing two or more items. You may identify several points of overlap or difference that should be illustrated, and you can organize your paper around those points. For example, if you want to argue that a vegetarian diet is healthier than a non-vegetarian diet, you might choose to highlight several points of comparison:

    - The risk of heart disease
    - The average time lost to sick days
    - The cost of groceries
    - The obesity rates among (non)vegetarians

- **Cause/Effect:** This pattern of organization is useful for showing a causal link between an event (or series of events) and the effects that came as a result. You do not necessarily need to begin with the cause, although beginning with an explanation of the cause would certainly make sense. You might want to start with a strong description of the effects and then proceed to reveal the causes. For example, a writer might begin by describing the terrible car wreck she was involved in: the mangled car, her injuries, and the financial aftermath. She might then reveal some of the things that helped contribute to this crash: the driver had been texting a friend or they may have not given themselves enough time to slow down before an intersection.

- **Problem/Solution:** This pattern of organization is very common for writers who are advocating for certain actions, perspectives, or policies. In this pattern, you would first explain the problem in detail for your readers. Show what has led to the problem, what negative effects it has, and so forth. Next, you present your solution or answer to this problem. It may be that you want your audience to change its mind about something, or you want to motivate them to take action.
- **Topical Order:** This pattern of organization is useful for writers who want to organize their writing around particular topics that are relevant to their larger point. The topical patterns of organization may be most useful for informative writing that describes or tells readers about the various aspects of a bigger subject. For example, if you are informing readers about types of higher education institutions, you might organize around the following topics:

  - Public universities
  - Private, liberal arts universities
  - Community colleges
  - Two-year public colleges

Organizational Paradigms

[Diagram showing overlapping circles labeled: Chronological Order, Comparison/Contrast, Problem/Solution, Spatial Arrangement, Cause/Effect, Topical Order]

Figure 1. Common organizational patterns.

These organizational patterns reflect traditional ways of arranging an essay or speech, but they should not be seen as a singular solution. Most rhetors will adopt various organizational paradigms to unite ideas throughout an argument, choosing multiple patterns to structure larger, more complicated claims. For instance you may use a chronological order to go over what happened at a UK Football game, and a cause/effect arrangement to explain why they won (or lost). However you choose to combine these patterns, you should strive to arrange your claims to communicate effectively. They are rhetorical techniques to be used to enhance your argument, so use them as you see fit.

Assembly: Constructing Your Claims

The next step in the Composition Process, and the one that gets most of the glory, is the actual construction of an argument: the development of an essay, the delivery of a speech, the design of an image, etc. After you've brainstormed your ideas and arranged them, it's time to start **Assembly.** Whether you call this writing, drafting, or something else, there will come a time when you must sit down and deliver an argument. And while this can be scary, the assembly of an argument is when you commit to a claim(s) and defend your perspective.

While Invention and Arrangement have their own difficulties, the actual drafting of an argument seems to be the most daunting step for students. Even professional writers have to train themselves to avoid the anxiety of a blank page. And the reason for this is more than understandable: when you write a paper, you are asked to artfully and effectively defend your thinking. But this *assembly* is something that you do on a regular basis. From talking with a friend, posting a comment online, or even waving hello across the quad, these are all arguments that you've committed to—even if you accidently embarrass yourself by greeting a stranger that looks like your friend (something we've all done before). But when the stakes are high (and a grade is attached), this becomes a more difficult proposition.

The next time you start constructing an argument, you can use the following to make this *assembly* a less intimidating process. And, hopefully, it'll make it easier to avoid procrastinating and commit to a rhetorical claim—if only the first draft of one.

Figure 2.

Drafting

As many of you know, assembly can be a tough step in the composition process—just ask your professors. Moving from a blank page to a defensible argument has a lot of risk built into it. But there is really no **one** right way that writers do their work. Some people love to sit in front of a computer in total silence, while others love to work with pen and paper in a coffee shop. Some prefer to knock out an essay in one (or two) dedicated writing sessions, and others tinker with an argument up until they hit "submit."

Whether you have a preferred way to write or not, most writers discover that adjusting how, where, and when you develop a draft can drastically change how they make their case. And adjusting your approach can prove more effective than rigidly following what has worked in the past. Try some of the following methods and compare how you feel. Do you find yourself working with more focus in one setting? Do you find that certain things distract you more than others?

Binge Writing

If you were to poll your classmates, I think that you would find that most college students prefer to write their essays all at once—to get it over with. This is not necessarily a bad choice. As Anne Lamott (1995) noted, "Very few writers know what they are doing until they've done it" (p. 22), and this idea is at the heart of *binge writing*. There are lots of reasons that students might put forth to justify this approach ("I write better under pressure," etc.), but one of the biggest reasons that this works is that, by focusing your efforts for an extended period of time, most find it easier to "find" an argument that works. Used in this way, this style of drafting is an extended free write and combines the generative impulse of Invention with the rhetorical expressiveness of Assembly.

Binge Writing, just like it sounds, is centered on an extended assembly period, in which you might write for two to eight hours or until you have a complete draft of your argument. If used purposefully and not out of necessity, this approach can help you (a) develop a stronger argument, (b) link your ideas together into a more coherent case, and (c) concentrate your efforts. But it has its drawbacks as well, as these arguments tend to take longer to revise, they can be very subjective, and the process itself is time consuming. So, *binge write* if you want to, but be aware that there are other methods of drafting.

Scheduled Writing

Professional writers often can tell you what times of day they prefer to write. I am a "morning writer," for example, because I love waking up early and getting my ideas down on "paper." Other writers are passionate about "night writing" because this is when their creative juices start flowing—after the world has calmed and distractions (internal and external) are at a low. Depending on your work schedule, it's not always possible to write exactly when you feel ready to do so. But you might try experimenting with writing at different parts of the day. How do you feel when writing in early or late afternoon? Do you like writing late at night? After you sit down for a session, make a mental note of how it felt to write at this time.

Some professional writers (and professors) will even schedule specific times throughout the week just for drafting. You might try this on your own. Pick a one to two hour period in which you plan to assemble your argument, develop an outline, or just free write/brainstorm. Try to choose a time when you can turn off notifications and focus, as that is the best method for taking advantage of a *scheduled writing* period. While this is not a great approach for everyone, it is a good technique for making sure that you do not let a writing assignment sneak up on you—among other long-term benefits.

Sprint Writing

While some students procrastinate and rely on *binge writing* to put an essay together, there is another option that allows you to develop a less panicked, more refined argument—*Sprint Writing*. Borrowing from the terminology of project managers, a *sprint* is a short, timed period in which an individual (or a team) completes a specific task or amount of work. Each intensive burst can last anywhere up to a month, but these sprints can be abbreviated even further and used to give yourself dedicated time to develop a smaller part of your larger argument. Instead of sitting for hours at a time in front of the computer, you can save yourself a lot of stress by breaking up the task into smaller pieces.

The intense focus that this approach encourages can generate more efficient and effective writing sessions—a nice counterpoint to the longer sessions of *binge writing*. Some researchers have even suggested that giving our brains set boundaries and deadlines can help to increase your ability to concentrate on the argument and, as a result, make for a more engaging essay, speech, etc. The **Pomodoro Technique** has become quite popular among many writers for just this reason. Here's how it works:

1. **Get a timer:** You can use an online timer, your phone's timer, or an actual timer.
2. **Set your timer for twenty-five minutes:** Write non-stop for twenty-five minutes. Don't get up to walk around. Don't stop to check your email. Just write for twenty-five straight minutes.
3. **When the timer goes off, take a full five-minute break:** Don't do any work. Now you can check your email, get some coffee, or just close your eyes. Take the full break.
4. **After your five-minute break is done, set the timer for another twenty-five minutes and write again:** Then take another five-minute break.
5. **Repeat the cycle for as long as you want to work.**

Writing in this way can prove useful for both your argument and your focus, as sustained/ *binge* writing tends to become sloppier and more hurried the longer that you keep working. But it takes time to develop a draft in this manner, and it is harder to reach a flow state if you are always checking the timer. That said, this is a useful way to approach more complicated arguments and to develop a draft over time. Try it out on your next essay and see if it helps.

Spartan Writing

Finding the perfect environment for drafting an essay can be difficult to do, but it is never a bad idea to take time to figure out what helps to put you in the headspace to write—for however long. Many people find that music can help generate just the right mood for writing and thinking—preferring familiar tunes or songs without lyrics (classical, low-fi, etc.). And others prefer a silent, dark space where they won't be distracted and can collect their thoughts. If you prefer to block out the world when drafting an argument, then you favor a *Spartan Writing* method.

This assembly style allows an intensity of focus that can help you develop a coherent and nuanced argument, but the specifics of developing a spartan writing space are completely up to you. The key is to avoid anything that might allow you to turn away from assembling the claim(s) at hand. You might need to experiment with the right conditions for getting work done. Do you favor a bright, spare room for writing? Or do you prefer to turn off your phone and the distraction(s) it offers? Will airplane mode help? What kind of music helps you stay focused? Try several different settings and note the results.

Framing Your Argument

Composing an argument can be an anxiety-inducing undertaking, even under the best of circumstances, and this is made even more of an issue if, as many of us were taught, you have to "hook" your readers with an engaging introduction and/or leave them satisfied with a compelling conclusion. These two sections of a traditional essay have a lot of extra rhetorical weight, offering context for the argument and engaging the audience more directly than most sections of a given text.

The opening and closing of any rhetorical text *frame* the claims that you are trying to make, and as a result, feel more important. But this does not have to be the case. The following section should help you start and end your essay, speech, or other rhetorical texts more effectively.

Introductions

If you find it difficult to craft an introduction for an essay, you're not alone—even experienced writers find it a challenging task. In just a handful of sentences (or paragraphs for longer pieces), you have to capture the attention of your reader, tell them why your paper matters, share a compelling thesis, and gesture towards the structure of your paper.

Though doing all of that is easier said than done, it's rewarding to craft a well-wrought introduction. It can even help improve the rest of your paper by encouraging you to think more actively about its structure and its main idea.

There are four main goals of any introduction:

1. Provide context on the issue.
2. State your thesis.
3. Preview the argument.
4. Capture the reader's attention.

Let's dive into each of those one-by-one:

◎ Provide Context

Imagine that I ask you to read a paper without telling you what it's about—what's the issue/topic. Looking at the document, you see that the introductory section is only one sentence:

> *I believe that golf courses must become more environmentally friendly.*

What is my paper about? Why am I writing about golf? Am I writing about golf, or am I writing about the environment? Are golf courses not environmentally friendly? Why should you care about this idea or about my perspective on this topic?

I may have provided an acceptable thesis statement, but it leaves too much to the imagination, doesn't it? A good thesis is useless without the context needed to understand it, and **good introductions provide context.** You need to bring your reader up to speed on your topic so that they understand the significance of your argument. A better introduction might look like this:

> *Despite the seemingly pastoral, natural landscape of American golf courses, many are, in fact, environmental blights. Golf courses, especially those in desert environments, are intensive water users, and golf course superintendents frequently use dangerous chemicals and weedkillers that run off into storm drains and river systems. Though I'm an avid golfer myself, this ongoing environmental negligence cannot continue, especially in a warming world. I believe that golf courses must become more environmentally friendly for the sport to survive.*

This introduction explains how I connected the two ideas together and explains why I, or anyone, might care about this issue. By the time the reader arrives at the thesis statement at the very end of the introduction, they have all the context they need to understand both why and for what my paper will argue.

When writing your own introduction, stop and ask yourself *what is the context for my thesis?* In other words, what key ideas must a reader understand in order to make sense of my argument? Why should they care about your thesis? By answering these questions, you'll provide the context (*stasis*) necessary for a strong, arguable thesis.

State Your Thesis

Every paper has to have a central, governing argument, typically called a **thesis**, and good introductions often feature a clear, concise **thesis statement.** In essence, this one to three sentence statement boils down the topic of your paper to a single idea. While a thesis is always dependent on the rhetor's argument and the rhetorical situation in which it will be received, here are a few rules of thumb for crafting a strong thesis.

First, a thesis must be **specific** and **defensible.** It might be helpful here to look at a thesis that doesn't work:

> *Golf courses have an impact on the environment.*

This is a bad thesis because it is too generic and inarguable. It's inarguably true: everything on earth has an impact of some kind on the environment, right? It's also very generic. Is that impact positive? Negative? Is it a major impact or a minor impact? We need more specificity in order to understand what point the paper is trying to make.

Here's what a better thesis statement could look like:

> **Weak thesis:** *Golf courses have a large impact on the environment.*
>
> **Acceptable thesis:** *Golf courses' intensive water use and chemical runoff have significant effects on their local environments.*
>
> **Strong thesis:** *As climate change makes water scarcer, golf courses must reduce their reliance on water and weed-killing chemicals to lower their environmental footprints and ensure the survival of the sport.*

This last thesis option is precise, concise, and defensible. It is a good distillation of a complex and compelling essay.

Often, writers will inadvertently craft an indefensible thesis in an attempt to play both sides, such as *"Lifting weights can be good for your body, but it can also cause health issues."* Instead of playing both sides, try to make an assertive statement. For example, even modifying this thesis to *"The physical benefits of lifting weights outweigh the risks"* turns a poor thesis into one that makes a case worth paying attention to, even if it is still pretty broad.

Make sure to keep an eye out for theses that offer clear, defensible, and specific arguments.

Preview the Argument

Let's take a look at the last thesis in the section above:

> *As climate change makes water scarcer, golf courses must reduce their reliance on water and weed-killing chemicals to lower their environmental footprints and ensure the survival of the sport.*

What do you think a paper with this thesis will discuss? In other words, what do you expect to read about in the following pages/paragraphs? If you made a list, it might include the following:
- A discussion of climate change's impact on water availability.
- A discussion of golf courses' environmental impacts, especially their water use.
- Closer investigation into the nature of the chemicals used by golf courses.
- A look at how golf courses might adapt to changing environmental conditions.

All of this can be gathered from a strong thesis that provides a "roadmap" for the paper that follows.

Ideally, this roadmap will be integrated into your thesis or in the background information used to establish context. Regardless of where (or how) you preview the argument, you want your reader to know what to expect from your paper—hopefully without ever feeling like they were explicitly told so. Sometimes, however, the roadmap might be more direct and clearly signposted, like it is here:

> *After an initial discussion of how golf courses' environmental impacts have evolved over time, I will look at both the negative and positive environmental effects of golf courses today. Then, moving into the future, I will argue that, as climate change makes water scarcer, golf courses must reduce their reliance on water and weed-killing chemicals to lower their environmental footprints and ensure the survival of the sport.*

Laying out a clear roadmap isn't just useful for your readers—it's also practical for you, as it can help you better structure the paper that follows.

◎ **Capture the Reader's Attention**

With some thought, attention to detail, and writerly elbow grease, any introduction can accomplish the first three of these introductory goals with relative ease. Doing those three things while also grabbing your reader's attention, though, is often the most difficult part. Try beginning your introduction with an **attention catcher** (see Chapter 12, "Beginnings"). A good opening might include (a) an intriguing example, (b) a surprising statistic, (c) hot take, (d) a personal anecdote, or (e) a thought-provoking question. Whatever you choose, your introduction should encourage your reader to want to know more about your topic.

A good *attention catcher* can be anywhere from one sentence to a full chapter, depending on the size of the paper and the audience being addressed. As an example, our paper on the environmental impact of golf courses might start like this:

> *It's seven in the morning at Newtown Golf Course, and the dewy grass glistens in the morning sun. Over the manicured green of the rolling hills, the day's first golfers tee off for eighteen holes that wind through ancient oak forests along the Jackson River. All is not as it seems, however. On the first hole, the golfers can already smell it, and as they approach the river beside the sixth hole, the odor is unbearable. There along the riverbank lie dozens, if not hundreds, of dead fish, poisoned by toxic chemical runoff from yesterday's thunderstorm. Their stench fills the air. The golfers look ahead to the eighth green, where they see a course employee spraying a bright green chemical onto the grass just feet from the riverbank.*
>
> *This incident is not an isolated one. Despite the seemingly pastoral, natural landscape of American golf courses, many are, in fact, environmental blights. Golf courses, especially those in desert environments, are intensive water users, and golf course superintendents frequently use dangerous chemicals and weedkillers that run off into storm drains and local river systems, poisoning riparian life. Though I'm an avid golfer myself, I believe this ongoing environmental negligence cannot continue, especially in a warming world. As climate change…*

In an essay, your introduction is your chance to make a good first impression. While a well-written introduction that includes each of these elements might feel like a lot, it is the rhetorical equivalent of turning heads. It can go a long way to ensuring a successful argument and an enjoyable experience.

Conclusions

Serving as the other half of your essay's "frame," a good conclusion is very similar to a good introduction, and, in fact, we can think of these as mirror images of each other. As noted above, an introduction first grabs a reader's attention, then provides context and a preview, and finally concludes with a thesis statement. A conclusion does the same things—just in reverse. When writing an essay, you should conclude with the following:

1. Restate the thesis;
2. Summarize the major points of the paper; and
3. Conclude with a thought-provoking ending.

As we did before, let's take a look at each of these components one-by-one:

- **Restate the Thesis**

   When you reach the end of your argument, you want your reader to think back on the overall point of your paper. What was your paper arguing for? Take a look at the thesis statement in your introduction and read it closely. Is that still the governing claim that your paper is organized around, or has the idea shifted slightly over the course of the paper? Oftentimes, an initial thesis might be slightly altered or become more nuanced through the very act of defending it in a series of claims/paragraphs, so keep in mind that the thesis you include in your conclusion may not match your introduction's thesis word-for-word (and, in fact, the very best papers will not restate it word-for-word).

   Just make sure to leave your audience with a clear sense of what they should take away from your essay. You want them to be able to clearly and without hesitation answer the question, "So what was that all about?"

- **Summarize the Paper**

   When you conclude a paper, you're essentially recapping the major ideas and evidence of your argument at a higher level. In essence, you should synthesize your case here by briefly reminding the reader of the myriad claims, evidence, etc. that they encountered while reading your paper. This is a chance to wrap everything up in a nice package so that your reader can clearly see how your argument (thesis) came together and made a compelling point (or three).

If you are struggling to put together a good summary, try reviewing the topic sentences of each paragraph in your paper. Those are typically the most important points you made to support your thesis. Walk your reader back through a "roadmap" of those points in your conclusion, tying these ideas together into a clear (or semi-clear) progression. A good summary shows the development of an idea—it highlights how your thesis was confirmed through the course of your paper.

◎ **Conclude with a Thought-Provoking Ending**

Lastly, just as an introduction should begin with an *attention catcher,* a conclusion should wrap up with a thought-provoking **capper.** If an introduction benefits from a good first impression, then its parallel is a conclusion that leaves the audience thinking about the claim(s) raised in a paper.

Here are three strategies for finishing your paper on a high note, though these are just a few of the myriad ways you might conclude a paper, script, or writing project of any kind:

- **A Parallel Claim:** Establish a parallel structure by returning to an idea, theme, or scenario from your introduction's *attention catcher.* If you began your paper with a scenario, you might hypothesize how that scenario would be different if they followed the direction suggested by your thesis.
- **A Glimpse of the Future:** What comes next for your topic or issue? For example, if you're writing a paper about AI-assisted writing, you might end by directing your reader towards what the future with AI might look like. Alternatively, you might encourage them to lobby their congressional representatives to pass tighter regulation of AI technologies—an effort to shape any potential consequence of your argument.
- **A Broader Appeal:** Connect your idea to an even bigger one, thereby showing your reader the significance of the topic and its implications. If I'm writing a paper about excessive water use by golf courses, I might end by suggesting that changing how golf courses are managed is just one piece of the puzzle to combat climate change—connecting a more precise or local issue (golf courses) to a larger, more global one (climate change).

Many students will rush through a conclusion in a final push to the finish line. But this is a significant section of any paper and can go a long way to making a lasting impression on your audience. If your goal is to change the mind of your reader, persuade them to act on this issue, or whatever you hoped to do with an argument, then a good conclusion is your final chance to appeal to them. It is your last word on the topic.

Revision: Improving Your Approach

After writers complete a rough draft, the work of **Revision** begins. Revising is not just editing or proofreading. In fact, this final step in the composition process is much more creative, critical, and exciting. During the revision process, many writers literally re-visualize their project. They get feedback from others, read their own work, and try to imagine ways of expanding their argument in areas that need more depth.

Assembly may get all the glory, but revision is where an argument is honed and perfected. When a writer drafts an essay, most of the attention is focused on making a clear and compelling argument—on *what* you are claiming. But when you turn to revision, the focus should shift to *how* you prove these claims. Reviewing the structure of the argument, the evidence that will support it, and how clearly claims are made, this step asks you to answer the question, "How will my reader respond to this essay *as they read it*?"

Some of the following revision questions are also worth asking yourself when re-visiting an essay, speech, or other rhetorical text:

- Does this draft actually fulfill the assignment? Have you strayed at all from what you were asked to do? Look back over the assignment prompt and try to determine whether or not you've managed to fulfill all parts of the assignment.
- What is your main point or central argument? Does the entire text actually support, explain, and make the case? Do you ever drift into unrelated tangents that don't exactly relate to your main point?
- Are there parts that seem confusing or unclear? Ask your readers to tell you if they get confused or lost at any points. If so, how can you revise those sections so that they address your readers' confusion?
- Are you able to clearly follow your own organizing structure of the whole paper? Try to make a "reverse outline" of your paper.
- Do you have an introduction that grabs your readers' attention? Does it set the tone for the rest of your work?

Good *revision* is focused on developing meaning—on helping your audience understand your claim(s). It is not solely concerned with cleaning up errors. So, the next time you are wrapping up an essay draft, take some time to make sure that your argument (your *thesis*) is as clear and as strong as possible.

Revising

Whether we're talking about peer review, multiple drafts, or simply reading over what you've written, the most important aspect of revision is making sure that your argument is well defined and that the audience can follow it. But this is easier said than done, especially as you learn how to make effective claims, etc., so to help you out, there are three specific aspects of any draft that you should examine and, if necessary, revise:[3]

The Argument's Structure

Successful essays have a clear, purposeful argument. This is one of the reasons that so much effort is put into *arranging* your claims into a coherent progression, as noted above. This structure is even more important in academic essays, where your audience does not have the opportunity to ask questions or seek clarification. Whether you write from an outline or just work from vibes, you should take the time to make sure your argument is organized around a *thesis,* progresses in a clear fashion, and includes appropriate evidence. In other words, *does it make sense?*

This may seem straightforward, but it is easy for writers—students and professionals—to look past the argument that they have put on the page and assume that everything is clear and organized. But there are tricks to get past this cognitive distortion.

The first thing you can try is **read your draft out loud.** This might seem too easy, but as noted earlier ("Responding"), we process arguments differently when we *hear* them. And this is a quick and easy way to actually find out what you wrote and how your reader might interpret it. The one issue—it can be embarrassing. But if you can get past this, then this is a simple tactic for effective revision.

The second thing you can do is play the "Believing Game." Developed by Peter Elbow,[4] this exercise asks you to take the time to read your text *as it is.* To do this, you need to give yourself twelve to forty-eight hours before you sit down with your draft (which means less procrastination, unfortunately). As you read, pay attention to the implications of your written argument by looking for the following:

- (Sub)Claims that might would help prove your claim(s).
- Further examples/claims that would complement your argument.
- Positive implications/inferences that could be derived from the draft.
- A rationale for why you made this argument (motivation/exigence).

This might seem weird—reading as if you believed yourself—but that is why you need the cognitive distance that 12+ hours provides (or however long you can afford). As you read, note where your argument can be strengthened or more evidence/examples can be added. This is where you should add *meaning* and develop a stronger claim(s).

The Auditor's Understanding

As noted in Chapter 3, a good writer or speaker will keep their audience's needs at the forefront of their mind as they develop an argument. But there is a lot to juggle as you write a paper (or speech), so one way that professional writers make sure that they make a strong claim and that their audience can follow along is to dedicate a great deal of time to "reading from the audience's perspective."

This exercise in empathy is an important step in making sure that your argument is meaningful and clear, but it requires a clear sense of how a skeptical academic reader might interpret your argument. You want to read this *as if* you were your primary audience. What questions would they have? Where would they want more information? Where would they be skeptical? Bored? Etc.

One way that you can build this skill is by playing the "Doubting Game"[5] by reading your draft with a highly skeptical eye and looking for the following:

- Unacknowledged or hidden assumptions about the argument.
- Imprecise descriptions, underdeveloped explanations, etc.
- Examples that might not be understood by your audience.
- Potential negative inferences that could be made.
- Obvious mistakes or misattributions.

Most of your readers will be more generous than a truly critical read will suggest, but if you can shore up aspects of your draft where your audience might need more clarification or your argument might need more refining, than you should be fine. Plus, this is a useful way to find out where more information (*and length*) is needed—if that matters.

The Writer's Style

While it is often looked down on, "mere rhetoric" is still important. The honest truth is that effective arguments are usually *stylistic* arguments. So, it is not a bad idea to take the time to review how good an argument "sounds." Where the earlier steps in Revision were focused on improving one's argument, this step asks you to take a closer look at how authoritative, relevant, and appealing an argument is. In other words, you want to look at *how* you make your case.

As noted above, reading a draft aloud is a useful way to hear what your argument sounds like. Does this draft sound like you? Does it use language that is appropriate to the rhetorical situation? Is it aligned with the expectations of the audience—with what they would appreciate in terms of tone, formality, etc.? If you can answer "yes" to these (and related) questions, then you are on the right path, but if there are any points in the essay where this could be improved, then you have a little more room for improvement.

Editing

If revising an essay asks you to focus on the overall argument, then *editing* asks you to carefully examine your work at a more minute level—to pay attention to the specific choices that contribute to your overall argument. That means when you edit, you should focus on awkward sentences, questionable word choice, and, yes, your punctuation tendencies. These smaller issues can be picked up on as you revise, but it is still a good idea to take time to look at the minutia of a given draft.

To do this, the best thing you can use is perspective. Given a little rhetorical distance from a completed draft of your essay or speech (4+ hours), it is easier to focus in on a single sentence (or section) and gauge whether you chose the right words, phrases, or clauses for the purpose. But even then, editing is a skill that needs to be developed.

> ### Revising on Screen versus Revising on Paper
>
> Some writers find it helpful to print out a draft on paper in order to revise and edit. Revising is sometimes easier to do with pen and paper, rather than online. Try it both ways to see which one you prefer.

Using Lanham's Paramedic Method

In his excellent book *Revising Prose,* Richard Lanham introduced what he calls the "paramedic method" for editing your own work.[6] This method is a great way to help find those awkward sounding sentences that might confuse (or annoy) readers. Lanham's method is designed to give your writing more punch, more power, and more persuasion. It's designed to make your prose more exciting to read. By following the paramedic method, you will eliminate boring, sluggish sentences and unnecessary wordiness. Here are the steps:

1. **Circle the prepositions.** Prepositional phrases often create wordiness and some s-l-o-w reading. (**Examples:** around, at, by, for, from, in, of, on, over, outside, through, since, under, up, with, etc.)
2. **Draw a box around the "to be" verbs.** This is a good way to catch passive voice construction that detracts from exciting, active prose. (**Examples:** am, is, are, was, were, etc.)
3. **Ask yourself, "Where's the action?" and "Who is kicking whom?"** Figure out who is actually performing the action in your sentences. Who or what is the main subject of each sentence? Revise each sentence to clearly show the actor in charge.
4. **Change the action into a simple verb.** Now that you know who is doing the action (who is doing the kicking!), revise each sentence to give that actor a simple action verb.
5. **Eliminate the slow wind-ups at the beginning of sentences.** Wind-ups are phrases like, "I believe that …" and "In my opinion …" These kinds of beginnings aren't necessary and they slow down the reader. Instead, jump right into the sentence.

In this paragraph is a demonstration of the use of good style in the writing of a report.

Action in sentence; eliminate slow wind-ups.

Revision
This paragraph demonstrates good style in reports (or) … good style in report writing. *The does is in the subject.*

Figure 3. An example of the Paramedic Method at work.

Example: Currently there *is* a project that *is* being done **to** help students **in** after school programs **to** further their learning and have educational resources made available **to** them.
- Who is doing the action? Who is kicking whom? *"A project"*
- What is the action? *Helping, furthering, and making*

Revised sentence: Currently, a project is helping students in after school programs by furthering their learning and making resources available to them.

Example: The point I wish **to** make **is** that the employees working **at** this company **are in** need **of** a much better manager **of** their money.
- Who is kicking whom? *Employees*
- What is the action (the kicking)? *Needing*
- Slow wind-up? *The point I wish to make is that ...*

Revised sentence: This company's employees need a much better money manager.

Here is an example from my own essay: Critical regionalism became widely theorized **in** the 1980s **by** several architectural theorists as a means of realizing, embodying, and building **upon** a community's political consciousness **through** local spaces.
- Who is kicking whom? Who is the actor? Architectural theorists
- What is the action/kicking? Theorizing (Redundant)

Revised sentence: In the 1980s, several architectural theorists developed critical regionalism as a way of realizing, embodying, and building upon a community's political consciousness in local spaces.

Exercise: Now It's Your Turn

Use the paramedic method to help this sentence:

It is widely known that the engineers at Sandia Labs have become active participants in the Search and Rescue operations in most years.

What is your revised sentence?

Using AI-Assisted Writing Apps

When you are running low on time (or want a quick once over from an "expert"), you should feel free to turn to a digital assistant like Microsoft's *Editor* or to *Grammarly* in order to highlight areas that can be improved or grammatical mistakes that you may have missed, but you will want to be careful. These programs can be very helpful, but they are not perfect. Watch out for the following if you turn to one of these services:

- **These apps make you sound generic.** The stylistic advice offered by these programs is derived from an algorithm that focuses on writing trends seen in the LLMs (Large Language Models) that an AI has been taught. These LLMs are not discriminating, highlighting the trends and common practices that emerge from comparing writers across the model(s). In other words, these programs favor *generic* changes. So, if you want to sound like everyone else, you should accept as many suggested changes as possible. But if you want to sound like yourself (as is the goal), then you should think through the suggested changes critically.
- **They have blind spots.** These apps are useful guides for clarifying your language and cleaning up the GSP errors (Grammar, Spelling, and Punctuation), but they tend to only catch what is initially flagged/scanned. The longer your document, the more likely these programs are to miss issues that the average reader will catch. This includes red flags like "a lot" vs. "allot" and many common uses of commas.
- **They are not adaptive,** *at least not yet.* The specific demands of your rhetorical document—the audience, the context, etc.—are not considered when these apps make a recommendation. They assume that all readers are the same and have similar linguistic preferences, but not all readers are the same—as you know. Each audience and rhetorical situation will call for different reference points, rhetorical appeals, and arguments, and a more adaptive approach will work better in most situations.

Unless directed otherwise by your instructor, you are welcome to use these apps to help you edit your drafts, but this is not the solution to all of your problems. Use these with care!

THE RECURSIVE COMPOSITION PROCESS

As you read through this chapter, you may have found yourself thinking, "But when I write, I just *write*," and you would not be wrong. Most people do not think of these as distinct steps with a clear progression; they just *write*. For example, invention rarely occurs only at the very beginning; most of us develop ideas over time. And anytime I stop writing—to text a friend, get a snack, or whatever—I take a minute to organize my thoughts before continuing to write. In fact, when rhetors talk about the composition process, we are usually referring to this as a *recursive* process.

Recursive Processes—like writing, swimming, or riding a bike—have a specific sequence of events, but this is a sequence that repeats itself continuously. *Brainstorm, Organize, Write, Revise. Repeat.* No matter when you start riding a bike, you will always move the pedals in the same sequence. Similarly, whenever most writers sit down to compose an essay (or any text), they go through the same sequence: *Invent, Arrange, Assemble, Revise. Repeat* (see Figure 4). And because few of us write in one fluid motion, most writers will stop, think about what they want to say (*invent*), fit it in with the sentence(s) before it (*arrange*), and then write (*assemble*) without taking time to (explicitly) revise their work. Every time you stop writing, you will spend some time making your way through these stages—or at least that is the theory. It does not usually feel like a carefully, segmented sequence.

Figure 4. The Recursive Composition Process

All rhetors have a composition process that reflects their own preferences and argumentative tendencies. One writer might refine their arguments as they write, adopting a highly recursive process that requires them to look back over their drafts continuously. Others might binge write a draft (or two) before they explicitly revise what they want to say. Still others might take a long time outlining and organizing their argument before they ever sit down to assemble their argument. However you choose to write, this recursive composition process should help you think through and refine your ability to develop nuanced and effective academic arguments—both for this course and later ones. Your ability to write is a skill that can be honed, after all, and knowing where there is room for improvement should help you do just that.

VIDEO RESOURCES

Mayor Jim Gray on Using Writing to Solve Problems

Mayor Jim Gray was elected Mayor of Lexington in 2010 and re-elected for another four year term in 2014. In 2016 he ran for the United States Senate against Rand Paul. Mayor Gray is also the former CEO of Gray Construction, which is a successful international construction firm. As part of his daily work in the Mayor's office, Mayor Gray uses writing in a number of ways. In this interview clip, he talks about how he uses the writing process as part of his regular problem-solving process as Mayor.

(https://vimeo.com/103940590)

Stella Parks on Her Writing Process

Stella Parks is a pastry chef (formerly the head pastry chef at Table 310 in Lexington), a blogger, and a cookbook author. Stella is a native of Louisville, but she has lived all over the world. As part of her daily work as a pastry chef and blogger, Stella uses rhetorical theory and writing in a number of ways. In this interview clip, she describes her own writing process.

(https://vimeo.com/103940582)

Stella Parks on Writing Proposals

Here, Stella Parks talks about her own process of writing a proposal for her new cookbook.

(https://vimeo.com/103938666)

Griffin VanMeter on Using Writing as a Creative Process

Griffin VanMeter is co-owner of the branding firm **Bullhorn Creative** *(http://bullhorncreative.com),* as well as the creative director of Kentucky for Kentucky (www.kentuckyforkentucky.com). Griffin grew up in Lexington, though he has also lived and worked around the country. As part of his creative work, Griffin uses writing and rhetorical theory in many ways. In this interview clip, he describes how he uses writing as part of his creative process.

(https://vimeo.com/104015855)

NOTES

[1] This has developed into a practice called "Sh_tty First Drafts" in which the initial formation of an argument, story, etc. is developed without revision or much structure. This longform free writing is often credited to Anne Lamott's influential *Bird by Bird (1995).*

[2] This is based on the work of Cicero, collected in his *Rhetorica ad Herennium* (I.iii.4).

[3] These are adapted from Donald Murray's *The Craft of Revision*, 1991.

[4] Elbow (2008).

[5] *Ibid.*

[6] Richard Lanham. *Revising Prose.* Pearson Longman, 2006.

WORKS CITED

Cicero, Marcus Tullius. *Rhetorica ad Herennium.* Translated by Harry Caplan, Harvard UP, 1999.

Elbow, Peter. "The Believing Game—Methodological Believing." *The Journal of the Assembly for Expanded Perspectives on Learning,* Vol. 14, 2008, pp. 1–11.

Lamott, Anne. *Bird by Bird.* Knopf Doubleday, 1995.

Murray, Donald. *The Craft of Revision.* Cengage, 1992.

Reading and Responding

Recommended for WRD 110/112

Chapter 5

CAN YOU THINK IN QUESTIONS?

Have you ever played the game Twenty Questions? Someone chooses an object—often one that people can see just by looking around—and has the other people guess what it is. Usually the other people try to narrow down what the object is, asking yes or no questions:

- Is it cold?
- Can you kick it?
- Is it alive?
- Can I touch it from where I'm sitting?

We tend to call these "narrowing questions" because they help us to eliminate a whole range of things that may fall into giant categories. For example, if I say that the object is indeed cold, then you know it's probably not the fireplace with a roaring fire. It's also not the space heater across the room.

Imagine if I didn't try to ask such narrowing questions. Instead, I just started guessing at random: *"Is it that eraser there? Is it my glasses? Is it Dmitri?"* Everyone playing would look at me in disbelief. Why? It's because we use questions that are not too broad and not too narrow to get a better sense of what the answer is. Without having questions, we'd have way too many possibilities to consider.

In other words, questions help us limit the information we have at hand.

Reading is the same way. Questions can help guide us through the reading process because they offer projections for how a text might turn out. Reading requires us to be *active* in thinking through its information. Reading passively will only let you look at the information, but reading by inquiry will let you absorb it and think critically about it. You'll get a lot more out of your time spent reading that way.

Think of reading as a conversation between two people. One person can't speak alone, or she'd just be talking to herself. Reading is **dialogic,** which means that it depends on the co-creation of at least two people to make its meaning. An author may write words, but they don't mean anything until a reader reads them. Between every two sentences is a gap that you have to fill in. Usually we do this intuitively—without thinking. But at other times we have to actively draw and imagine connections between an author's ideas.

Author's Statement #1 _____ (gap) _____ Author's Statement #2

Look at the gaps between the sentences in these initial statements from Wendell Berry's essay, "Why I Am Not Going to Buy a Computer":

> *Like almost everybody else, I am hooked to the energy corporations, which I do not admire. I hope to become less hooked to them. In my work, I try to be as little hooked to them as possible. As a farmer, I do almost all of my work with horses. As a writer, I work with a pencil or a pen and a piece of paper.*[1]

First, he's talking about energy corporations, and then he suddenly mentions that he works with horses. There's not a direct link, but as inquiring readers, we supply the connection since we know that the difference between big businesses and agrarian life will lead to his stance about technology which is given to us in the title. Some connections will be made for us by the author, but often we have to actively pursue the text's meaning.

So reading is more than just letting the words pass under your eyes. It means engaging in a dialogue with the author by seeing if her words make sense to you, if you agree with them, if you can follow their meaning from one section to the next, if they create a new idea in your mind that wasn't there before, or if they repeat or emphasize things you've learned already.

Not only will asking questions help you complete the conversation with the author through the text, but it will also give you a great way to take notes, especially if you write down the questions and jot down possible answers as you go.

READING REPORTS AND EDITORIALS

Choosing the kind of questions you ask while reading is just as important as choosing to ask questions in the first place. Some genres that you read encourage certain kinds of questions, and you're probably already familiar with some of these. Tweets respond well to the question, *"What's happening?"* Facebook status updates explicitly ask the question in their dialogue box, *"What's on your mind?"* which pushes people to compose a wide range of posts. Most texts you read or listen to can be thought of in terms of responding to a specific question or set of questions.

Newspaper reports are often written in response to the formula questions *"Who? What? When? Where? Why?"* By asking those questions about informational reports, you can easily follow the material presented. Facts tend to drive these articles, leading the reader along a path of causation in which the answers to those questions form a narrative that makes sense.

Reports may be full of opinions, but they tend not to be the main focus. Instead, we often see opinions in reports in place of facts. So asking the questions "Who? What? When? Where? Why?" means not only getting answers to those questions from the report, but also trying to figure out other answers to them that the report may not include.

Reports usually have a clear structure, explain their method, and present information as facts. They often marshal statistics, eyewitness accounts, and logical methods to arrive at some kind of cut-and-dried conclusion. In "Program Targeting Fraternities, Sororities Has Little To No Effect On Alcohol Use," we see a report that has a more empirical basis to it, the kind you will often find in the sciences (find it here: "Program Targeting Fraternities, Sororities Has Little To No Effect On Alcohol Use." DATA: The Brown University Digest of Addiction Theory & Application 18.12 (1999): 6. Academic Search Premier. Web. 15 Aug. 2013. Read it and decide what about it makes it seem "factual."

On the other hand, editorials (including the one we'll look at below) often respond better to the two-part question, *"What's wrong, and what do I think about it?"* since they take issue with something previously said. Usually engaging with hot topics, editorials are full of emotion as opposed to full of facts. They may provide facts to clarify a problem in the original viewpoint they are disagreeing with, but it is the emotions that organize their information. In addition to the question above, you might ask, *"How does the author feel about X and why?"*

Be aware that the questions you choose to ask are going to determine the kind of information you get. So you might ask editorials questions about their exigency (*What are the authors writing in response to?*), standpoint (*What's the angle on the topic?*), reasoning (*Why do the authors think they're right?*), or credentials (*Why should you believe them?*). You can also search a text for questions that are a bit more distant from its primary purpose, such as *"What about this article made the newspaper want to publish it?" "How is this editorial's point similar or different from other arguments in the debate?" "What can I learn about stylistic technique by looking at this editorial as a good (or bad) model of writing?"* These questions develop a specific aim into your reading.

Consider the following **editorial by Brooke Myers written for the University of Oklahoma's student newspaper, the OU Daily, on Feb. 3, 2010** *(http://www.oudaily.com/opinion/column-fraternities-cleaning-duties-rush-and-the-quest-for-brotherhood/article_fef503e7-a3fb-550b-9a40-56221c4545f4.html)*. As you go through, jot down questions you have, from the very first paragraph down through the last. And don't rush! Remember that quality inquiry comes from a sustained and focused reading of a text.

FRATERNITIES, CLEANING DUTIES, RUSH, AND THE QUEST FOR BROTHERHOOD

There is no bond like the bond of brothers. It is a bond made infallible. The word "brothers" connotes the dripping, sweet glue that binds men, young and old, together for life.

Together. For. Life.

Brotherhood has no limit, it has no age. It is an unconditionally bound relationship.

Let this be the eulogy to your days as an only child in this great, big world, dear newly-initiated fraternity boys.

Look, men. Look at the days that have passed. Remember them well, those preliminaries. Remember the beginning, when many of you were taken out to fancy dinners. Remember the delicious free meals and the kind smiles that were flashed at you. Remember the petty conversation that may or may not have reeled you in to your respective house. Remember being a chosen one, how good it must have felt to know you were wanted.

The Sorting Hat had done its bit, and you became another component in the category you apparently fit well. Some of you were jocks, some of you were cowboys, some of you were smart, some of you were stupid, some of you were attractive, some of you spent money in great amounts, some of you wore Polo well, some of you had impressive fluid capacities, some of you were good at getting girls, some of you really knew how to party. You all truly had your uses for your respective houses.

As new initiates, we can look back together on all the things you've had to do to make yourself worthy of admission. It has been a brutal trek, but you have made it.

When you were just wee little monkeys (we can't call you pledges, since it's illegal, and I rather like the name "monkey"—it has a cute little dehumanizing effect), you were made to do awful things. But those awful things were intelligently and symbolically designed so you would feel brotherhood seeping from your pores as you sweat while doing your duties, such as cleaning up the after-party leftovers in a fraternity bathroom while dressed in a nice suit.

You were asked to be humiliated for a noble cause, making right-angle turns and speaking to no one but your pledge brothers for a week. You were deemed house-keeper at any hour of the morning, be it 2 or 5 a.m.

Boys, you were disrespected by the guys you would call your brothers, and you trusted they had dignified intentions; they trashed the house and yelled in your face while you were made to clean it all up. Your older brothers taught you lessons in presentation, forcing you to wear a suit everyday for a week without washing it. You were stripped of your identity, given no choices, brought down to a lowly level. You memorized names and numbers and more names and "star facts" about all the members of your respective houses. You were sleep deprived, abused, belittled, humiliated and asked to love it.

I envy you, though, for all that you gained from the experience. You formed a brotherhood with those experiencing the same struggles you were. You have learned, from deprivation, to appreciate so fully the honor bestowed upon you to be a part of something so much greater than yourself. You are one of them now.

You have truly accomplished something in life. You can now proudly display those prized Greek letters. You have been given a number—and it represents you! You are now four digits that say one thing: "I made it, I'm somebody!" And you are. You are somebody.

You've come so far. Your traits have blossomed. In fact, you might have added some you didn't have in the first place.

Many of you have truly been changed. And it's only the beginning.

Maybe, if you didn't once sport Polo and Sperrys, you do now. Maybe, if you didn't have long, side-swept hair under a backwards cap, you do now. Maybe, if you didn't wear cowboy boots originally, you do now. Maybe, if you didn't dip before, you do now. Maybe if you couldn't do the frat snap, you can now. Maybe, if khaki wasn't your color, it is now. Maybe, if getting chicks in bed wasn't on your agenda before, it is now. Maybe, if you didn't drink then, you do now. Maybe, if you cared more about school work than Greek letters, you don't now.

Maybe, if you were different from everyone else, you're not now.

Congratulations, guys, you're a whole lot like everybody else! [2]

How do you respond to this article? Does it make you want to kick your desk? Stand up and applaud? Laugh violently? It made many students at the University of Oklahoma submit editorial responses to Myers that were published. Some attacked it for its strong, parodying tone, while others rushed to its defense with facts and evidence. Others got defensive and argued for the longstanding tradition of fraternities. Why did the article inflame so many different responses, and how do we deal with those responses?

Once again, questions come to the rescue. You can diffuse your own outrage or delight (or possibly indifference) to this article by approaching it with a series of questions to help you understand it. Now that you've read it, go back over the questions you jotted in the margin. Did they help you understand the article? How can you revise the questions you asked to better analyze the text? As you develop your own style of reading and questioning, you should get better and better at revising and adapting the kinds of questions you ask.

THE "SO WHAT?" QUESTION

Just because a text lends itself to certain kinds of questions for its production does not mean that other questions can't be used to understand it in different and possibly better ways (in fact, both editorials and reports often benefit from flipping the questions we ask about them, since they usually don't fall neatly into the categories of "facts" or "opinions"). For example, one of the most important questions in academic writing, *"So what?"*—which deals with the significance of a text—can be applied to any of the genres mentioned above. Think about a newspaper story—how would you read the story differently looking for the answer to "So what?" Or Facebook status updates—how many will you have to sift through to find a satisfying answer to that question? Choosing different questions to ask texts is encouraged by the textual genre itself, but also gives the reader latitude to search for what is important to him/her while reading.

This leads to another point about the kind of answers you'll find after asking these questions. The answers will change based on your own views and the context in which the text is published. Whether or not you care or know about a topic will influence your own judgment, but you also want to be aware that others may have very different cares or very different knowledge from you. So when reading a text through certain questions, you want to keep in mind both your own standpoint and what you know about others' standpoints. You may be a member of the main audience for some texts but part of a very peripheral one for others. Have you ever read a Facebook status or a tweet that didn't even make sense to you? The intended audiences of a text come from where and when it is published, and this shapes both its content and how we should read it.

> ## Exercise: Different Questions for Different Genres
>
> Find a newspaper editorial and ask the questions you would normally ask for a newspaper story. Write a paragraph about whether you were able to get answers to your questions and what that says about the genre of editorial. After you do that, come up with the questions you'd ask to understand the following newspaper genres:
>
> - Comics
> - Advertisements
> - Weather forecast
> - Dear Abby columns
> - Classifieds
>
> Put your questions together in a chart and see if you can find any patterns, such as commonly asked questions, among the newspaper genres.

How Do Emotions Fit In?

As Myers's extreme example of polemical rhetoric demonstrated, even the most objective reading is not free of emotions, since every stance taken by the author adopts a position that we may not agree with, that we may put up barriers against, or that we may agree with and accept happily. You should try to discover what emotions the text is trying to provoke by the text and use your own emotive responses as a guide to making sense of the author's goals. Remember to maintain a grasp on the text's claims at the same time—what its argument and reasons are. We must combine emotional awareness with logic to imagine others' responses to a text, to gauge its rhetorical power.

Our position as an ethical audience leads to what rhetorician Peter Elbow calls "The Believing Game," in which we tacitly accept what an author says as true until we have read his/her rationale.[3] The notoriously divided Congress at present in Washington, D.C., might better reach compromise if they adopted this kind of reading and listening posture. Imagine a Republican arguing before the House for the benefits of closing abortion clinics and having all the Democrats present with rapt attention, nodding as they try to understand the speaker's position as if they were he/she. Or suppose the compromise that might be more quickly reached if the benefits of a lesser dependence on coal were jotted down while a Democrat spoke, rather than a list of arguments against it. Critical but ethical reading begins by acknowledging the values of the speaker's stance, not by simply rejecting them.

We've looked at two examples of factual-based reports and opinion-based editorials, but as noted, the distinctions are not always so clear in most examples. Many authors will have heavily-slanted facts or strongly neutral opinions. Although some articles come close to relying exclusively on one or the other, such cases are rare and most examples will mix the two. Don't be fooled by the genre it claims to be part of, either. A report isn't any more true just because it claims to be news.

Exercise: Fact or Opinion?

Read the following report from the respected journal *The Chronicle of Higher Education* (Katherine Mangan, **"Colleges Confront the Perils of Frats,"** *The Chronicle of Higher Education,* Aug. 30, 2017. https://www.chronicle-com.ezproxy.uky.edu/article/Colleges-Confront-the-Perils/241055?cid=RCPACKAGE.)

Which of the two genres does it seem to lean more toward? Why do you say that? Which sections come across as factual? Which as opinion? Identify parts that seem as though they're being passed off as facts but are really weighted opinions. Are there opinion sections that seem grounded in objective statements? Based on these questions, compose a paragraph in which you analyze the article for its logic, how it thinks. Remember to use your own questions that you've found useful to guide your reading and your evaluation.

Exercise: A Report and a Reply

Imagine you had to turn Katherine Mangan's editorial into a report. How would you do it? Write up a plan with at least five steps for how you would go about making changes. Then do some research and write your own report based on Mangan's topic. Finally, read back over both documents and make a list of the major differences you see.

Do you agree with Mangan's view of the Greek system? Write an editorial in response to hers. What questions will guide your reply? How will they help structure your points? Make an outline of what you will say, using questions as your major headings. Now, write the reply. Finally, look at the two documents. What similarities and differences do you find?

PREPARING QUESTIONS FOR PEER REVIEW

Whether bringing your work to a university writing center or to a required in-class peer review session, you are more likely to use your time effectively if you know what type of feedback you are seeking as opposed to starting the session without an idea of what you want to accomplish. For example, if you already feel confident about your grammar or plan to review it on your own at a later stage of revision, you might not want your peer reviewer to spend much time critiquing grammar. If you are instead, for example, primarily concerned about whether your introduction is engaging to readers, you can specifically tell your reviewer to focus their comments upon your introduction. Before beginning peer review, reflect upon your work and come up with a question or set of questions to direct your reviewer's attention.

There are two key traits to useful questions for peer review: specificity and relevance. Regarding specificity, it should be clear based on your question what areas of concern you want to point out to your reviewer. If you would like to know if your project is "any good," try to be more specific by identifying for yourself the traits of good writing and asking your reviewer if your writing has those traits. Relevance is also key; the questions you ask should pertain to your goals for the project, meaning they should be targeted at fulfilling the assignment's guidelines and/or enhancing your writing skills in areas you deem important. To explain relevance further, if assignment guidelines specify, for example, that you should not use outside sources, it would not be relevant to ask your peer reviewer if you have cited sources properly. To ensure your questions are tailored to the particular assignment, it is a good idea to review assignment guidelines before formulating your questions.

Some examples of useful questions are:

- What are the strengths of my project?
- How can I make my draft more concise?
- After reading my draft, what ideas do you wish I had explained further or are there ideas you feel I overlooked?
- I want to use this quote, but how can I smoothly integrate it?
- Can you help me check for incomplete sentences and give me advice on how to complete them?
- Looking at the rubric, are there any requirements I am not yet meeting?

> ### Exercise: Question-Based Peer Review
>
> Take a look at a piece you have been working on for this class. Identify specific areas of concern you have about what you have written, and write a question to ask a partner. When you first pair up, share your question, share your writing with your partner, and receive their response to their specific question. Then listen to the question they wrote, review their writing with an eye for answering their question, and give them feedback specific to their question.

RESPONDING TO PEERS' WORK

"Your first point has a well-developed structure."

"That word didn't make sense because it's not specific enough."

"Your tone seemed a little aggressive."

"The poor grammar in the fourth paragraph obstructs your point."

If you've received feedback on a paper, you're probably familiar with the language of critically evaluating essays, but it's not always clear how to provide that kind of feedback. In this section, we'll offer some skills that you can use to edit your peers' work.

Remember that making comments on your peers' work helps them with the process of writing. The reason papers written the night before the assignment is due don't turn out well is because good writing takes time and collaboration to develop. The more views and opinions you can get on your writing, the better you will know how your piece comes across to others and what you can change to improve it. It may take others saying that they didn't understand your fifth paragraph or that your best point was one you just tagged on near the end to get you to realize the real center and power of your work.

While we need others' help to make our writing stronger, most people are timid to make strong comments on others' work. Don't think that you're grading your peers, but that you're making their papers better by helping them improve their weaker parts. To do that, you'll want to give comments that are as specific as possible. Don't just say *"your words are vague"*—say which words in which paragraph are vague, why they're vague, and how your peer can make them less vague. Always identify the paragraph and sentence that your impression comes from. Always give a brief rationale of *why* a revised version of that part could be stronger than the current version. Always offer suggestions for how to solve the problem.

Students and teachers alike are not always clear when they give feedback. So if a sentence seems awkward to you, don't just write "awk" in the margin—explain why it is awkward and how it can be corrected. If the tense is off, don't just jot "tense problems" but explain which tense the problematic area is in and why it should be changed to another. In short, clarity in your comments should mirror the kind of clarity you expect in your peers' writing. And of course, the clearer you write for your peers, the more precise and understandable your own essays will be.

Since the previous section offered some ways to use inquiry to actively read reports and editorials critically and ethically, let's see how you might apply those skills to editing your peers' work. Although the core aspects of reading and questioning will not change from published work to peers' work, your peers' work differs from published texts in that it is in process, and so your goal is to read, believing and questioning, with an end toward identifying areas that need more clarity, that lead the reader along, taking him or her through the gaps between sentences, from initial question to presented answer. When you are unsure of your peers' intent, consider offering feedback in the form of a question rather than an assertion. For example, instead of writing "this sentence makes no sense," consider asking your peer "what do you mean by this sentence?" By asking your peer to clarify their purpose for writing, you can demonstrate your aim to support them in more effectively achieving that purpose; they retain creative control over their own work.

Now, just because your peer's work is still in an early stage of development does not mean that it will leave a single trail of breadcrumbs for the reader to follow—in fact, more advanced works often make the reader do more of the work or are open enough to let the reader imagine several possible and equally valid interpretations—but in general the connections between each point should be identifiable. Making sure the text is cogent and easy to follow is not always as simple as it sounds. It involves looking at the major ways language communicates.

The aspects of your peers' work that you'll want to look at may vary based on your instructor's specific requirements, but whatever those may be, thinking of the peer review at two different levels, global and local, will help you understand the kind of comments you're making on your peers' work.

- **First, think of *global*, or large-scale, changes to suggest.**

    Before worrying about grammar, look at the essay's thesis, argument, and main points. Does the argument make sense? Do all the points fit together? Does anything need to be added? Also ask about the order of the points. Does it follow some kind of arrangement model (for example, from most important to least important)? Once these broader and more important questions are answered, the smaller, stylistic components will gain relevance.

◉ **Next, identify *local,* sentence-level problems.**

Grammar and style are best modified only after the ideas themselves are well established. Though second, these aspects can be critical in both the understanding and persuasiveness of an argument. Mechanical mistakes or stylistic dullness can easily overshadow the power of good ideas. Recall the editorial above: if its tone turned you off from the article, then you missed out on its ideas. Strong style that anyone will find compelling is one of the hallmarks of good writing.

For the first kind of remarks, think about what your peer's purpose is—and not just "to get a good grade on the essay." What is s/he trying to accomplish or say? Summarize the main point as succinctly as you can. In the rest of your questions, ask about how your peer unpacks the main point, asking for a logical organization and strong evidence.

For the second kind of remark, think about *how* your peer accomplishes that purpose. What does your peer do in the essay that successfully communicates his or her purpose? What about the style, tone, choice of examples, numbers of statistics, etc. are appropriate for following through with the main goal of the essay?

Use the checklist below to make sure you've covered the major parts of the essay.

Peer Review Checklist

Global

Thesis/ Argument	Is the point stated clearly?	Do all the points contribute to the main argument?	Is each point well supported with evidence?
Structure	Are the points clearly divided and without unnecessary overlap?	Are the points in the best possible order?	Should any paragraphs be moved or deleted? Should others be added?

Local

Content	Is the information about one main topic?	Is the language of the content as specific and narrow as possible?	Are transitions used to get from one piece of information to the next?
Style	Do paragraphs contain topic sentences, details to support the topic, and a concluding or transition sentence?	Are sentences formed with a variety of constructions, including different lengths, clauses, and subjects and verbs?	Is the style appropriate to the context of the assignment? How might tone or word choice be changed?
Grammar	Are tenses consistent?	Is punctuation correct? (Check especially for correct use of commas and correct combining of sentences.)	Is the third person maintained, except for the times when the information requires a shift?
Format	Are MLA conventions such as parenthetical citations used?	Is all information clearly designated from which source it has come?	Is the Works Cited page formatted correctly?

Remember that reading is a powerful act. Besides being a way of gaining information, reading may even reveal parts of a person much more intimate than those we glimpse in a face-to-face meeting. Part of the reason for this directness is due to the persuasive bent of rhetoric and part is because a piece of writing establishes the values of the author, values that may be different from your own. Immediately, reading is a process of judging these values, negotiating them in ethical terms even while we are making sense of the lines of thought themselves. By practicing intelligent questioning of the texts we read, we can both have a better understanding of what they are trying to say and provide ways of helping others say what they want to say.

Exercise: Write a Peer Review Paragraph

Before writing anything, take your peer's essay and go through the process described above by looking first for global problems and then moving to local issues. After you have several ideas in your head, write a paragraph describing the main ways the essay could be improved. Be sure to write well yourself by referring to specific points in the text that can benefit from revision.

Exercise: Positive Feedback

Peer review is not all about critique. One of the most delighting parts is to receive your own paper back with comments indicating how well you communicated. Identify three aspects of your peer's text that stand out as having been done well and write a paragraph explaining what they are and why they are done well.

Exercise: Rewriting Peers' Work

Rewriting your peers' work can give them ideas for better phrasing or pinpointing ideas. Try rewriting the following parts of a peer's paper:

- Come up with a new opening sentence for your peer's paper that gives a stronger introduction to the main points.
- Rewrite the thesis so that it is more concise.
- Change each opening and concluding sentence to each of the body paragraphs so that it introduces and wraps up the material in the paragraph and also transitions between paragraphs.
- In the concluding paragraph, come up with a new way of summarizing the main points without simply repeating them.
- Compose a new final sentence to the essay so that it ends with a strong sense of finality and closure.

NOTES

[1] Wendell Berry. "Why I Am Not Going to Buy a Computer." *What Are People For?: Essays,* Counterpoint Press, 2010. p. 170.

[2] Brooke Myers. "Fraternities, Cleaning Duties, Rush, and the Quest for Brotherhood." *OU Daily* (Norman, OK), Feb. 3, 2010.

[3] Peter Elbow. *Writing Without Teachers.* Oxford University Press, 1986.

Rhetorical Analysis

Recommended for WRD 110/111/112

Chapter 6

ANALYZING TEXTS

You've probably been asked to "analyze" texts, images, advertisements, or arguments. But what exactly does that mean? The term analysis comes from the Greek word *analusis,* which means to break apart. Whenever you analyze something, you are literally taking it apart to inspect its finer details.

When you analyze a song, for example, you might focus on its rhythm, harmony, lyrics, and vocals.

When you analyze a painting, you might break it into the colors, brush strokes, use of light, symmetry, and artistic genre.

Analyzing a rhetorical text requires the same kind of "breaking apart." What are the parts that comprise a rhetorical text? We can start with the elements involved in any rhetorical situation:

- Exigence
- Audience
- Author/ethos
- Text

The **exigence** is the situation, problem, or incident that caused the text to be written. If the text is a birthday card, then the exigence is obviously a birthday. However, if you're examining a card that says "I'm sorry" on the front of it, you might rightly imagine that someone did something they now regret. To find the exigence of a text, ask yourself some of the following questions:

- Does this text respond to something that came before?
- Is there some kind of problem that this text is addressing?
- Is this part of a larger public conversation?
- Does this text fill some kind of need?

The **audience** for this particular text may or may not be immediately obvious to you. In fact, there may be several different audiences. To identify the audience(s), ask yourself the following questions:

- Whom does the text seem to target through its language? (For example, is the language written at a basic level or in very specific jargon that only makes sense to experts?)
- Does the text use language that would make one kind of audience angry, happy, excited, or sad?
- Where does this text appear? Is there a certain kind of person who would usually read this magazine or website (or watch this TV program, listen to this podcast, etc.)?
- What kind of people are more likely to be invested in this topic?

The **author(s)** may be listed by name, or the text may be anonymous. Either way, you can decipher some important details about how the author tries to establish a certain kind of ethos in the text. The author/textual ethos is the kind of reputation or persona interpreted by the audience.

Some authors want their texts to be read as highly professional or official. Other authors want their texts to be read as familiar, friendly, fun. One author may try to seem provocative and tough, while another author may want to seem approachable and non-threatening. To identify the authorial ethos, ask yourself the following questions:

- Is the author identified? If so, does she or he have a reputation already? Does this text fit with his or her reputation?
- Is the text identified with a certain brand (like a corporation or company)? Does this text seem to fit coherently with this brand's previous reputation?
- What kind of *persona* or *impression* does this text try to achieve or cultivate? Would you call this text cool, tough, friendly, informal, official, bureaucratic, etc.? What makes you say so?

The **text** itself can be analyzed according to its style and genre. An advertisement online is quite different from a television ad for the same product. Likewise, a speech delivered to a room full of teenagers will use very different language, style, and visuals than a speech delivered to shareholders of a major corporation. When examining the text, ask yourself the following:

Chapter 6   Rhetorical Analysis

> - What are the stylistic features of the text? Is the language vivid or very neutral?
> - Are there images that accompany the text? What is the ratio of text to image, and what difference does that make?
> - What is the context of this text? Is it part of a website? Is it a billboard on the highway? Is it a commercial shown during the Super Bowl? How does the context affect how an audience might read it?

Let's create a short rhetorical analysis of an advertisement by asking ourselves the questions above.

What seems to be the exigence for this text? For several years, Dove® has launched a public campaign to help fight the notion that women must be young and skinny to be considered beautiful. This advertisement is responding to a cultural notion that models (if not all women) should look a certain way (for example, "size 8"). In this way, the advertisement is part of a much larger public conversation happening about women's bodies and cultural standards of beauty.

Figure 1. Dove's campaign for real beauty.[1] *(Image Courtesy of the Advertising Archives.)*

The audience for this particular advertisement is most likely women in their 20s and beyond. We can assume this because this ad (and others like it by Dove) appears in magazines and websites typically read by that demographic. The image included also shows an adult woman with whom other adult women can identify.

The ethos cultivated by this advertisement is best described as positive and empowering, yet it also aims to create the impression of joining a debate. Rather than making direct statements, the language of the advertisement uses questions ("Fat?" "Fit?" "Does true beauty only squeeze into size 8?"). The image of a smiling, happy, strong woman who does not look like a "traditional" model seems to imply Dove's answer: beautiful bodies come in all sizes.

The text is simple, even sparse. There are few words, and those words are phrased as questions. The largest two words ("Fat?" "Fit?") are written as check boxes, as if the reader is supposed to "vote" on which term best describes the smiling, happy woman to the left. The negative connotation of the word "fat" forms a stark contrast with this joyful image. The fact that this advertisement appears in women's magazines, where there are ads with "traditional" models (extremely thin and young), may add to the overall sense that this text is part of a conversation.

ANALYZING ARGUMENTS

When you are analyzing arguments, you can include some additional elements that are present in any type of persuasive text. Consider the following questions involved in any argument:

> What are the claims being made either implicitly or explicitly?
>
> What types of evidence or support help make the case for this claim?

When looking for the **claims** in any argument, you might make a distinction between the main claim and any smaller claims also being implied or suggested. Try to decipher what it is that the author wants her or his audience to do, think, believe, change, or buy. What is the big point of this text?

Once you identify the claims, you want to then look for what kinds of evidence help to support these claims. In the language of rhetorical theory, what kinds of **proofs** are offered in support of the main claims?

Remember that rhetorical proofs (from the Greek term for "belief," *pistis*) are usually divided into three types:

> **Logos:** The type of reasoning used in making an argument.
>
> **Ethos:** The type of persona communicated by the author.
>
> **Pathos:** The emotional, visceral, experiential elements of a message.

Arguments do not simply use only one of these types of proof. Rather, every message has elements of reasoning (even if they're fallacious), a type of persona, and emotional or experiential elements.

RHETORICAL ANALYSIS EXERCISES (THE PROGYMNASMATA)

If you find yourself in need of more practice in rhetorical analysis, you may want to turn to the progymnasmata. The progymnasmata is a structured sequence of 14 types of rhetorical exercises, which will be discussed below. It was designed in ancient Greece around the 5th century BC and used to teach students in ancient Greek and Roman schools, although its influence extended for centuries in Greek, Roman, and later European rhetorical education.[2]

Although the progymnasmata is an ancient sequence of exercises, it is still helpful today. The progymnasmata is designed to guide you through multiple patterns of thinking and multiple perspectives through multiple genres, all of which we still use in some way.[3] But considering our modern context, how do we use it?

Generally, the progymnasmata would be taught over a series of years during what we would now consider middle and high school years.[4] However, as a university student, you may use the exercises of the progymnasmata more readily for your own purposes. To use the progymnasmata for rhetorical analysis, first select a text for analysis. Then follow these 4 steps, which correspond roughly to how a student would have been taught the progymnasmata.[5]

- Read your text.
- Determine the exercise(s) that corresponds to your text.
- Evaluate the success of your text.
- Rewrite the text in your own words.

Sometimes your text will have multiple components that correspond to multiple exercises. For example, an essay may present an account of events by an important figure (narrative) before arguing against this version of events (refutation). In these cases, divide your text into different sections for analysis.

Historically, the 14 exercises below would detail structures for constructing speeches or pieces of writing in imitation of other texts. However, for the purposes of analysis, you will find concepts, questions, and directions relevant only to the evaluation of your text's success.

Fable

In the fable exercise, a student would read, evaluate, and rewrite a folk tale (fable). Fables were generally not evaluated to the extent of other genres but for analysis you might consider whether it has the structural components of an effective narrative.[6]

- Actor—Who is doing the action?
- Action—What is the actor doing?
- Time—When is the action happening?
- Manner—How is the action happening?
- Cause—Why is the action happening?

Narrative

In the fable exercise, a student would read, evaluate, and rewrite the telling of an event (narrative) that has happened. To evaluate a narrative, consider the following.[7]

- Clarity—Does the action of the narrative have clear cause/effect relationship?
- Concision—Is the narrative an appropriate length?
- Plausibility—Is the action of the narrative likely to have occurred?
- Diction—Is the language of the narrative appropriate for the audience?

Chreia

In the chreia exercise, a student would read, evaluate, and expound on a concise anecdote or saying (chreia) that could be attributed to a specific person. To evaluate a chreia, you may do the following.[8]

- **Praise** or **condemn** the speaker.
- **Paraphrase** the chreia.
- Explain the **opposite** of the chreia.
- Make an **analogy** to the chreia.
- Provide an **example** of the chreia.

Maxim

In the maxim exercise, a student would read, evaluate, and expound on a wise saying (maxim) that cannot be attributed to a specific person. To evaluate a maxim, you may follow the same steps as those in the chreia exercise.[9]

Common Topic

In the common topic exercise, a student would evaluate and expound on a particular vice or evil attribute in a piece of writing similar to a speech. This exercise is less suited to rhetorical analysis of a text, since a student would learn the structure of such a piece of writing rather than evaluate a particular text.[10]

Refutation

In the refutation exercise, a student would read, evaluate, and rewrite an argument **against** one or more given facts/events of a narrative. To evaluate a refutation, you may consider the following, noting you must note **how** the argument answers each consideration in the negative.[11]

- Clarity—Is the relationship of cause/effect between the fact and the narrative clear?
- Plausibility—Is the fact likely to have occurred?
- Possibility—Is the fact possible to have occurred?
- Consistency—Is the fact consistent with the actor or the narrative as a whole?
- Propriety—Is the fact moral?
- Expediency—Is the fact beneficial/helpful to the actor?

Confirmation

In the confirmation exercise, a student would read, evaluate, and rewrite an argument **for** one or more given facts/events of a narrative. To evaluate a confirmation, you may use the same considerations as the refutation, noting you must note **how** the argument answers each consideration in the affirmative.[12]

Encomium

In the encomium exercise, a student would read, examine, and rewrite a speech in praise of a specific person. Similar to the common topic, this exercise is less suited to rhetorical analysis, since a student would be taught the structure of a such a speech rather than evaluate a particular text.[13]

Invective

In the encomium exercise, a student would read, examine, and rewrite a speech in condemnation of a specific person. Similar to the encomium and common topic, this exercise is less suited to rhetorical analysis, since a student would be taught the structure of a such a speech rather than evaluate a particular text.[14]

Comparison

In the comparison exercise, a student would read, examine, and rewrite a speech in which two people or objects are contrasted in some way. Similar to the common topic, encomium, and invective, this exercise is less suited to rhetorical analysis, since a student would be taught the structure of such a speech rather than evaluate a particular text.[15]

Characterization

In the characterization exercise, a student would read, evaluate, and rewrite a speech which imitates the character of a specific person. To evaluate a characterization, you may consider the following.[16]

- Clarity—Do the actions in the speech have a clear cause/effect relationship?
- Concision—Is the speech of an appropriate length?
- Floridity—Is the speech's language appropriate to the speaker?
- Finish—Does the speech have a clear focus?
- Intricacy—Is the speech attentive to details about the speaker?

Description

In the description exercise, a student would read, evaluate, and rewrite a vivid description of a person or object. To evaluate a description, you may consider the following.[17]

- Order—Does the description proceed from beginning to end, outside to inside, etc.?
- Style—Is the style appropriate to the person or object being described?
- Figure—Does the description use any figures of speech for ornamentation?

Thesis

In the thesis exercise, a student would read, evaluate, and rewrite an argument about some question being considered (thesis). To evaluate a thesis, you may consider the following about the thesis's solution to the question.[18]

- Legality—Is the solution one that is legal or will require legal action?
- Justice—Is the solution one that accomplishes justice, and for whom?
- Expediency—Is the solution one that is beneficial/useful, and for whom?
- Possibility—Is the solution one that can occur?
- Counterposition—Does the thesis address any counterarguments?

Law

In the law exercise, a student would read, evaluate, and rewrite a proposal **for or against** a law. To evaluate such a proposal, you may consider the following.[19]

- Legality—Is the proposal one that will be overruled or challenged?
- Justice—Is the proposal one that accomplishes justice, and for whom?
- Expediency—Is the proposal one that is beneficial/useful, and for whom?
- Possibility—Is the proposal one that can occur?

RHETORICAL ANALYSIS OF SPACES

So far, we've talked about how to analyze texts and words. But it is also possible to analyze other kinds of rhetorical artifacts. Rhetoricians are fond of saying that "everything is an argument," which means that *everything has been designed by someone to accomplish a goal.*

Take a look around the room you're sitting in right now. What kinds of choices did the designers make? Are the windows big or small? Are the walls painted in vibrant colors, or are the walls neutral colors? How is the room set up? Are the chairs in rows, or are they arranged in a circle? What effects do all of these different choices make? You might say that these questions—and your answers—get us closer to a rhetorical analysis of a place. Even in the most mundane of spaces, like a classroom, someone has made specific choices to achieve certain effects on an "audience."

When you find yourself in a particular place, try asking the following questions to analyze the rhetorical choices used in that place:

- Is this a "man-made space" or a "natural space"?
- If this is a "natural space," are there man-made signs that help to "explain" this space?
- What are your eyes drawn to in this space? What are the areas that attract the most attention?
- Is this space designed for you to look, sit, move, or stand in particular ways?
- What colors are used in this space? What kind of effects do these colors have? How might entirely different colors affect you differently?
- Are you prevented from entering certain spaces or areas?
- What is the history of this place? Does the building or space have a sense of "timelessness," or does it seem to reveal a certain time period?
- How do you think the designers want visitors to feel in this space? What makes you say so?

A QUICK USER'S GUIDE TO RHETORICAL ANALYSIS OF TEXTS

When you are asked to create a rhetorical analysis, use this chart to help get started. You might find additional elements that are worth mentioning. If so, add those into your analysis! Remember that an analysis requires you to take apart a text to inspect its finer details.

Exigence	◎ Does this text respond to something that came before? ◎ Is there some kind of problem that this text is addressing? ◎ Is this part of a larger public conversation? ◎ Does this text fill some kind of need?	Give examples of how you came to this conclusion.
Audience	◎ Whom does the text seem to target through its language? (For example, is the language written at a basic level or in very specific jargon that only makes sense to experts?) ◎ Does the text use language that would make one kind of audience angry, happy, excited, or sad? ◎ Where does this text appear? Is there a certain kind of person who would usually read this magazine or website (or watch this TV program, listen to this podcast, etc.)? ◎ What kinds of people are more likely to be invested in this topic?	Give examples of how you came to this conclusion.
Author	◎ Is the author identified? If so, does she or he have a reputation already? Does this text fit with his or her reputation? ◎ Is the text identified with a certain brand (like a corporation or company)? Does this text seem to fit coherently with this brand's previous reputation? ◎ What kind of persona or impression does this text try to achieve or cultivate? Would you call this text cool, tough, friendly, informal, official, bureaucratic, etc.? What makes you say so?	Give examples of how you came to this conclusion.

Text	◉ What are the stylistic features of the text? Is the language vivid or very neutral? ◉ Are there images that accompany the text? What is the ratio of text to image, and what difference does that make? ◉ What is the context of this text? Is it part of a website? Is it a billboard on the highway? Is it a commercial shown during the Super Bowl? How does the context affect how an audience might read it?	Give examples of how you came to this conclusion.
Claim	◉ What are the claims being made either implicitly or explicitly?	Give examples of how you came to this conclusion.
Evidence	◉ How does the author use logos? What types of reasoning are used in making the argument? Are there any fallacies or logically troubling aspects of his or her reasoning? ◉ How does the author communicate his or her persona? What kind of ethos does the text convey? ◉ What elements of pathos are involved? How does the text use emotional words or images to convey the message?	Give examples of how you came to this conclusion.

NOTES

[1] Kylee Plummer. "PR Practice: Dove Campaign Presents 'Tick Box' Messages." *Dove Campaign for Real Beauty: The Real Truth about Beauty,* last modified June 9, 2013, http://blogs.uoregon.edu/j350the-dovecampaignforrealbeauty/posts/.

[2] Fleming, David J. "The Very Idea of a 'Progymnasmata.'" *Rhetoric Review,* vol. 22, no. 2, 2003, p. 110.

[3] Hagaman, John. "Modern Use of the Progymnasmata in Teaching Rhetorical Invention." *Rhetoric Review,* vol. 5, no. 1, 1986, p. 25.

4. Penella, Robert J. "The 'Progymnasmata in Imperial Greek Education." *The Classical World,* vol. 105, no. 1, 2011, p. 79.

5. Fleming, David J. "The Very Idea of a 'Progymnasmata.'" *Rhetoric Review,* vol. 22, no. 2, 2003, pp. 110–111.

6. Fleming, David J. "Apthonius *Progymnasmata.*" *University of Massachusetts,* n.d., https://people.umass.edu/dfleming/E388%20Aphthonius%20Progymnasmata.pdf.

7. Ibid.

8. Ibid.

9. Ibid.

10. Ibid.

11. Ibid.

12. Ibid.

13. Ibid.

14. Ibid.

15. Ibid.

16. Burton, Gideon O. "Impersonation." *Silva Rhetoricae,* Brigham Young University, n.d. http://rhetoric.byu.edu/Pedagogy/Progymnasmata/Impersonation.htm.

17. Fleming, David J. "Apthonius *Progymnasmata.*" *University of Massachusetts,* n.d., https://people.umass.edu/dfleming/E388%20Aphthonius%20Progymnasmata.pdf.

18. Ibid.

19. Ibid.

Argument

Recommended for WRD 111/112

Chapter 7

Argument seems like one of those things that you wouldn't necessarily need to learn. After all, even children know how to argue with their parents. We are all probably pretty good at being argumentative at certain times. But there is an important difference between what we mean by rhetorical argumentation and what might better be defined as "bickering." Rhetorical argumentation begins with what is called an exigency or an issue. There is some kind of stasis question that multiple interests are examining. At its most basic, argument has a claim and some kind of evidence to support that claim. Rhetorical argumentation always takes place in some kind of rhetorical situation, with particular audiences and constraints.

When students begin to learn rhetoric, the first question many of them ask is "How can I be more persuasive?" Although no one can guarantee how to teach another person to always be persuasive, this chapter will look at two important aspects of rhetorical argumentation. First, we will look at the elements of argumentation in order to help you analyze and discuss the arguments of others. By understanding how effective arguments and ineffective arguments are constructed, you will have the power to better respond to the arguments of others. Second, by understanding how to construct a sound and compelling argument, you will increase your own ethos in a variety of situations where you want to persuade others. So, while we can't guarantee that you will win every debate or argument, the information here can definitely increase your effectiveness as a rhetorician.

ARGUMENT BEGINS IN AGREEMENT

Where does an argument begin? Take a minute to think about how you might respond to this question. You might say something like the following:

> An argument begins with a disagreement.
>
> An argument begins whenever two or more people have different ideas about the right way to think about something.
>
> An argument begins in moments of conflict.

All of these responses point to what we might call **stasis**: a point where we find ourselves standing at various distances from others who are concerned with the same question. For example, you may have an argument with a friend about whether or not it should be socially acceptable to illegally download music online. Maybe you feel like it is okay to do because it does not hurt anyone (like physically stealing something from someone). However, your friend has a different position on this question. Perhaps she feels that, over time, downloading music does hurt the artists who depend on music sales to make a living. You are both concerned with the same question—is it socially acceptable to illegally download music?—but you both stand on different positions where the answer is concerned.

Your argument about downloading music may take all kinds of twists and turns. It may stay friendly, or it might turn serious. Maybe your friend gathers together some statistics about how much new or relatively unknown artists lose because of music downloads. She may even be so persuasive that you find yourself shifting your position. With enough evidence and compelling discussion, you might find yourself sharing her outlook on this question. Or, after arguing your own position, you may indeed be even more convinced that your position is correct. No matter what happens, however, you and your friend share a mutual concern for the same question: *Is illegally downloading music socially acceptable?*

Ideally, when arguers share the same stasis questions, the deliberation and debates can be relatively productive. Perhaps you won't change people's minds on an issue, but you can contribute to new ways of thinking and an expanded knowledge base. Many rhetorical scholars believe that productive argument can be socially positive, even when there are no shifted positions. If you and your friend debate different issues relating to illegal music downloads, you might end up discussing such issues as how "stealing" should be defined, if breaking the law is ever socially acceptable, and even the ways that "property" should be defined when talking about digital material. This kind of debate could be an edifying conversation, regardless of whether or not your friend persuades you to stop downloading music.

> Beginning an argument with agreement might sound strange, but it's the only way to ensure that the process of argument is fruitful.

Chapter 7   Argument

Sometimes, however, you might find yourselves in an argumentative situation that seems pretty unproductive. You have probably at least heard or witnessed these kinds of public arguments: people shouting at each other without listening, slogans that substitute for any real dialogue, even insults hurled back and forth. It might also seem as if two parties are "talking past" each other during an argument. One diagnosis of such unproductive argument is that the arguers are not truly in stasis. That is, they are not concerned with answers to the same questions.

Arguments about climate change show why it's important to begin an argument in agreement. Some writers, such as sociologist Kari Marie Norgaard, say that "sociological theory and insights are urgently needed" in an interdisciplinary effort to speak to the public about natural science research as we move forward in responding to climate change.[1] Others suggest that "facts aren't what changed people's minds. Viable solutions are what people can often agree on first."[2] Still other voices contend that we should focus on the economic benefits of curtailing carbon emissions.[3] Some want to focus on the rising ocean temperature, but others want to focus on carbon emissions or economic gain. While all these writers are speaking about *what* can be done about climate change, each has a different reason for *why* we should respond to climate change. Their reasons *why* affect their methods and approach. Because they can't come to stasis as to *why* or *what* we need to do to mitigate climate change, they are arguing past each other. Essentially, they are all three having a different conversation. It is important to come to stasis in order to argue the same thing and to come up with a solution for that narrowed-down problem.

Figure 1.   United Nations' webpage on the UN Climate Change Paris Agreement.[4]

Other countries have found stasis in their climate change arguments to form the Paris Accord. Though it may not be possible to come to stasis on every argument under the vast umbrella of climate change, it is possible for 174 countries to come to stasis on limiting the global temperature and responding to pollution. They have come to the agreement that they *will respond,* yet the countries have various approaches to *how* they will respond. Here, we see how important coming to stasis can be in order for people to work towards a common goal on a problem they might not agree on 100%. If either side is unwilling to engage with the other's question, then they may end up "talking past each other" in a debate.

Exercise: Beginning an Argument in Agreement

Think of the last time you heard an argument that you found unproductive. What seemed to be the questions that each side was asking? Were they concerned with the same question, or were they talking past each other? Could the argument have been improved if the two sides had more explicitly agreed upon the question that they both wanted to answer?

ARGUMENT REQUIRES A CLAIM

To be productive, arguments must begin in some kind of agreement about the main question under debate. More technically, however, arguments usually begin with a **claim.** There is no argument without a claim. Rhetorical claims are what you put forward in any text (written, spoken, visual) to persuade an audience to believe or do something. Your claim may be explicitly stated, or it may be implicit.

An example of an explicitly stated claim:

- "You should vote for candidate X because she supports reforms in education!"

An example of an implicit claim:

- "3 out of 4 dentists recommend Toothies brand toothpaste." (Implicit claim: You should use Toothies toothpaste.)

Claims are sometimes also called your *thesis,* your *point,* your main idea. No matter what you call them, claims are the propositions or assertions you offer to your audience in any written, visual, or spoken text.

Chapter 7   Argument

Claims may be minor, requiring relatively little development. For example, if you tell a friend that she should go see a movie with you instead of sitting alone at home, that is a claim. She may agree with you, but she might also disagree. Maybe she has too much homework, or maybe she simply wants to be alone.

On the other hand, claims may be major, requiring a great deal of support and development. If you want to convince your bank to lend you $10,000 to begin a small business, you will find yourself making a major claim about your business's feasibility, profitability, and sound business plan. The bank may agree with your claim that you are capable of successfully using $10,000 to launch a profitable business, but they may also disagree with you.

Whether minor or major, claims are almost always *debatable*. While you may find your claim 100% convincing and persuasive, there are people in your audience who might present reasonable objections to your claim.

Think of how many claims you have made or heard in the past 24 hours. If I could list all the claims I've made recently, they would include the following:

- We had no real winter this year.
- I should start making my own lunches in order to save money.
- Beyoncé's *Lemonade should have won Album of the Year at the Grammys.*
- *The cost of housing on campus is too expensive to be worth the convenience.*
- *They need to hire more people at the coffee shop.*

Not all of these claims are controversial. It's hard to imagine someone trying to passionately debate me about whether or not making my own lunches really saves money. (However, my friend did recently send me an article that questioned how much money you can save by making your own lunches!) Some of the claims, of course, are very controversial. Adele's win over Beyoncé for Album of the Year sparked quite a debate with impassioned responses from both detractors and supporters. Additionally, many members of the UK community have voiced strong opinions about the construction and lease agreements for newer housing on campus.

EVIDENCE

Few audiences simply accept claims without much evidence or support. Evidence is a crucial piece of every claim. If you make a claim without evidence, you are simply making a statement. Consider the differences between these scenes.

Scene One

Amelia: You shouldn't buy that car.

Rocky: Why not?

Amelia: You just shouldn't.

Scene Two

Amelia: You shouldn't buy that car.

Rocky: Why not?

Amelia: It gets horrible reviews online.

In the first scene, Amelia tells her friend Rocky that he shouldn't buy a certain car, but she gives him no real evidence that buying the car would be a mistake. By asking "Why not?" Rocky is asking Amelia to give him some kind of evidence that would make her claim sound reasonable to him. In other words, he wanted some evidence that he should take Amelia's claim seriously. She doesn't provide any evidence, however. Chances are low that he will simply take her word for it.

In the second scene, however, Amelia does provide Rocky with evidence. She tells him that the car he's hoping to buy gets horrible online reviews. This is a small piece of evidence in support of her claim, and it might not initially be enough to persuade Rocky against buying the car. However, it does offer some kind of evidence that Rocky should take Amelia's claim seriously.

Notice that by providing evidence, Amelia is not guaranteed to convince Rocky of her claims. Rocky may be extremely skeptical of anything that appears online. Or he might want to know more about where these reviews are found and who is writing them. Providing evidence is not a guarantee that your argument will be persuasive, but it might prevent listeners from dismissing you right away.

Chapter 7   Argument

If you were to visualize most arguments, they would probably look something like this:

[Diagram: Claim → Evidence, linked by (Because)]

The word "because" links the claim and evidence, since the evidence is what explains any argument's claim.

For example, Amelia's second argument above would look something like this:

[Diagram: You shouldn't buy that car ... → ... it gets horrible reviews online., linked by (Because)]

Even in instances of implicit claims, you can draw this argument diagram to see if evidence is actually being offered. Earlier, I gave an example of a common type of implicit claim: "3 out of 4 dentists recommend Toothies brand toothpaste." What would this implicit claim look like as a diagram?

[Diagram: You should buy Toothies ... → ... 3 out of 4 dentists recommend it., linked by (Because)]

156   Town Branch Writing Collection

Many claims are more complex than the examples above, of course. In real world arguments, several pieces of evidence may be offered in support of a claim. For instance, the language of the Kyoto Protocol argues that developed nations should bear a greater portion of responsibilities for correcting climate and environmental damage. If we tried to diagram this argument, it might look something like this:

To check and see if you are providing evidence for your claims, try the following exercise. Look over your argument and use the "because" diagram above to draw your major claim and evidence. Do you offer a "because" to support your claims?

WARRANTS

Unfortunately, even if you offer the strongest possible evidence you can find in support of your claim, your audience may remain unconvinced. Why is this? Is this because your audience doesn't understand your argument? Are they just being stubborn? Chances are, when you have really made the strongest possible argument you can make and you *still* find opposition, you are experiencing someone with a different **warrant.**

Warrants are the third part of any argument. Claims and evidence are held together in a bond, and warrants are the glue that holds those claims and evidence together. Warrants are the underlying beliefs, opinions, ideas, and feelings that allow for your evidence to logically support your claim (or not).

Warrants are usually unstated and unnoticed by everyone involved in an argument. In fact, you might not even think about your own warrants until you find yourself questioning whether certain claims and evidence really work together.

For example, Amelia's claim that Rocky shouldn't buy a certain car because it gets horrible reviews online might not convince Rocky. He might argue that he doesn't believe online reviews. In fact, he finds them very unreliable and even shady. Amelia disagrees, however. She finds online reviews a very credible and reliable way to decide on products.

The argument between Amelia and Rocky might look something like this:

- You shouldn't buy that car ... (Claim)
- ... it gets horrible reviews online. (Evidence)
- Online reviews are reliable. (Warrant)

For Amelia's claim to be persuasive to Rocky or anyone else, they must share Amelia's warrant that online reviews are reliable. However, Rocky does not share this warrant. He feels that online reviews are unreliable. Therefore, the warrant does not "glue" Amelia's claim and evidence together in a way that persuades him.

Warrants can be described as cultural, social, religious, and ideological beliefs that allow us to believe certain things and not others. If your warrant is radically different from your audience's, then you may find that making a claim and providing persuasive evidence is very difficult. Consider, for example, those who make arguments with others based on the Christian Bible.

- You should not steal. (Claim)
- The Bible forbids stealing. (Evidence)
- The Bible contains actual commandments from God and should be obeyed. (Warrant)

If both parties share the same warrant that the Christian Bible is true and infallible, then this evidence may indeed be persuasive enough to convince the other party. However, if one party in the argument is not Christian, then the warrant may not be shared.

If I do not believe that the Bible contains actual commandments from God and therefore should be obeyed, then the evidence that the Bible forbids stealing will not necessarily persuade me that stealing should be avoided.

On the other hand, you might be able to offer me different kinds of evidence for this same claim. Perhaps you want to draw on my sensitivity to others and my sense of compassion. Therefore, you might change your argument to look more like this:

- You should not steal. (Claim)
- Stealing can mentally and materially hurt others. (Evidence)
- Hurting others mentally and materially is unethical, and it should be avoided. (Warrant)

This different warrant may be one that I do indeed share with the arguer. In this case, I would find the evidence offered in support of the claim ("stealing can mentally and materially hurt others") to be very compelling.

LOGICAL ARGUMENTATION

Another way to think about arguments is to think about them in terms of simplified claims that logicians and philosophers call "statements." While rhetorical claims are concerned primarily with persuasion, statements are concerned with facts. A **statement** is any simple sentence that is either true or false. Therefore, a logical statement *must* be a declarative sentence or part of a sentence which could stand alone as a declarative sentence. Here are a few examples:

- The sky is blue.
- You are likely to need an umbrella today.
- Pizza is not a vegetable.
- No students ever cheat on their papers.
- Plenty of rest helps you retain information better.

Each of these sentences can at least in theory be determined to be true or false. The first two are true or false depending on the time of day and weather conditions. The third sentence is false based on the definitions of "pizza" and "vegetable." The fourth sentence can be determined to be false by just one counterexample (i.e., one student who cheats one time). The fifth sentence can be determined to be true or false by scientific study.

However, there are some statements which do not have this capacity to be determined true or false at all. These include questions, commands, suggestions, opinions, and so forth. These are certainly grammatical sentences, but a sentence is not always a statement. These are examples of sentences which are not statements:

- Do you know the way to Memorial Hall? (question)
- Be quiet and put away your phones. (command)
- I think you need a haircut. (suggestion)
- I like tacos more than burgers. (opinion)
- Let's go to the basketball game! (proposal)

Sometimes the use of questions, proposals, and commands can be rhetorically persuasive in terms of ethos and pathos, but these kinds of sentences are counter-productive if you want to focus on logos. Strictly speaking, then, an **argument** is a series of statements where one or more statements called **premises** provide support for usually one statement called the **conclusion.**

In an essay, we use the word "conclusion" to refer to the final paragraph or the ending of the essay. However, an **argumentative conclusion** is somewhat different: The conclusion in an argument is the statement that you are trying to prove to be true with the use of the other statements. The conclusion is the whole point of the argument, the reason you are offering an argument in the first place, or the thing you want to persuade other people to believe. Usually we use signal phrases to indicate that a certain sentence contains our argumentative conclusion. These include words and phrases like **therefore, thus, consequently, accordingly, hence, it follows that, it implies that, so,** and more. However, just because an author uses one of these signal phrases, it doesn't always mean there is an argumentative conclusion. Sometimes, writers use the words illogically or simply to sound important. In your own writing, be careful to avoid using signal phrases to skip a step in your thinking. Instead, connect one statement to the next and show your audience how you reach your conclusion. Use a signal phrase as a flag to the reader for where the conclusion is, rather than as a cover for a gap in your argument from one point to the next.

Similarly, we have many different meanings for the words "premise" and "premises," including the starting point in the plot to a story (the "premise" of a movie) and the grounds of a building (the "premises" of the University). However, **argumentative premises** are again somewhat different. The premises in an argument are the statements that you are using to prove your conclusion. Premises include both warrants and evidence, and are the reasons why the conclusion is supposed to be true. With premises the rhetor provides justification for the claim they are trying to assert is true. If the conclusion is the "what" behind what the rhetor is saying, the premises are the "why." Premises also have signal words and phrases, including **since, because, for, given that, for the reason that, as indicated by,** and others.

Again, however, you should remember that these can be used without any care for their logical significance.

Signal Phrases

Argumentative Conclusions	Argumentative Premises
◎ Therefore	◎ Since
◎ Thus	◎ Because
◎ Consequently	◎ For
◎ Accordingly	◎ Given that
◎ Hence	◎ For the reason that
◎ It follows that	◎ As indicated by
◎ It implies that	
◎ So	

Arguments in ordinary language are not always clear and logical exactly because they are in ordinary language. When we speak to our family and friends, we make assumptions about what they know, believe, and value, and so we leave many of the claims in our arguments unstated. We also make complex arguments, where the point of one series of reasons leads to another point, and so on. These kinds of arguments can be translated into clear, categorical language that reveals their structure and makes it easier to spot logical flaws or fallacies. Translating arguments into simpler language also helps us to critically analyze the arguments we receive from others.

There are several ways to criticize an argument. The two primary methods are 1) analyzing the content of the premises and 2) analyzing the structure of the premises. Consider the following examples:

- All cats are mortal.
- Katy Perry is a cat.
- Therefore, Katy Perry is mortal.

In this example we have a true conclusion (Katy Perry is mortal) based on a true premise (cats are mortal) and a false premise (Katy Perry is a cat). In responding to this argument, we can say that it is a bad argument because one of the premises is false. The facts are different; Katy Perry happens to be a human. Compare this example with the next:

- All humans are mortal.
- Katy Perry is a mortal.
- Therefore, Katy Perry is a human.

In this example we have true premises (All humans are mortal; Katy Perry is a mortal) and a true conclusion (Katy Perry is a human). However, there is still something wrong with this argument. Just because those premises are true does not prove anything about the conclusion. Sure, all humans are mortal, but so are butterflies and trees. Just because Katy Perry is mortal, this does not prove that she has to be human. Thus, there is a structural problem with this argument. In responding to this argument, we can say that it is a bad argument not because of a false premise, but because the conclusion does not *follow from* the premises.

This is a structural or *formal* logical problem, and it is a bit trickier than simple truth or falsity because this is a matter of **validity** or **strength.** Again, in ordinary language, "valid" (and "strong") has a number of different meanings, including legitimate, right, and acceptable. However, **argumentative validity and strength** apply only to the structure of the argument, and whether the way the premises fit together actually allows them to build the conclusion. This means that a single statement cannot be valid or invalid, nor can just any group of statements, nor can just any argument. If you want to sound like you know what you are talking about, do not use the words "valid" or "strong" to simply describe a legitimate opinion or a good point.

Logicians divide arguments into two groups: deductive and inductive. **Deductive arguments** are determined to be **valid or invalid** on the basis of the structure and relations between the premises and conclusion. Deductive arguments include arguments based on definitions, arguments based on mathematical proofs like in geometry, and syllogisms. Syllogisms are typically arguments with two premises and one conclusion and include categorical syllogisms, disjunctive syllogisms, and hypothetical syllogisms.

A categorical syllogism relies on the structure of categories and will usually have statements like "All cats are mammals" or "Some fish are not freshwater animals." By contrast, disjunctive syllogisms rely on the structure of "or" statements like "Either he knows French or he knows Spanish," and hypothetical syllogisms rely on the structure of "if/then" statements like "If you do not turn in your excuse, then you cannot make up the work." The quality of deductive arguments depends on the form or shape of the arguments, which piece is where in relation to the others, and so forth.

By contrast, **inductive arguments** are determined to be **strong or weak** on the basis of the structure and quantity of the premises in relation to the conclusion. These are more familiar arguments because they provide the basis for much of our daily lives. Inductive arguments include predictions, generalizations, causal inferences, and analogies, as well as arguments based on signs or the authority of the source.

A few examples of these include weather forecasting (prediction), statistics based on surveys (generalizations), diagnoses of the reason you are sick (causal inferences), using the behavior of one city to support policy change in another similar city (analogies), concluding that there is no class today because there was an email or a literal sign in the classroom (argument by signs), and claiming that the Big Bang occurred a certain way on the basis of Stephen Hawking's work (argument from authority). The quality of inductive arguments depends on the form or shape of the argument as well as the sheer quantity of evidence. More examples cannot improve a deductive argument, but an inductive argument can often be improved by adding more and more examples, provided they are of good quality.

FALLACIES

A flaw in an argument is called a **fallacy** and may be formal or informal. Deductive arguments with structural or formal flaws are invalid; inductive arguments with structural flaws are weak. However, both deductive and inductive arguments can have informal flaws as well, and these do *not* make the arguments invalid or weak; instead, a deductive argument with an informal fallacy is unsound, while an inductive argument with an informal fallacy is uncogent. **Soundness** and **cogency** are evaluations of the overall quality of the argument, not just the structure, but also the truth of the premises, the truth of the conclusion, and the other considerations raised by informal problems.

Rhetorical fallacies tend to be fallacies of the informal type. These informal rhetorical fallacies are present in many arguments, though they may not be immediately obvious to the audience. Sometimes, the evidence offered in an argument may sound perfectly reasonable, at least until you really pay attention to what's being said. The value of recognizing a fallacy is that you can draw attention to the faulty logic being passed off as solid reasoning. At the same time, you can also work to consciously avoid using fallacies that might land you in trouble with a savvy audience. The following pages offer definitions and examples of common rhetorical fallacies.

Chapter 7   Argument

Deductive Fallacies

Of Relevance

- **Ad hominem:** Making a personal attack to distract one from the substantive issue.

    Example: *Hillary Clinton shouldn't be president because she wears terrible pantsuits.*

- **Ad populum:** Appealing to desires, fears, and prejudices of the audience to arouse mob mentality and distract from the issue.

    Example: *Everyone in my class thought* The Hunger Games *was an awesome movie, so it must be an excellent film.*

- **Red herring:** Misleading information designed to pull the audience off track from the main point under discussion.

    Example: *Yes, my son committed sexual assault, but he's a diligent student and a dedicated athlete. Everyone who knows him would call him a good kid.*

- **Poisoning the well:** Planting accusatory or negative information in misleading questions or statements.

    Example: *Would you still vote for Cady for Spring Fling Queen if you knew she was a mathlete?*

- **Straw man:** Distorting the position of the opponent and then attacking the distortion instead of the opponent's actual position.

    Example: *The Senator has argued against prayer in public schools. Clearly, he is an atheist, and he is trying to make all our children atheists as well.*

Of Presumption

- **Begging the question:** Using circular reasoning; creating the illusion that the premises support the conclusion by restating the premise in the conclusion.

    Example: *Kale is healthy because it's good for you!*

- **Complex question:** Asking two or more questions simultaneously in the guise of a single question, thus generating a single answer to the multiple contained questions.

    Example: *When did Beyoncé join the Illuminati?*

- **False dichotomy:** Using a disjunctive statement ("either/or" statement) which presents only two options where there are many.

  Example: *You are either for gun control or against it!*

Of Grammar

- **Amphiboly:** Using an ambiguous statement to draw faulty conclusions.

  Example: *Dr. Smith donated, along with his wife, about $200,000 at the charity event. The organization is grateful, but they have no place to keep Mrs. Smith and had to send her home.*

- **Equivocation:** Using a word or statement in two completely different ways in premise and conclusion.

  Example: *The U.S. Constitution says all men are equal, but women are not men. Therefore women are not equal to men.*

Inductive Fallacies

Of Weak Induction

- **Unqualified authority:** Using authorities or witnesses who have little or no credibility with regards to the argument in question.

  Example: *Coach Cal gets his coffee at Dunkin' Donuts, so it must be the best place to get coffee in Lexington.*

- **Appeal to ignorance:** Using the absence of evidence as the evidence of absence.

  Example: *No one I know has ever seen God. God must not exist.*

- **Hasty generalization:** Drawing a conclusion from too few examples, or too little evidence.

  Example: *I found an article that said boys at a middle school in Arizona had lower test scores than the girls, so all boys must have lower test scores than girls.*

- **Post hoc, ergo propter hoc:** "After this, therefore because of this." Assuming that because one event preceded another, it must have caused the other.

  Example: *When I wear my Ulis jersey, the Cats win.*

- **Slippery slope:** Alleging a simplified chain reaction in complex situations where the proposed chain of reactions has little to no connection to the original cause.

    Example: *If we allow people to marry others of the same gender, then soon people will be asking to marry dogs and cats, corpses and children!*

Of False Analogy

- **Faulty analogy:** Using unlike terms in an analogy.

    Example: *Raising a baby is like raising a plant. If you can't even raise a plant, then you shouldn't have children.*

- **Composition:** Transferring the attributes of the parts to the whole.

    Example: *My high school English teacher was unqualified. Therefore, we need to heighten the standards for all teachers in the public education system.*

- **Division:** Transferring the attributes of the whole to the parts.

    Example: *Car engines are very heavy things. I have to pick up an air filter and spark plugs today, how on earth do you expect me to bring those home on the bus?*

You can find many more lists of fallacies by simply searching the web for rhetorical fallacies!

Exercise: Identifying Logical Fallacies in Visual Media

There are many examples of logical fallacies in the visual media that we consume everyday. Whether on YouTube or cable television, we encounter faulty logic in people's arguments. Spend ten minutes watching ads, political campaign debates, and/or sports interviews on YouTube. Make a list of all the fallacies you identify. Take five of those fallacies and write a few paragraphs on why you identified the example as a specific fallacy and a way that the rhetor could avoid that fallacy in the future.

For more information, see Chapters 1 and 3 of *A Concise Introduction to Logic* (10th edition) by Patrick J. Hurley (Belmont: Thomsom Wadworth, 2008).

STAKEHOLDERS

Sometimes we mistakenly think of argument as a black-and-white debate between two sides: pro and con. We even talk about trying to see "both sides" in an argument. But, in actuality, this is not how arguments over public issues play out. Instead of "two sides," there are different kinds of **stakeholders** who are invested in or affected by the problem being discussed. Stakeholders are those who may participate in an argument with different perspectives.

Consider the public debates over whether or not adults should be allowed to carry concealed weapons on university campuses in Kentucky. Many different stakeholders have weighed in on this question, all bringing new perspectives to the conversation.

- The University of Kentucky has strictly enforced a "no gun" policy on campus.
- A local student group called "Students for Concealed Carry" has lobbied the University to allow concealed permit holders to carry guns on campus and even into classrooms.
- UK faculty members have declared their opposition to concealed handguns on campus.
- UK students who do not hold licenses may object to sharing classroom or dorm spaces with guns.
- Parents who send their children to UK hold various opinions on whether concealed weapons make everyone safer or put more people at risk.
- Dorm resident assistants and directors have indicated that the presence of guns would require them to "police" deadly weapons.
- The Kentucky Supreme Court ruled in 2012 that UK students and staff may keep licensed weapons in their cars on school property, though they may not carry them anywhere else on campus.
- The city of Lexington must also deal with potentially thousands of new guns flowing into Lexington, thanks to students who now live on campus with guns. How will these guns and their sale be regulated?
- National pro-gun organizations, such as the National Rifle Association, have been very vocal in their support for concealed guns nearly everywhere, including campuses.
- National gun control organizations, such as the Brady Campaign, have also been very vocal in their opposition to guns in schools and other public spaces.
- Several survivors of the Virginia Tech shooting massacre have spoken out against guns on campus. See the documentary *Living for 32*.

As you can see from this list, there are many different groups invested in or affected by the question of whether or not guns should be allowed on UK's campus. Not all of these stakeholders can be easily categorized as "pro" or "con." Some stakeholders bring entirely different perspectives or issues to the table. For instance, the Kentucky Supreme Court has been an important voice in this debate through its interpretation of the law.

Likewise, dorm directors may not be opposed to guns per se, but they may not want the responsibility of "policing" guns among dorm residents. Likewise, faculty may not be opposed to gun ownership, but they may not feel comfortable with students carrying guns into the classroom.

How Do You Find Stakeholders?

Finding stakeholders is a process of finding all organizations, individuals, groups, professions, and people who would be affected by this topic or have spoken up about it. List as many as you can think of, and then search for additional stakeholders. You might search the web for organizations or groups who have something to say on the matter. Are certain people or groups quoted in newspaper articles about this subject?

It might help to actually draw, or map, these stakeholders to get a sense of their relationships to one another. Furthermore, your map can also represent their potential impact in this debate. Which stakeholders have the loudest voices, so to speak?

If I was going to map the various stakeholders in the UK concealed guns debate, it might look something like the image below:

STAKEHOLDER ANALYSIS

After you identify all the stakeholders you possibly can, now it is time to engage in a **stakeholder analysis.** A stakeholder analysis is a genre quite common to businesses and organizations that are trying to identify those who may be allies or adversaries in advancing some argument. By knowing how to create stakeholder analyses, you will have an advantageous and useful skill for whatever career you enter. The following will lead you through the steps to conduct a stakeholder analysis:

1. For each stakeholder, list its characteristics. What does this group, organization, or person value the most? What are its priorities? What does this stakeholder most want? What are its fears? How will this situation impact them?
2. Next, list this stakeholder's rhetorical characteristics. What kinds of texts does it use to make its case? What type of language does it use? What types of rhetorical appeals are especially evident in their discourse?
3. Finally, analyze this stakeholder's main claims. What claims does this stakeholder make (about your chosen topic)? What types of evidence are offered in support of these claims? What kinds of warrants are "bridging" this argument for the stakeholder?
4. When you are finished with your analyses of all stakeholders, see if you can identify any points of agreement, disagreement, similarities, or patterns among the various stakeholders. Even among those who disagree, are there rhetorical similarities in their discourse or rhetoric? Do they rely on similar or different types of arguments? Are their warrants different, or are they generally shared?

DEALING WITH OPPOSING ARGUMENTS[5]

Any time you make an argument, no matter how controversial or mundane, there will be people who disagree with you. In an age where anyone can alter a Wikipedia page or publish a blog post or Tumblr thread on any given subject, it's very easy to find lots of opposing viewpoints on even the simplest of subjects. We've learned how to address these opposing viewpoints when we're having an argument in person—the other person says something and you respond with your own ideas about why they are wrong. But how do we deal with counterarguments and opposing viewpoints when we're writing a paper, recording a podcast, or making a documentary, when the people who disagree with us may not be physically present to share their thoughts?

Perhaps a better place to start with the question of how to deal with opposing arguments is why we bother acknowledging them at all? Isn't it better to focus our research on people who agree with and support our positions and not mention the people who may think differently? The answer is no. We want to acknowledge opposing arguments and address them in our own work. Why?

Think about dealing with opposing arguments in terms of what they do for your own ethos, pathos, and logos. Acknowledging opposing arguments shows that you've done your research, that you know about all of the other people who disagree with you and that you're aware that your own ideas are part of a larger, much more complex conversation around your chosen topic. You will come across to your audience as well prepared and thoroughly informed, therefore building your own ethos as a speaker.

Furthermore, because those opposing viewpoints exist whether you address them or not, by bringing them to your audience's attention first, you can shape how they view those opposing arguments and bring them back around to your way of thinking. You've already thought about how you want your audience to feel and how you want to use pathos to appeal to your audience, so you can cast an opposing argument in a light that makes them feel something else.

You can also point out the logical fallacies, false premises, or lack of evidence in an opposing argument. Demonstrating how an opposing viewpoint fails to make a logical argument, you can undermine that viewpoint's use of logos while impressing your audience of your own logical mastery.

So even though it may seem more worthwhile only to talk about your own argument and the evidence that supports it, you have good reasons to deal with opposing arguments preemptively. Addressing viewpoints that do not align with your own will help you seem prepared and give you the chance to dismantle those viewpoints before they start attacking your ideas. We deal with opposing arguments by going through four steps:

- Identifying Them
- Acknowledging Them
- Critiquing Them
- Proposing Your Own Solutions

Identifying Opposing Arguments

We can't begin to deal with opposing arguments before we know what those opposing arguments are. Luckily, identifying opposing arguments is a fairly simple process. As we mentioned before, it seems like everyone who has an opinion has a way to share it on the Internet. A simple search for almost any topic is bound to return lots of articles, tweets, threads, and other informal rants from many sides of the argument. However, you do not have to identify and deal with every opposing argument out there. In some contexts, it is appropriate to seek opposing arguments in informal sources, while other situations might call for using scholarly sources.

When might you look to informal sources? Informal sources include social media posts or personal interviews with friends or family members. First, ensure that your professor, supervisor at work, or any audience for whom you are writing allows the use of this type of source. Then, ask yourself whose concerns you are hoping to address or whose perspectives are especially relevant to your paper. If your argument might address the concerns of people outside of scholarly sources, your composition might be more effective if it were to address those people. Say, for example, that you are writing a paper arguing that students tend to get less value out of online classes compared to in-person classes. As you are sharing your ideas you come across a classmate who disagrees with you. After receiving their consent to do so, you might record some of their ideas and include them in your paper. In this circumstance, the classmate would be a fitting source for an opposing argument, because their perspective is relevant to the issue you are addressing.

You might also look to scholarly sources for opposing arguments. Authors of scholarly sources demonstrate their ethos by avoiding logical fallacies or inconsistencies and providing evidence beyond emotion.

You can find credible sources for opposing arguments in a number of places:

- News articles or reports from respected newspapers or magazines
- Peer-reviewed journals
- Books written by experts in their fields
- Polls conducted by trustworthy organizations

The UK Library offers online access to two databases that are particularly useful for identifying opposing arguments: CQ Researcher and Opposing Viewpoints in Context. CQ Researcher provides detailed reports written by experienced journalists on important or controversial issues of the day. Their full-length articles include an overview of the topic, historical background, a pro/con feature, and resources for additional research. The pro/con feature will pose a question about the topic of the report and then give you a debate in which one side argues in favor of the question and the other argues against it. Opposing Viewpoints in Context also provides articles on a wide range of topics including such varied subjects as deforestation, slavery reparations, vaccines, the culture of beauty, and live streaming of violent acts. Each of these articles includes an overview of the topic and links to academic journals, images, videos, and other resources that you can peruse to identify opposing arguments.

A quick note on identifying opposing arguments: remember that every argument begins in stasis. An article that you think may be expressing an opposing viewpoint to your own may not, in fact, be useful to you because it deals with a slightly different topic. Make sure to read the arguments you find closely and carefully so you know that you're actually talking about the same issue.

Exercise

Think of a topic that's been in the news lately. Do a quick Google search for that topic and see what comes up. Identify ONE argument from your Google search that you think is credible and one that you think is not credible. What is the difference between the two? Why should you trust one but not the other? Now go to CQ Researcher or Opposing Viewpoints in Context and search for the same topic. What kinds of opposing arguments did you find on these databases?

Acknowledging Opposing Arguments

Once you've done your research and identified some credible viewpoints that disagree with your own positions, you need to acknowledge these viewpoints either in writing or orally in your podcast or documentary. When you're acknowledging an opposing argument, it's important to remember that you should summarize the argument accurately but briefly. You should lay out the basics of the argument, but don't make your opponent's argument for them. This will require you to use your skills at synthesizing evidence just like the evidence was your own. However, you do not want to explain your opponent's argument and evidence in so much detail that you are distracting from your own ideas.

When you're summarizing an opposing argument, it's important that you be careful not to misstate your opponent's position. It can be tempting to cast an opposing viewpoint in an overly negative light, but it's very easy to take that negative light too far and end up mischaracterizing what your opponent is actually saying. If you describe the opposing argument too broadly or inaccurately, you could end up committing the logical fallacies of a hasty generalization or the straw man.

You also want to make sure that you quote selectively but accurately. In 1995, the ad copy for New Line Cinema's thriller *Se7en* included a quotation from *Entertainment Weekly* critic Owen Glieberman in which he allegedly called the film "a small masterpiece." Anyone who saw the ad copy would believe that Glieberman had given the film a positive review. However, Glieberman actually gave the film a lukewarm review; he only used the words "small masterpiece" to describe the opening credits, and even then the full quotation was "a small masterpiece of dementia" (Levine 584). So Glieberman did say the words "small masterpiece," but New Line Cinema chose the part of his otherwise mediocre review to make it seem like he thought the film was wonderful. This is something you should avoid. Don't pull apart what your opponent says to make it seem like they are saying something else. Quote from parts of the argument that are particularly important, but otherwise rely on your own accurate summary of the position.

Critiquing Opposing Arguments

Critiquing opposing arguments works the same way that you critique the arguments that agree with you when you're trying to determine which evidence you want to use to support your own claim. However, when you're critiquing evidence that supports you, you want to make sure that the evidence is free from logical fallacies and comes from credible sources. When you're assessing opposing arguments in order to critique them, you're actually looking for these problems so you can point them out to your audience as a part of your rationale for disagreeing with the opposing argument.

Begin your critique by aiming to understand the concern behind the opposing argument and any merits to that argument. Imagine that your audience is the person making the opposing argument. By acknowledging the concern that person has and any valid aspects of their argument, you demonstrate to them that you have thoughtfully engaged with and care about their perspective. A person who believes that opposing argument is more likely to listen to your rebuttal if they feel heard. Furthermore, if you are open to seeing the merits of opposing arguments, you can minimize your own bias and remain open to nuances.

Continue by identifying the stakeholders. Who cares about the opposing argument and who might agree with that argument? What kinds of characteristics, such as values, priorities, desires, or identities, might those stakeholders share? Why do you think that they might agree with the opposing argument? Stakeholder analysis can help you identify some problems with the opposing argument that don't arise within the argument itself but rather lie underneath the argument. For example, you might find that only people of a certain background or educational status agree with an opposing position, or that people who have had particular life experiences are more likely to share an opposing viewpoint. Point out these stakeholders in your project and explain their limitations to your audience.

Next, move on to critiquing the argument itself by thinking about the three rhetorical appeals of ethos, pathos, and logos. When assessing the argument's ethos, think about the background and qualifications of the person or group making the opposing argument. Consider their gender, class, race, sexuality, education, or profession. What kinds of biases might that person or group have that could affect their argument? Identify any potential problems with ethos and explain them to your audience. Then think about pathos—does the opposing argument rely too much on emotion and not enough on actual evidence? What do they want their audience to feel? Break this down for your audience as well. Finally, look for logical problems in the forms of fallacies, faulty premises, or insufficient evidence in your opponent's position. Explain these flaws in logic to your audience.

Once you have assessed and critiqued the opposing arguments, you will be in good position to refute the to your audience. This requires you to explain to your audience exactly what is wrong with the opposing argument. We're used to doing this when we're arguing in person, so when we're addressing an audience in a paper, podcast, or documentary, we might need to be a little more thorough in explaining what our opponents are saying and why the audience should not believe or agree with that position. In this step, you'll take all of the research and assessment that you've done in the previous steps and present it to your audience in your own words. In refuting an opposing argument, you could answer as many of the following questions as are relevant:

- How credible is the person or group making the opposing argument?
- What warrants or biases could be at play?
- What factual errors does the opposing argument make?
- What logical errors or fallacies does the opposing argument make?

The basic structure of a refutation of an opposing argument should read something like this:

- My opponent says this …
- However, you should not believe my opponent because …

Proposing Your Own Solutions

By this point, you've identified important opposing viewpoints, summarized them for your audience, and explained your critique of that position. Why don't we just stop here? Why do we bother with a fourth step in the process?

To redirect your reader from the opposing argument to your own argument, the last step in dealing with opposing viewpoints is to explain why, in light of them, your own argument still stands. We conclude the process of dealing with opposing arguments by proposing our own solutions for a number of reasons. First, this lets you end the debate on a positive note. Second, and more importantly, it makes sure that the last thing your audience hears is *your* perspective, not the perspective of your opponent. Even though you will have critiqued and refuted the opposing argument in your own terms, that argument is still the last position your audience will hear unless you go one step further and bring the audience back around to hearing your own ideas.

When proposing your own solutions, you offer an alternative to your opponent that you believe is better based on your own evidence and your own opinions. It gives your audience something positive and productive to walk away with. Furthermore, it shows your audience that you have thought not only about differing perspectives on your topic, but also about why your position is compelling.

Exercise

Choose ONE of the articles that you found on CQ Researcher or Opposing Viewpoints in Context that you believe is credible and deals with a topic that interests you but that expresses an opinion you don't agree with. Go through the three remaining steps for dealing with an opposing argument. First, acknowledge it by summarizing it briefly and only quoting from it selectively and accurately. Next, assess it by identifying its flaws in ethos, pathos, and logos. Then, refute it by explaining to your audience what is wrong with the opposing argument. Finally, propose your own solution and end the debate with your own original ideas.

NOTES

[1] Watson, Robert, James J. McCarthy, and Liliana Hisas. *The Economic Case for Climate Action in the United States.* FEU-US Report, September 2017, https://drive.google.com/file/d/0B9whT-2Ezzu7UUNUS3ZielhROFk/view.

[2] Hayhoe, Katherine. Interview, "There Must be More Productive Ways to Talk About Climate Change." *NPR Morning Edition,* May 9, 2017, https://www.npr.org/2017/05/09/527541032/there-must-be-more-productive-ways-to-talk-about-climate-change.

[3] Norgaard, Kari Marie. "Climate Change is a Social Issue." *The Chronicle of Higher Education,* Jan. 17, 2016, https://www-chronicle-com.ezproxy.uky.edu/article/Climate-Change-Is-a-Social/234908.

[4] Figure 1: UN website on the Paris Agreement. http://newsroom.unfccc.int/paris-agreement/.

[5] Levine, Timothy R., ed. *Encyclopedia of Deception.* SAGE Publications, Inc., 2014.

Using Evidence

Recommended for WRD 111/112

Chapter 8

The phrase "using evidence" sounds like it belongs more in a courtroom or a crime scene than in a writing classroom. When we think of this word, a whole host of images might pop into our head:

- A police officer putting on gloves and picking up an object in an area cordoned off with yellow crime scene tape.
- A reporter squinting at a computer screen or shifting through stacks of paper in search of a piece of information for a story.
- A lawyer in a courtroom holding up a weapon in a numbered bag and using it to prove his case to a jury.

Of course, when we hear **"evidence,"** we might also think of more traditional synonyms or definitions, such as an object or document that includes the following:

- Provides **proof** or **corroboration.**
- Functions as a form of **validation** or **authentication.**
- Acts as a vehicle of **persuasion.**
- Serves as **documentation.**
- Indicates **truth** or **accuracy.**

The item that the police officer finds at the crime scene; the information that the reporter uncovers; the weapon that the lawyer holds up to the jury in the courtroom: while each may be physically different, they all function in a similar way because they all serve as a kind of **evidence.**

It's kind of comforting to know that people like police officers, reporters, and lawyers all have to find enough evidence to make their case or their argument. But it can be unsettling when we're asked to do it ourselves—especially in our writing.

As we discussed earlier in this textbook in the chapter on rhetoric, **artistic arguments**—arguments that use ethos, pathos, and logos in some form or fashion—allow us to use the credibility, emotional connection, and sensible structure that is largely our own invention to make our point.

But the kind of evidence that we're discussing in this chapter is the kind most often used in **non-artistic arguments**—in other words, it's the kind of evidence that isn't our invention. It's the kind of evidence that we have to seek out from other people and other reliable sources, the kind of evidence that changes from assignment to assignment and genre to genre. Sometimes that evidence might come from a personal interview or an article from an academic journal; other times, it could be an excerpt from a novel or a newspaper article.

Sometimes when we're asked to use evidence in a piece of writing, we have a visceral reaction to this request. If we don't have much experience doing research or incorporating evidence into our writing, it can be intimidating, even a little frightening. What, we think, is my word not enough? Where am I supposed to find this "evidence"? How will I know if it's any good? And what on earth am I supposed to do with it once I have it?

Why do we react this way? Because, first of all, it's natural to be a little nervous about writing something in a different format than we're used to, especially if it requires more steps and more rigorous analytical thinking than we may have used in the past.

In addition, writing is too often portrayed culturally as some kind of magical, mysterious, mystical process that some people are good at and some people aren't, and we often assume that if we don't know how to do it right away, then we must be the person who isn't good at it.

But as natural as the nervousness is, this perception of writing as some kind of magic is a myth. In truth, clear, effective writing is largely achieved by learning to implement a few rules and putting in some hard work. This, too, is the key to using evidence effectively.

In this chapter, we'll outline and explain four steps in this process, which will help you with the following:

- Determine which sources are best for your piece of writing.
- Understand what your sources are arguing.
- Incorporate those sources into your writing so that they bolster your claim.
- Revise your work so that your use of evidence is most effective.

STEP ONE—REVIEW: WHAT DO I HAVE?

Looking for sources can be both time-consuming and tedious—hours in the library sifting through the stacks for that perfect book or journal, hours on the Internet reading link after link, trying to find the best piece of relevant information. Although it's sometimes frustrating, doing research and doing it well does require the dedication of some time. And when you finally sit down to write that paper, you don't want to stare at a stack of books or articles or links and wonder, what do I have here? Before you pick up a pen or open that Word document, you need to have a good idea of what you have in your possession, so you have to **evaluate your sources.** Here are a few tips on how to do that:

> Be discriminating: Make sure you are using the best, most reliable and trustworthy sources possible.

Although Wikipedia might seem like a go-to for gathering some quick research on a topic, a crowd-sourced website that allows anyone to edit its entries isn't as trustworthy as, for example, a website run by a college or university or a government agency.

It's certainly better to get information about the resurgence in measles or the latest Ebola outbreak in Africa from, say, the National Institutes of Health, the nation's top medical research agency which is staffed and run by some of the world's best doctors, rather than from the Wikipedia entry for either of these topics, which could have been edited by anyone (and chances are, it isn't someone with a medical degree). For more on why choosing the most reliable sources is so important, you'll find a real-life example in Case Study 1 on pg. 183.

> If a source doesn't seem to work for you, the bibliography might.

It's frustrating to realize that sometimes a source that you've worked hard to find isn't the best source for you at all (see the box "The Pain of Tossing out Sources" on pg. 181). However, that doesn't mean that the source is completely useless. Before you toss that source, make sure you check its bibliography: many times, you'll find a host of new sources on your same topic, and chances are there may be one that you hadn't found through other means.

Because you're using the bibliography of a source that had some relationship to your topic, you have a better chance of striking gold with something on that list. Even *Wikipedia*, which is questionable as a source by itself, can prove fruitful: if you check out the pages on Ebola, for example, and look for the numbers at the ends of a sentence, that indicates that the sentence has a source for its information. That source is listed at the bottom of the page in the "Reference" section:

Figure 1. Images from Wikipedia, accessed June 28, 2014.

Often, that source information includes a hyperlink that allows you to link directly to the original primary or secondary source on the Wikipedia page. But you have to be careful: sometimes, the link is to a personal blog or website instead of a reputable organization or agency. Before you use that information, double-check the source itself for credibility and accuracy.

> ### The Pain of Tossing out Sources
>
> So here's an uncomfortable fact about research that many people don't like to talk about: yes, you are going to have to read things you won't end up using in your paper. It's difficult to admit, but you will spend valuable time throughout your college career reading a host of sources that you will realize, in the end, aren't what you're looking for, and you'll have to scrap them. The first time you do this, it will feel a little bit like throwing away a $20 bill (after all, your time is worth something, and you just flushed it away!).
>
> But what you'll discover is that learning to let go sometimes will help you to become much more effective at using evidence well. The pain of tossing away a source that you've spent time on is counterbalanced by your growing understanding of how to distinguish valuable sources from ones that aren't as valuable. And, in the end, you'll become a better writer because your professors will see that you didn't just throw in every source and the kitchen sink to get a paper done, but instead you tried to choose the best possible sources to bolster your particular claims. And getting the good grades that come along with that realization is a pretty great pain reliever.

> If a source does work for you, again, the bibliography also might.

Just as the bibliography of a source that you discard might be valuable, so might the bibliography of a source that you deem helpful—likely, even more so. Be sure to read through them to see what other research gems you might uncover that you may have overlooked.

> Make sure you are using a diversity of sources.

Although you may have gathered 10 sources, if they are all sources by the same author or from the same publication, you're not getting a representative sampling of the diversity of research available out there on your topic. No matter how unbiased we attempt to be, humans are fundamentally biased; although we all try to keep our biases out of our work, none of us are perfect. So if you consult only one author or one publication for your information on a topic, you run the risk of falling prey to their individual biases, which might lead you to miss crucial considerations. If you draw from a diversity of sources, however, chances are your pool of sources will balance one another out—what one misses, another will see clearly.

> Make sure your sources aren't all from the same time period.

Unless you are researching a topic whose development stalled during some period of time, it's generally not a good idea to have sources that were all written during the same period. If you do, generally you'll end up missing critical information.

For example, reading research on Dwayne Johnson after 2004 would not be very helpful for writing a paper on the eight-time WWF/WWE Champion. You would be fully versed in his acting success, but not his wrestling career. But if you expanded your research further back, you would learn that Dwayne Johnson earned his wrestling name, "The Rock," from his father, and was the first third-generation wrestler in WWF history.[1] His trademark move was the "Rock Bottom"; no, it had nothing to do with *SpongeBob SquarePants*. You might not even know that the WWE was the WWF until 2002. As you can see, it's incredibly important to broaden the pool of your research to cover both historical and contemporary time periods because a lot can change on a topic in just a few years.

> After you've noted all of these issues, looks for obvious gaps in your research.

Once you've narrowed your list of sources and noted the patterns listed above, look for the gaps and try as best you can to fill them in. If there's a gap or a concentration for some reason, make sure you can justify it—for example, if you have a host of valuable sources from the year 1996, maybe there was a surge in research on your topic that year that advanced knowledge about your topic in some fundamental way. Or if you have several sources from the same author, perhaps that person is a noted and reliable scholar who deserves a little more textual landscape than some others. Don't be afraid of gaps and don't feel like your sources have to be perfectly balanced—just be prepared to justify those gaps to yourself and your audience.

Case Study 1: Judith Miller's Reporting on Weapons of Mass Destruction

Even researchers with a reputation for vigilance can sometimes make mistakes when it comes to distinguishing reliable sources from unreliable ones. Judith Miller, a Pulitzer Prize winning reporter for the *New York Times,* found that out the hard way.

Figure 2. Judith Miller (NYT).

Miller, in conjunction with journalist James Risen, won the Pulitzer Prize for Explanatory Reporting in 2002 for their 2001 coverage of global terrorism before and after the September 11 attacks. Despite winning the highest accolade for journalism in the country, Miller was still susceptible to making a mistake with a source. Much of her coverage of the Iraq War and the country's supposed "weapons of mass destruction" in 2002 and 2003 was later proven to have been based on incorrect information.

The source of at least some of that incorrect information was Ahmed Chalabi, an Iraqi politician and former oil minister who was initially a trusted intelligence informant for the United States government. Chalabi's information linking Saddam Hussein to Al-Quaeda and weapons of mass destruction, however, was later proven false, and his position as informant and his relationship to the United States grew sour.

Trusting the wrong source had a dramatic impact on Judith Miller and on her career: by October 2005, even the *Times* Public Editor Byron Calame was stating publicly that because of the inaccuracies in her reporting, it would be "difficult for her to return to the newsroom as a reporter."

For any other reporter, this kind of inaccuracy would probably be a career-ender, but winning the Pulitzer Prize does still hold some weight: Miller continued to write for other publications and eventually was offered a job at Fox News, which she still holds today. Still, the legacy of not being discriminating enough about her source is one that will follow her name throughout the remainder of her career and likely her life.

Chapter 8   Using Evidence

Read more about Judith Miller here:

From *the New York Times*, **"Threats and Responses: The Iraqis; U.S. Says Hussein Intensifies Search for A-Bomb Parts"** *(http://www.nytimes.com/2002/09/08/world/threats-responses-iraqis-us-says-hussein-intensifies-quest-for-bomb-parts.html?module=Search&mabReward=relbias:r,[%22RI:5%22,%22RI:18%22]).*

From the *New York Times*, **"The Miller Mess: Lingering Issues among the Answers"** *(http://www.nytimes.com/2005/10/23/opinion/23publiceditor.html?pagewanted=print&_r=0).*

Exercise: Case Study

Read some of the additional reporting from and about Judith Miller's reporting on Iraq in the early 2000s. What could and/or should have Miller done differently in order to verify the accuracy of the information she was receiving from Chalabi?

Consider your own approach to verifying information for a paper. What are you doing now to make sure that the information you are gathering is accurate? What could you do differently to improve upon this process?

STEP TWO—REFLECT: WHAT DOES IT MEAN?

Now that you have a good idea of what kind and what variety of sources you have, you also need to have a good understanding of what those sources are saying. That stack of books or articles might be intimidating, but again, you'll have a much better grasp on where your paper is headed if you have an understanding of what the larger academic and cultural conversation is about your topic. So, again, before you start to write, make sure you **understand the content of your sources.** Here are a few tips that will help you move through that process smoothly and effectively:

> Understand the ethos of your source's author.

Before you even begin reading a source, it's a good idea to do a little cursory reading about the author. Read his/her bio in the back of the book; perhaps Google his/her quickly to see what you can find. As we noted in Step One, we're all biased—it's unavoidable—so it might be a good idea to know what your author's history is related to the subject he/she is writing about.

For example, Dr. Mehmet Oz, host of the "Dr. Oz Show," might seem like a reputable source to quote on the medical value of green coffee beans or garcinia cambogia. But a little research shows that he has been called before a congressional subcommittee on consumer safety, and the committee has stated that both green coffee beans and garcinia cambogia have been promoted as tools for weight loss on Dr. Oz's show, but that neither product has any scientific evidence to back up those statements.

> Don't quote from sources with which you aren't familiar.

It might seem easy to simply flip to a page in a source and to pull a quote out to use in your paper, but it's also a very risky maneuver. When you pull out a quote at random that looks good—an action called "contextomy"—you risk two important things. First of all, you risk misunderstanding the context of that quote. What that means, in essence, is that if you haven't read the entire chapter or section that a quote comes from, chances are you're going to miss an important part of the argument. Second, if you don't read the entire article or book, there's a good chance that you're going to miss out on a quote that might be even better than the one you're choosing.

> Similarly, have a good understanding of each source's argument.

This is a challenge, but it's absolutely worth it, and it goes hand-in-hand with the previous suggestion. Make sure that you actually read your sources and that you try to pinpoint the arguments the authors are making. If it is an article, what is the one takeaway that the author is attempting to prove? If it is a book, what is the overall point that ties the chapters together?

> Learn how to skim and scan effectively.

Reading an article or two for an essay seems pretty reasonable, but an entire book? Or two? Or more? This kind of research is daunting to most students to say the least. But learning to skim and to scan effectively will help you move through large volumes of text while still gathering pertinent information.

Skimming is essentially a method of reading where you move your eyes quickly over a source while attempting to gather information that will help you better understand the source's main points. Read for these informational clues while skimming:

- The source's title
- Chapter headings
- Sub-headings for sections within chapters
- The introductory paragraph in full
- The first and last sentence of each paragraph (if the source is not book-length)
- The concluding paragraph in full
- Unusual words
- Words that provide concrete answers to the "five w" questions and "how"
- Any words that are italicized, in bold, or set apart in any way
- Any graphics

Scanning is essentially a method of reading where you read over large volumes of information in a source while looking for particular information. Read for these informational clues while skimming:

- Main ideas (typically in an introductory paragraph or a topic sentence)
- Facts or statistics
- Quotes
- Dates
- Other information related to a person, thing or event

> Take notes on your sources.

Reading through your sources is valuable, but when it comes time to write your paper, you'll frustrate yourself to no end if you don't have notes on those sources to which you can refer. Note-taking, which can include writing down memorable points on a separate piece of paper or adding margin notes to a text (also called annotation), is a valuable skill that not only gives you a quick reference point for what you've read, but it also helps you to retain that information a bit better. Here are a few tips on note-taking and annotation:

- Take notes on the same categories and clues that you skim and scan for.
- Make sure to write down page numbers for quick reference.
- Use different-colored highlighters to identify different points in the text.

- Write down a summarizing word or phrase next to a particularly relevant paragraph or passage.
- At the end of your notes on a source, write down a quick paragraph or sentence synopsis with the most important take-away.
- Group the notes of similar sources together.

Case Study 2: Media Misunderstands Supreme Court's Obamacare Vote

Major news networks usually take great pains to get their facts right, but sometimes even they misunderstand their source material in their haste to get a news story out to the public. The Supreme Court's June 28, 2012, decision on the Affordable Care Act, known colloquially as "Obamacare," is case-in-point.

The Supreme Court's decision on Obamacare was revolutionary in a number of ways: it upheld a very controversial piece of legislation that changed Americans' relationship to their healthcare and their healthcare system, but it also showcased a major flub on the part of two prominent media outlets.

In the minutes following the release of the decision, networks and media outlets—including Reuters, the Associated Press, and Dow Jones—attempted to wrestle their way through the nearly 200-page decision and concluded that the Supreme Court had upheld one of the legislation's most controversial components: the individual mandate that requires all United States residents to have health insurance. Both CNN and Fox News reported that the mandate had been struck down. Why did this error occur? There's no doubt that the reporters and producers on the story were rushed and eager to get their information out first and didn't take the time to review the primary source document—the ruling itself—in enough detail. According to a story issued by Poynter on June 28, CNN issued a correction about 90 minutes after the error occurred and said that the network "regrets that it didn't wait to report out the full and complete opinion regarding the mandate." Fox News also issued an apology to its viewers.

This kind of error by major media organizations illustrated that no one is immune to making this kind of mistake. CNN was embarrassed publicly and compounded its problems by not only reporting the error on the ruling on its live broadcast, but also on its website, by email, and on its social media sites. Its tweet about the ruling, for example, was retweeted hundreds of times by the time the network realized its error and sent out a correction over 10 minutes later. Fox News was also embarrassed by its error on live TV, but because at the time it hadn't

Chapter 8   Using Evidence

fully integrated its method of distributing information digitally, it did not deal with as many retractions as CNN had to cope with. The moral of the story? Make sure you read your source thoroughly and get your information right, even if you don't get it out first.

Figure 3. Poynter's screenshot of CNN's website.

Read more about CNN and Fox News' error on Obamacare here:

From Poynter.org, **"CNN, Fox News Err in Covering Supreme Court Healthcare Ruling"** *(https://www.poynter.org/reporting-editing/2012/were-cnn-fox-news-mistakes-on-supreme-court-ruling-part-of-process-journalism/).*

From SCOTUSblog, **"We're Getting Wildly Different Assessments"** *(http://www.scotusblog.com/2012/07/were-getting-wildly-differing-assessments/).*

Exercise: Case Study

1. Read the SCOTUSblog article, particularly the section under the time 10:08:30 where journalist Tom Goldstein talks about his skimming approach to reading the Supreme Court's opinion. What did he do well in this exercise? What could he have improved upon to make his skimming more effective?
2. Consider the apology that CNN and Fox News offered their viewers after they realized their mistake. What would you do if you realized that you had made a serious error in your assessment of a source for a paper? How would you approach your professor to discuss it? How could you keep yourself from making that kind of error in the future?

STEP THREE—RESPOND: WHAT DO I DO WITH IT?

Now that you've evaluated your sources and understand their content, you're ready to start writing. Once you get your introduction and your thesis crafted, you'll probably be looking for source material to use to bolster your first point, so you're also ready to begin to **integrate sources into your paper.** This is an exciting point in the writing process, but it's also tricky—many students get frustrated when they begin to put source material into their work because they're not quite sure how to do it effectively. Here are a few tips for you on how to make sure that that source material works to both bolster your claim and push you to make it even stronger:

> Draft freely.

Although this isn't a point that is directly related to using evidence, it's a point that, if executed well, will allow you to integrate your evidence more effectively. Try your best to turn off your internal editor and just write. Get your ideas down on paper to the best of your ability so that you aren't judging your work harshly while it is still in an early draft stage and so that you can feel confident about your initial ideas. This will give you more courage to reach out during the revision process to integrate your source material.

> Use shorthand to designate places in your paper where you'd like to include source material.

Don't feel compelled to integrate your source material seamlessly on the first try. Most effective writers have worked with and revised their source material numerous times in order to integrate it smoothly. Sometimes the easiest way to begin the process is to simply put a note to yourself in the text of your paper about what source you want to use and what point you'll be highlighting from it in parentheses next to your claim. You can come back later and work on polishing it.

> Let your sources inform your thesis and your claims.

When you write a paper, remember that you aren't starting off with an ironclad idea for which you need to find absolute and unequivocal support. Your thesis is not static—it's elastic, and it should be flexible and receptive to change based on what source material you've discovered. In other words, you aren't making an inflexible argument and then looking for sources to support that idea—you are actually testing your argument similar to the way that scientists test a hypothesis; and as a result, you need to be willing to adapt that argument to new discoveries and information just as scientists do. That does not mean, however, that you shouldn't have confidence in your argument or that you should scrap it at the first sign that one of your sources might disagree with you. You are looking for support, but you are also looking for people who might have more in-depth information than you do to inform your argument and improve it.

> Don't let your sources overburden your work.

Excellent source material is great, but overkill is also always a possibility. A paper that relies too much on source material can cause the voice of the paper's author to disappear. This happens sometimes because people don't have enough confidence in their ideas, so they lean on source material as a kind of crutch. It's very important to place your ideas in the larger conversation about your topic, but you don't want your ideas to be completely drowned out. The answer? Make sure that you surround every instance of source material with your own ideas. We'll explore some concrete ways to do this below.

> At the same time, don't lose sight of your sources.

The flip side of the problem above is that some students don't rely enough on the larger conversation on their topic and can end up with an argument or ideas that get out of their control. Work hard to maintain your focus on your ideas and how your source material can support those ideas because if you deviate too far, you could lose control of your paper and your message.

Case Study 3: CaroMont Regional Medical Center's Rebranding Campaign

There are a number of examples out there that illustrate how easy—and damaging—it can be to lose sight of your source material, but the example of North Carolina's CaroMont Regional Medical Center's rebranding campaign is a painful and memorable one.

In the spring of 2013, CaroMont—located in Gaston, North Carolina—announced a name change for the Gaston Memorial Hospital and a rebranding. The hospital, which would now be known as CaroMont Regional Medical Center, would also abandon its former tagline "In Love With Life." Its replacement? "Cheat Death."

Figure 4. The Gaston Gazette's photograph of the infamous slogan reveal. (*http://www.gastongazette.com/caromont-rethinks-cheat-death-updated-1.123327*)

The new tagline drew rapid and unrelenting critique from members of the public and from national news media outlets like *The Huffington Post* and *NPR*. Some were merely uncomfortable with the tagline's negative connotations; others mocked it and treated it as if it were a joke. Local residents, however, who had lost relatives at the hospital felt like the message was both demeaning and insulting: after all, they said, no one cheats death, and nowhere is that more apparent and more inescapable than at a hospital.

So what went wrong with this new campaign? In part, the fault lay with the hospital's board of directors who gave the job of creating the new tagline to Immortology, a Chapel Hill-based marketing and branding firm which many said did not do a sufficient job of vetting the proposed rebranding internally, much less among public focus groups, before launching it.

But also problematic was the fact that the impetus for changing the tagline was lost in the shuffle. Hospital board members had recently been made aware that Gaston County had scored near the bottom of the state's 99 counties and on a national level on an assessment of community health conducted annually by the University of Wisconsin Population Health Institute and the Robert Wood Johnson Foundation. A new tagline and associated campaign, they thought, just might spur county residents to improve their health.

Chapter 8   Using Evidence

What made headlines here, however, was not the good intentions of the hospital board but instead the failed attempt of a firm that, according to its website, believes that "safe is for sissies," a firm that creates only "immortal" brands that "lead rather than follow." Unfortunately, the only thing that's lasting about this particular story is a public relations disaster that the hospital will never quite live down.

Read more about CaroMont's PR disaster here:

From *Charlotte Business Journal*, **"CaroMont's 'Cheat Death' Slogan Drawing a Sharp response"** *(http://www.bizjournals.com/charlotte/news/2013/04/05/caromonts-cheat-death-slogan.html?page=all).*

From *Modern Healthcare*, **"Outliers: New Slogan Dies Quick Death"** *(http://www.modernhealthcare.com/article/20130413/MAGAZINE/304139958).*

Exercise: Case Study

In the *Modern Healthcare* article, CaroMont CEO and President Randy Kelley says the hospital's intent was "never to offend or incite." How do you think CaroMont could have handled this differently that would have kept the public's focus more on the health report that spurred their desire for change?

Consider what would happen if you lost sight of source material in a paper. What steps could you take to revise your paper so that your argument connected effectively with your source material again?

> For every major claim you make in support of your thesis, try to have at least one source.

This is less a hard-and-fast rule than a suggestion. If possible, try to see if you can find a source that will support each major claim that you make in your paper. This is a challenge, but if you aim for this standard, it will help you maintain balance in your paper between reputable sources and your own ideas.

> Make sure you indicate whether your source material is quoted, paraphrased, or summarized.

It's very important to indicate in your paper whether you are using source material that is a quote, a paraphrase, or a summary. Here's a brief description and example of each to help you understand the difference between these classifications:

- **Quoted source material** is material that is replicated word for word in your paper. This material is always set apart by quotation marks.

    Example: In his 1955 essay "Stranger in the Village," James Baldwin wrote "but some of the men have accused *le sale negre*—behind my back—of stealing wood and there is already in the eyes of some of them that peculiar, intent, paranoiac malevolence which one sometimes surprises in the eyes of American white men when, out walking with their Sunday girl, they see a Negro male approach."

- **Paraphrased source material** is generally a passage whose general intent and meaning is restated succinctly and faithfully in the writer's own words. Paraphrasing is typically confined to a small amount of quoted text. This material is also usually afforded some kind of introduction, and no quotation marks are typically used unless the writer feels the need to retain some of the author's original vocabulary.

    Example: In his 1955 essay "Stranger in the Village," James Baldwin wrote that male residents of the Swiss village still accuse him of stealing behind his back and silently radiate the same fear and hatred that he has seen in the eyes of American men.

- **Summarized source material** is material that attempts to put the main ideas of a text succinctly and faithfully into the writer's own words. Typically, summarized source material incorporates a much larger section of text, such as a paragraph, chapter, article, or book. As with others, this material is also afforded some kind of introduction, and no quotation marks are typically used unless the writer feels the need to retain some of the author's original vocabulary.

    Example: In his 1955 essay "Stranger in the Village," James Baldwin wrote about the unsettling experience of being the only African American man in a village of 600 white Swiss villagers, the odd quietude associated with living in a remote village in the Alps in the middle of winter, the dramatic difference between the village and his hometown of Harlem, and the inescapable history of race and racism.

To integrate a quote, paraphrase, or summary effectively, follow these three steps: introduce, insert, and explain.

The process of quote integration can be a bit tricky, especially for new writers. Although there's no real formula for doing this effectively, we've outlined a three-step process below with examples that can serve as a guide. Once they are comfortable with this approach, advanced writers can feel free to deviate from this process and use these steps in varying ways to help them construct a more complex argument.

Introduce

Try offering a two-part introductory statement that indicates to your reader important information about your source material:

Part I

This part of the introduction should introduce us to the text. It can include the title, date, or author, or if it feels relevant or important, all three.

Example: In *The Great Gatsby,* written by F. Scott Fitzgerald in 1925, …

Typically, you only need to offer this much information once in your paper. After the first mention, and any time you include another quote, you can simply refer to the title of the book or the author or, in some cases, you may not need to mention the title at all because it will be understood contextually.

Example: Fitzgerald's novel … or In the novel …

Part II

This part of the introduction should introduce us to the relevant quote itself. It should be a statement that gives us the context for the quote.

Example: In *The Great Gatsby,* written by F. Scott Fitzgerald in 1925, Gatsby's great love Daisy Buchanan and her friend Mrs. Baxter are introduced to the reader …

Insert

Adding Citation

After you've written your two-part introductory statement, you are ready to insert your quote, paraphrase, or summary. Make sure you follow all correct citation rules (see Step Four—Revise: How Do I Make It Better? on pg. 198).

Example: In *The Great Gatsby,* written by F. Scott Fitzgerald in 1925, Gatsby's great love Daisy Buchanan and her friend Mrs. Baxter are introduced to the reader "in white, and their dresses were rippling and fluttering as if they had blown back in after a short flight around the house" (27).

Explain

Now that you've given relevant information about the text, relevant information about the quote, and provided your quote, you can provide a two-part explanation for the quote.

Part I

This part is your explanation of what the quote means to you. Consider the details, images, and description in the original quote and try to put them into your own words and explain their meaning.

Example: In *The Great Gatsby,* written by F. Scott Fitzgerald in 1925, Gatsby's great love Daisy Buchanan and her friend Mrs. Baxter are introduced to the reader "in white, and their dresses were rippling and fluttering as if they had blown back in after a short flight around the house" (27). This description depicts Daisy and Mrs. Baxter as birds, swans perhaps, elegant in white, ornamental, flighty, unable to stay in one place for too long.

Part II

This part is your explanation of why this quote is relevant to your claim. How does it support your argument? Err on the side of providing too much explanation, if possible; it's always easier to cut text out of a paper rather than try to come up with additional information.

Example: In *The Great Gatsby,* written by F. Scott Fitzgerald in 1925, Gatsby's great love Daisy Buchanan and her friend Mrs. Baxter are introduced to the reader "in white, and their dresses were rippling and fluttering as if they had blown back in after a short flight around the house" (27). This description depicts Daisy and Mrs. Baxter as birds, swans perhaps, elegant in white, ornamental, flighty, unable to stay in one place for too long. Although it seems at first like merely a frivolous and perhaps derogatory depiction of the novel's women, in fact, it hints at the the true nature of Daisy's character—her lack of sincerity and focus and her utter inability to care about more than appearances—that makes her one of the most damning and damaging characters in the novel.

> Avoid these common missteps because they violate the three-step process for source material integration.

There are lots of rules that we could cite here, but these are three common mistakes that new writers make that run contrary to the three-step process we've just outlined. Read them through so that you can be aware of them and avoid them.

- **Try not to let a quote stand on its own in a sentence.** Some writers feel like they shouldn't tamper too much with an author's words because they speak for themselves, but that's not the purpose of using them in a paper. You are using them to bolster your argument. In order to do that effectively, you have to provide context and connections to what you're writing, so it's much more effective to provide an introduction to a quote that links it seamlessly to your work.
- **Don't end a paragraph with a quote.** It's another common mistake that new writers make: end with a quote, and you'll end with the strongest possible sentiment, right? Wrong. In the end, you end up weakening your own argument because you're relying on the words of someone else to fully explain your point rather than using those words to supplement and bolster your own. Whenever possible, try to end with some kind of explanation of the quote.
- **Don't use quotes in your topic sentences.** Topic sentences are places for you to work your writerly magic—not places for the words of others. These are the sentences where you need to set forth your claims succinctly using your own thoughts and ideas. If you use source material here, you run the risk of having that source material monopolize the conversation.

> Attribute your material appropriately—or, in other words, cite your sources.

This rule is one that's paramount. Just as you want to be given credit for your original words and thoughts, so do others. Make sure that you always cite words and ideas that are other than your own. And if you're not sure you're doing it correctly, look it up.

Case Study 4: The Fabrications of Stephen Glass

Most people think of plagiarism as primarily a problem among high school and college students, but not so: in fact, there is a long and unsettling pattern of plagiarism and fabrication in the professional world, particularly in the field of journalism, that can teach us some valuable lessons about why it's so important to cite the work of others—and to tell the truth.

One of the most infamous examples of this rising trend is *Republic* magazine. One of Glass' most appealing qualities was his uncanny ability to find the most incredible stories: about teenage computer hackers who extorted money from corporations and a conference for drunk and angry young conservatives that boasted orgies and drug fests. The only problem was the stories were almost all fabricated.

In fact, once the *New Republic's* editorial staff finally made their way through an investigation and fact-checking of all of Glass' 41 bylines for the magazine, they discovered that 27 of his pieces contained fabrications. The staff noted that in a few cases, entire stories were invented.

Figure 5. Stephen Glass photo used in 1998 *Vanity Fair* profile. Photo by F/Stop Studios.

Glass, of course, is not the only writer to be branded as a fabulist or a plagiarist. Former *New York Times* reporter Jayson Blair and columnist Maureen Dowd have both been accused of plagiarism, and *A Million Little Pieces* author James Frey has also been accused of being a fabulist. Although there will always be people who will complete this disturbing pattern, the resulting public humiliation and guilt should be enough of a motivator to remind most of us of how important it is to credit the ideas of others and to stick to the truth.

Read more about Stephen Glass:

From *Vanity Fair,* **"Shattered Glass"** *http://www.vanityfair.com/magazine/1998/09/bissinger199809.*

Exercise: Case Study

Read "Shattered Glass." What do you think Stephen Glass' reasons were for fabricating his stories? Why not just find genuine stories to write about?

Think carefully about the pitfalls associated with plagiarism. What steps can you take when writing your next paper to keep yourself from even accidentally plagiarizing?

> Know which style of documentation you need to utilize.

Most professors will tell you clearly what they're looking for, so pay attention, and if you're not sure, ask. Most humanities classes, for example, use MLA style, and most social sciences use APA. The rules for these methods of documentation are clearly outlined in numerous books and on numerous websites, so the answers you might be looking for are readily available.

STEP FOUR—REVISE: HOW DO I MAKE IT BETTER?

Your paper is drafted, so it's ready to turn in, right? Not so fast—**revising and editing** are both fruitful and necessary, and you will be well served to follow at least a few steps before turning your final draft in to your professor. In fact, many students find that their best writing happens during the revision process. Give yourself enough time to go through your paper at least once before you turn it in—you'll be glad you did.

> Be your own fact-checker.

This is a simple step but incredibly important. Check for the following:

- Spelling, grammar, and punctuation errors.
- The spelling of names in particular.
- The accuracy of source page numbers.
- The accuracy of quotes.

> Make sure your use of source material is balanced.

You don't want to turn in a paper that's heavily dominated with sources in one area and then devoid of sources in other areas. You want those sources to be used effectively and to be distributed relatively evenly so that your claims are supported equally by material. Remember—the use of sources is less about the number than it is about how effectively and artfully they are incorporated.

> Polish your integration of sources.

In other words, make sure that when you integrate your source material using accurate and effective punctuation:

- Use ellipses to shorten a quote.
- Use parentheses for in-text citations and to indicate an error in an original quote (for example, "sic" to indicate incorrect spelling).
- Use brackets to help clarify or explain a quote.
- Alter your grammar so that it matches the grammar in your paper.

NOTES

[1] "Dwayne 'The Rock' Johnson: Bio," *WWE,* http://www.wwe.com/superstars/the-rock.

Research

Recommended for WRD 110/112

Chapter 9

Chapter 9   Research

When I first moved to Kentucky, I found myself driving to Versailles in order to visit a restaurant I had heard about. The drive was lovely and relaxing, but there wasn't much to see along the way. Suddenly, in the middle of nowhere was a giant castle that looked like it belonged in a European countryside.

Figure 1. What is this castle doing in the middle of Kentucky?[1] Image by Christina Ramey. Licensed under a Creative Commons Attribution-Share Alike 2.0 Generic license. *https://flic.kr/p/5BBNGe*.

"Did you see *that*?" I asked my husband.

"I have no idea," he said. "What the heck *is* that thing?"

When we arrived at the restaurant, I immediately pulled out my iPhone and did a quick online search to try and figure out what a giant castle was doing in the middle of Kentucky. I chose some keywords that I thought might get me the results I wanted.

I typed in "*castle + Versailles + Kentucky.*" The first several links that came up were links to sites about something called "CastlePost" and a *Wikipedia* entry for "Martin Castle."

Figure 2. What your Google search might look like if you searched for information about Kentucky's mystery castle.[2]

202   Town Branch Writing Collection

I clicked on the Wikipedia entry and discovered that this was the strange site I'd seen. According to the Martin Castle Wikipedia page, the castle was built in 1969 in Versailles, Kentucky. A local contractor named Rex Martin built the castle after returning from a trip to Europe, where he was smitten with the castles dotting the European landscape. Unfortunately, Rex Martin and his wife divorced in the 1970s, and the castle was left unfinished. It still sits, relatively unused, on the roadside in Versailles, Kentucky.[3]

Figure 3. What you might see if you search Wikipedia for "Martin Castle."[4]

The entry mentioned that the current owner has been criticized by locals for failing to devote much attention to the landscaping on the sprawling property. My husband and I found ourselves continuing to talk about the castle and the history we had just learned.

I asked, "What do you think people around here think about the castle?"

"I don't know," he said. "Look it up."

But how could I look up public opinion easily? My previous search didn't seem to turn up lots of details about local opinions on this huge piece of architecture. Maybe the local newspaper has a story on the castle. I knew that local papers not only have archives of stories online, but they often archive reader responses to online stories.

I went to the *Lexington Herald-Leader's* website at Kentucky.com, and I immediately found a story about Woodford county approving CastlePost to open as a restaurant. There were fourteen reader comments to the story.[5]

Figure 4. Some of the comments posted on the news story about CastlePost's approval as a restaurant.[6]

Some people thought the restaurant was a good idea, but other comments showed that people in the area weren't too happy about the castle at all. One reader even called the castle a "land scar" instead of a "landmark."

As my husband and I finished our sandwiches, we talked about how funny it was that we had learned such an interesting—and strange—piece of local history just by doing a little research during lunch.

HOW DO YOU START RESEARCH?

Although my castle search might not seem like the kind of research you do in school, it really is very similar. Research isn't always complicated or hard. In fact, we do research every day without really knowing that we're doing it! Whenever I see or hear something strange, I tend to immediately reach for a computer or book so that I can look up more information about it. Think of the ways in which you already act as a researcher:

A researcher starts with some kind of question or observation:

- *That's strange! What is that?*
- *Why isn't my car starting?*
- *How do I make peanut butter fudge?*
- *Why did World War I start?*
- *Have there ever been any unmarried U.S. Presidents?*
- *Is organic food really healthier for you?*

A researcher then goes searching for some kind of answer or clue:

- Doing online searches.
- Asking experts or people who might know an answer.
- Reading books.
- Doing experiments and trying out various possibilities.
- Observing and noticing other clues.

Think of how many different questions you've researched in the past week. Did you do a search for any recipes or for price comparisons on something you want to buy? Have you asked any friends about their background knowledge of a topic? Have you called your parents to ask them any questions? All of this is *research!*

Exercise: Strange Happenings

Think of the last *strange* thing you saw or heard. Would you like to know more about it (like how it started, who made it, etc.)? Do a quick online search to get the background story. You can use my castle search as an example. When you finish, share what you discovered with the class.

Research is the act of looking for information, stories, facts, evidence, histories, or details that help to answer a question or solve some kind of problem.

DIFFERENT KINDS OF RESEARCH: PRIMARY VERSUS SECONDARY

Earlier, we defined research as the act of looking for information, stories, facts, evidence, histories, or details that help to answer a question or solve some kind of problem. This definition shouldn't sound too complex since research is something we all do every day. Broadly speaking, there are two different kinds of research: **primary research** and **secondary research.**

Primary research is information that you gather from *firsthand accounts*. You take words, quotes, observations, histories, or facts directly from the actors involved in the situation. Primary research includes interviews, ethnographies, observations, archival documents, oral histories, surveys, etc.

Secondary research is information that has been gathered firsthand by someone else and then reported in an essay, article, book, or other publication. Secondary research includes newspaper articles, academic journal articles or essays, reports of studies or surveys, media reports, etc.

In academic situations, both primary and secondary forms of research are important. You will find that you need to do both at different times.

Exercise: Song Lyrics

Sometimes song lyrics are fun to research. Do a quick search and listen to the following songs. Each of these songs tells a story about events that really happened, even though you might not know about them. After listening to the song online and/or reading the lyrics, do some online searches with a partner and try to uncover the background stories.

- "Hurricane"
- "Ohio"
- "Sunday Bloody Sunday"
- "Biko"
- "Strange Fruit"

Doing Primary Research

Authors use primary research when their question or problem would most benefit from direct evidence gathered from **primary sources.** Authors might visit archives or somehow gather direct quotes from people who are involved in the situation under discussion. They might also survey a small number of people who are part of the population being studied. When you seek firsthand accounts about your subject, you might consider the following primary research strategies.

Sometimes primary research involves what is called "fieldwork." **Fieldwork** may sound like a very technical or complicated activity, but it's actually quite enjoyable. In fact, you probably do some kind of fieldwork on a regular basis, though you might not think of it in these terms. Any time you take a picture of something strange, cool, weird, or amazing, you are doing a kind of fieldwork.

Some of us like to share these photos online with friends. When we share these photos, we're basically saying, *"Hey. Here's something cool I noticed."* Your friends might ask questions about it or they might comment on it. This conversation might lead you to look up more information or learn something new.

Here are two photos I shared online with friends. The first photo is a hand-painted sign I noticed stapled to a telephone pole in downtown Lexington. On a piece of notebook paper were the red painted words, "TEAR THE WHOLE THING DOWN." What could this mean? Tear *what* down? Who wrote this and why? I shared the image on my Facebook page, and some friends replied that they had seen similar messages around Lexington. Together, we began to speculate on where the messages were coming from and whether or not they were a joke. I decided to keep my eye out for similar messages downtown.

Another photo I shared online was much less mysterious, but still really interesting to me. As I walked across campus one day, I suddenly noticed blue doors sitting in the middle of the sidewalk. I shared them online and many friends described their experience of discovering the doors.

The doors remained on campus for about a week, and one day I decided to sit and watch how people interacted with the doors. How many people would try to walk through them? How many people would take pictures of them? How many people would walk right past them without even giving them a glance? I sat outside with my lunch and watched the doors for about an hour. During that time, a few people took pictures and stopped to look at them. But many more people walked right by them without stopping.

I may have been killing some time during my lunch break, but I was also doing fieldwork. I started with an observation *("Hey! Look at this door in the middle of the sidewalk!"),* and then I formed a question from this observation *("Does anyone else find this door interesting enough to stop and look?").* I did a little bit of observation in order to help answer this question. I was doing research.

When doing fieldwork, you can use **observations, surveys,** or **interviews** to help answer your question. But the first step is usually noticing something interesting enough to grab your attention.

Exercise: Observations

Go for a thirty-minute stroll outside. If you have a phone or device that can take digital pictures, take that with you. Take images of anything that you find strange, curious, funny, weird, cool, interesting, fascinating, etc. Don't stop to comment on them right now. Just collect as many images (or written descriptions) of interesting things that you can find.

When you get back from your stroll, pick one or two of your favorite. For ten minutes, write as many questions as you can think of about these images. What do you want to know about them? What do they make you curious about? (Don't edit anything just yet. Write *everything* down for now.) After you finish, pick out the question that is most interesting to you. Would this make a good research question?

Using Observations

Observation can be a powerful form of research. Sociologists and anthropologists have long used observations as a central part of their studies. Sometimes the researcher will interact with the community or place being studied. For example, a researcher studying first-year high school teachers might sit in on a class being taught by a first-year high school teacher. Observations can also happen online. When I wanted to study how people argue about current events online, I observed several Facebook and online groups to see how participants argued back and forth.

Before observing a specific group, however, be sure that you have permission from the individuals you are studying. *This is essential if you are participating in a group or event that involves people sharing personal information of any kind.* For example, if you want to observe a support group for teenage mothers, you would need to ask for permission in advance. Make clear why you are asking to observe, what your project includes, and how the research will be used. *(See below for model permission forms.)*

If you observe a public space (like I did when I was sitting on campus, watching people walk past the blue doors), then you do not need to gain permission. For example, let's say you are interested in observing whether people at the mall tend to text on their phones even when they are physically with other people. You might sit at the mall for an hour or two in order to observe people's behaviors with their cell phones. This would not call for permission from those individuals.

Creating Surveys

You might also find **surveys** are a good way to help you discover more information about your topic. Before you decide to do a survey, you should ask yourself the following questions:

- Is there any other way of finding credible sources who might have done similar research?
- Is the audience I'm surveying likely to give me a unique perspective or insight into this topic?
- Am I asking the right people?

If I am interested in finding out whether or not Kentucky's horse racing industry is growing or shrinking, I probably wouldn't find it very helpful to survey a group of 100 random UK students. On the other hand, I could survey a group of people who participate in the horse racing industry to get a unique perspective on the topic.

You should also consider whether or not you are asking questions about **opinions,** questions about **behaviors,** or questions about **demographic information.**

- Questions about **opinion** ask about people's perspectives and opinions on certain topics. This might help you to better understand what a group thinks about your topic, but remember that the responses might not be factually correct. For example, if you survey 100 UK students to ask whether they think a Caesar salad has more or less calories than a hamburger, 80% might say that they believe that a Caesar salad has fewer calories than a hamburger. But (depending on the salad), this is not always the case! Caesar salads can easily have more calories than a Big Mac®!
- Questions about **behavior** ask about daily routines and habits. If you want to know how many hours of sleep UK students get per night, you can give out a survey asking people to tell you their sleep average.
- Questions about **demographic information** asks background details about individuals: age, gender, number of siblings, birthplace, etc.

In order to create strong survey questions, keep in mind the differences between **open-ended** and **closed-ended questions. Open-ended questions** are worded so that respondents actually have to *explain* their answers. These kinds of questions are best on surveys where you want the responses to offer you a narrative. **Closed-ended questions** are worded so that respondents can simply offer you a "yes" or a "no," or one-word reply.

Conducting Interviews

You can interview people directly involved with your topic, or you can interview people who may have some kind of important knowledge. Interviews are great ways of finding information from firsthand accounts. In order to have the most useful and productive interview experience, ask yourself the following questions:

Does My Topic Really Call for an Interview?

Not all topics are likely to benefit from an interview. Will interviewing a particular person give you information that you could not otherwise find? For example, if I want to know the history of the University of Kentucky, I probably do not really need to interview one of my professors. It is more likely that I can find relevant information in University-related sources, including in the archives and in publications. On the other hand, if I want to know what it is like to be a filmmaker living in Kentucky, I could probably learn a lot by talking with someone who makes films in Lexington.

How Can I Find the Right Expert?

You are surrounded by knowledgeable experts on your college campus. But how do you know the best person to interview? You will want to do some research in advance to see if a particular person has the background or expertise to answer your questions. Has he/she written about this topic? Does he/she work in a field that is relevant to your topic? Does he/she have firsthand experience or knowledge about your topic?

How Do I Ask for an Interview?

Let's say you have identified the perfect expert for interviewing purposes. Now comes the tricky part: asking for an interview. Keep in mind that the interviewee is doing you a favor by taking time to sit for an interview. You will need to approach the interview request with a very coherent phone call, email, or visit. Make sure you clearly explain who you are, why you are contacting him/her, and what you are requesting. You will also need to explain why you think they would be particularly ideal for this interview. State your available days and times, and then ask if you could arrange a time (according to his/her own schedule) to meet. See the example email below:

> *Dear Dr. Sykes:*
>
> *My name is Joel Tyler and I am a student at the University of Kentucky. I am currently researching the subject of amateur beekeeping in Lexington, and I was given your name as someone who is interested in beekeeping. I know your time is valuable, but I wonder if you would allow me to interview you about your hobby. Over the next two weeks, I am available every afternoon after 3:00. The interview should only take approximately 20–30 minutes, and I would be willing to meet you wherever is most convenient. If you have any questions, or if you would be willing to be interviewed, please contact me at joel.tyler27@uky.edu.*
>
> *I appreciate your time,*
>
> *Joel*

Chapter 9   Research

How Do I Interview Well?

A good interview starts with the interviewer's questions. Some of the worst interviews are ones where the interviewee answers closed-ended questions: "Yes." "No." "Maybe." A little boring, right? When interview questions are too closed-ended, the person being interviewed does not have a chance to elaborate or expand on his/her stories or ideas. By making the questions more open-ended, you invite the interviewee to share interesting, vivid, and memorable details with you.

Consider the following two interviews I conducted with former small business owners who lost their businesses. What are the differences between the two kinds of questions?

CONVERSATION 1

Jenny: *I wanted to talk with you today about your experience with owning a small business. How long did you own your business?*

Amy: *Two years.*

Jenny: *And did you go out of business for financial reasons?*

Amy: *Yes.*

Jenny: *Was it hard on your family when you had to close?*

Amy: *Yes. Very hard.*

Jenny: *How long ago was that?*

Amy: *About five years ago.*

Jenny: *Do you think you'll ever go into business again?*

Amy: *Hmm. I'm really not sure. I don't know.*

CONVERSATION 2

Jenny: *I wanted to talk with you today about your experience with owning a small business. How long did you own your business?*

Rick: *Almost five years.*

Jenny: *Can you describe the events that led to your business closing?*

Rick: *We had been struggling to pay our bills for about a year. My wife and I had to either take out additional loans, or just close the business. We stayed open for as long as we could, and then we just finally decided to give in.*

Jenny: *Do you remember the day you actually closed the business? What happened?*

Rick: *Oh sure. It wasn't really all that dramatic. We printed up a sign to hang on the door that said we were closed. We still had to go back and pack up, clean. It was pretty unexciting, except that it felt like we had just blown it.*

Jenny: *How did that struggle and the closing affect your family life?*

Rick: *There was definitely a lot of tension at home. We argued a lot because we were both stressed out, and I think we both sort of went through a mild depression when the doors closed.*

Jenny: *Can you think of one specific example of how you and your wife handled that stress differently or similarly?*

Rick: *Well, I found myself really unable to go out with friends. It was harder and harder for me to talk with people because the stress was overwhelming. I think my wife found herself wanting to talk about her stress with me, but I just didn't want to.*

My interview with Rick provided much more details and insight into his story. Amy's story, however, remains a little unclear. I did not give her an opportunity to expand on her answers. When I interviewed Rick, I tried to keep in mind some good rules of interviewing:

- **Ask open-ended questions that go beyond one-word answers.**
- **Frame your questions by asking for an example.** ("Can you think of one specific example of how you and your wife handled that stress differently or similarly?")
- **Try to ask people to describe memories of events or situations.** This helps people provide you with interesting stories and narratives that are filled with useful information. ("Do you remember the day you actually closed the business? What happened?")
- **Follow up on responses by asking for examples.** When you get one-word responses, try asking your interviewee for a specific example of what they're describing.

Using Archives

Another good way to find primary research is to visit the archives. If you've never been to library archives, this idea might sound a little intimidating. However, archives (sometimes called *special collections* in the library) are extremely fascinating. Universities and historical societies keep historical documents and artifacts in their archives as a way to preserve the historical record about various people, places, events, and topics. **Archives** keep things like letters, original photographs, rare books, diaries, clothing, memorabilia, business records, and all sorts of other unique materials that help give researchers some insight into specific topics.

The archives at the University of Kentucky have collections of memorabilia and documents relating to a wide variety of topics, including the histories of coal mining, UK athletics, segregation in Kentucky, the bourbon industry, tobacco and hemp growing, Kentucky politics, and many, many other topics.

Before you physically step foot into any archive, it is a good idea to first visit the archive's website. Many special collections are available for viewing online, which might help to give you some additional ideas about what you want to research. For example, the **Kentucky Digital Library** *(http://kdl.kyvl.org)* is a searchable website full of historic newspapers, images, books, and oral histories.

Let's say that you were interested in researching the history of segregation in Kentucky. If you go to the Kentucky Digital Library site and type in the term "segregation," you will find over 1,200 results that include historical photos of segregated hospitals, oral histories of African-Americans who lived in Kentucky during the era of segregation, UK yearbook pages that address the issue of racial segregation, newspaper articles, and many other fascinating sources that give some perspective on the history of segregation in Kentucky. Of course, you don't need to stop there! You may contact special collections librarians directly in order to ask for help finding materials that relate to your specific topic.

Exercise: Using the Archives

Go to the **Kentucky Digital Library** *(http://kdl.kyvl.org)* right now and type "Buell Armory." What results do you see? Look to the left and identify what types of materials are available for viewing: photographs, postcards, and what else? Notice the different publication dates of the available materials. Click to view the oldest available image. What do you notice about the UK campus? What is interesting to you about this image? Click on the photo from 1918. Read the description and describe what is happening in this image.

Most students enjoy doing archival research because it's a bit like opening up a time capsule. It can be fun to find old photographs, read personal diaries from centuries ago, or even see advertisements from bygone eras. More than just a fun experience, archival discoveries can also tell us something about our history.

Take a look at these two historical advertisements, for example. What do you find interesting about them? What kinds of questions do they leave you with?

Figure 5. What kinds of questions does this historical ad for cigarettes leave you with?[7]

Figure 6. What is interesting/different about this historical ad for Wrigley's?[8]

A Word about Ethical Primary Research

Doing primary research—interviews, observations, surveys, fieldwork, archival research—is lots of fun. When you are working with other people, however, be sure to approach them in an ethical and respectful manner. Be sure to recognize that your interviewees are sharing something important with you.

- Always ask for permission before quoting an interviewee in your text. Make sure that he/she knows who will see this project and how his/her name or identifying information will be used. Before beginning to work with any interview subjects, please ask him/her to complete a permission form, **like this one from the Nunn Center for Oral History at UK** (https://libraries.uky.edu/sites/default/files/2022-08/372_NunnCenter-Release-Master-2018_v2-2.pdf).
- If you are dealing with very sensitive topics or groups that may need an extra level of protection (e.g., children, elderly people, trauma survivors, etc.), please talk with your instructor about the best ways of working ethically with them.
- Always be honest and respectful in your observations. Remember that you probably wouldn't like someone to stand over your shoulder and suddenly start making notes on what you're doing. Conduct your research in a way that does not make anyone feel like a "lab rat."

Student Writing Example: "The Men Behind the Dust" by Sheldon Parrott

University of Kentucky undergraduate student Sheldon Parrott wrote "The Men Behind the Dust" for his WRD course. This ethnographic essay, which examines the lives of coal miners in Harlan County, Kentucky, draws upon primary research methods, including interviews, pictures, and observation. As you read Parrott's essay, identify the different kinds of research he uses. How does the primary research enhance your overall experience as a reader? Do the interviews and pictures give you a richer sense of the details?

Doing Secondary Research

Authors use **secondary research** when their question or problem would benefit from the findings and conclusions gathered by experts, journalists, or others who have collected and analyzed research on the topic. Authors find credible sources that summarize and describe the primary research that someone else has done. Some of the most common forms of secondary research include the following:

- **Academic journal articles:** Academic journals are places where academic scholars share the results of their studies and their research. These are not "popular" journals, but are written for an audience of fellow academics and researchers interested in that scholarly field. Academic journals can be helpful to you because they often share results of important research. However, because academic journal articles are written for professional academics who are already in those fields, these articles are usually more technical and detailed than a popular magazine article.

  You can find academic journals in particular fields through the library's online databases. Several of the most popular databases are easy to find from the main UK Library homepage. Each of these databases can be used to search for a huge number of journal essays. Each database hosts slightly different journals, so you may want to search in a few of them to find what interests you:

  - Academic Search Premier
  - EBSCOhost
  - JSTOR
  - LexisNexis Academic

- **Newspaper and magazine articles:** Newspapers and magazine articles can also be useful sources of information for a number of reasons. Not only do newspapers and magazines report current events, but many of them offer argumentative journalistic pieces that offer perspective on various issues. For example, the editorial pages of the *New York Times* have featured essays written by famous politicians, celebrities, and even past U.S. Presidents.

- **Books and other media:** Certain topics may lead you to find books and other media (like documentaries) that address some of your questions. Be sure to pay close attention to the author and the time of publication. If the book (or documentary) is not new, have there been later developments on this topic that you should consider?

Chapter 9   Research

> ### Exercise: Using Primary and Secondary Research
>
> Together with a partner or group, come up with one question or problem you would like to explore. This can be a big issue (like whether or not the University of Kentucky can afford to lower tuition for students) or a small issue (like what the best cheap restaurant is close to campus). Come up with two primary sources and two secondary sources that might help you to answer this question.
>
> Which of these sources might help to answer your question most effectively?

Sites for Secondary Research

Libraries

Like all research universities, the University of Kentucky contains a number of libraries, archives, and collections, both general and particular to disciplines and professions. Information about them is readily available: on the Internet, you can follow a link to Libraries from the UK home page (head to the Site Index, look under "L"), or go straight to **the Libraries homepage** *(http://libraries.uky.edu)*, and surf to the peripheries of collections here and elsewhere.

We needn't duplicate information that's so readily accessible elsewhere. Rather, we'll take a verbal tour of libraries most likely to be of use to you in your writing courses, giving impressions of their character and possibilities—since the very act of embarking on secondary research, of wading into the stacks, is a powerful form of direct experience, if you keep your eyes open.

The big one, clearly, is the **William T. Young Library.** It looms up in its own broad lawn like a giant horse stable, dwarfing the adjoining pasture. If you're new to UK, you're advised to wander in there right away. You'll see that the stable motif is no accident: consider the tapestry mural of the philanthropist Young stroking his horse's nose, located to the right of the long, curving circulation desk. Then look up toward the faraway ceiling, the glassy cupola above, cathedral-like. If the configuration of a stable were elevated to the condition of a shrine, in some religion indigenous to the Bluegrass state, this library could serve as its St. Peter's.

What's enshrined here is not thoroughbred, but rather the thoroughness of scholarship, which seeks to preserve everything. With the advent of electronic archiving devices—first microfilm, now digital—that take up next to no space, this impulse grows less physically obvious. But in a big library like this one, it's still imposing. Take a stroll through the stacks of periodicals, which fill the third floor. This is *time travel,* the closest you'll get. Not only do you have the records, the information and reflections of decades before you, you have the very objects these past people handled. Find an old magazine of news, entertainment, popular science, design, something from when your grandparents were young or before; pull out a bound volume, sit on the floor, and leaf through it. These words and images were on coffee tables, in train stations, before other eyes, on vanished tongues. It's another world—the roots of yours.

You can rest assured that the moving stacks on their little trolley tracks will not crush you as you browse: they are fitted with electronic eyes and will discern the intrusion of your form. Once you figure out what you're after, you'll press the lit arrow buttons and shift those stacks with purpose.

If you want to take notes and copy passages in the stacks, a laptop computer may come in handy. You can check one out at AV Services on the basement level. Show a valid UK photo ID and the machine is yours for four hours, renewable if nobody's waiting for one (no reservations; first come, first served). Return it on time, as the late fee is steep, more than ten dollars an hour.

While you're in the Young Library, head down to the basement and locate **the Hub,** which houses the **Writing Center.** It's not easy to find, tucked in one of the classrooms on the side (**B-108B**), but there are signs to direct you, and once you reach it, it's a pleasant space, with friendly, accomplished writing consultants awaiting you there, smiling and with red pencils poised. It's worth seeking out.

Though UK's more specialized libraries (at the Law School, the Medical School, the College of Agriculture, the Equine Research Center) aren't the sort most undergraduates will frequent, a few warrant special mention, since their holdings may pertain to research your writing course requires or invites, and they are interesting places to visit in themselves:

- The **Fine Arts Library,** closer than the Young to the campus center, is a handsome, peaceful two-level facility holding art and photography books and collections, with music and movies as well. It's a good place to study since it's not crowded, and when you're tired of reading, you can look at the pictures.
- The **Design Library** in Pence Hall houses collections on architecture, interior design, and historic preservation. As befits its subject, it's a visually arresting space: Art Deco in style with wood and wrought iron features. Since some writing instructors favor assignments that call for exploring constructed environments, the Design Library may hold information that will come in handy.

◎ The **Margaret I. King Library** was UK's main library until the Young Library opened. In the large room at its east entrance across from the Fine Arts Library, there are interesting, mildly peculiar exhibits pertaining to UK and Kentucky history—worth a look with notebook in hand. At a desk you'll see the gatekeeper to the Special Collections, UK's repository for rare, antiquated, and collection-specific holdings, a place you can't just walk into but must have good reason to access. Though most undergraduates won't have such reason, you never can tell; your interests may develop in directions that lead you to the Special Collections, and you have as much right to these holdings as anyone.

Since written texts are not all that researchers look into or libraries hold, you should know about the **UK Audio-Visual Archives,** located in the William T. Young Library, basement level. It's described on the Library website as "one of the largest university-based collections of archival film, video, and audio recordings in the United States,"[9] containing local TV and radio programming, Kentucky-related independent films, and 400,000 still photos, among other holdings.

For visual resources, you can also visit the **UK Art Museum,** our primary site for art and photography archives. The Art Museum, of course, has a sizable exhibit space in the Singletary Center, with special and continuing exhibits; plus it has significant collections of archival materials that can be surveyed online and examined by request. **Its website** *(http://finearts.uky.edu/art-museum)* can brief you on these materials: Click on Collections. A few digital images are available there, too—images of major works from the gallery, plus photos from the Works Projects Administration.

Electronic Archives

Electronic resources for research are proliferating—a moving target. Our list is suggestive, not exhaustive. We'll start with archives linked to UK and Kentucky, then fan out.

Many instructors give assignments that ask students to focus on home places or sites in local communities. A rich electronic archive for such work is the **Kentucky Digital Library,** which UK manages on behalf of libraries, archives, museums, and historical societies across the state. You can reach its website at *kdl.kyvl.org,* or follow a link from the **UK Libraries home page** *(http://libraries.uky.edu/).* At this site, you'll find links to materials under eight categories: books, newspapers, journals, manuscripts, maps, oral histories, images, and finding aids. Most are comprised of old documents that have been scanned and reproduced online: articles, narratives, letters, diaries, scrapbooks, and the like, plus whole books and newspapers.

Oral histories are interviews with people conducted to preserve their memories and experience of the past, then transcribed and put online—a powerful, accessible form of primary research that students can readily use and also contribute to through their own interviews of family and community members (more on this below).

Images are photos, illustrations, and such, scanned and posted. These materials are organized and described so they can be located throughout the archives.

Finding aids are designed to be keyed to information of various sorts, from overviews of whole collections, to biographical information on collectors, down through descriptions of individual items. The holdings are extensive and growing—more than a thousand oral histories, 80,000 images, and hundreds of thousands of book and newspaper pages—yet easy to maneuver through and access, with images from searches delivered ten thumbnails at a time. They're fascinating to use, like rummaging through boxes in an attic.

The Kentucky collection is the tip of a growing iceberg of digital resources available through UK. Here's the simplest way to get to troves of this material:

1. Go the UK website's Site Index.
2. Click on the letter "A."
3. Scroll down to "Archives," and click on it.

From the Archives site, you can go in different directions. Of the four choices before you, two are likely of most interest.

The topmost link is the **UK Audio-Visual Archives,** the web extension of the Young Library archive mentioned above. Click on that link, then on "Collections" at the top of the screen, and *voilà!* An enormous list of collections appears, most with online images to peruse. A variety of these can be traced out to nearly any locale and period in the Commonwealth. It's worth half-an-hour of your time just to browse about and get a sense of what's there.

Bottommost of the hyperlink choices is "University Archives and Records Program." Click on this, then on **University Archives,** then on "Archival Collections/Holdings." What you'll come upon are voluminous digital materials regarding UK itself: its history, buildings, past presidents and faculty and such. Again, the best way to find out what's there is to explore the site.

The Nollau F Series Photographs are there, for instance: a remarkable batch of digitized photos showing buildings, people, features, and artifacts from UK, Lexington, and elsewhere, from the first half of the twentieth century—the work of an engineering professor who doubled as UK's first quasi-official photographer.

The Archives website links to the **UK Libraries Oral History Project,** too, through a link to the Charles T. Wethington, Jr. Alumni/Faculty Oral History Collection, named after Lee Todd's predecessor as UK President. There's a link to the Kentucky Digital Library there, and much, much more (check out the photo of the 1916 UK football team—all with concussions, probably—in the Margaret Ingels Collection).

Though you aren't able to copy and paste these images from your screen, it's simple to request copies of images you might use in a project—the procedures are set forth right there. These materials are there for researchers—which for the time being, at least, is what you are.

Beyond archives particular to the University and region, the **UK Libraries home page** provides links to numerous research sources, including these key ones:

- **InfoKat:** The main UK library catalog and search engine.
- **LexisNexis:** The premier database for legal, news, public records, and business information.
- The full-text **E-Journals Database:** Containing entire articles from a range of scholarly journals.
- **EBSCOhost:** A search engine for such journals, plus guides on these and a host of other databases, research tools, and search engines. Some, like LexisNexis, are available by institutional subscription only, thus accessible only from campus computers or through proxy servers for qualified off-campus users. Such powerful archival resources are expensive to subscribe to: it's a privilege of University life to have access at your fingertips.

Among the services available from the UK Libraries home page is **Ask-a-Librarian**—a link off of the Help section of the home page. There's a "chat" function open during business hours on weekdays, with a real librarian fielding instant-message questions; there are provisions for emailing or phoning in questions as well.

Linked to the Library website (just type it into their search line) you'll find **ARTstor** (http://www.artstor.org), a site run by the Mellon Foundation to provide art images and information for noncommercial, scholarly, and educational use. The site holds some 700,000 images at present, along with tools to help users locate and make use of them. Like LexisNexis and other subscription databases, ARTstor is most readily accessed through campus computers, though instructions are available for proxy server access by UK faculty, students, and staff off campus. This site is a remarkable trove of images, not just fine art but design, illustration, decoration of all sorts, even tattoo. It's a pleasure to surf, and its potential extends well beyond art history, to cultural phenomena of all sorts—a profusion of material for assignments in classes focusing on close readings of popular culture.

Here's a Sampling of E-Archives Beyond the UK Library's Links

◎ **The Library of Congress website** *(http://www.loc.gov)* contains a remarkable digital archive called **American Memory,** with texts, images, audio, and video of cultural artifacts in all sorts of areas. It lists these topics, with numerous links for each: advertising; African-American history; architecture, landscape; cities, towns; culture, folklife; environment, conservation; government, law; immigration, American expansion; literature; maps; Native American history; performing arts, music; presidents; religion; sports, recreation; technology, industry; war, military; women's history. It's all readily searchable and browsable—a national digital treasure.

◎ If you're working on an assignment about a place, you might go to **ePodunk** *(https://web.archive.org/web/20191202130708/http://epodunk.com/),* a website devoted, it says, to "the power of place."[10] It has information, maps, and links to further sites on some 46,000 communities across the United States, detailing parks, historic sites, museums, schools, cemeteries, and other features there and nearby. "Podunk" has long been a slang term for a generic tiny, obscure town; but there really is a Podunk, in upstate New York, and ePodunk's founders lived nearby, having retreated there from their former lives as journalists in order to create this site. It's a compendious labor of love, worth surveying.

◎ You may be enrolled in a class that takes citizenship and democracy as themes for exploration and research. A stimulating electronic source for such themes is **OpenDemocracy.net** *(https://opendemocracy.net),* described as "an online global magazine of politics and culture."[11] While this site is progressive in outlook (since democracy, after all, remains a progressive ideal), it is not partisan or doctrinaire but seeks, rather, to "publish clarifying debates which help people make up their own minds."[12] And it is indeed restlessly global in scope, providing wider, more varied coverage and perspectives on world affairs than we are accustomed to find in our news media. More than 1,500 articles are indexed at this site, representing writing on a range of themes (these categories are listed: arts and cultures; conflicts; democracy and power; ecology and place; women and power; faith and ideas; globalization; media and the net; people), from voices across the world, both celebrated and obscure. These voices may inform your own; you might even seek to join them, publishing your views on this site or others like it.

- A broadly useful electronic research source is **the Brookings Institution** *(http://www.brookings.edu)* website. The Brookings Institute is one of the best-known, most prestigious public affairs research institutes in the United States. The plethora of subject areas listed on its Research page indicates their great range of interests: business; cities and suburbs; defense; economics; education; environment and energy; governance; politics; science and technology; social policy. There are all sorts of leads for assignments like those common to writing classes. Some of our country's best minds, working on our most pressing issues, can be tapped in an instant here.

- Another prestigious research institute, conservative in outlook, is **the Hoover Institution** *(http://www.hoover.org)*, located at Stanford University. Its website contains Library and Archives links useful for various projects. Other valuable information can be located through the site's Publications and Multimedia links. Publications include full texts of books and journals the Institution publishes. Multimedia includes access to *Uncommon Knowledge,* a weekly program of public policy discussion broadcast until 2005 on public television and since then as a webcast. The site offers full transcripts, streaming video, and downloadable MP3 files.

DOING ONLINE RESEARCH: WHY *WIKIPEDIA* IS NOT BAD FOR YOU

Increasingly, we tend to use online resources in our research process. Even professional writers and academic scholars use the Internet as part of their very serious research. Like anything else, the trick to using online sources is to use them *wisely*.

Wikipedia

I probably visit *Wikipedia* at least once a week. Maybe I am curious whether a celebrity is dead or alive. Or maybe I want to know everything I can about a certain holiday that is celebrated in another country. Or maybe I am trying to remember what year the first desktop computer was advertised. I have found answers to all of these questions on *Wikipedia*. I use it because I want quick answers to my questions.

Wikipedia is an ideal place to begin your research because the community of *Wikipedia* users regularly cite their sources of information. In fact, citation is one of the community standards that *Wikipedia* fans insist on. For this reason, you might begin by searching for a topic on *Wikipedia* and then scroll down to the bottom of the page to see what kinds of primary and secondary sources have been cited.

Let's say that you were interested in finding out the story of the great Kentucky meat shower of 1876. That's right. *The Kentucky meat shower.* According to *Wikipedia,* On March 3, 1876, chunks of raw meat fell from the sky for several minutes over Bath County, Kentucky.[13] Could it be that this strange event actually happened? Did Kentucky experience a meat storm over a century ago? If you scroll down to the bottom of the page, you will discover a footnote that sends you to a *New York Times* article from March 10, 1876 (**"Flesh Descending in a Shower: An Astounding Phenomenon in Kentucky—Fresh Meat Like Mutton or Venison Falling from a Clear Sky"** *[https://timesmachine.nytimes.com/timesmachine/1876/03/10/81687268.pdf]).*[14] If you find that *New York Times* article, you will learn that the meat was reported to be approximately the size of snowflakes and it reportedly tasted like mutton. It is certainly a strange story—and it makes for a great joke—but even in this strangest of *Wikipedia* entries, we can find reference to an important historical newspaper article. Even if the great Kentucky meat shower was a hoax, its 1876 nationwide reporting is worth noting.

Exercise: Using *Wikipedia* Wisely

Together with a group, choose a subject and look it up on *Wikipedia*. Your subject could be almost anything, but try to choose something that achieved some attention from a large number of people. (**Examples:** World Cup Soccer, emotions, home schooling, ADHD, President John F. Kennedy, etc.)

Read the *Wikipedia* entry and pay close attention to the footnotes. Choose one article that is cited in a footnote and try to find this source in the library's online databases.

Evaluating Online Sources for Credibility

Students often want to know how to evaluate the credibility of online sources. It's easy to Google your topic and find many kinds of websites that *seem* to address your topic. But are these websites the kind of sources that give you reliable information about your subject? If you have questions about whether or not online sources have strong *ethos,* ask yourself the following questions:

- What is the website or source of this material? Is this a website for a reputable organization? Is it a personal website? Look around the rest of the website and see if it contains questionable material.
- Is the source biased toward one particular opinion? Does the author or the website seem to have a particular goal in mind? If so, keep in mind that you are not getting an unbiased piece of information.
- Does the author have some kind of special qualifications or expertise on this subject? If the author is not listed, consider what it means that this piece is anonymous.
- When was this information published online? Is it outdated? Is newer information available?

VIDEO RESOURCES

Kevin Patterson on Doing "Research"

Kevin Patterson manages The Beer Trappe, a craft beer specialty shop in Lexington. Kevin is a native to eastern Kentucky, and he is an active participant in social media discussions of craft beer. As part of his job, Kevin uses rhetorical theory and writing in a number of ways. In this interview clip, he describes how he researches every day, as part of his job.

(https://vimeo.com/103939687)

NOTES

[1] Sarah Altendorf. "074 | 365 August 11, 2011," *Flickr,* Uploaded on August 11, 2011, https://www.flickr.com/photos/46732441@N06/6033957917/.

[2] "Castle + Versailles + Kentucky." *Google Search,* accessed June 27, 2014, https://www.google.com/webhp?tab=iw&ei=wPSxU4ffD8fOsATuiYG4Cg&ved=0CBcQ1S4#q=castle+versailles+kentucky&spell=1.

[3] "Martin Castle." *Wikipedia,* last modified March 24, 2014, http://en.wikipedia.org/wiki/Martin_Castle.

[4] Ibid.

[5] Greg Kocher. "Woodford Votes to Approve Restaurant at CastlePost." *Lexington Herald-Leader,* last modified January 8, 2013, http://www.kentucky.com/2013/01/08/2468960/woodford-fiscal-court-votes-to.html.

[6] Ibid.

[7] "Viceroy, Filter the Smoke." *Flickr,* last modified July 6, 2007, https://www.flickr.com/photos/behindthesmoke/6012416034/.

[8] Frank H. Jump. "Wrigley's Spearmint Gum—Vintage Print Ad 1911." Image, Uploaded March 27, 2012, http://www.fadingad.com/fadingadblog/2012/03/27/wrigleys-spearmint-gum-vintage-print-ad-1911-st-louis-fading-ad-1999/.

[9] "Audio-Visual Archives." *University of Kentucky Libraries,* last modified September 19, 2013, http://libraries.uky.edu/libpage.php?lweb_id=391&llib_id=13.

[10] "About ePodunk." *ePodunk,* last modified 2007, http://www.epodunk.com/about.html.

[11] *OpenDemocracy,* accessed June 27, 2013, http://opendemocracy.net.

[12] Ibid.

[13] "Kentucky Meat Shower." *Wikipedia,* last modified April 25, 2014, http://en.wikipedia.org/wiki/Kentucky_meat_shower.

[14] Ibid.

Citation

Recommended for WRD 110/111/112

Chapter 10

WHAT IS CITATION, ANYWAY?

One of the most difficult things to do when writing is to cite.

What is citation? **Citation** is the quotation or paraphrasing of others' words, images, or ideas. Typically, we indicate citations by putting other writers' ideas and words into quotations and by indicating the page and source of the citation.

But why do writers cite each other's work?

Often, citation is the result of research. We've read a lot for a project, and we want to incorporate some of what we've read into our writing. To do so, we need to cite.

Figure 1. The punctuation marks we typically associate with citation.

But why do that? There are a number of reasons to cite:

1. **To give credit where credit is due:** This is the most repeated reason for citing. A writer gives credit to the original source in order to avoid being accused of plagiarism.
2. **Ethos (credibility):** Citation allows a writer to show that he/she knows the information at hand well. In fact, he/she knows it so well, he/she shows the ideas by citing them from their original sources. The reader will then find the writer to be credible (i.e., the writer isn't making all of this information up).
3. **Context:** Citation shows context. By context, we mean the larger picture. No idea exists in a vacuum. Ideas are part of larger conversations. Context shows where and how the writing being read fits within larger conversations.
4. **Reference:** Citations might note well-known ideas or make allusions to known people, sayings, events, moments, texts, etc. These citations can anchor the idea or writing in a reference so that the reader understands the writing's focus better.

5. **Service:** When a reader comes across an interesting idea in a given piece of writing, he may want to know where that idea came from so that he can read it completely at its source. A citation (and the accompanying Works Cited page) allows the reader to track down that source and read the idea in its original form.

There are two basic premises for including citations that we can note here:

- **In-Text Citation:** Referring to the source in the writing.
- **Works Cited:** Listing the writings, interviews, videos, films, songs, etc. used in the text when citing.

> **In-Text Citation**
> Jay Kesan notes that even though many companies now routinely monitor employees through electronic means, "there may exist less intrusive safeguards for employers" (293).
>
> **Entry in the List of Works Cited**
> Kesan, Jay P. "Cyber-Working or Cyber-Shirking? A First Principles Examination of Electronic Privacy in the Workplace." *Florida Law Review 54*.2 (2002): 289–332. Print.

Figure 2. Here's an example of both an in-text citation (top) and a Works Cited citation (bottom).

USING SOURCES

With these reasons for citing in mind, we might ask: what does a citation look like? Where do we get citations from?

What it shouldn't look like is a quotation lifted from an online citation site, such as **Quotations Page** *(http://www.quotationspage.com)*.

And why not do this kind of citation? Because when you take a quotation from a quotation site, it is obvious that the quotation has been taken out of context, doesn't fit with the overall writing you are doing, has been jammed into your writing, and is not relevant. Instead of using a quotation site, cite from relevant material you have, material that shows you ideas, shapes your ideas, or performs any of the above items we've listed for citing. Cite from what you have:

> - Read (books, magazines, journals, archival material, newspapers, magazines, websites)
> - Seen (movies, videos, advertisements, posters)
> - Heard (songs, interviews, podcasts)

Use the source for material. A citation page is not a source. Otherwise, your ethos (number 2 above) can be damaged. Readers won't believe you since they will know you lifted from citation websites and that you are not familiar with the source you are using.

This is where the difficulty comes into play. Many writers, when citing for the first time, struggle to figure out how to incorporate the citations into the body of writing. On the one hand, we want to use citations for the reasons outlined here. On the other hand, we don't want our citations to be awkward or merely jammed next to one another in a given paragraph or body of writing.

When citing from sources, we can first think of a number of roles citations play, and then we can consider how to weave them together in order to write. That is, we don't want our citations to be an afterthought; we want them to be the writing itself.

Think of the weaving metaphor when citing in your writing. You are weaving, making fit, not jamming together quotations.

Figure 3. Wikipedia entries are woven together by citations. Sources are listed by footnotes.[1]

Some online sources you are familiar with do a good job with citation. They do so to prove where their ideas come from. Contributors to *Wikipedia*, for instance, footnote each source they use for information. The citations build the encyclopedic entry for viewers. Readers of the entries can follow up with the sources if they want to read more. If a source is not cited, other contributors often demand citation as evidence.

Some of the examples in this chapter come from published work, but they don't have quotation marks nor do they have page numbers of their sources. The reason is because of style. In the style section of this chapter, we'll discuss how style determines the ways you cite. In the meantime, keep in mind that the usage of quotation marks and the indication of page numbers are not consistent throughout publications. In fact, many mainstream publications do not show their citations. This is a problem, of course. See above regarding service. Without page numbers, how can we follow up on the writer's ideas?

In the university, we do use quotation marks, indicate page numbers and sources within the writing itself, and include a Works Cited. You will do this kind of citation not only in WRD 110 and WRD 111, but in many other courses you take at the University of Kentucky. In academic writing—the bulk of writing you will likely do at the University of Kentucky—you'll use quotation marks, indicate page numbers and sources within the body of your writing, and include a Works Cited.

Sources for academic publications can be found in **UK's library** *(http://libraries.uky.edu)*. In the Humanities, two major databases where you can find academic journals are JSTOR and Project Muse. They are accessible via UK's website.

ROLES OF CITATION

There are a number of ways we can use citations. Let's call these the "roles" of citation. The "roles" indicate different usages of a citation. Here are a few:

> 1. **Evidence:** The writer is making an argument. An argument needs evidence (proof) to demonstrate why it should be believed. The writer cites from statistics, examples, anecdotes, moments, common beliefs, or other forms of evidence by citing them from sources.

Example: To support a claim that films have become extremely violent in recent years, a writer might cite *Kill Bill's* The Bride versus Crazy 88 fight scene in which The Bride (Beatrix Kiddo) is able to single-handedly kill all of the members of the Crazy 88 gang over an eight-minute time period.

As evidence, the scene might be used to showcase the immense violence in a popular film, a film seen by millions of Americans.

Example: In sports, a controversial issue is the NBA rule that a player cannot be drafted until he is at least one year removed from high school. In 2012, former NBA player and Phoenix Suns general manager Steve Kerr **wrote an argument against removing the draft age limit** *(http://grantland.com/features/steve-kerr-problems-age-limit-nba/).* If a writer wanted to argue for the current rule, she could cite Kerr's positions on maturity, costs, player development, marketing, and mentoring as evidence. These five points could be cited as evidence a veteran of the NBA offers against removing the draft rule.

> 2. **Context:** One of the reasons we gave for citation was context. Context is also a role citation can play; it can provide a scene or setting for a piece of writing.

Example: You are writing about the struggle to be understood or to overcome obstacles in life (a fairly common experience). You need an example to show the context for what you've experienced (others have experienced it too, and it is important that the reader understand this point). You might cite Eminem's song "8 Mile" or the film *8 Mile,* which shows Rabbit's movement from the stamp factory to winning the rap battle. Rabbit overcomes all odds. You feel you've overcome all odds. Your experience has context, so you cite the film or song.

Example: In **"The Kentucky Derby Is Decadent and Depraved"** *(https://sensitiveskinmagazine.com/hunter-s-thompson-the-kentucky-derby-is-decadent-and-depraved/),* Kentucky's Hunter S. Thompson cites newspaper headlines to show the context of the time period he is writing about. The depraved Derby is put into context with a depraved time period of war. By reading the citations next to the Derby, the reader is supposed to read a larger context of depravity:

> He grabbed my arm, urging me to have another, but I said I was overdue at the Press Club and hustled off to get my act together for the awful spectacle. At the airport newsstand I picked up a Courier-Journal *and scanned the front page headlines: "Nixon Sends GI's into Cambodia to Hit Reds"... "B-52's Raid, then 20,000 GI's Advance 20 Miles"... "4,000 U.S. Troops Deployed Near Yale as Tension Grows Over Panther Protest." At the bottom of the page was a photo of Diane Crump, soon to become the first woman jockey ever to ride in the Kentucky Derby. The photographer had snapped her "stopping in the barn area to fondle her mount, Fathom." The rest of the paper was spotted with ugly war news and stories of "student unrest." There was no mention of any trouble brewing at a university in Ohio called Kent State.*[2]

3. **Showing the conversation:** Often, writers need to show that a larger conversation exists, and that the writer is trying to be a part of that conversation. Citations show the conversation by weaving together relevant quotations (similar ideas, differing ideas) so that the reader sees how others have approached the topic.

Example: Grantland **writer Steven Hyden describes the importance of Led Zeppelin** *(http://grantland.com/features/the-winners-history-rock-roll-part-1-led-zeppelin/)* by showing a conversation among fellow writers Chuck Klosterman and Jon Landau as well as Jimmy Page. Notice how Hyden cites a little bit from each person to show a larger conversation regarding Led Zeppelin's sound. Hyden weaves together three sources to create the writing:

> If it's still true (as Grantland's Chuck Klosterman once wrote) that every teenage male goes through a "Zeppelin phase," it is due to two things, and one of them is The Sound. Rock critic (and future Bruce Springsteen manager) Jon Landau once described The Sound upon seeing Led Zeppelin perform in 1969 as "loud … violent and often insane," but this is only two-thirds true as it pertains to Zeppelin's records. In reality, The Sound was the conscious and mentally competent creation of Jimmy Page in his role as Led Zeppelin's producer. Utilizing a coterie of well-chosen studio tricks—including something called "backward echo" and what he dubbed "the science of close-miking amps"—Page ensured that unlike practically all of his contemporaries in the late '60s and early '70s, his records would not be diluted by the passage of time.[3]

Example: Writing about the demise of alternative media *(https://pitchfork.com/features/oped/9093-alt-weeklies/#:~:text=In%201969%2C%20at%20the%20height,in%20his%20book%20Smoking%20Typewriters.)*, Pitchfork's **Damon Krukowski** weaves together several sources in one paragraph to show that alternative media often lost money:

> In 1969, at the height of the underground press era, "72% of underground papers reported [making] no profit whatsoever," historian John McMillian points out in his book Smoking Typewriters. "Though they worked feverishly, most of them were jaundiced to the very idea of profit-making." Many operated as collectives without owners, some without editors. "There wasn't a hierarchical structure to what we were doing, so anybody could come in and get involved," says a contributor to Austin's The Rag in the colorful oral history of the 60s underground press, On the Ground. "All the underpinnings were different than they were in straight society," remembers one of the producers of Chicago's

Seed. "There was a saying in the *Seed,* which I always believed: 'Work is love made visible.'" [4]

> 4. **Definition:** When defining, the temptation is to turn to a dictionary and write something like "According to *Webster's* . . . ." But since anyone can open a dictionary and find a basic definition, a better approach is to cite from a text (written, filmic, visual) that shows the meaning you want to share. This way, you demonstrate for the reader that the definition exists in actual ideas (and not just in a dictionary).

Example: Malcolm Gladwell, **writing in "The Ketchup Conundrum"** *(http://www.newyorker.com/magazine/2004/09/06/the-ketchup-conundrum?currentPage=all),* defines ketchup accordingly:

> Tomato ketchup is a nineteenth-century creation—the union of the English tradition of fruit and vegetable sauces and the growing American infatuation with the tomato. But what we know today is ketchup emerged out of a debate that raged in the first years of the last century over benzoate, a preservative widely used in late-nineteenth-century condiments. [5]

Gladwell defines ketchup by drawing on a historical citation. He doesn't show us where he got it from, but we can assume that this is not common knowledge he has in his head; he must have read it somewhere.

> 5. **Appeal:** To persuade a reader to believe in a given idea, a writer may want to show an emotional example. The writer may, then, appeal to the reader's emotions or beliefs by citing a source.

Example: In 2012, **a video showing "pink slime"** *(https://www.youtube.com/watch?v=dCqKl4Q3hW4),* meat processed mostly for fast food consumption circulated on the Internet. By showing fast food meat as a pink sludge of animal parts, the video meant to appeal to people's distaste for food that looks and sounds unappetizing. In turn, it meant to dissuade people from eating fast food.

> 6. **Balance:** Some writers want to navigate an issue by citing from differing and conflicting positions so that a pro/con argument is not presented. Instead, various sides are shown to present a more complex response than the limited pro/con binary.

Example: Reporting on the "pink slime" controversy associated with fast food and processed meat, **the website Snopes** *(http://www.snopes.com/food/prepare/msm.asp)* cites a number of published documents in order to navigate "a mixture of true and false information."[6]

Thus, the citations provided balance to an otherwise controversial idea.

> 7. **Repetition:** Often, ideas repeat in a number of contexts. A writer may feel that showing a specific repetition will produce a specific effect for the reader. Therefore, the writer cites the repetitions.

Example: *The Daily Show* introduced Barack Obama's 2009 inaugural speech by showing it was a repetition of George Bush's inaugural speech. The citation of a repetition was meant to underscore how little difference there was between the two presidents.

Example: Musical artists often use repetition to cite other songs, muscially or lyrically. The songs may not explicitly state the origin of what is repeated, but they repeat an idea to create new meaning.

Go on **YouTube** *(https://www.youtube.com)* and look up the following repetitive usages of "Try a Little Tenderness" by the following artists:

- Bing Crosby
- Solomon Burke
- Aretha Franklin
- Otis Redding
- Tom Jones
- Kanye West and Jay-Z

How does each artist repeat the basic elements of the original? How do the meanings change in each new context?

> 8. **Introductions:** A writer may want to introduce an idea by citing another source. Such citations can be better beginnings to an idea than clichés (*"Since the beginning of time …"*) or vague generalities (*"A lot of people think different ideas about this topic …"*). The citation can offer a specific entry into the idea you want to convey.

Example: In a 2013 essay on Syracuse University's men's basketball team's run for the Final Four (http://www.theatlantic.com/entertainment/archive/2013/03/sorry-syracuse-why-the-hot-hand-in-basketball-maybe-isnt-a-real-thing/274489/), the *Atlantic's* Ashley Fetters introduces the concept of the "hot hand" by citing a 1991 study. While Fetters paraphrases her source, she does cite the concept ("hot hand"), the authors (Gilovich, Tversky, and Vallone), and the source (the *Wilson Quarterly*). This citation introduces readers to the concept in order to argue against the idea of a "hot hand":

> *In 1991, psychologist Thomas D. Gilovich and his colleagues Amos Tversky and Bob Vallone conducted the classic investigation of the phenomenon of the "hot hand"—that is, when a player gathers shooting momentum or gets "in the zone" to the extent that he or she seemingly can't miss a shot—and published their findings in* The Wilson Quarterly. *They discovered it didn't exist anywhere outside of players' and fans' imaginations; rather, the research team found, the "hot hand" happens when an optimistic interpretation and some funky psychology are applied to a statistically average outcome of shots missed and shots made.*[7]

WEAVING

To be effective, citations have to be the writing itself. That is, the citations are the writing, not added to the writing. Thus, we introduced the metaphor of weaving to better express how to work citations into your writing. You don't drop them in awkwardly; instead, you weave them into the writing so that they are the writing.

Sometimes students think: *"I'll just throw in a citation here or a citation there."* But that kind of approach comes off as awkward.

If you follow up on the preceding examples, you'll see that these citations make up the body of the writing. The writers don't add citations as if they were seasoning a meal; these writers build a piece of writing out of the information that they have researched.

In a 2013 *New Yorker* piece on Guantánamo Bay (http://www.newyorker.com/news/daily-comment/a-hundred-hungry-men-at-guantnamo), Amy Davidson weaves together a question asked of President Obama at a press conference and his answer:

"Is it any surprise, really, that they would prefer death rather than have no end in sight to their confinement?" a reporter asked during a White House press conference on Tuesday. President Obama was aware: *"It is not a surprise to me that we've got problems in Guantánamo,"* he said, and then talked about how he said so back in 2007, and how that was part of his campaign, and how Congressional Republicans had made things very hard. They have; but he, for a couple of years now, has made it easy for them to do so. He said he knew that it wasn't *"sustainable."* [8]

In a 2013 *Atlantic Monthly* **article** *(http://www.theatlantic.com/national/archive/2013/04/will-new-teacher-evaluations-help-or-hurt-chicagos-schools/275415/)* on teacher evaluations in Chicago public schools, Sara Neufeld weaves a statistic from the *New York Times* with a quotation from an expert:

> *The* New York Times *recently reported that only 3% or fewer of teachers under new systems in Florida, Tennessee, and Michigan were rated unsatisfactory, raising questions about how effective that agenda will be. "The hope of the business folks is that this ... will identify more failing teachers so they'll be gotten rid of. I'm just not sure that's going to happen," said Sue Sporte, research operations director at the University of Chicago's Consortium on Chicago School Research, which is studying the implementation of the evaluations in the Windy City. "If only 2.5% is rated unsatisfactory, I don't know how satisfactory that will be to the constituency that believes that kids are failing because teachers are awful."* [9]

When you read—whether in popular publications such as the *New Yorker* and the *Atlantic Monthly* or in academic publications that you might find via the library—notice how authors weave together their citations. How do they create a fluid writing from citations?

CITATION STYLES

It's too easy to get hung up on **style.** Citation style mainly means the ways you note the citation, where you put the page number and source, and how you construct a Works Cited. Styles aren't holy. They are discipline/profession specific. Styles allow us to format our citations in a way that is readable to a specific audience. If you write in the university, you are often expected to use a specific citation style, depending on your audience.

You've likely noticed that a great deal of what you read outside the classroom—newspapers, websites, novels, magazines—often lacks stylistic citations. That is, even if the writer conducted research for the writing, there often isn't a Works Cited or even a page number and source. This is also true for many of the examples presented in this chapter.

The citation styles are largely academic. They are professional ways of indicating sources. Thus, when you use a citation style, you are engaging with the professional way of doing something. Every profession has its own ways of presenting ideas, documents, and sources. In the university, the professional way of citing sources is to use one of the academic citation styles.

Style is the easiest part of citation. Style is merely the way you format and present your citation. It does not reflect the quality of your citation. How do you know which style to use? The key is knowing who your audience is. Each style is based on an academic audience:

- **MLA:** mostly humanities (English, foreign languages)
- **Chicago:** history
- **APA:** mostly sciences (psychology, physics, biology, technical writing)

Nobody can memorize the styles for citing books, movies, articles, interviews, etc. And there are enough online resources that make this information available that you can find the proper style easily.

Some Style Resources

- **Purdue OWL** *(https://owl.english.purdue.edu):* all of the styles are documented here.
- **Zotero** *(https://www.zotero.org):* a free tool that allows you to gather online sources.
- **MIT Overview of Citation Software** *(https://libguides.mit.edu/cite-write/citetools):* an overview of some popular citation management tools.

To practice working with citations, here are a couple of exercises. The exercises are meant to give you some familiarity with identifying and working with citations.

Chapter 10   Citation

Exercise: Reverse Citation

The reverse citation exercise asks you to take a piece of writing that has citations—the writer obviously has used outside sources to write—but doesn't indicate where the citations came from. The reason for doing the exercise is to try to understand how writers use citations in their work.

This exercise asks you to find the citations that likely informed the writer.

Using the following essay, **"Dissed Fish" by Calvin Trillin** *(http://www.newyorker.com/magazine/2004/09/06/dissed-fish?currentPage=),* identify places where Trillin is likely using an outside source. You can tell if he is using an outside source by asking yourself: *"Could someone know that on his/her own?"* If the answer is "no," then you need to find the source.

Use the following tools to guess where the writer got his information. The keyword here is *guess*. We don't really know if the writer used these texts. But the guess will allow us to figure out how a writer might find a source and then use information from that source in his/her own writing. Here are some places where you might want to start your search:

- **Google Books** *(https://books.google.com/?hl=en)*
- **Google** *(https://www.google.com/?gws_rd=ssl)*
- **Magportal**
- **UK's Library portal**

Make a list of the sources you find. Then compare them to how Trillin uses the information to write "Dissed Fish." Did you find the exact source (i.e., what you found matches his writing) or something that might be the source (the same idea)?

Town Branch Writing Collection   241

Exercise: Citation Profile

This exercise asks you to build a profile of a public figure by researching and then citing sources related to that figure. The citations you find will show a reader who that person is. You are not writing a biography as much as you are building a profile via citations. A public figure may be one of the following:

- A celebrity
- A politician
- An artist
- Someone else in the public eye
- An entertainer
- Activist
- A business person

The first thing you need to do is identify a person. Then, research as much as you can about that person on the following:

- His/her beliefs
- Hobbies
- Background
- Other's views on that person
- What he/she has done
- Habits
- Successes or failures

Use magazines, newspapers, public records, interviews, online books, websites, and other similar sources in order to find information for your profile.

With each source you find, identify a few passages that demonstrate that point. For instance, if you were reading the *New Yorker's* **profile of Whole Foods CEO John MacKey** *(http://www.newyorker.com/magazine/2010/01/04/food-fighter)*, you would see that MacKey is interested in the following:

- Yoga
- Veganism
- Libertarianism
- The writings of Ayn Rand

If you were doing a citation profile of John MacKey, these could have been four items you researched and found citations about.

Your next step would be to compose a paragraph or two about John MacKey from the citations.

You could have multiple citations for each item. By weaving the citations together, you will be able to build a profile. The reader will know more about the person you chose to profile by the strength of your citation choices.

HOW TO CREATE A WORKS CITED PAGE AND CITE COMMON SOURCES USING MLA

Works Cited

"Works Cited" (or "Work Cited" if only citing one source) appears on a separate page from the essay, centered at the top of the page.

Sources are listed **alphabetically** by author's last name. If the citation is longer than one line, insert a "hanging indent" for the second+ lines of each entry. For more information/help outside of this guide, head to (all MLA citation guidelines below are from Purdue Owl's MLA Guide): *https://owl.english.purdue.edu/owl/resource/747/01/.*

When deciding how to cite your source, start by consulting the list of core elements. These are the general pieces of information that MLA suggests including in each Works Cited entry. In your citation, the elements should be listed in the following order:

1. Author.
2. Title of source.
3. Title of container,
4. Other contributors,
5. Version,
6. Number,
7. Publisher,
8. Publication date,
9. Location.

Each element should be followed by the punctuation mark shown above.

Author

Begin the entry with the author's last name, followed by a comma and the rest of the name, as presented in the work. End this element with a period.

> Said, Edward W. *Culture and Imperialism.* Knopf, 1994.

Title of Source

The title of the source should follow the author's name. Depending upon the type of source, it should be listed in italics or quotation marks.

A book should be in italics:

> Henley, Patricia. *The Hummingbird House.* MacMurray, 1999.

A website should be in italics:

> Lundman, Susan. "How to Make Vegetarian Chili." *eHow,* www.ehow.com/how_10727_make-vegetarian-chili-html.

A periodical (journal, magazine, newspaper article) should be in quotation marks:

> Bagchi, Alaknanda. "Conflicting Nationalisms: The Voice of the Subaltern in Mahasweta Devi's Bashai Tudu." *Tulsa Studies in Women's Literature,* vol. 15, no. 1, 1996, pp. 41–50.

A song or piece of music on an album should be in quotation marks:

> Beyonce. "Pray You Catch Me." *Lemonade,* Parkwood Entertainment, 2016, www.beyonce.com/album/lemonade-visual-album/.

Title of Container

The container is the larger whole in which the source is located. The container may also be a television series, which is made up of episodes; or a website, which contains articles, postings, and other works.

> Kincaid, Jamaica. "Girl." *The Vintage Book of Contemporary American Short Stories,* edited by Tobias Wolff, Vintage, 1994, pp 306–07.

Sometimes, a container might be within a larger container. You might have read a book or short stories on *Google Books* or watched a television series on *Netflix*. You might have found the electronic version of a journal on JSTOR. It is important to cite these containers within containers so that your readers can find the exact source that you used.

> "94 Meetings." *Parks and Recreation,* season 2, episode 21, NBC, 29 Apr. 2010. *Netflix,* www.netflix/com/watch/70152031?trackId=200256157&tctx=0%2C20%2C0974d361-27cd-44de-9c2a-2d9d868b9f64-12120962.

Other Contributors

In addition to the author, there may be other contributors to the source who should be credited, such as editors, illustrators, translators, etc. If their contributions are relevant to your search, or necessary to identify the source, include their names in your documentation.

> Foucault, Michel. *Madness and Civilization: A History of Insanity in the Age of Reason.* Translated by Richard Howard, Vintage-Random House, 1988.

Version

If a source is listed as an edition or version of a work, include it in your citation.

> *The Bible.* Authorized King James Version, Oxford UP, 1998.

Number

If a source is part of a numbered sequence, such as a multi-volume book or journal with both volume and issue numbers, those numbers must be listed in your citation.

> Quintilian. *Institutio Oratoria.* Translated by H.E. Butler, vol. 2, Loeb-Harvard UP, 1980.

Publisher

The publisher produces or distributes the source to the public. If there is more than one publisher, and they are all relevant to your research, list them in your citation, separated by a forward slash (/).

> *Women's Health: Problems of the Digestive System.* American College of Obstetricians and Gynecologists, 2006.

Note: The publisher's name need not be included in the following sources: Periodicals, works published by their author or editor, a website whose title is the same name as its publisher, a website that makes works available but does not actually publish them (such as *YouTube, WordPress,* or *JSTOR*).

Publication Date

The same source may have been published on more than one date, such as an online version of an original source. For example, a television series might have aired on a broadcast network on one date, but released on *Netflix* on a different date. When the source has more than one date, it is sufficient to use the date that is most relevant to your use of it. If you're unsure about which date to use, go with the date of the source's original publication.

In the following example, Mutant Enemy is the primary production company, and "Hush" was released in 1999. This is the way to create a general citation for a television episode.

> "Hush." *Buffy the Vampire Slayer,* created by Joss Whedon, performance by Sarah Michelle Gellar, season 4, Mutant Enemy, 1999.

However, if you are discussing, for example, the historical context in which the episode originally aired, you should cite the full date. Because you are specifying the date of airing, you would then use WB Television Network (rather than Mutant Enemy), because it was the network (rather than the production company) that aired the episode on the date you're citing.

> "Hush." *Buffy the Vampire Slayer,* created by Joss Whedon, performance by Sarah Michelle Gellar, season 4, episode 10, WB Television Network, 14 Dec. 1999.

Location

You should be as specific as possible in identifying a work's location.

An essay in a book or an article in a journal should include page numbers.

> Adiche, Chimamanda Ngozi. "On Monday of Last Week." *The Thing around Your Neck,* Alfred A. Knopf, 2009, pp. 74–94.

The location of an online work should include a URL.

> Wheelis, Mark. "Investigating Disease Outbreaks Under a Protocol to the Biological and Toxin Weapons Convention." *Emerging Infectious Diseases,* vol. 6, no. 6, 2000, pp. 595–600, wwwnc.cdc.gov/eid/article/6/6/00-0607_article. Accessed 8 Feb. 2009.

A physical object that you experienced firsthand should identify the place of location.

>   Matisse, Henri. *The Swimming Pool.* 1952, Museum of Modern Art, New York.

Citations should be in alphabetical order; however, sometimes sorting and citing authors can be tricky.

For More Than One Work by an Author

If you have cited more than one work by a particular author, order the entries alphabetically by title, and use three hyphens in place of the author's name for every entry after the first:

>   Burke, Kenneth. *A Grammar of Motives.* […]
>
>   ---. *A Rhetoric of Motives.* […]

For Work with No Known Author

Alphabetize works with no known author by their title; use a shortened version of the title in the parenthetical citations in your paper. In this case, Boring Postcards USA has no known author:

>   *Boring Postcards USA.* […]

For More Than One Author

When a book has more than one author, order the authors in the same way they are presented in the book. The first given name appears in last name, first name format; subsequent author names appear in first name, last name format.

>   Gillespie, Paula, and Neal Lerner. *The Allyn and Bacon Guide to Peer Tutoring.* Allyn and Bacon, 2000.

If there are three or more authors, list only the first author followed by the phrase et al. (Latin for "and others") in place of the subsequent author's names. (Note that there is a period after "al" in "et al." Also note that there is never a period after the "et" in "et al.")

>   Wysocki, Anne Freances, et al. *Writing New Media: Theory and Applications for Expanding the Teaching of Composition.* Utah State UP, 2004.

Citing Electronic Sources

Citing an Entire Website

Editor, author, or compiler name (if available). *Name of Site.* Version number, Name of institution/organization affiliated with the site (sponsor or publisher), date of resource creation (if available), URL, DOI or permalink. Date of access (if applicable).

> Felluga, Dino. *Guide to Literary and Critical Theory.* Purdue U, 28 Nov. 2003, www.cla.purdue.edu/english/theory/. Accessed 10 May 2006.

A Page on a Website

For an individual page on a website, list the author or alias if known, followed by the information covered above for entire websites. If the publisher is the same as the website name, only list it once.

> "Athlete's Foot—Topic Overview." *WebMD,* 25 Sept. 2014, www.webmd.com/skin-problems-and-treatments/tc/athletes-foot-topic-overview.

An Image (including a painting, sculpture, or photograph)

Provide the artist's name, the work of art italicized, the date of creation, and the institution, and city where the work is housed. Follow this initial entry with the name of the Website in italics, and the date of access.

> Goya, Francisco. *The Family of Charles IV.* 1800. Museo Nacional del Prado, Madrid. *Museo Nacional del Prado,* https://www.museodelprado.es/en/the-collection/artwork/the-family-of-carlos-iv/f47898fc-aa1c-48f6-a779-71759e417e74. Accessed 22 May 2006.

If the work is cited on the web only, then provide the name of the artist, the title of the work, and then follow the citation format for a website. If the work is posted via a username, use the username for the author.

> Adams, Clifton R. "People relax beside a swimming pool at a country estate near Phoenix, Arizona, 1928." *Found,* National Geographic Creative, 2 June 2016, natgeofound.tumblr.com/.

An Article in a Web Magazine

Provide the author name, article name in quotation marks, title of the web magazine in italics, publisher name, publication date, URL, and the date of access.

> Bernstein, Mark. "10 Tips on Writing the Living Web." *A List Apart: For People Who Make Websites,* 16 Aug. 2002, alistapart.com/article/writeliving. Accessed 4 May 2009.

An Article in an Online Scholarly Journal

For all online scholarly journals, provide the author(s) name(s), the name of the article in quotation marks, the title of the publication in italics, all volume and issue numbers, and the year of publication. Include a URL, DOI (digital object identifier), or permalink to help readers locate the source.

Article in an Online-Only Scholarly Journal

If the journal you are citing appears exclusively in an online format that does not make use of page numbers, indicate the URL or other information.

> Dolby, Nadine. "Research in Youth Culture and Policy: Current Conditions and Future Directions." *Social Work and Society: The International Online-Only Journal,* vol. 6, no. 2, 2008, www.socwork.net/sws/article/view/60/362. Accessed 20 May 2009.

Article in an Online Scholarly Journal That Also Appears in Print

Cite articles in online scholarly journals that also appear in print as you would a scholarly journal in print, including the page range of the article. Provide the URL and the date of access.

> Wheelis, Mark. "Investigating Disease Outbreaks Under a Protocol to the Biological and Toxin Weapons Convention." *Emerging Infectious Diseases,* vol. 6, no. 6, 2000, pp. 595–600, wwwnc.cdc.gov/eid/article/6/6/00-0607_article. Accessed 8 Feb. 2009.

An Article from an Online Database (or other electronic subscription service)

Cite articles from online databases (e.g., LexisNexis, ProQuest, JSTOR, ScienceDirect) and other subscription services as containers. Thus, provide the title of the database italicized before the DOI or URL. If a DOI is not provided, use the URL instead. Provide the date of access if you wish.

> Alonso, Alvearo, and Julio A. Camargo. "Toxicity of Nitrite to Three Species of Freshwater Invertebrates." *Environmental Toxicology,* vol. 21, no. 1, 3 Feb. 2006, pp. 90–94. *Wiley Online Library,* doi:10.1002/tox.20155.

E-mail (including e-mail interviews)

Give the author of the message, followed by the subject line in quotation marks. State to whom the message was sent with the phrase, "Received by" and the recipient's name. Include the date the message was sent. Use standard capitalization.

> Kunka, Andrew. "Re: Modernist Literature." Received by John Watts, 15 Nov. 2000.

A Listserv, Discussion Group, or Blog Posting

Cite web postings as you would a standard web entry. Provide the author of the work, the title of the posting in quotation marks, the website name in italics, the publisher, and the posting date. Follow with the date of access. Include screen names as author names when author name is not known. If both names are known, place the author's name in brackets.

> Editor, screen name, author, or compiler name (if available). "Posting Title." *Name of Site,* Version number (if available), Name of institution/organization affiliated with the site (sponsor or publisher), URL. Date of access.

A Post on X (formerly Twitter)

Begin with the name of the account user. If their handle differs substantially from their name, you may include the handle in brackets after the name. If the post includes text, use a portion of the text in quotation marks to identify the post. Posts that contain images and/or videos but no text can be identified by a description. Include the date and time of posting, using the reader's time zone; separate the date and time with a comma and end with a period. Include the date accessed if you deem necessary.

> Brokaw, Tom. "SC demonstrated why all the debates are the engines of this campaign." *X,* 22 Jan. 2012, 3:06 am., twitter.com/tombrokaw/status/160996868971704320.

A *YouTube* Video

Video and audio sources need to be documented using the same basic guidelines for citing print sources in MLA style. Include as much descriptive information as necessary to help readers understand the type and nature of the source you are citing. If the author's name is the same as the uploader, only cite the author once. If the author is different from the uploaded, cite the author's name before the title.

> "8 Hot Dog Gadgets put to the Test." *YouTube,* uploaded by Crazy Russian Hacker, 6 June 2016, www.youtube.com/watch?v=WBlpjSEtELs.

Other Common Sources

Interviews

PERSONAL INTERVIEW

Personal interviews refer to those interviews that you conduct yourself. List the interview by the name of the interviewee. Include the descriptor "Personal Interview" and the date of the interview.

> Smith, Jane. Personal Interview. 19 May 2014.

PUBLISHED INTERVIEWS (PRINT OF BROADCAST)

List the interview by the full name of the interview. If the name of the interview is part of a larger work like a book, a television program, or a film service, place the title of the interview in quotation marks. Place the title of the larger work in italics. If the interview appears as an independent title, italicize it. For books, include the author or editor name after the book title.

> Gaitskill, Mary. Interview with Charles Bock. *Mississippi Review,* vol. 27, no. 3, 1999, pp. 129–50.

For sources outside of the types listed in this chapter, please refer to Purdue Owl's MLA Formatting Guide.

NOTES

[1] "Rhetoric." *Wikipedia,* last modified June 13, 2014, http://en.wikipedia.org/wiki/Rhetoric.

[2] Hunter S. Thompson. "The Kentucky Derby is Decadent and Depraved." *Scanlon's Monthly 1,* no. 4, 1970.

[3] Steven Hyland. "The Winners' History of Rock and Roll, Part 1: Led Zeppelin." *Grantland*, January 8, 2013, http://www.grantland.com/story/_/id/8821559/the-winners-history-rock-roll-part-1-led-zeppelin.

[4] Damon Krukowski. "Alternate Ending." *Pitchfork*, March 27, 2013, http://pitchfork.com/features/oped/9093-alt-weeklies.

[5] Malcolm Gladwell. "The Ketchup Conundrum." *New Yorker*, September 6, 2004, http://www.newyorker.com/archive/2004/09/06/040906fa_fact_gladwell?currentPage=all.

[6] "Pink Slime and Mechanically Separated Chicken." *Snopes*, last modified March 22, 2012, http://www.snopes.com/food/prepare/msm.asp.

[7] Ashley Fetters. "Sorry, Syracuse: Why the 'Hot Hand' in Basketball (Maybe) Isn't a Real Thing." *Atlantic*, March 29, 2013, http://www.theatlantic.com/entertainment/archive/2013/03/sorry-syracuse-why-the-hot-hand-in-basketball-maybe-isnt-a-real-thing/274489/.

[8] Amy Davidson. "The Guantánamo Hunger Strikes: An Unprecedented Hundred Hungry Men." *New Yorker*, May 1, 2013, http://www.newyorker.com/online/blogs/comment/2013/05/guantanamo-hunger-strikes-hundred-hungry-men.html.

[9] Sara Neufeld. "Will New Teacher Evaluations Help or Hurt Chicago's Schools?" *Atlantic Monthly*, April 30, 2013, http://www.theatlantic.com/national/archive/2013/04/will-new-teacher-evaluations-help-or-hurt-chicagos-schools/275415/.

Writing with Style

Recommended for WRD 111/112
or as needed for WRD 110

Chapter 11

You have an implicit understanding of rhetoric: you know that you must adapt your language to suit your audience and the particular occasion. If you want to explain to your friends why you didn't like a movie, you will make one argument; if you want to contribute to a discussion of the same movie in your film theory class, you will make a different one. Your conclusion—that the movie was a poor one—will likely remain consistent. But you might choose to highlight different elements of the movie—and you will almost certainly use a different vocabulary and tone in making your point to these two different groups. These decisions you make about word choice and tone are stylistic ones, and they are every bit as rhetorical and important to your success in convincing your audience as the choices you make about content.

THE APPEAL OF STYLE

Although stylistic choices can make a piece of writing "sound good," an effective style is not just a beautiful one. Style also effects an audience's perception of a text's reasonableness and the character of the writer. One way to understand the impact of style is to consider it in terms of the three primary rhetorical appeals:

- **Logos:** An appeal based on good reasons (logic).
- **Pathos:** An appeal to the emotions or to values (personal and cultural).
- **Ethos:** An appeal based on the character (authority and credibility) of the writer.

In order to be successful, a writer must construct a text that appeals to readers through their logic, their emotions, and their sense of the writer's character. And an impactful style (diction, voice, syntax, etc.) is necessary to accomplish all of these ends. Put more specifically, an effective style makes an argument easier to follow (makes a logos appeal); it creates a mood and a sense of aesthetic pleasure (makes a pathos appeal); and it convinces the audience the writer is knowledgeable and trustworthy (makes an appeal to ethos).

If the stylistic choices of the writer are ineffective, a text can fail to win over the audience regardless of its content; the writer may seem unkind, or the mood may feel inappropriate. Consider, for example, this piece by Prachi Gupta for *Salon.com* on **"The 15 Most Hated Bands of the Last 30 Years."** *(http://www.salon.com/2013/08/10/15_most_hated_bands_of_last_30_years/)* Gupta chooses a biting, humorous tone, as in her justification for John Mayer's inclusion on the list:

John Mayer is that insufferable bro—you know, the one who wears a pukka bead necklace, is always shirtless, toting around a guitar at that house party you didn't want to go to, anyway. He'll suck the humor out of a joke and ruin the punch line every time, but no one else seems to care, because he's a shirtless bro with a guitar. He probably likes Dane Cook. And misogyny.

Gupta might describe her ethos, her persona for the piece, as trendy and humorous, but the comments below the piece suggest that much of her audience would have described it differently. Few commenters disagreed significantly with Gupta's choices (which included Creed, Nickleback, Limp Bizkit, and 98 Degrees), although they often added to the list. But the article nevertheless aroused a good deal of vitriol. One commenter, Local Area Man, claimed, "I feel like I'm reading an eyeball rolling, impatient teenager who is bored and angry." Tejana, another commenter, scoffed, "Who elected you the taste Czar?"

For many of her readers, Gupta creates a dislikeable persona through her writing: she fails to build an effective ethos. More importantly, we could point to elements of her text that led her readers to describe the piece as "insipid" and "self-indulgent." The repetition of the word "bro" and short sentences at the end make the paragraph seem not just humorous but snarky—humor at the expense of a group of people (those who attend house parties, use the word "bro," and play guitar for others unsolicited). To further associate this group with misogyny seems both unnecessary and unfair. She also uses the second person, "you," suggesting that the reader must automatically share these opinions.

Gupta's missteps in this article are mistakes less of content than of style—of tone and word choice. You could make an argument that her piece is "link bait" or "troll bait"—deliberately antagonist in order to entice people to repost the link or comment. However, those readers who found her ethos to be off-putting are unlikely to click on Gupta's articles in the future. Any short-term success may mean long-term failure.

No one style will be effective for all contexts, let alone effective for all audiences. Instead, the key to success is learning to make informed stylistic choices that will enhance the content of your writing. This chapter will help you make choices that will meet the needs of your text and your audience's expectations.

VOICE

I have used the word ethos to describe Gupta's writerly persona in her piece. When we judge a writer's ethos, we consider both the content and stylistic features of the text: our sense of how informed they are; our ability to identify culturally and personally with their persona; and their **voice,** which is most deeply connected to style.

You likely already have a sense of what the word voice means in writing—the personality of the writer as it comes through on the page. But we can be much more specific in analyzing what makes an impactful and appropriate voice if we consider the stylistic elements that create it—particularly its perspective, tone and diction, and use of figurative language.

Perspective

Perspective, or point of view, is the stance that you take up to address your topic. Do you want your position to come across as very personal (first person)? Objective or impersonal (third person)? Or do you want the piece to seem conversational, by directly addressing the reader (second person)?

First Person	Second Person	Third Person
I, we (my, me, us, our)	you (your)	he, she, they, it (his, her, their, him, her, them, its)

The table above lists the pronouns associated with each perspective. The perspective you choose should depend on your topic, the particular context of the piece, and your sense of the ethos you want to develop. For example, Deb Perelman uses a first person perspective in her blog, *Smitten Kitchen*:

> *Look, I came around on kale, I did! I realized that I didn't dislike* it *so much as much as I was suspicious of fervor around it, as if there had never been any other healthy vegetables before it, as if it its renaissance was the result of the kind of PR team only a certain troubled mayoral candidate could dream of right now. And the kale chips of 2010 didn't do much to convince me (ducks; sends self home from the internet in disgrace). But it turns out, I like kale the way I like my slaws—raw, finely slivered, not overwhelmed by dressing and with just the right extra punches to round it out.* ("Kale Salad with Pecorino and Walnuts"; http://smittenkitchen.com/)

The first-person perspective is standard for the blog genre. It helps the audience to identify with Perelman as a lover of food, rather than a chef (amateur or not). This approach allows Perelman to portray cooking not as an exact science but as an experience that the audience can share from their own kitchen—from picking the recipe and ingredients to preparing the dish. We move with her through the process of culinary creation, thanks largely to her first-person stance.

Tone and Diction

Perspective, however, is only the first decision you'll need to make in developing a powerful voice for a piece of writing. The stylistic elements of a text that will be most important in making your voice appropriate or distinctive are your tone and diction. **Tone** reflects a stance, attitude, or emotional investment in a topic. **Diction** is word choice, which helps to build a particular tone.

Your tone and diction should supplement your choice in perspective and be appropriate for the content and rhetorical situation. Business reports, for example, are usually written in third person, with a tone that is straightforward rather than humorous, cheerful, or angry. Blogs, like Perelman's above, often supplement their first-person perspective with an informal diction and an intimate or funny tone.

But there's more to creating the right tone than simply labeling it with an adjective. Let's compare Perelman's voice to that of Megan Carter in another food-related blog, *Verdant Nation*:

> [H]ow can cooking our own meals help the obesity epidemic? Meals and snacks eaten outside of the home generally have more calories than those made in the home. Simplistically, if you consume more calories than you expend on a regular basis, you're going to gain weight. There is also some evidence that eating more frequently outside of the home is related to an increased body weight. Preparing your own meals also cuts down on packaging, particularly if you eat a lot of fast food, which is better for the environment. And preparing your own meals means just that—as Yoni Freedhoff recently commented, nuking something doesn't count. ("Is Cooking the Silver Bullet to the Obesity Epidemic?" http://verdantnation.blogspot.com/)

The first thing that we notice is that Carter's paragraph uses a third-person perspective, as opposed to Perelman's first-person. (The "you" in this case is less a direct address to the individual than a synonym for the overly formal "one" or "an individual.") This choice in perspective gives Carter's piece an analytical, authoritative tone, rather than the intimate, playful tone of Perelman's. The perspective of each piece suits its purpose: Perelman hopes to make the art of cooking a part of her readers' everyday lives; Carter aims to relay scientific research on food and obesity to a non-scientific audience and reflect on its significance.

But we could highlight further stylistic elements that distinguish the tones of these blogs. Perelman's piece includes an exclamation, a parenthetical aside, and interjectory words ("look," "well"). All of these elements give the piece its more informal feel. By contrast, Carter's piece uses a standard argumentative technique: Ask a question in the first sentence, then answer it. It does not include the stylistic features that Perelman's does. Instead, it opens sentences with transitional adverbs ("simplistically") and uses abstract subjects ("there is"; "preparing your own meals"). These choices create a more authoritative, formal tone.

The diction of each piece further defines the voice. Certainly, both blogs use standard or everyday diction, if by standard we mean non-specialized. But if we look carefully at each paragraph, we can see more subtle differences. Perelman frequently uses phrasal constructions, where multiple words are used to convey a single idea ("came around"; "turns out"; "round out"). And, of course, she makes jokes and uses slang ("PR team"; "kale chips of 2010"; "sends self home"). Because these are features of quite informal texts, Carter uses them less frequently in discussing scientific topics. Perspective, tone, and diction work together in both texts to create a voice that is coherent and appropriate.

Figurative and Descriptive Language

Perhaps the most imposing element of creating a strong voice is using figurative and descriptive language. **Figurative language** is language that compares two things in a non-literal (and hopefully unique) way. **Descriptive language** creates a mood or paints a picture by playing on the audience's senses.

Sam Sifton draws his audience into his discussion of summer cooking with both figurative and descriptive language:

> *Peak summer is upon us, the corn as high as an elephant's eye, tomatoes fat and nearly bursting on the vine. On the East Coast, down in the shallows of low tide, you'll find people doing the shimmy with their bare toes, or pulling hard with a rake, looking for clams. There is basil in the window box and bacon in the fridge. This is the time of year to make like a chef: Embrace the simplicity of this, and allow the ingredients to talk for themselves.* (http://www.nytimes.com/2013/08/18/magazine/for-summer-cooking-embrace-simplicity.html?ref=dining&_r=0)

The piece opens with a familiar simile ("high as an elephant's eye"). While such a stock simile would not normally be successful, in this case it makes the image feel universal. Then, he quickly progresses to a series of images of summertime using rich descriptive language. He invokes particularly touch ("bare toes"; "pulling hard with a rake") and sight ("basil in the window box and bacon in the fridge"). This series of images creates a particular mood, a sense of nostalgia, from the opening lines of the piece.

While using figurative and descriptive language may sound difficult, you use both all the time. You use metaphor ("a breath of fresh air"); simile ("strong as an ox"); hyperbole ("it took an eternity"); and even metonymy ("the White House" to stand for the presidential administration) and synecdoche ("wheels" to stand for a car). These figures are already a part of your everyday discourse. Creating new figures involves nothing more than making new and unusual comparisons: these new creations will help you continue to develop your own unique voice.

It would be impossible to discuss all of the many tropes and figures available to you in the confines of this chapter. However, the table below lists some common tropes that will be useful to you, along with a definition and an example.

Figure	Definition	Example
Metaphor	Describing one object using the characteristics of another.	The sunflowers bobbed their heads in the strong Midwest breeze.
Simile	Comparing two things using "like" or "as."	The creek bustled with the same energy as a busy city street.
Alliteration	Repeating the same sound in nearby words.	The lake lapped against my legs, lulling me to sleep.
Metonymy	Referring to something by naming an object associated with it.	The Crown issued a proclamation when the new heir was born.
Synecdoche	Referring to an object by naming one of its parts or attributes.	We take only cash or plastic.
Anaphora	Repetition of the same word(s) at the beginning of consecutive clauses or sentences.	I came; I saw; I conquered.
Traductio	Repeating the same word in various points of a sentence.	Desperate times call for desperate measures.
Anastrophe	Shifting normal word order to create effect and emphasis.	Against the vast blackness hung a brilliant full moon.

You can find many more tropes and figures using online resources; Silva Rhetoricae is particularly useful in this respect *(http://rhetoric.byu.edu/)*.

Exercise

Choose a paragraph from an article or blog that you enjoyed. Rewrite the paragraph, keeping the content but re-imagining the voice. In other words, change the tone, diction, and perspective so that is differs from the original. It can help to imagine an entirely new context for the paragraph. If the paragraph came from a magazine, perhaps imagine it as an angry letter to the editor; if it came from a blog, imagine it as a front-page news article or a brochure.

Breaking the Rules

Perspective, tone and diction, and use of figurative and descriptive language can be used as identifiers for your favorite authors. Consider the short, concise sentences of Stephen King, or the down-to-earth tone of Kurt Vonnegut. But authors become even more distinguishable as they venture away from generally accepted features of written English. Take, for example, Cormac McCarthy's minimalist style. By removing most punctuation and writing with the tone and diction of speech, McCarthy achieves a unique voice that fans could recognize anywhere.

While technical writing is often thought of as a place where the rules must never be broken, there is a bit of leeway. Linguists, folks who study language, divide grammar rules into two categories. **Descriptive rules** are ones that people follow without thinking about it; for instance, there is a descriptive rule in English that sentences must have a verb.[1] Take the following sentence: *We taco soup.* It's completely impossible for an English speaker to make sense of this sentence without a verb. **Prescriptive rules,** on the other hand, are ones that have been set by grammarians and dictionary-makers that describe what we *should* do. Take the following phrase from the opening sequence of the television series *Star Trek,* as spoken by William Shatner: *To boldly go where no man has gone before.* While most readers/listeners don't notice anything wrong with the phrase, English has a *prescriptive* rule that says you should not split an infinitive verb (like *to go*). So when the captain of the Enterprise crammed the word *boldly* in between *to* and *go,* he broke the rules.

With some exceptions from the world of creative writing, it is virtually never acceptable to break the *descriptive* rules of English in your writing. As you might expect, breaking descriptive rules makes it difficult for the reader to understand what you are trying to convey. However, many writers find that there is often room to break some of the *prescriptive* rules. In fact, *following* some prescriptive rules can actually make it harder for the reader to understand. Take the following sentences for example:

- With whom do you plan to walk to the class to which you are going?
- Who do you plan to walk with to the class you are going to?

Many readers would be thrown off by the complicated syntax of the first sentence while the second sentence would be much easier to read. However, while the first sentence is prescriptively correct, the second sentence breaks the prescriptive rule that the object of a preposition must come immediately after it. You may have heard of this rule, simplified as "don't end a sentence with a preposition."

So when can we break the rules? When writing for a general audience, it's usually acceptable to break some of the prescriptive rules such as the split infinitive rule and the preposition rule, as long as the sentence is easy to understand. However, if your writing needs to be very specific, such as writing the Terms of Agreement for a smartphone app, it is often best to stick more closely to all rules and be as clear and concise as possible. For a more in-depth discussion of when to and not to break the rules based on your audience, see the *Appeal to Language* section of Chapter 3: "Audience."

Writing with Dialect

Consider the following terms. The first two are discussed in greater detail in Chapter 3.

- **Dialect:** A regional or social variety of speech.
- **Register:** A variety of language determined by the social setting; often the level of formality.
- **Feature:** Something about a variety of speech that makes it different from other varieties.

While strong dialect or register features may appear in some genres and rhetorical situations more than others (see the chapters on genre and rhetorical situation), such as truncating *-ing* words like *fishin'* and *walkin'*, less distinct features are practically guaranteed to appear. To explore this further, consider the following sentences:

- Cornhole is a popular game played at barbecues and camping trips.
- Bags is a popular game played at barbecues and camping trips.

Both words, *cornhole* and *bags,* refer to the same popular lawn game played by throwing bean bags at a wooden raised platform. However, depending on where you are from, or more accurately, which dialect of English you speak, at least one of these names will likely be foreign to you. This can be problematic if the reader is unfamiliar with the word chosen by the author. It's also worth pointing out that the author may not even be aware that the feature they are using is specific to their dialect. In this way, the existence of dialogue can present nuanced challenges and extra considerations when attempting to produce writing that is intelligible to the widest possible audience.

On the opposite side of that coin, however, is the fact that dialect feature use, when consciously applied, can be used to great rhetorical effect. Consider the following excerpts from the speeches of former U.S. President Barack Obama.

> We live in a time of extraordinary change—change that's reshaping the way we live, the way we work, our planet and our place in the world. It's change that promises amazing medical breakthroughs, but also economic disruptions that strain working families. It promises education for girls in the most remote villages, but also connects terrorists plotting an ocean away. It's change that can broaden opportunity, or widen inequality. And whether we like it or not, the pace of this change will only accelerate.
>
> January 12, 2016

> There's an extra spring in my step tonight. I don't know about you guys, but I am so relieved that the whole birther thing is over. I mean, ISIL, North Korea, poverty, climate change—none of those things weighed on my mind like the validity of my birth certificate. And to think that with just 124 days to go, under the wire, we got that resolved. I mean, that's a boost for me in the home stretch. In other breaking news, the world is round, not flat. Lord.
>
> September 8, 2016

It should be easy to notice the difference in tone even without being able to hear the stark difference in pronunciation exhibited by the president in these speeches. Both speeches, delivered only months apart from one another, were given in the face of an impending election. Both speeches shared the similar goal of increasing the morale of the audience and improving the audience's views of the president and his party. The primary difference in the two speeches is that the first was given as the 2016 State of the Union Address, delivered to Congress, while the second was given as remarks at the annual Phoenix Awards dinner hosted by the Congressional Black Caucus Foundation, where a significant portion of the audience would have indeed been black.

Many linguists who study **code-switching**—the act of transitioning from one register, dialect, or language to another—have pointed out the fact that politicians like Barack Obama tend to change their manner of speaking depending on the crowd they are speaking to. Why would someone use a different **dialect** of English when speaking to a certain group? Because the way a person speaks **indexes** them as a member of a certain community. So, by using a register of English that is commonly associated with the black community, Barack Obama is able to claim membership within the community. As in speech, dialect features can be used in writing to index the author as a member of a certain community, which can in turn be used as a rhetorical strategy as an ethical appeal. Much in the way using jargon such as *carcinogen* can make you seem more qualified to discuss medical topics, using dialect features such as *crawdaddy* (as opposed to crayfish) can make you seem more qualified to discuss Southern-style cooking, for example.

Whether you are breaking prescriptive rules of English to make your writing more clear (Can you find the times we've broken them in this section?) or indexing yourself as a member of a community for rhetorical effect, dialect should factor heavily into your decision-making process when determining the most appropriate and effective language to use in your writing.

Chapter 11   Writing with Style

> ### Exercise: The Way Grammar Rules Change a Text
>
> The following sentences, while *prescriptively* correct, are a bit difficult to understand because they break some of the *descriptive* rules of most readers' variety of English. Rewrite each sentence in two ways: once without breaking the prescriptive rules of English and once without concern for prescriptive rules, focusing only on making it as intelligible as possible.
> - People with whom it is worthwhile to talk are those that have the least to say.
> - The parrot cleaned in its cage flew.
> - The governor the president the queen hated supported likes maple syrup.
> - Toasted toasts toast toasted toast.

SYNTAX

If a strong writerly ethos depends on developing an appropriate voice, then a successful logos appeal, or appeal to reason, is grounded in an effective use of syntax. **Syntax,** or sentence structure, involves not just using correct grammar—but building sentences that accurately reflect the meaning that you want to convey.

As you read through this section on syntax, it is important to remember that there is no one right way to build a sentence. Any standards of "good" and "bad" English have varied significantly over time. English-speakers during the Renaissance highly valued a writer's ability to use tropes and figures and applauded what we would call flowery language. By contrast, contemporary English-speakers (particularly denizens of corporate America) value efficiency in prose, or the "skimmability" of a piece of writing. These two standards call for different types of syntax.

However, just because there are many ways to write a good sentence doesn't mean that all sentences will be equally effective. First, different types of sentences signal different kinds of relationships between ideas, so some sentences will better reflect what you mean than others. Second, you have an obligation to your readers to make your writing clear. They are investing time in your writing, so it's your job to make their reading experience as smooth and pleasurable as possible. The table below outlines four general principles—four "rules of thumb"—for using syntax effectively.

The Four Principles of Syntax

1. English speakers prefer simple, concrete subjects.
2. English has simpler verb forms than other languages like Spanish and French, so take advantage of this and use the simplest language necessary to get your point across.
3. Subjects and verbs should be placed close together and only occasionally separated by modifying phrases and clauses.
4. English sentences (usually) branch to the right, toward the end the sentence. The simplest and most concrete elements of the sentence should be at the beginning, while complex modifiers are added at the end.

This section will discuss these principles in more detail and give you strategies for implementing them in your own writing. Great writers are those who develop a unique and impactful voice, while abiding by the principles of effective syntax; it is these writers that both engage their audience and meet their expectations.

Choosing Effective Subjects

Principle 1 of the Principles of Syntax states that "English speakers prefer simple, concrete subjects." In other words, sentences are easier to read when they begin with subjects that can actually *do* something—or that we can at least see: I, my mother, the ball, the university administration, etc. These types of subjects are easily followed by simple action verbs: I wrote; my mother left; the ball rolled; the university administration attempted, etc.

However, all writers sometimes allow their sentences to be taken over by relatively "empty" subjects. The most common empty subjects are found in the table below, along with their most common verbs. Sentences that begin with these expressions have a filler for a subject, such as "this," "it," or "there," rather than a real subject that can do something. These expressions are syntactical fillers: They have no meaning but merely give the sentence a grammatical subject and verb.

Empty Subject and Their Verbs

- It is/was
- This is/was
- There is/are
- It seems
- I think
- I believe

Writers tend to use these expressions because they occur in conversation. But because we value efficiency so highly in writing, these same subjects cause problems when they are put on paper. First, English is a verb-driven language, and strong verbs require strong subjects. A vague subject like "it" often leads to a weak verb like "is." Second, they make a sentence wordy and complicate the sentence structure. An expression like "this is" at the beginning of a sentence merely fills in for the actual actor of the sentence—the real subject. The real subject then gets buried further along in the sentence, making it harder to read and leading to grammatical errors.

Writing Strategy

One effective means of revising at the sentence level is to focus on empty subjects. Try rewriting the same problematic sentence with two or three different subjects. Which sounds best? Choosing new subjects is just an easy way of brainstorming different ways to state an idea: more than likely, one of the sentences on your list will work for you.

Consider, for example, this sentence:

- **There are great resources available to student organizations when it comes to facilitators and presenters.**

The sentence begins with the empty words, "there are," and more importantly, the sentence is unclear and vague. So we want to give it a better subject that more clearly expresses the idea.

> ### Writing Strategy (continued)
>
> The subject of the sentence should be most important actor in the sentence—the person or thing that *does* something. The easiest way to find the "actor" of a sentence is to consider its most important nouns. In this sentence, the most important nouns are resources, organizations, facilitators and presenters. With this in mind, we can begin crafting alternative sentences, based on our new subjects:
>
> - **Facilitators and presenters can serve as important resources for student organizations.**
> - **Student organizations can plan presentations to meet the academic or professional needs of its members.**
>
> We might also have a "hidden" subject that doesn't appear in the original sentence:
>
> - **The Office of Student Affairs can help student organizations find facilitators and presenters that will appeal to their members.**
>
> Obviously, these sentences say different things, and the writer would have to choose the one that best expresses his or her meaning. But all of these sentences are clearer and more specific than the original, largely because they have a strong subject.
>
> You don't need to rewrite every sentence multiple ways—just those that seem awkward. Best of all, you do not always need to know *why* a sentence isn't working in order to improve it. Oftentimes, these awkward sentences don't even have grammatical mistakes—they are just wordy, and a better subject will eliminate the problem indirectly.

Choosing Impactful Verbs

Principle 2 of the Principles of Syntax states that "English is a verb-driven language: The verb of the sentence should always be in the simplest tense that is appropriate." In other words, your verbs should, if possible, be in simple present, past, or future tense: jumps; jumped; will jump. Certainly, you frequently will need other verb tenses, such as progressive forms (was jumping), to express certain ideas, but you should be selective in your use of them. Sentences are clearer and often richer with strong, simple-tense action verbs.

This section addresses two common writing problems that may impede your ability to build sentences with strong, impactful verbs: passive voice and nominalizations.

Chapter 11   Writing with Style

Passive Voice

Undoubtedly, you've had a teacher warn you of the dangers of passive voice. Passive voice occurs when the real object of a sentence becomes the subject, and a simple action verb is replaced by a form of the verb "to be" and a participle. Passive voice inevitably causes the writer to break Rule 2: "wrote" becomes "was written," and "cook" becomes "was cooked."

> - **Active:** My ball broke the window.
>   Subject   Action Verb   Object
> - **Passive:** The window was broken by my ball.
>   Subject   "to be" + participle   prepositional phrase with the real actor

As you can see in the example above, the passive voice sentence, although expressing the same idea, is wordier and has a more complex verb. Moreover, it buries the real actor of the sentence: "The ball" is hidden in a prepositional phrase at the end of the sentences, rather than holding its rightful place as the subject. The window, real object of the sentence—the thing being acted upon—fills in as the subject, where it does not belong. When you are trying to express a more complicated idea than the one above, this convoluted structure causes even more problems.

A sentence will almost always read more clearly if the main actor in the sentence is the subject. However, like most rules of writing, there are exceptions to the rule that we avoid passive voice. The passive voice may be more appropriate when:

1. The passive construction simplifies the subject of the sentence.

   For example, consider one of the clauses that I wrote above:

   - A simple action verb is replaced by a form of the verb "to be" and a participle.

   The verb of this sentence—"is replaced"—is in passive construction; it includes a form of the verb "to be" and a past participle, "replaced." I could have written the sentence in active voice:

   - A form of the verb "to be" and a participle replaced a simple action verb.

   This version of the sentence has a simple past-tense verb, "replaced," but it also has a very long subject: "a form of the verb 'to be' and a participle." I decided that the passive construction was a "lesser evil" than the overly long subject. In other words, a simple subject takes precedence over an active verb.

2. The audience expects passive construction as a convention.

   In some cases, an audience will expect a passive construction, whether it simplifies the sentence or not. For example, scientists will always use a passive construction when describing their experimental method. They will not say, "I diluted the solution," but "the solution was diluted." This structure buries the true actor ("I") but does so for rhetorical and ideological reasons. The passive construction implies that it does not matter who dilutes the solution—the results should remain the same regardless: it implies that the scientific process is "objective" and the results "true."

Nominalizations

While passive voice is a common problem, we often have to look beyond the main verb of the sentence when we are revising our prose. Nouns are a very flexible part of speech, one that can often mutate into other forms: In particular, both verbs and adjectives can often be turned into nouns. These words are called **nominalizations.**

Writers often use nominalizations in an effort to "sound smart" or more formal because they are more abstract. But more often than not these words just confuse the primary action happening in the sentence. Consider the following sentence:

> *While the meta-**analysis** will yield a mathematically sound **synthesis** of the studies included in the **analysis**, if these studies are a biased sample of all possible studies, then the mean **effect** reported by the meta-**analysis** will reflect this **bias.*** (https://www.meta-analysis.com/downloads/Intro_Criticisms_optim.pdf)

This short sentence includes several nominalizations, bolded in the sentence above: analysis could be analyze; synthesis could be synthesize; effect could be affect; bias (n.) could be bias (v.) or biased (adj.). These nominalizations make the passage sound sufficiently "scholarly" but make it far more difficult for the audience to understand.

> ## Writing Strategy
>
> The English language contains so many nominalizations that you will use them regularly. Rather than avoiding them completely do the following:
>
> 1. Primarily avoid using nominalizations as the actor of the sentence or clause.
> 2. Identify and eliminate nominalizations as a means for revising problematic sentences.
>
> In the sentence above, the main subject is "the mean effect," a nominalization. Rather than using effect as a noun, we might consider revising our sentence by beginning with the verb affect.
>
> Next, we must choose a subject for our new sentence. What is affecting the analysis? In this case, it is a biased sample. Now we have the beginning of a solid sentence: **"A biased sample will affect …"** We can continue to build the sentence from this foundation:
>
> ◎ **A biased sample of studies will affect the results of the meta-analysis, even if it accurately synthesizes those studies included by the author.**
>
> The sentence above eliminates most of the nominalizations, although "meta-analysis" remains. More importantly, it conveys the same information to the reader in a much clearer way.

Building an Effective Sentence

To this point, we have addressed the first two Principles of Syntax: choosing effective subjects and impactful verbs. In order to address Principles 3 and 4, we need to consider the basic building blocks of sentences—clauses.

A **clause** has a subject and a verb. We can further divide clauses into two types:

- **Independent clauses:** Contain a subject and a verb and form a complete idea.
- **Subordinate (or dependent) clauses:** Contain a subject and a verb and do not form a complete idea. Begin with a subordinating conjunction (**Example:** because, if, when, which, etc.).

An independent clause contains the most important idea in a sentence; the subordinate clause contains a less important idea.

Understanding the difference between independent and subordinate clauses can improve our grammar and mechanics, but even more importantly, it can help us better convey our ideas. We signal to our reader the relationship between our ideas through the types of clauses we choose. *In other words, our syntax—our sentence structure—conveys our logic—the way we connect our ideas and points.* It creates our logos appeal for the audience.

It can be overwhelming to talk about syntax because there are so many ways to build a sentence. However, a good sentence does not mean a long or complex one. Our audience will judge our writing less on the complexity of our syntax than on our content, diction, tone, and the variety of sentence structures that we use.

In fact, most sentences fall into one of eight types, which I discuss in the remainder of the section.

Eight Sentence Types

- SV.
- SV, and SV.
- SV; SV.
- S V and V.
- S and S V.
- Sub, SV.
- SV, Sub.
- S, Sub, V.

Simple Sentences

Simple Sentences contain only one independent clause—a single idea. A typical paragraph will usually contain at least a couple of simple sentences.

- SV _____.

    Many educators have pointed out the lack of medical evidence to support the existence of learning disabilities and the problematic nature of the "discrepancy method" in labeling a child.

The simple sentence above is relatively long but still easily readable. Notice that the subject and verb come immediately at the beginning of the sentence, as Principle 4 suggests. The sentence contains a long predicate with modifiers, but because these modifiers come at the end of the sentence, it is not confusing.

Compound Sentences

Compound Sentences contain two independent clauses. Because these clauses are both independent, the ideas they contain are of *equal* importance.

- SV, and (but/or/yet/so) SV.

    This process assumes that underlying biological impairment causes the learning disability, but medical examinations cannot detect such subtle differences in brain function.

- SV; SV.

    Some individuals with a learning disability may "get by" until they reach college; other individuals with a more severe disability may remain unable to process basic words throughout their lifetime.

These sentences require a punctuation mark to separate the two clauses: a semicolon; or a comma with a conjunction. If you choose to use the semicolon, you should not include a conjunction.

Writers often make one common mistake when they are building a compound sentence: they use the word, "however," as a conjunction. However, the word, "however," is not a conjunction but a transitional word, as I have used it in this sentence. It cannot connect two independent clauses. The word, "but," reflects the same relationship between ideas and can be used to connect independent clauses.

Compound Subjects and Verbs

Compound Subjects and Verbs contain only a single clause, a single idea, because there are not two subjects or verbs.

- S and SV.

    Neurologists and educational professionals have been studying learning difficulties for more than two centuries.

- SV and V.

    Other terms besides learning disability were proposed during the Foundation Phase but did not gain general acceptance.

Notice that these sentences do not contain any commas because they include only a single clause. *Another common mechanical error is to separate a compound verb with a comma.* However, this usage sends a wrong message to the reader—that there are two separate ideas when there are not.

Subordination

Subordinate clauses begin with subordinating conjunctions (after, because, if, when, which, etc.). Subordinate clauses are less important than independent clauses. Therefore, the less important idea goes in the subordinate clause.

- Sub, SV.

    If they have the appropriate documentation, students on campus can be provided with modifications such as extended time on tests or a note-taker.

- SV, Sub.

    The group approved the term, learning disabilities, which rapidly gained acceptance in educational circles.

- S, Sub, V.

    The current term, which was embraced by educators and parents alike, was the product of a grass-roots effort to gain support for struggling students.

We can write many sentences with a subordinate clause multiple ways. For example, we could rewrite the final example above:

- The current term, which was the product of a grass-roots effort to gain support for struggling students, was embraced by educators and parents alike.

Neither version of this sentence is better than the other at the level of style or content. However, the first version emphasizes the idea that the term, learning disabilities, was the product of a grass-roots effort. This version therefore might be the superior choice for a paragraph about grass-roots advocacy in education. The second version emphasizes the idea that the term was embraced by both educators and parents. This version therefore might be the superior choice for a paragraph about coalition building in education.

Rule 3 of the Principles of Syntax is particularly significant when discussing sentences like this final example, which include subordinate clauses between the subject and verb. Sometimes, this type of sentence is necessary, when the subordinate clause modifies the subject. In the above example, the subordinate clause modifies the single word, "term," and must immediately follow it. But these subordinate clauses should remain relatively short: the more words between the subject and verb, the more difficult it will be to read.

Writing Strategy

You can make revision (and grammar) more concrete by listing the eight sentence types on a piece of scrap paper and comparing it to your own sentences. This process can help you to identify improper comma use, run-ons, and fragments without feeling overwhelmed with grammar rules. More importantly, it can help you determine why a sentence is not working and break down ones that are overly wordy.

In addition, the following guidelines can help ensure that your prose is as reader-friendly as possible:

1. *Limit your sentences in most cases to two clauses.* If it has more than two clauses, a sentence is far more likely to be wordy, awkward, or ungrammatical.
2. *Separate clauses with commas.* If it isn't a new clause, it probably doesn't need a comma (with the exception of lists and certain situations where they're optional).
3. *Do not overuse subordinate clauses at the beginning of sentences.* You can move some of these clauses to the end of the sentence, as they will often read clearly in both places. This strategy will also increase your sentence variety.
4. *Limit subordinate clauses at the beginning or middle of sentences to about 5–7 words.* A long subordinate clause at the beginning of a sentence will make it much harder to read.

Exercise

Choose a paragraph from a piece of writing you are currently revising. Analyze its syntax:

1. Determine the structure of each sentence: Which of the eight types is it?
2. Tally the number of each type: how many are simple sentences? Compound?
3. Which sentence structure do you use most frequently? Which do you not include at all?
4. Combine two simple sentences, or change one sentence into a different type.
5. Shift one subordinate clause at the beginning of a sentence to the end.

RHYTHM AND ELEGANCE

An audience often judges the success of a piece of writing on its logos appeal, both at the level of content and style. Paragraphs and sentences need to be built in a way that is orderly and efficient for reading. But as readers, we also recognize elegance in language and are drawn to a piece of writing because we recognize its beauty.

You don't need to be Virginia Woolf to write sentences that will appeal to your audience at the aesthetic level. Elegance in prose requires not an artistic gift but a sense of balance, emphasis, and rhythm. In other words, it is in large part our ear that determines the pathos appeal of a piece of writing.

This section addresses three characteristics of prose that create elegance and appeal to the aesthetic sense of the audience: emphasis; punctuation; and balance.

Emphasis

In a sentence, the primary point of emphasis occurs at the end of the idea. This characteristic of the language is called **end focus:** it stresses certain content and helps build normal sentence rhythm. Consider this short passage by Tom Junod:

> *Once upon a time, a long time ago, a man took off his jacket and put on a sweater. Then he took off his shoes and put on a pair of sneakers. His name was Fred Rogers. He was starting a television program, aimed at children, called Mister Rogers' Neighborhood. ("Can You Say … Hero?";* http://www.esquire.com/entertainment/tv/interviews/a27134/can-you-say-hero-esq1198/*)*

The final words of each sentence are impactful and significant: sweater, sneakers, Fred Rogers, and *Mister Rogers' Neighborhood*. More importantly, these words are carefully chosen: Junod's piece is a profile of Mr. Rogers, and no words invoke a more powerful image of the man than a sweater and sneakers. Only at the end of the sentence would these words gain such significance.

You were likely told at some point in your academic career that you should not end a sentence with a proposition like "of" or "to." Like most rules of style, this one has exceptions, but the advice is generally sound. If you conclude with a preposition, you've lost the opportunity to end your sentence with a striking and meaningful word.

You can improve your end focus and manipulate the emphasis within a sentence by adopting four strategies:

1. *Focus the end of the sentence by trimming unnecessary words.*
2. *Shift peripheral phrases* (like "Once upon a time" or "After our visit") *to the beginning of the sentence.*
3. *Shift new ideas to the end of the sentence.*
4. *Avoid repeating the same words at the end of nearby sentences.* A sentence will seem flat if it ends with a word that you used nearby, because your voice will trail off. **Example:** Instead of repeating the noun, use a **pronoun.** The reader will at least hear emphasis on the word just before **it.**

Correctly using end focus not only places emphasis on the most important ideas in a passage but creates rhythm.

Strategies for Shifting Emphasis

Ordinarily, you will want to eliminate empty words from your sentences. However, strong writers often break this rule to change which ideas in a sentence get stressed. This strategy can be extremely effective—but only if you use it sparingly.

When empty words begin a sentence (specifically "it," "there," or "what" expressions), the emphasis changes to the word or phrase immediately following them.

- "It ..."
  - **End focus:** The dog ripped *my favorite scarf.*
  - **Empty words:** It was *my favorite scarf* that the dog ripped.
  - **Empty words:** It was *the dog* that ripped my favorite scarf.

- "There …"
  - **End focus:** A crocodile is living *in the sewer.*
  - **Empty words:** There is *a crocodile* living in the sewer.

- "What/Where …"
  - **End focus:** We heard *a colony of bats.*
  - **Empty words:** What *we heard* was colony of bats.

Queen Latifah uses this strategy in a passage from her memoir, *Ladies First:*

> *I* am not a *psychologist or* sociologist. *I don't have any* degrees, *and I'm not an expert on* life. What I am *is a young black woman from the inner city who is* making it, *despite the* odds, *despite the obstacles I've had to face in the* lifetimes that have come my way.

The passage is emphasized through the use of italics, in most cases through the use of end focus. However, Latifah manipulates the third sentence by adding a "what" clause, emphasizing the phrase, "I am." This passage is primarily about her sense of identity, so this choice highlights the main idea of the passage. But more importantly, it also helps create rhythm by varying the sentence structure.

Punctuation

Our ability to manipulate the emphasis in a sentence is perhaps our most important tool in building rhythm—but not our only one.

Punctuation between clauses and phrases can be used to build rhythm and give more (or less) emphasis to the secondary parts of the sentence. In other words, punctuation builds meaning and serves a rhetorical function.

We use three primary types of punctuation to help us build rhythm, each of which sends a different signal to the audience about the emphasis that should be placed on a clause:

- **Dashes:** Clause or phrase has more than ordinary emphasis.
- **Commas:** Clause or phrase has ordinary emphasis.
- **Parentheses:** Clause or phrase has less than ordinary emphasis.

Commas are the foundational mid-sentence punctuation, separating clauses, phrases, and series. Dashes and parentheses, however, can be used as alternatives, giving a passage more variety and greater rhythm.

Dashes and parentheses can be used in two primary ways:

1. *Dashes and parentheses can be used as an alternative to replace commas.*

   - The black-eyed-susan (prolific and hardy) brightens any early summer garden.
   - The rose—beautiful but fickle—is the bane of any gardener.

2. *Dashes and parentheses can be used to connect full sentences in a compound sentence, unlike a comma.*

   - The storm swept across the Midwest—it left fallen trees and flood waters in its wake.
   - The tomato is Nature's greatest gift to mankind (only garlic can claim to be its equal in the kitchen).

The use of punctuation to build rhythm is subtle but significant. Consider the following passage by Gloria Anzaldúa:

> *I will no longer be made to feel ashamed of existing. I will have my voice: Indian, Spanish, white. I will have my serpent's tongue—my woman's voice, my sexual voice, my poet's voice. I will overcome the tradition of silence. ("How to Tame a Wild Tongue")*

The passage begins with a simple, direct sentence with only an ending period. The following two sentences share a similar structure—an independent clause followed by a series of three items. The second sentence uses a colon to introduce the list, which contains single words. The third sentence uses a dash to introduce the list, which includes longer phrases. The passage gains rhythm through this repetition, but it also builds to a climax. As readers, we feel the passage build in intensity, both through the choice of the dash and the longer list. The final sentence, the most significant, brings the essay to a dramatic close. But without her use of punctuation in the second and third sentences, Anzaldúa would have been less effective in her use of climax.

> ### Exercise
>
> Choose a paragraph from a text that you have been reading—preferably not a textbook or similarly "bland" genre.
>
> Rewrite or type the paragraph without any punctuation. Add in your own new punctuation, without looking at the original version. There are many possibilities, so be creative!
>
> How did your new punctuation change the rhythm of the paragraph?

Coordination and Balance

Our use of emphasis and punctuation helps us construct sentences with rhythm; sentences that are pleasing to the ear. But in order to have a fluid rhythm, a sentence must also be symmetrical—balanced.

Coordination (or parallel structure) is the repetition of syntactical structures: strings of nouns; strings of prepositional phrases; strings of predicates; strings of subordinate clauses; a series of sentences with the same subject and sentence structure; or even a series of paragraphs that begin with parallel sentences.

While a sentence must be "parallel" to be grammatical, coordination in a sentence (or parallel structure) is about so much more than grammar:

1. *Coordination helps to emphasize the relationship between ideas:* It makes the equality of different parts of the sentence visible and audible to the reader. In other words, balanced sentence parts look and sound the same—so they share the same level of importance.
2. *Coordination builds rhythm in prose*—that elusive quality, "flow."

Because it is so important in creating rhythm and linking ideas, coordination occurs within sentences, across multiple sentences, and even across multiple paragraphs. There is no limit to the ways in which this syntactical repetition can be used.

At the sentence level, coordination is most commonly used to:

1. *Balance parallel ideas in a series.*

    Example: Attending a hockey game is a unique auditory experience: The rhythmic **whisper** of the blades across the ice; the loud **crack** of the puck against the glass; the harsh **ping** of the puck off the goalpost; and the crowd roaring happily.

In the sentence above, the final item in the list is not parallel with the other items. It has a noun-present participle structure, while the others have an adjective-noun structure. In order to have a pleasing rhythm (and to be grammatical), the final element would have to be changed to, "the happy roaring of the crowd."

2. *Balance parallel ideas presented as pairs with coordinating or correlative conjunctions.*

   Example: The puppy was not only a cuddly ball of fur but also destroying the house.

In the sentence above, the parallel structure revolves around the pair of correlative conjunctions, "not only … but also." However, the second element of the sentence differs in structure from the first. The first element ("cuddly ball") has an adjective-noun structure, while the second has a present participle-object structure. In order for the sentence to be effective and grammatical, we would have to change the second element to, "a wrecking ball in the house." This revision would make the sentence not only more symmetrical but also more rhythmic, with the repetition of the word, "ball."

Conjunctions

- **Coordinating conjunctions:** and, but, or, nor, for, so, yet
- **Correlative conjunctions:** not only … but also, either … or, neither … nor, both … and, whether … or

We can also use coordination and parallel structures in my complicated ways. The following passage appeared in Sarah Adams' short oral essay, "Be Cool to the Pizza Dude" on NPR:

I am the equal of the world,

>> not because of the car I drive,

>> the size of the TV I own,

>> the weight I can bench-press, or

>> the calculus equations I can solve.

I am the equal to all I meet because of the kindness of my heart.

(http://www.npr.org/2005/05/16/4651531/be-cool-to-the-pizza-dude)

Adams' passage uses two different parallel constructions. First, she builds to a climax through a parallel list of "unimportant" possessions and skills, each of which is longer than the previous one. Second, she echoes the phrase, "I am the equal," in the first and last sentence; this strategy further builds the sense of climax and creates symmetry. This use of balance and coordination is crucial to Adams' piece because its oral form requires not only correct grammar but also a sense of rhythm for the radio.

> ### Writing Strategy
>
> To check for parallel structure, first identify the type of sentence you are looking at. Does it have compound verbs? Is it a compound sentence or a string of independent clauses? To answer this question, identify the main subject(s) and verb(s).
>
> Once you know which type of sentence you are looking at, you can begin to circle any conjunctions and repeated words—those elements around which a sentence will be coordinated. Particularly when a sentence is complex, you should diagram the sentence, listing the series of parallel elements beneath each other.

CONCLUSION

Sentence-level revision often seems imposing. Hopefully, this chapter provided you with strategies for revision, but the process does take time. You will need to build time into your writing process to revise at the sentence-level. I suggest that you revise only a couple of pages at each sitting, reading the paper aloud. Highlight sentences that you stumble over or have to read twice, and revise them after you are finished reading. Before long, you will develop both a process for your revisions and a stronger ear for prose.

It might seem that elegant prose is only a necessity for those who imagine themselves to be writers. But a sense of style is crucial in building our ethos, constructing a logical argument, and pleasing our readers' ear. In other words, style is crucial in writing texts that are audience-friendly, meant to be read by others rather than just to express our thoughts. It is our obligation as writers (and you are a writer!) to provide our readers with work that is both efficient and, hopefully, beautiful.

Exercise: Using Your WRD Skills in Your Field

What do we want to be when we "grow up"? Many WRD students know their chosen career path, but some might still be questioning. No matter your path, the skills discussed in the previous chapters will help you in your future career.

For this exercise, research your chosen profession, or any profession that sounds interesting. Using UK's library system and the research skills you've learned, find an article published in your field. Look at the title, citations, and bibliography. Can you tell in what style this article is formatted? Cite the article using the same format. Go around the classroom and talk to classmates about their citations styles. How are they different or like your chosen formatting and citation styles? Have you noticed which professional fields tend to utilize MLA or APA style? Have you encountered a formatting style you haven't heard of before? It is important to understand how formatting guidelines are unique.

Now you've successfully practiced research in your chosen or interested field. Throughout your college career, you'll gain familiarity and practice in using this style. Because professionals in your field have used this style, you know it's one you'll need throughout your professional career.

NOTES

[1] Note that this rule does not always apply when answering questions: *Where did you go?* **Idaho.**

Public Speaking

Recommended for WRD 111/112
or as needed for WRD 110

Chapter 12

As scholars who present at professional conferences in our field and as instructors of classes with a significant public speaking component, we have seen many presentations. And some of the most memorable presentations we have seen over the years begin by using narrative, by telling a story. So in the spirit of those noteworthy openings, this chapter also begins with a story: In this instance, a story about why there is a public speaking chapter in a book about writing and rhetoric in the first place.

To tell that story, one has to go back several years, to around 2007, to the time during which our University as a whole was rethinking its priorities by overhauling undergraduate general education curriculum. At that time, the University of Kentucky general education program had not been reconsidered for several decades, so much of the discussion during this moment centered on what students in our classes would need in order to leave our campus ready to confront the challenges of life, work, and citizenship in the 21st century. The result was the *UK Core*, a substantial portion of which is fulfilled by the Department of Writing, Rhetoric, and Digital Studies Composition and Communication courses, which recognize the interconnectedness of written, spoken, and visual communication.

The logic behind WRD's Composition and Communication course design was to give students the bedrock of skills that they would need to become effective communicators in any modality—be it the written word, a podcast or audio essay, a video, a speech, or even in a medium that does not yet exist. The foundational knowledge set behind all of these modes of communication is *rhetoric*. As you may have read in Chapter 1, rhetoric has been defined in various ways over the years, from Aristotle's classical definition of rhetoric as the ability to see the available means of persuasion in a situation to Krista Ratcliffe's contemporary notion that rhetoric is "the study of how we use language and how language uses us."[1] However one defines rhetoric, the production of meaning and its relation to language takes center stage. With that being the case, rhetoric in the written word and rhetoric in public speaking have been closely linked. Indeed, for almost its entire history of formal study in the West, rhetoric has concerned itself with public speaking, even to the point of leading a first-century Roman rhetorician Quintilian to say, "Rhetoric is the art of speaking well."[2] Therefore, to give students experience in a broad range of rhetorical situations, the skill of speaking before a live audience becomes integral to the mission of Composition and Communication.

ORGANIZATION

In many, if not most ways, the process for composing a speech closely mirrors the process for writing anything else. The writing process in general is explained in more detail in Chapter 4, "Strengthening Your Writing Process." On the whole, however, a quick overview of the writing process reveals several steps that occur as a person creates: invention, organization, drafting, and revision and editing. The steps in the writing process are often nonlinear, occurring and recurring at different times throughout the life of any project. For example, when I am drafting a speech, new ideas occur to me even as I try to document existing ideas, which means that even though I am ostensibly in the drafting stage of the writing process, I am also in the invention stage, coming up with new ideas as I go. Given this recursive nature of the writing process, you might find yourself revising portions of your speech as you plan an organizational pattern. Even so, our main focus in this section is to give you strategies to organize a presentation effectively.

Speeches differ from most other forms of communication because they are often delivered live, which does not afford the audience the opportunity to rewind or reread a portion that might be difficult to understand. With that being the case, the organization of ideas in any presentation must be easy to follow because it is important that your audience understand each main point the very first time they hear it. To help you with such considerations, it is sometimes beneficial to think of your speech as existing in three distinct sections: a beginning, which gets the audience's attention, introduces your topic, and gives an overview of main points; a middle, which develops those points; and an end, which summarizes the presentation's main ideas and leaves a lasting impression.

Beginnings

"All beginnings are difficult," taught the Rabbinic sage Ishmael ben Elisha. A similar Irish proverb opines, "Making the beginning is one third of the work." American expatriate and poet T. S. Eliot wrote "In my beginning is my end." Though perhaps these maxims are not specifically referring to the opening of a speech, they nevertheless seem relevant, and the general consensus is in: getting a speech started is a challenge. Notwithstanding this difficulty, there are some general qualities that the introductory portions of good speeches often share, and including them in your presentation as a way of structuring your ideas can often help you set your speech off with a bang.

◎ **Good speeches get our attention.** Sometimes, half of the battle in a presentation is connecting with an audience, and experienced public speakers realize that most audience members decide, consciously or not, within the first minute of a talk whether to tune in or to tune out. The most well-thought-out research and the most compelling argument on a topic will still fall flat if a speaker does not interest their audience right from the start. To accomplish this, many speakers use **attention catchers,** brief, often colorful openings designed to entice an audience into listening. The audience, the occasion, and the topic of a presentation often dictate the kind of attention catcher a speaker will use, but they often range from the humorous—a short joke or anecdote—to the shocking, to the unexpected, to the pressingly relevant. Similarly, many speakers will rely on the eloquence of others, starting their talks with a pertinent quotation. Take a look at the YouTube video below, which contains examples of various attention catchers. What rhetorical appeals are these speakers using to connect with their audience early in the speech? *(https://www.youtube.com/watch?v=2_VvIr1KkLo)*

◎ **Good speeches often clarify their topic right from the start.** Just like many writers often do not wait until the end of an essay or website to let readers know the main focus of their project, skilled speakers most often present their topic and or argument clearly and succinctly right from the start of their speech. Doing so can help to increase your audience's comprehension by helping them identify a clear area of focus for the talk. Of course, there may be instances in which a speaker wants to work deductively, arriving at a conclusion or thesis after careful consideration of particular instances. However, even in these situations it is wise not to leave the audience guessing at your topic and motives for too long; such uncertainty can result in a talk that seems too unfocused to be effective.

◎ **Good speeches give an overview of what is to come.** Since the primary audience for many speeches only gets to hear a speaker's talk once, it is important that they be able to follow the logic and organization of the talk. Towards that end, experienced speakers frequently included a **preview of main points** in the speech as a way of helping the audience understand the main ideas that the presentation will consist of. Such previews do not have to be elaborate or complex, but including a short sentence or two that highlights the most important ideas in a talk before you develop them will help make the presentation more memorable through repetition.

- **Good speeches build good ethos for the speaker early.** The most effective presentations are ones delivered by speakers an audience feels they can trust. In classical rhetoric, this phenomenon is known as *ethos*—an appeal based on the perceived character and credibility of the rhetor. Many factors influence an audience's impressions of a speaker's ethos—from appearances, to manner of speaking, to seeming familiarity with the subject matter. And while a speaker will most likely never be able to account for every factor affecting her ethos, she can nevertheless get the speech started on the right foot by speaking confidently and showing genuine engagement with her subject matter.

Middles

The middle of a speech, also called the body of a speech, is where most of the speech resides. The content and organization of these middle sections can vary wildly from one speech to another, depending on purpose and occasion. However, there are some general guidelines you can apply to most public speaking occasions that will help you organize the body of your speech.

- **Good speeches are organized around main ideas.** When organizing the content you have generated for your speech, it helps to single out the ideas that you believe are most important to conveying your message and achieving your goals. Think of these main ideas as the building blocks of your speech, as something akin to body paragraphs in an essay.
- **Good speeches make effective transitions between main ideas.** If part of a successful speech is presenting your ideas and research in a manner that the audience can follow, some of the most important tools toward that end are **transitions**. The best transitions perform two distinct functions simultaneously: they summarize important information that has just been conveyed, and they provide a preview for the next main point. Consider for example this transition statement, taken from a speech about cultural standards of beauty: "Now that we have spent some time examining the ways that the media constantly bombard us with unrealistic representations of beauty, we can begin to articulate the ways that people's daily lives are negatively affected by these representations." Reading this transition now, without even hearing the rest of the speech, we can clearly understand the main point that preceded it

(media representations of beauty) and the main point that will follow (negative effects on people's everyday lives). Providing such summary and preview in between your main points provides the repetition and reinforcement needed to keep your audience engaged and easily able to follow your talk.

- **Good speeches continue to build good ethos in the middle.** Consciously or not, audiences continually keep tabs on a speaker's credibility. Building credibility does not depend solely on any one aspect of the speech, but instead consists of a network of indicators: familiarity with the subject matter, citing authoritative and reliable sources, documenting your logic and reasoning, and showing that you are invested in your topic are all ways to improve your ethos. Being mindful of the way your credibility is established or undermined by your main points and how you develop and support them is crucial to the success of the body of a speech.

Endings

Just as it is crucial to draw an audience into a speech by capturing their attention at a presentation's outset, the way a speaker ends her speech also makes an important impression on an audience. When drafting a conclusion for a speech, here are some ideas to keep in mind.

- **Good speeches often conclude by reiterating important points.** Think of this reiteration as a mirror version of the preview of the main points you shared in the beginning of the speech. Proficient speakers realize that repetition is one tool that helps increase retention, so it stands to reason that summarizing the main ideas of your talk will help emphasize the main take-away points for the audience.
- **Good speeches end memorably.** You have put a lot of time into your talk. You have come up with a topic, conducted research, organized and drafted a quality speech, and you have rehearsed the presentation until your delivery is smooth and confident. Even so, the overall effect of your presentation can be seriously diminished if the speech ends with a whimper. To avoid this all-too-common pitfall, make sure that you craft an ending for your speech that will leave the audience thinking about your topic for the right reasons: that the last few sentences resonated with them, impressing upon them the importance of your topic, rather than a speech that ends abruptly with no conclusion at all. The concluding sentences are called **perorations,** and they perform the same function for the end of a speech that an attention catcher does at the start.

Organizing a Group Presentation

All of the above qualities of good presentations are applicable to group speeches. Good group speeches still have a beginning, middle, and an end. They still get and keep their audience's attention and still build good ethos. In contrast, however, group speeches present their own set of challenges unique to multi-speaker coordination. Here are some tips to help you organize such a team-delivered talk.

- **Decide on the main points of your speech as a team.** Even though you will eventually assign speaking roles for your group speech, make sure that the preliminary work—the invention and prewriting—is done collaboratively. Making sure each group member has a say in the direction and content of a speech right from the start will ensure a smoother process overall.
- **Organize your speech around main points.** This step is no different from how you would approach a solo presentation. Even so, as you begin to organize around the main talking points, individual speaking roles will begin to suggest themselves. For example, one person might feel most comfortable delivering introductory material, while another speaker might feel herself best suited for summarizing the background and related research the group has gathered. It is difficult to assign speaking roles before the main beats of the presentation have been worked out.
- **Monroe's Motivated Sequence is your friend.** In the 1930s at Purdue University, a speech teacher named Alan Monroe pioneered an organization pattern for presentations and marketing campaigns that drew upon the rhetoric of persuasion. In this style of organizing a speech, orators walk an audience through a five-stage organization pattern that is seemingly simple yet still proves to be effective. To persuade an audience to take action on an issue, Monroe argued a presentation needed to do five things: garner the audience's attention, establish that a problem exists, propose a solution for that problem, help the audience visualize what that solution might be like, and finally, issue a call to action that informs the audience what they can do about it. Consider the following preliminary outline that uses Monroe's Motivated Sequence on a speech about a single payer healthcare system.
    - **Attention catcher:** What if I told you that our nation could spend considerably less on healthcare while simultaneously enjoying a longer, healthier life?
    - **Establish problem:** Even after the Affordable Care Act, thousands of Americans suffer without adequate healthcare.
    - **Propose solution:** One approach to this issue is what is called a single payer health care system.

- **Visualize solution:** Consider the success of the single payer health care system as shown by the increased life expectancy and lower healthcare costs in these nations who have adopted the model.
- **Call to action:** Support legislation and candidates who are in favor of single payer healthcare.

To be sure, the content of this speech is not quite there yet, but after organizing the speech into categorical sections based on Monroe's Motivated Sequence, individual speaking roles have already begun to become apparent.

When organizing a speech using Monroe's Motivated Sequence as a group, it is often a good idea to designate one group member as a **moderator.** A moderator's role during the delivery of a presentation is usually to begin and end the speech and to introduce each new speaker along the way. In the above example, the moderator could begin the talk by capturing the audience's attention before introducing the group member who will establish the problem. Coming after an attention catcher, such an introduction and transition might look something like this:

> *To better acquaint us with the continuing need for healthcare reform, Hannah will now walk us through some of the problems with healthcare as it now exits.*

Similarly, after Hannah has established the problem, the moderator might sum up her main points and transition to the next speaker and section of the talk:

> *Thanks Hannah. Now that we have seen how healthcare reform is still needed because of continually rising healthcare costs and gaps in insurance plan coverage, Tyra will explain the ways in which a single payer healthcare system might be a solution.*

The group speech moderator often continues on in such a manner, alternating between speakers, summing up and looking ahead, until finally concluding the speech. A well-rehearsed group speech moderator can generate the unity and cohesion that a group presentation really needs to shine.

AUDIENCE ANALYSIS

Chapter 2 of this book covers audience more extensively than does this chapter, and everything mentioned about audiences and the two-way street of communication in that chapter holds true for speeches you will deliver. Nevertheless, the specific rhetorical situation of delivering live speeches merits a few additional words on audience.

Your WRD class will prepare you for and perhaps give you opportunities to speak to a number of different audiences. However, in most instances, you'll deliver speeches to audiences limited to the classroom environment: namely, the instructor and your fellow classmates. On the surface, that might appear to be all you need to know about the audience for a speech in your WRD class. Think of some of the things you can likely assume regarding this audience: They are college students or faculty at the University of Kentucky, most of them probably live in Lexington or nearby, they have been exposed to the same ideas you have in the class this semester, they most likely have a high school diploma or the equivalent. All of these common factors, taken together, begin to provide us an idea of who we will be talking to, which in turn, clues us in on some of the design choices we can make when crafting a speech—things like what level of vocabulary we can use and what cultural references might be understood or not. However, closer examination of this audience can be enlightening because, even in a classroom that appears to be filled with many commonalities, there can still be vast differences in life experiences: everything from large differences based on the race, class, or gender of an audience member, to seemingly small but nevertheless consequential things, such as whether or not your neighbor has eaten breakfast that day.

Knowing that the audience for a message can have a powerful influence on the ways a speaker composes and delivers that message, how can rhetors analyze their audience when such groups can vary so vastly as individuals? Speakers in these situations develop their material to be delivered to what is known as a **target audience,** which consists of the individuals the speaker intends to connect with or persuade through a presentation. The notion of the target audience is an often fictitious but nevertheless educated guess at who will be reached through a particular rhetorical exchange. Therefore, when drafting a speech, speakers often use a list of generative questions to help them pin down to whom they will be speaking and which design strategies would be best to reach that audience. Such a list of questions appears on page 36.

Chapter 12   Public Speaking

> ### Exercise: Considering Audience through Interview
>
> Pair up with a partner in your class and conduct a short interview with him or her regarding a potential topic for a speech. What does this person already know about your topic? What would this person like to know about your topic? Does she or he have any strong opinion on the matter? Why or why not? After noting your interviewee's answers to such questions, you will begin to have a better idea of who the person is as an audience member and how you might best present your topic to such an audience member. Finally, ask yourself if this person's knowledge or experiences with your topic might be typical for other audience members or unique to him/her.

WORKING WITH VISUALS AND PRESENTATION AIDS

Audience First

When possible, many speakers choose to incorporate visuals and other presentation aids into their presentations. Because you'll be thinking about your audience from the moment you begin designing the presentation, continue keeping their needs in mind as you choose presentation aids and work within your constraints. Every member of your audience will have different needs and abilities, and you may not know just by looking at your audience (or even asking them to complete a survey) what those needs and abilities are. Think about this:

- If an audience member is unable to see or read visual content, will he/she be able to understand my presentation?
- If an audience member cannot hear or understand the auditory content, will he/she be able to understand my presentation?
- Does my presentation require any active participation that makes assumptions about the physical abilities of my audience (e.g., that they can run or walk, that they can eat a snack I bring in, etc.)?

Some of these questions you can answer by polling your classmates or your audience. However, sometimes you can't do this, and sometimes you don't know exactly what questions to ask. For this reason, strive to create presentation aids that will work for all abilities. This is a principle that scholars of teaching and learning call Universal Design.[3] You can incorporate elements of Universal Design by the following:

- Adding captions to video clips or songs
- Making typefaces large and easy to read

- Adjusting images for clarity and sharpness
- Commenting on and discussing images; not just leaving them on the screen
- Offering multiple ways to participate in your presentation

One of the great things about Universal Design is the evidence that it helps all kinds of learners, not just those with physical or learning disabilities. For instance, captioning will allow audience members who are deaf or hard of hearing to understand auditory content used in your presentation, but the captions are also helpful for learners who retain written information more easily than spoken and English language learners. In addition, captions can reinforce for all of the hearing audience the content they're receiving through audio. Everyone wins!

Constraints

Audience needs won't be the only factors you'll need to consider. Like all rhetors in all rhetorical situations, you will have constraints. The length of time you'll be speaking, whether you can use notecards or an outline, what kinds of presentation aids you can use: These constraints will probably be determined by the assignment. These and other constraints, such as the size of your presentation space and the available technology, will shape how you develop presentation aids. Consider the following:

- What technology is available in the room I'm speaking in? Can I use PowerPoint? Prezi? Show video clips?
- How reliable is that technology? Should I have a handout or other backup plan?
- Will I be able to connect to the Internet? What if Internet access is disrupted during my presentation?
- How big is the room? Will I be able to move around?
- Can I use a clicker or a pointer?

Think about your constraints before and during your process of creating the presentation aids, and, equally important, have a back-up plan. It's no fun to spend time creating an elaborate and beautiful presentation in Google slides only to discover that the computer you've got to work with won't connect to the Internet.

Chapter 12   Public Speaking

Presentation Aids: Media and Design

In today's classroom and professional settings, mention of a presentation often connotes the use of PowerPoint, Prezi, or other digital slideshows. Presenters may embed photos, videos, sound and video clips within their slideshows, but the overall format remains dominant. The ubiquity of PowerPoint and its ilk has given rise to a condition professional speakers, business people and comedians alike call "Death by PowerPoint." Death by PowerPoint occurs when a presenter uses slideshow software ineffectively, creating text-dense, hard to read, redundant, uninformative, and/or aesthetically unpleasing or "busy" slides. The boredom instilled in the audience by these kinds of presentations results in "death": the complete and total loss of the audience's attention.

Watch these videos for two different takes on what constitutes "Death by PowerPoint."

- TED Talk on Death by PowerPoint *(https://www.youtube.com/watch?v=Iwpi1Lm6dFo)*
- Comedian on Death by PowerPoint *(https://www.youtube.com/watch?v=MjcO2ExtHso)*

No one sets out to commit Death by PowerPoint (or Prezi), but it happens. One reason it occurs is that presenters sometimes begin to think of the PowerPoint *as* the presentation, rather than one part of it. This can result in gaffes like reproducing on the slide word for word what you plan to say, reading from the screen, and creating far too many slides. Another reason Death by PowerPoint occurs is the opposite problem: taking the PowerPoint for granted, assuming your speaking is the presentation and the PowerPoint is just what you're required to project behind you. Avoid both of these mistakes. Your presentation is everything you do in front of the audience; presentation aids and speaking are inextricably connected. A few basic principles can help you avoid Death by PowerPoint.

Simplicity

Keep your presentation aids simple so that your audience can focus on you. Simple PowerPoint slides will attract rather than distract your audience.

- **Keep text to a minimum.** Some presenters suggest no more than six words on a line, no more than six lines per slide. Others reject this so-called 1-6-6 rule in favor of no more than 15 words on a slide or even no more than six words total.[4] There is no hard and fast rule, but less is often more in this case. Stick to key words and main ideas; avoid scripts and multiple subpoints.

◎ **Many presenters favor sentence fragments,** beginning with active verbs, to avoid too much text. You can see below how Figure 1's text, "Promotes active learning" is more succinct than Figure 2's text. Figure 3's text is even shorter, "Active learning," a key term that you can explore more fully as you're speaking. Whether you use fragments, single words or phrases, or short sentences, be consistent. Continue using the same verb tense and basic structure.

Figure 1.

Figure 2.

Figure 3.

- **Allow plenty of white space on slides with text.** Consider using blank space, such as a black slide projected behind you, when you want to call attention to what you're saying at that moment.
- **Limit your total number of slides.** Even a well-designed presentation with limited text, lots of interesting images, and appropriate animations will be undermined by too much clicking.

Continuity

As with keeping your presentation simple, maintaining continuity in your design will also help your audience focus on you rather than an ever-changing array of fonts and colors on the screen behind you.

- **Use a single theme or color scheme for your entire presentation.**
- **Limit yourself to two fonts:** One for your titles and one for any text beneath. You may use just one for both, adjusting size and boldness. Choose sans serif fonts that are easier for your audience to read on a screen.
- **Limit animations and transitions.** Using the fanciest fly-ins for text or pictures might backfire if you project on a computer different from the one you designed on; they may appear too slowly or not at all. It can also be distracting.

Variety

It might seem a bit contradictory, but some variety in your slides is a good thing. Vary your use of text and images. Don't click through four slides in a row filled with the maximum amount of text. A text dense (or image dense) slideshow can become monotonous.

- **Use different kinds of visuals:** Video, infographics, charts, pictures. See below about how best to use these.
- **Incorporate other kinds of presentation aids and avenues for participation.** Kristi Hedges of *Forbes* magazine suggests using social media, props, handouts, and group discussion to avoid Death by PowerPoint.[5] You might not be able to have a four-minute group discussion about your topic during your presentation for class, but you can ask a question or two that the audience can respond to briefly.

Visuals

Choosing smart visuals for your presentation is not an easy task. A Google image search for "cancer research" will bring up lots of options, from the very specific and technical diagrams of cancer cells to the stock images of white-coated scientists swirling blue liquids in test tubes and flasks. You might choose the former so that you can explain to your audience how immunotherapy targets cancer cells differently than traditional chemotherapy and radiation. With the proper citation of the image (discussed a bit later), that's a fine use of the image. However, you might also be tempted to use the white-coated scientist, who is probably not a scientist at all, to fill space, to have something on the screen other than text, to meet a visual requirement. This is not a great use of a visual; it's somewhat relevant to your topic, and, if you cite it properly, you haven't done anything unethical by using it. However, stock images like this are usually unoriginal and uninteresting. Even more importantly, stock images are often evidence that presenters haven't thought much about how they want the audience to interact with the image.

Figure 4. Stock images don't always grab your audience's attention and are seldom memorable. Photo credits: Getty images and Shutterstock.

Remembering that the presentation is *everything* you're doing in front of the audience, you might realize that there's more than one way for audience members to interact with an image. When you pair an image with sound, whether through using a video clip or through your own speaking, you increase the possibilities for interaction even more. Scholars of film and the movies recognize that there can be different relationships between what moviegoers see and hear. Siegfried Kracauer made distinctions between what he called "parallel" and "contrapuntal" sound.[6] Parallel sound matches the image on the screen, such as when an eerie-sounding theremin plays during a tense moment in a horror movie. Contrapuntal sound offers a counterpoint or contrast to what the image reveals. A famous use of contrapuntal sound occurs in Stanley Kubrick's *A Clockwork Orange* when the protagonist, Alex, happily sings the upbeat "Singin' in the Rain" while attacking a man and a woman in their home. Though Kracauer focuses especially on sound, the terms parallel and contrapuntal refer to the relationship between sound and image more so than just sound. These categories are not the only options for relationships between visuals and sound (see below), but the categories should make you pause and reflect: Not every image is the same, nor do they have to be used in the same way in a presentation.

Going back to our immunotherapy and cancer research topic above, you can imagine a presentation using both parallelism and counterpoint. If you wanted to emphasize the rigors of traditional cancer treatment (e.g., radiation and chemotherapy), you could achieve parallelism by showing an image of a person with cancer who is suffering from some of the side effects, such as hair loss. As you spoke, your audience would see that the effects you describe match the image they are seeing projected. On the other hand, you could project an image of former President Jimmy Carter while discussing the side effects of chemotherapy and radiation. As your audience pays attention to your speech, they may wonder why President Carter is being projected. Because you're using the image as a counterpoint to what you're saying, you can touch briefly on how Jimmy Carter survived brain cancer (at age 90) without enduring chemotherapy, thanks to immunotherapy. The contrapuntal image can be just as memorable and evocative as the parallel image.

Figure 5. A memorable contrapuntal image. Photo credit: Erik S. Lesser, European Pressphoto Agency.

Informative Visuals

Photographs and videos are, of course, not the only kind of visual available to you as a presenter. Depending on the context and the topic, many presenters choose to incorporate informative images such as charts, graphs, and diagrams. These kinds of images take us back to the principles of Universal Design: They're meant to convey information in a new way so that more audience members understand the content and understand it better than they would without it.

When creating or choosing an informative image, you want to consider the best format for doing so. Different kinds of figures illustrate different points about data. For instance, if you wanted to illustrate a trend, such as the fluctuations in the average amount of student loan debt carried by undergraduates upon graduation over the past twenty years, a line graph is appropriate. A pie chart, which is used to distinguish the constituent parts that make up a whole, wouldn't illustrate this information effectively. When creating an informative figure, consider the following guidelines:

- Use bar graphs when you want to compare and contrast several different entities that are not part of a whole; e.g., to compare student loan debt for mathematics majors to expected income.
- Use pie charts when you want to explain and represent the different parts that make up a whole. For instance, if you wanted to, you could create a pie chart that illustrates what you spend money on each month. The pie (the whole) is all of the money you spend in a month, and the slices of the pie represent different categories or items of expense.
- Use line graphs to show trends and changes over time. For example, the line graph mentioned above showing the average student loan debt each year for twenty years would illustrate whether that average has increased or decreased.

Other Props

When they're feasible, props can be great alternative presentation aids. If you're giving a presentation on the history of photography, photographs of a stereoscope might be appropriate (and interesting), but bringing in your grandmother's stereoscope and allowing the audience to view images in 3-D through it would be more memorable. Of course, not every presentation lends itself to this type of prop use, and you should always consider your audience's needs and other constraints when bringing in a prop. However, small uses of props can frequently be incorporated. Getting your audience's eyes off the projection screen (and on to you) can increase their attention and engagement with the presentation.

> ### Exercise: Plan B
>
> With a partner, brainstorm back-up strategies for technological and other difficulties you might have on presentation day. Sketch briefly for your partner what presentation aids you're going to use: PowerPoint, videos, props, etc. Then, your partner will suggest one possible mishap that could occur: e.g., campus-wide Internet blackout. Come up with a strategy that will allow you to present in spite of this difficulty. Run through five mishaps and five solutions each.

> ### Exercise: Contrapuntal PowerPoint
>
> Using your outline or speech notes, brainstorm five contrapuntal images or videos you could use in place of images you have now planned. What other changes would you need to make to your presentation to make sure the counterpoint was understood by your audience?

Verbal Citations

Using visuals almost always requires giving credit to a source: a photographer, videographer, or even the authors of a study who provided you with the data for the pie chart you made. However, images are not the only sources you'll be citing in your presentations. Often, you will use summaries, paraphrases, and quotes of outside material to support/develop/explain the points you make in your presentation; you may even be asked to give a research update or present on the research you've done while working on a larger project. Just like when you cite your sources in written work, you need to cite sources in spoken work as well.

Captioning Images

When you use an image created by another person, include a caption on the slide citing the source in the format your instructor requests. In MLA format, images are captioned with parenthetical citations, just like the ones you create for your written work. As a general rule, you should not substitute a URL for a properly formatted caption. A URL isn't very much use to your audience, while a caption with the photographer's last name or the name of the image, might be useful.

Citing Sources

When you reproduce text from a source on a slide, cite it as you would if it were written in an essay. Whether you quote or paraphrase that text, it deserves a citation. Keep in mind, however, that you want to keep text to a minimum.

More likely, you'll be speaking aloud quotes and paraphrases from the sources you use. When you do this, you'll want to introduce and signal the use of your source. Audience members should be able to tell when you are speaking for yourself and when you are quoting or paraphrasing a source. Introducing a source is an opportunity for you to build ethos by introducing the source's author, date of publication, venue, etc., and any details that will show the audience you know your sources and you know why they're relevant. Signaling the use of the source, saying "The authors argue ..." can act as the open quotation marks (or the verbal parentheses for your citation) that let listeners know you're speaking for the source now. Some presenters will say, "Quote" or otherwise overtly indicate a quote is coming before quoting a source. Be wary of doing this. You want to show familiarity with your sources by paraphrasing often and quoting selectively. Plus, there are more imaginative (and subtle) ways to signal the use of a quote.

Finishing Up with Sources

Just like with your written work, you don't want sources to overwhelm your voice. Make sure that after you've introduced, signaled, and quoted/paraphrased a source, you discuss it. Make sure it's clear to your listeners that your voice has returned; you can consider using I-language or taking a brief pause (or both) to signal the end of the quote or paraphrase and the beginning of your thoughts.

Once you've done that, though, you're not through with your sources. You should include a Works Cited page (a slide or a handout, or another method your instructor requests) with the citation information for all of your sources, visuals and verbally cited.

Chapter 12   Public Speaking

> ### Exercise: Yoda Citations
>
> Familiarize yourself with the great character of Yoda, Jedi master of *Star Wars* fame. Use internet research to find out some of Yoda's better known aphorisms. With this list of quotes (and the sources for them), compose a 60-second speech advocating for (or against) Yoda's worldview. In this speech, quote and paraphrase Yoda at least once. When you quote Yoda, do not imitate or mock him. Imagine that your audience takes Yoda very seriously. Perform your speech to a group of 3–4 classmates. Ask them to evaluate how well you introduce and verbally cite your sources.

DELIVERY

When UK basketball coach Mark Pope drills his athletes on a play, he does not just have them run through it once. Instead, like all good coaches, Pope realizes that successful execution of all the elements of a complex play need to be rehearsed, time and time again, in order to refine each element until it has worked its way into a player's muscle memory. The importance of repetition in the delivery of a speech is the same and while the likelihood of you being body checked during a presentation is significantly lower than it would be on a basketball court, without repeated rehearsal of individual elements in the delivery of your speech, you might experience the emotional equivalent of one.

The embodied delivery of a speech can often be one of the last things we think about. Between coming up with a topic, researching, planning, and drafting a presentation, the way that we will look and sound during a talk can easily take a back seat to what seem to be more pressing concerns. However, classical rhetors thought about delivery quite a bit. Indeed, Roman philosopher and political theorist Cicero believed delivery to be such an important part of the success of a message that he singled it out as one of the five canons of rhetoric in his book *Rhetorica ad Herennium*. To become an expert on all the varied nuances of the craft of delivery might take a lifetime, but there are nevertheless several important aspects of delivery that you should be mindful of as you rehearse your talk.

- **Consider the space and your body.** Much of the labor of composing a speech happens from the shoulders up, so it is easy to forget about the other 90% of your body. For this reason, it becomes important to rehearse delivering your speech exactly as you plan to in front of the audience. What will the room for your speech look like? Will you be standing or sitting? Will there be a podium or lectern in the room? How will you incorporate visual aids? Are there planned gestures you wish to make at particular times to emphasize points? Will you need to use speaking notes? All of these are considerations that might affect how you hold yourself during a speech, and recreating these environmental constraints as you rehearse will help you make the most of your rehearsal time.

- **Plan to be nervous.** During the pressure of a live speaking engagement, many (if not most) speakers experience some degree of performance jitters. Such nervousness is OK and is perfectly natural. However, the well-prepared public speaker will be mindful of these nerves and will not allow them to manifest themselves in a nervous tick. As you rehearse your speech, practice planting your feet firmly and speaking without shifting your weight from foot to foot. Similarly, as you prepare for the talk, practice what you will do with your hands to fight the urge to fidget with clothing, notecards, etc. Have a plan for how you will position yourself in the speaking space, and then practice, practice, practice that plan.

- **Make eye contact.** Professional public speakers know that one of the ways they can connect with an audience and build rapport is to talk *to* them, not *at* or *around* them. One of the ways to convey that you are speaking not to a general audience but to individuals within the audience is to practice making eye contact. A goal to shoot for when rehearsing eye contact is to strive to look 90% of your audience in the eyes during 90% of your speech. Obviously, with larger audiences or in some spaces, such a lofty goal might be unachievable. Nevertheless, as you practice your delivery, try to imagine yourself looking at the people to whom you are speaking.

- **You have good ideas; make sure they hear them.** Air conditioners. Jackhammers. People in the hallway. Flatulent trucks. Audience members packing up their backpacks early. That guy eating a cheese Danish out of a crinkly cellophane wrapper. When we deliver a speech, there is often background noise that seems unavoidable. If you have a particularly deep voice or are a soft-spoken person, all the great points you worked so hard to develop might be at risk of getting lost in a sea of static. Because of that, one important aspect of delivery you can rehearse is **vocal projection.** Practice speaking from your diaphragm, not the top of your lungs, and envision yourself projecting your voice to the very back row of the audience. Relatedly, many speakers consciously rehearse speaking at a slow, moderate pace as they practice because of the tendency to speak more quickly under the pressure of a live performance. Rehearsing projection and a slow delivery can go a long way towards ensuring your message gets through to the audience.

The benefit of these rehearsal sessions is difficult to overstate: They give a speaker the chance to practice all of the above aspects of delivery, but they also increase familiarity with the subject matter, which in turn lowers speech day anxiety, boosts confidence, and bolsters credibility. Good public speaking is rarely easy, but setting aside time to practice your delivery can at least make things easier.

PRACTICING AND PREPARATION

A music teacher of mine once said: "Practice doesn't make perfect; *perfect* practice makes perfect." This might seem like a cynical piece of advice if you're struggling to overcome pre-presentation nerves while finishing up your Prezi, formatting your Works Cited, and working on your assignments from your other classes as well. Who can be "perfect" in these circumstances, especially just on a rehearsal day? Nonetheless, there's truth to it. Practicing your presentation is essential, and any amount of practice will pay off. However, practicing without the ability to correct any of your bad presentation habits will not help you pull off a (close to) perfect presentation when the time comes. To practice perfectly, you need to practice prepared, practice with an audience, and practice with specific goals in mind.

Your practice sessions will have greater impact on your performance the closer your presentation is to completion. Should your instructor set aside class time for rehearsal, there are several ways he or she might approach it. Some classes might focus just on introductions or conclusions, while others perhaps give you time to practice individual elements of delivery, such as making eye contact or projecting your voice. Generally speaking, however, you should come to an in-class rehearsal prepared as though you had to give the presentation for a grade that day. This means a thorough outline (or speaking notes) and a completed PowerPoint or other presentation aids. If you come to this session with an incomplete presentation, you might be able to get some good feedback from your classmates and instructor about some parts of your presentation, and you may be able to ad lib the missing pieces. However, this rehearsal will not really prepare you for the experience of giving the presentation in full. If you haven't rehearsed it, you might not realize that you don't know how to pronounce the name of a source you decide to add at the last minute; or that your audience doesn't find your opening anecdote as amusing as you had anticipated; or that the transition between your second and third points is a bit awkward; or that you run over (or under) on time when you present the whole thing. Having a complete presentation for each rehearsal can help you find these problems early.

An audience for your rehearsals will also help you improve your performance. A small audience (ideally of your classmates or other people who will be there when you give the actual presentation) can help you overcome jitters by giving you experience on a smaller scale. Rehearsal audiences are also invaluable tools for learning what the audience finds most interesting and engaging. If your rehearsal audience smiles or laughs when you want them to, makes consistent eye contact, or otherwise uses backchannels (nonverbal cues, such as head nods or concerned expressions) to indicate they're paying attention, you know that your presentation is engaging them. On the other hand, if they seem confused or inattentive, you can ask them after your rehearsal if there was anything they didn't understand or had questions about. If you didn't notice much about your audience's reaction, you need to keep rehearsing; you've either not made eye contact with them consistently enough to notice them, or you're still too nervous about/unfamiliar with your presentation to focus on the audience. If an audience isn't available, record yourself presenting with a stable camera (on a phone you can prop up or a webcam; don't attempt to take one long selfie during a rehearsal). If you don't have a camera, rehearse in front of a mirror. Deliver the presentation just as you would for an audience; half-hearted rehearsals don't constitute "perfect" practice.

Finally, make the most of your rehearsals by setting specific goals. Professional public speakers offer a range of "ideal" numbers of rehearsals for perfecting a presentation, with some advising six and others over fifteen. There probably isn't a magic number that will make all speakers equally prepared to present in all contexts. Nonetheless, more practice is probably better than less practice, so try to rehearse your presentation a minimum of five times. Set aside blocks of time that will allow you to rehearse the entire presentation multiple times at a stretch. Begin each rehearsal with a completed presentation (you can rehearse parts of your presentation before the whole thing is completed, but those don't count towards the goal of five) and an audience (or a camera or mirror). Your presentation aids should be ready to go. Have a mechanism in place to time your rehearsal; if your presentation doesn't meet the time constraints, don't count that rehearsal towards your goal of five. Additionally, if you make any major changes to content, set your rehearsal counter back to "1."

Below are some goals you can set for each rehearsal. Add your own goals based on your individual strengths and weaknesses.

- **Rehearsal #1:** Rehearse the entire presentation without stopping.
- **Rehearsal #2:** Make eye contact with each member of your audience at least twice during the presentation.
- **Rehearsal #3:** Be able to continue speaking while transitioning slides, notecards, pages, etc. (Try to memorize what's at the bottom and top of your note cards/pages; make sure you know exactly the order of your slides.)
- **Rehearsal #4:** Play the "Babble game."[7] Instead of speaking actual words, say "Blah blah" or some equivalent (e.g., "Yadda yadda" or "Rah rah") throughout the entirety of your speech. The goal is to use your tone of voice, gestures, and other nonverbal communication to emphasize your points. It should help you think about which words and phrases you want to emphasize and how you want to do it.

- **Rehearsal #5:** Dress rehearsal. Try to replicate the atmosphere of your actual presentation as closely as possible. Wear what you plan to wear that day. This might help you anticipate minor issues, like the difficulty of making eye contact if you're wearing a baseball cap. Try to rehearse in a similar location at a time similar to when you'll actually present. You'll get a good feeling for how the environment might affect you.

Finally, establish a cut-off point for rehearsals and spend your energy in other kinds of preparation. Try to get a good night's rest before and make sure to eat well the day of the presentation. Make your handout copies in advance. Have a backup of your PowerPoint on a jump drive (and/or email it to your instructor). Do something small to make yourself feel confident and relaxed: practice Power Poses, get to class a little early, talk to your parents or a friend about how much you've practiced and how smoothly you're anticipating it will go.

Visualize yourself finished with the presentation and feeling awesome. Think about what you'll do afterwards: get a fancy coffee, Skype with your younger siblings, reward yourself with Netflix. You're ready, and your presentation will be finished sooner than you think.

SELF AND PEER EVALUATIONS

When you receive written work back from your instructor with comments, what do you do? Oftentimes, students will read over their own work again as they digest their teachers' feedback. It's a bit more difficult to do this with your speeches and presentations. However, with preparation, you can be a better self- (and peer-) evaluator of your verbal work.

Self-Evaluation

Part of self-evaluation will take place before your presentation; when you're rehearsing and setting goals. You'll have a sense when you finish presenting whether or not you hit those goals. However, you shouldn't take your initial emotions when you finish presenting as the sole indicator of your performance. Sometimes, we're way too hard on ourselves (and sometimes we're way too easy on ourselves). If possible, try to have your presentation recorded. Your instructor may be able to arrange this for you, but if not, you can ask the instructor if it's okay for you to record (video or audio) your presentation.

Before you watch the recording, jot down some notes about your performance. Try to do this as soon as possible after you've presented, even if you don't plan to watch or listen to your recording right away. Make note of what you think went well and what didn't work out the way you wanted. Only after you've done this writing should you view the recording. The initial notes you take can be useful. They can tell you if your experience of the presentation was wildly different from the reality your audience experienced, but they can also help you watch the recording with a grain of salt. Remember that the video (or audio) is a mediated representation of the presentation, not the real thing. How you felt it went does in fact matter.

Note discrepancies between your initial feelings and what you observe in the recording. Did you feel like you were making eye contact frequently, but the tape suggests you turned towards the projection screen … a lot? Do you have trouble hearing yourself? Are you speaking too quickly? Does it seem like you're reading from your notes rather than speaking? It's easy to note these issues when you view a video of your presentation. You can also prioritize working on these issues for your next presentation. For instance, if you have trouble making eye contact, add another rehearsal dedicated to working on eye contact. You can also deprioritize things that went really well. If you're great at eye contact, but speaking way too fast and monotonously, focus on the Babble Game rather than eye contact in your rehearsal.

Peer Evaluation

Whether you're asked to give feedback to your peers or not, preparing to give comments to your classmates is a useful task. It can help you self-assess, as when you notice a peer pausing too long between slides, and remind yourself to memorize transitions. It can also help you cultivate good listening skills, a really underrated, but vitally important talent. Chances are good that you'll end up working with some of your classmates in group projects during the semester. Listening to their presentations can tell you a lot about their interests, knowledge, and skills.

When listening to your peers' presentations, the first thing to remember is to respect them. If you've already presented, you know how difficult it can be to be at the front of the classroom, trying to impress your class and instructor, and trying not to do anything to embarrass yourself. You may have noticed a classmate who looked bored or inattentive, maybe even one who was checking his or her phone or looking at flashcards for another class. Perhaps you understood that this person's inattention probably had nothing to do with the quality of your presentation. When you're giving a presentation, though, even the most neutral look of boredom on an audience member's face can be devastating. Try to emulate the behaviors of an attentive audience member.

- *Attentive audiences arrive on time and stay seated during the presentation.* If you're late (or need to leave early) wait for the applause following a presentation to enter (or leave).
- *Attentive audiences silence and put away phones and tablets.* Clear your desk of electronic devices unless you need them to follow the presentation.
- *Attentive audiences make eye contact with the presenter.* Remember that the presenter is trying to make eye contact; it's a two-way street.
- *Attentive audiences participate in the presentation.* When you're asked to respond, respond. Take notes so that you can formulate questions to ask during the Q&A (if applicable) or offer feedback (if you're watching a rehearsal).

Your instructor (or your peers) may ask you for more substantial feedback during rehearsals or presentations. If so, remember that you shouldn't focus exclusively on the presenter's delivery. You may notice a lack of eye contact or numerous vocalized pauses ("uhhs" and "ums"), but don't let that stop you from learning something from the presenter. Your instructor may give you specific criteria for evaluating your peers. If not, consider the following questions in formulating your response:

Feedback on Content

- What did you learn from this presentation?
- What would you like to learn more about following this presentation?
- Which sources did you feel contributed most to the presentation?
- What visuals did you find most memorable, appropriate, or interesting?

Feedback on Organization and Structure

- How did the presenter begin the presentation? Was it engaging and memorable?
- Could you list the major points of the presentation? Did the presenter list these at any point in the presentation?
- How did the presenter conclude the presentation? Could you tell when the presentation was ending? Were the final words/sentences memorable?

Feedback on Delivery

- Did the presenter make eye contact with the audience?
- Were the presentation aids visible and aesthetically pleasing?
- Could you hear and understand the presenter's voice?
- Could the presenter do anything to make the presentation more accessible for all people?

You might not have time to answer all of these questions or to talk to the presenter about all of them. If you have the opportunity, tell the presenter something important he/she did well and one or two important things he/she can work on. You can also work in your interest in the presentation topic, but make sure you prioritize helping the presenter. Remember that an audience is an invaluable tool for presenters looking to improve their performance.

NOTES

[1] Ratcliffe, Krista. "The Current State of Composition Scholar/Teachers: Is Rhetoric Gone or Just Hiding Out?" *Enculturation* 5.1, 2003. Web. 29 February 2016.

[2] Quintilian. qtd in "American Rhetoric: Definitions of Rhetoric." *American Rhetoric: Definitions of Rhetoric*, Web. 18 March 2016.

[3] Sheryl Burgstahler. "Universal Design: Process, Principles, and Applications." *Disability, Opportunities, Internetworking, and Technology,* University of Washington. N.d. Web. 11 March 2016.

[4] John Zimmer. "PowerPoint Math: The 1-6-6 Rule." *Manner of Speaking,* http://mannerofspeaking.org/2010/03/04/powerpoint-math-the-1-6-6-rule/.

[5] Kathy Hedges. "Six Ways to Avoid Death by PowerPoint." *Forbes.* N.p. 14 November 2014. Web. 11 March 2016.

[6] Siegfried Kracauer. *Theory of Film: The Redemption of Physical Reality.* Oxford UP, 1960.

[7] Nick Morgan. "Seven Ways to Rehearse a Speech." *Public Words,* 26 July 2012. Web. 11 March 2016.<http://publicwords.com/2012/07/26/seven-ways-to rehearse-a-speech/>.

Visual Rhetoric and Design

Recommended for WRD 110/112

Chapter 13

Chapter 13   Visual Rhetoric and Design

> *We are all designers. We manipulate the environment, the better to serve our needs. We select what items to own, which to have around us. We build, buy, arrange, and restructure: all this is a form of design.*
>
> —Donald Norman, from "Epilogue: We Are All Designers," *Emotional Design*[1]

This chapter focuses on visual literacy, visual design, and visual rhetoric. **Visual literacy** is the ability to observe and interpret visual information. This draws on our skills of visual observation, our abilities to notice and recall small and subtle visual details. We use our visual literacy to interpret the storyline of a film, or to laugh at the humor in a comic. When we use a website, we use visual literacy to infer what is a button that can be clicked, and we infer from the button's color and shape what that click might do or lead to. **Visual design** is the practice or profession of using design elements, like light, color, or shape, to make those films, comics, or websites into something we can interpret. **Visual rhetoric** combines visual literacy and design with rhetoric to make a branch of rhetorical studies concerned with the persuasive use of images, whether on their own or in the company of words.

In this chapter, we will practice and sharpen our observational skills. We will look closely at visual artifacts made by artists, photographers, filmmakers, author-illustrators, advertisers, and designers; and we'll talk about how writing and images can work together to form a narrative or argument.

We'll also show you tools and skills that will help you design your own visuals from scratch. Feel like you are not a visual designer? *Au contraire!* We all have some hand in the design of our own homes, rooms, or appearance. You may not sew your own clothes, but you make choices about what clothes you wear.

In 1917, Marcel Duchamp submitted a urinal, signed "R Mutt," as a work of art to be exhibited at the Society of Independent Artists in New York. It was not accepted (but also not officially rejected—it was dumped behind exhibition screens where it could not be viewed), and instead shown at the studio of his friend, Alfred Stieglitz. Duchamp called the urinal and other works like it, including a bottle rack and a bicycle wheel on a barstool, "readymades."[2] Duchamp did not make any of these sculptures. Instead, he claimed that art does not stem from what is made by the hands, but through the choices made in the mind of the artist:

> *... you can cut off the artist's hands and still end up with something that is a product of the artist's choice since, on the whole, when an artist paints using a palette he is choosing the colours. So choice is the crucial factor in a work of art. Paintings, colours, forms, even ideas are an expression of the artist's choice.*[3]

Masterful painting skills or an expert understanding of computer animation code aren't prerequisites to being an artist or a designer. We all have the potential to make art, to design, or to create visual stories or arguments. The potential lies in the choices we make. This chapter will guide you through those choices, how to interpret those choices made by another, and how to make your own choices when creating a visual artifact.

Why did you wear what you are wearing today? You may have chosen something chic and color-coordinated because aesthetics are important to you. Maybe you're wearing shorts with several pockets because it's warm out, and you have a lot of gadgets to keep on hand. If so, then functionality is important to you. You might be dressed in business wear for an interview, or in your favorite team's jersey for game day. If so, then you are conscious of an audience around you—you chose your outfit to send a message.

If you're not sure of a strong purpose behind your choice of clothes, consider this: "Why *aren't* you wearing something else?" Why gray running shoes and not yellow flip-flops? Why a t-shirt with a lion's head instead of plain black? Why an oxford shirt and slacks and not a bathrobe and spandex leggings? Why not go to class naked? Are these choices made for aesthetic reasons, practical functional reasons, or due to audience consideration?

> Not every visual object is visual rhetoric. What turns a visual object into a communicative artifact—a symbol that communicates and can be studied as rhetoric—is the presence of three characteristics. The image must be symbolic, involve human intervention, and be presented to an audience for the purpose of communicating with that audience.[4]

Using the three characteristics in the quote above as a guide, do you think there are parts of your wardrobe that constitute visual rhetoric? Why or why not? Similar questions can be used to examine and interpret visual artifacts, and to help us design our own. Why use a drawing instead of a photo? Why use bright color instead of black and white? Our first answers might be *"because it looks better,"* but often, that's not the reason. As with well-planned works of writing, well-planned visuals are created with a purpose in mind, and the choices made in the design of the visual build up to achieving this purpose.

Chapter 13   Visual Rhetoric and Design

CLOSE LOOKING

If we practice close reading to understand and interpret how a text communicates a message, then to understand and interpret how a visual communicates a message, we practice close looking. The readings and activities in this section will help you sharpen your observational skills.

Exercise: Sherlock Holmes

Clothes are a part of appearance that a person can choose. Even if choices are limited by authority or available resources, we may personalize, adapt, or search for a better option. Whether intended or not, clothes give our audience (everyone around us) clues about occupation, age, regional identity, and even aspects of personality.

View or **read** the opening scene from "The Adventure of the Blue Carbuncle" in *The Adventures of Sherlock Holmes*. The famous detective makes detailed description of an unknown person based on a hat. Some of his conclusions are based in the era of the times. Which conclusions could still apply today? Which seem too far-fetched or highly assumptive?

Holmes uses steps of logical reasoning to draw conclusions about the person's life and habits. His mind combines an observation, of things seen on the hat, with a generalization, something learned from life experience, and then reaches a conclusion. This is an example of inductive reasoning. (**Note:** We're used to hearing about Sherlock Holmes' powers of deductive reasoning, but the techniques the character employs are often inductive … maybe the "Inductive Detective" didn't have that snappy alliterative quality Doyle wanted.) Here's a few of Holmes's "deductions" broken down:

Exercise: Sherlock Holmes (continued)

Table 1. A table of Holmes's "deductions," showing how he made them from observations.

Observation	Generalization	Conclusion
There are grizzled hairs stuck to the inside of the hat.	When wearing a hat, one's loose hairs come off inside.	The wearer of this hat has grizzled hair.
It has a flat brim with curled edges.	These hats were all over London a few years ago.	This hat is a few years old.
The hat material is of good quality.	Hats of this quality cost money.	The wearer has money.
The hat is battered and dirty.	Most people would throw out a hat this worn.	The wearer has no other hat, perhaps cannot afford it.
The hat is very large.	Large headed people are smart.	The man is intellectual.

The catch here is in the generalization. Generalizations may come from life experience or may be told to us by someone else. If we use a faulty generalization, our conclusion will be wrong. In the last row of the table above, Holmes observes that the hat is large and draws the conclusion that the man is intelligent. The television adaptation plays this moment as a conversational joke, but phrenology, a theory that claimed to determine personality characteristics from the shape of the skull, was a debated science throughout the 1800s.

All of us use steps of logical reasoning. (Did you catch that generalization?) Our minds usually move through the process quickly, so we don't always note each step of making an observation, combining it with a generalization, and coming to some conclusion. Breaking the process down into steps can help us see what visual details we observe and what past experiences might have led to true or false conclusions.

Exercise: Sherlock Holmes (continued)

Try your hand at playing Sherlock Holmes, and see how much you can guess about someone based on an object. Select an object you use often and have with you: a shoe, watch, hat, backpack, keychain, pair of glasses, etc. Whatever the object is, you should be comfortable having a stranger examine it inside and out. Avoid objects like notebooks or journals where someone can simply open and read all about you. If the object is a cell phone, lock the phone so no one can see your contacts or messages. Trade your object with another person or group of people.

After you've traded objects with someone else, make a table on a piece of paper with three columns labeled "observations," "generalizations," and "conclusions." Look at the object given to you, and start listing all the different traits the object has in the observations column. No trait is too simple to matter, so start with the obvious. Note what the object is, and the object's size, color, texture, shape, and weight. Look closer. What condition is it in? How old is it? Does the object have a specific physical function? What is it, and can it perform it well? Are there other objects attached or inside? Is there a particularly well-worn area of the object? Is the object right-handed or left-handed? What does the object smell like? Is there writing on it? Has anyone altered this object to change it from its original design? Is there anything about this object that has a specific cultural association (for example, a sports logo, cartoon character, brand name, election slogan, etc.)?

Clothes are a part of appearance that a person can choose. Even if choices are limited by authority or available resources, we may personalize, adapt, or search for a better option. Whether intended or not, clothes give our audience (everyone around us) clues about occupation, age, regional identity, and even aspects of personality.

Figure 1. An illustration of Holmes examining the hat in "The Blue Carbuncle."

Exercise: Sherlock Holmes (continued)

After you've looked as closely as you possibly can, make conclusions based on each observation. If you can, provide the generalization that led you to this deduction. (You may find yourself thinking of the conclusion before the generalization!) Allow yourself freedom to go out on a limb, to write down what may seem like a far-fetched idea. Try to fill up the entire table.

Now for the spine tingling part! Share your conclusions with the class. After sharing, ask the owner to reveal which deductions are correct and which are incorrect. Make note of the incorrect deductions.

Discussion and Questions

What assumptions or false generalizations may have lead to incorrect deductions? In our example, Holmes deduced that the owner did not also own a laptop or smartphone. They assumed that a person wouldn't own two or three items that perform the same task. They correctly deduced that the owner used math in class but was not a math major, and that the owner has a busy lifestyle and is a little careless. Many of Holmes' deductions seem plausible but aren't correct because they assumed the object had not been owned by anyone else in the past.

- While playing Sherlock Holmes, what conclusions did you make that were incorrect, and where did the logical reasoning process go wrong?
- What incorrect conclusions were drawn about you when your own object was examined? How do you think the person playing Holmes came to this conclusion?
- What observable aspects of your object did you, the owner, intentionally choose or design? Why?
- Write about or talk about a time in your life when either a) you made a false assumption based on someone's appearance or b) someone made a false assumption about you based on your appearance.
- We've talked a lot about how false generalizations can get us into trouble. When might observations, generalizations, and conclusions help us out in a positive way?
- How can we regulate our own logical reasoning processes so they stay useful? How do we keep it from causing bias or discrimination?

Chapter 13   Visual Rhetoric and Design

LEARNING TO SEE

The same close-looking skills used in the Sherlock Holmes activity can also be applied to visuals and works of art. These skills are important enough that one of the largest police forces is training its officers to see with more skill. Through a special program at the Metropolitan Museum of Art, Amy Herman teaches a course called "The Art of Perception." New York police officers observe and discuss artworks from the museum to practice observation skills and communication skills. Let's try our hands at "the art of perception" and describe what we see.

Figure 2. Photograph by Mark Steinmetz.

Exercise: What's Going on Here?

Take a look through **the following gallery of images by the photographer Mark Steinmetz** *(https://www.josephbellows.com/artists/mark-steinmetz).* To boost your observation skills, try looking at the image and drawing it on a piece of paper. The drawing doesn't have to look anything like the original for this to help. This process will slow down your eyes and cause you to focus on specific areas of the image. With each picture answer and discuss: What is going on here? What time of day is it? Who is this person, and what is his/her life like? With each question and answer, be precise about what exact part of the image gives you a clue. Make notes on your drawing, if you wish. Look closer. Are your conclusions correct? Are there alternative conclusions that can be drawn from your observations?

... and How to Talk about It

Observing is just one part of visual literacy. To really understand how visuals communicate, we need to know how they carry a message. The message might be in its subject matter or content: what the picture is of—such as a dog—or what the subject matter might symbolize—such as loyalty. This message will differ based on the image's context, its surroundings: a cute puppy on a grade-schooler's notebook has one purpose, and a cute puppy on a poster at a rescue shelter has another. Media may change the message: A photograph says something different than a finger painting. The message can also be molded by formal elements like light, color, shape, and texture. A dog in bright light gives the viewer a different feeling than a dog in darkness.

CONTENT AND CONTEXT

Content is the subject matter of an image, or what the image is about. No image is without content. Even an abstract painting of one large blue square has content: that of a large blue square.

Context refers to the varied circumstances in which a work of art is created and interpreted. Think of context as anything happening outside the boundaries and surface of the image. The painter's life, the materials available, the time and place in which it was made, the history and culture of that place and time, and the potential audience of the painting, who may have even hired the painter to make it.

Context includes all of those aspects of the image's making, as well as those same aspects of the image's viewing and interpretation. When I step in front of a painting from 1660 and give my interpretation, I become part of the painting's context, outside the image's boundary looking in. My life, the time and place in which I view it, the history and culture of that place and time, and even the setting in which the image sits, such as an online thumbnail gallery or a large museum hall, all become part of the painting's interaction with me, its viewer.

When looking at **Claude Lorrain's Sermon on the Mount** *(https://collections.frick. org/objects/220/the-sermon-on-the-mount)*, one NYPD officer who participated in "The Art of Perception" said the image resembles that of a potential suicide victim, a "jumper."[5] In reality, this painting is of Jesus Christ on a high plateau preaching a sermon. How did this happen? The painting's context has changed. Its viewer, or audience, is now a police officer. Every day his job puts him in situations that many other people see few times, if ever, in their lives. He may have been called to save potential suicide victims or had extensive training in this area. Perhaps current events that happened recently in his own local sphere put this topic on his mind. Maybe the fact that he saw the painting as part of a police training exercise, and not while visiting the museum on the weekend, changed what he saw in the expressions of the faces in the crowd watching Jesus.

In 1656, Claude Lorrain definitely did not intend the police officer's vision of a suicidal jumper to be part of the painting's content. This is through no fault of his own because of the great shift in context. He couldn't foresee a New York City police officer viewing this image in a museum in the twenty-first century anymore than he could imagine New York City existing. Lorrain most likely did intend to create a dramatic scene of an individual drawing a crowd through uncommon acts and speech. Perhaps the body language and facial expressions of onlookers seemed similar to the officer. Or, maybe the visual traits Lorrain used to create this dramatic scene, like a dark, backlit landscape, somehow touched a chord in the police officer's mind.

This leads us to a third crucial part of any image or artwork: its **form.**

Exercise: Photo Pictionary, Round One

In the game Pictionary®, players guess a word or phrase from pictures drawn by a teammate. In Photo Pictionary, players guess a word or phrase from a photograph. Each team will create a photo, using a smartphone or digital camera.

First, form into teams. Next, randomly select a word. For this game, avoid simple words and names of objects that are easily found in your area. Uncommon action words, adjectives, or more abstract nouns work great: "panic," "hero," "revenge," or "apathy." Try this **game word generator** *(https://www.thegamegal.com/word-generator/),* set to hard or really hard, for inspiration.

Teams get ten minutes to take a walk, discuss a plan, and shoot a photo that illustrates their word. Players can pose, use props, or photograph something in the environment. Text of the word is, of course, not allowed. Only one photo can be used for guessing.

Once photos have been taken, teams trade photos with another team. Players on each team discuss possible guesses for what word the photo is illustrating, then submit to the class their best guess. Take one or two attempts at guessing the word (don't reveal the answers just yet!), then move on to Photo Pictionary, Round Two.

FORM

Form can be difficult to talk about because it is so simple. Formal elements of art and design usually sound like something we learned from *Sesame Street:* shape, color, light and dark, size, texture, to name a few. We can also think of form as what's left when we ignore the subject matter. Form is all the parts of an image that are not of semantic significance. Form has nothing to do with visual symbols that we translate to meanings with our minds and everything to do with sensations we perceive physically with our eyes and bodies. Varying the formal elements of a visual can completely reframe or even overturn the content of the image.

These images portray similar subject matter: a Doberman Pinscher looking at the camera. There are a few content differences: The ears are in different positions. To viewers who are familiar with dog body language, or with the practice of cropping Dobermans' ears, this content may mean something. Is the dog alert? Angry?

Figure 3.

Figure 4.

Now, let's look at differences in form. Which picture is darker? Darkness can trigger a feeling of the unknown, or even potential danger. Which picture has more color? Color can make something more inviting, or add warmth or coolness. What textures do you see in the picture? How might they contribute to the viewer's interpretation?

One of these pictures is taken from a different point of view. Point of view is a particular aspect of the design element of space: the real or illusional space and distance in the image. How does this point of view change what message might be in this image of a dog?

Reading: Formal Elements of Visual Design

To include form in our toolbox of visual literacy, we need a good grasp of the different formal elements of visual design. Most of us have had reading and writing in school. We were taught the basic forms of language: letters, sounds, words, meanings, sentences, tenses, etc. We were taught that words have a meaning (content), and that the meaning can be flexible or changed, that the words may have different connotations to different people or connotations that change over time (context).

We also learn that writers might choose a word for an aesthetic, sensory-based purpose: to make a rhyme, or a harsh clacking sound, or a smooth swooshing sound, when writing poetry. The formal elements of visual art are like poetry, they play on our most basic reactions to visual stimulation. Darkness is mysterious; we can't see objects in it. Large objects have power, especially when they are bigger than us. The natural world is curvy; the man-made world is angular and square.

These tutorials *(https://ukwrite.wordpress.com/tutorials/visual-literacy/)* cover the formal elements of visual design. Examples from a wide range of media are included, such as photographs, film stills, paintings, sculptures, maps, diagrams, and architecture. (We'll cover things like unity, emphasis, and grids later on, so skip those for now.)

Exercise: Photo Pictionary, Round Two

In round two of Photo Pictionary, teams can use a photo-editing program to alter design elements, like lighting and color, to better illustrate subtle connotations of the word. For example, if a team's word is "explore" and the guesses were "lost" and "stranded," the team might alter their photo to add some more *positive* connotation.

This can be a fun time to play with Photoshop®, but online photo editors like PicMonkey or Pixlr work great, too. Just be aware of pre-made filters that change several formal elements at once. Make sure that every change is one that nudges the guessers into the right direction.

Exposure, brightness, and contrast will adjust lights and darks. If the word has a dangerous or mysterious connotation, darkening the image might help. Color balance, white balance, hue, and saturation can adjust color or color intensity. If the word is playful, bright colors might help. Rotating and cropping will change the direction of major lines. For example, if the word describes dynamic movement, a slight rotation tilting the horizon and edges of objects on a diagonal might help. If the word describes something massive and overwhelming, a quick collage job that changes the scale of things will help. Adding text is not allowed!

After editing the photos, try a new round of guessing. Did the changes in design elements give the guessers the hints they needed?

Form and Content Activities

Exercise: Whose Font Is This?

The tutorial **"Communicating with Shape"** explores the world of typography. Typefaces come in a wide variety of shapes: some curvy and organic, some blocky and mechanical. One of the tasks of a graphic designer is to create or choose typefaces that subtly send the right message or set the right tone.

Compare the typefaces of brands that are selling similar products, such as two Internet search sites or two soft drinks. How do their typefaces differ from each other? What image or identity do you think the company is trying to project with this typeface?

Exercise: The Formal Side of Humor (NSFW!)

The tutorial "Communicating with Shape" also contains a link to *McSweeny's Internet Tendency*. *McSweeny's* uses a typeface that connotes serious, studious thinking, and yet, essays like **"It's Decorative Gourd Season, Motherf%$#^rs!"** are anything but serious and studious. It's as if the content of the writing is wearing the visual design, or the "clothing," of another kind of content. Does this "clothing" make the article funnier than it would be **if it were in another font** *(http://www.mcsweeneys.net/articles/im-comic-sans-asshole)?* When a message is wearing an *unexpected visual look,* the result could be very inappropriate, or, depending on the context, very humorous.

Satirical television shows, parodic websites, and other humorous multimedia outlets perform this kind of visual design dress-up to combine content with form in unexpected ways. The **Onion** *(http://www.theonion.com)* wears the visual design of a mass-marketed newspapers. The **Colbert Report** *(http://thecolbertreport.cc.com/videos/3vijkd/the-word---color-bind)* uses all the visual elements of cable news shows, and in particular, The *O'Reilly Factor* **from Fox News.**

Kick back and take a look at some of your own favorite multimedia satires and parodies. What is the content in the piece? What choices have been made about formal elements, like lighting, color, shape, texture, scale, or point of view? How does dressing this content in this form affect the rhetoric of the piece? What cues, visual or verbal, let us in on the joke?

After studying the visual rhetoric of your favorite spoofs, satires, and parodies, try making one of your own. What spoken or written message can you dress in new visual "clothes" for a wildly different effect?

Exercise: Close Looking at Content, Context, and Form

In this section, we've learned to observe visual details closely, to check our observations and deductions for false generalities, and we've explored the three aspects of any visual artifact: form, content, and context. Let's practice what we've learned so far.

Find a visual artifact that holds your interest for several minutes. Look for visual artifacts:

- at online visual archives such as the Library of Congress or the Kentucky Digital Library;
- around your own environment in the forms of posters, flyers, book covers, and magazine articles;
- in your own community in billboards, sculptures, or murals;
- in the media in the form of sets, stills, and shots from film, video, and TV (choose a still or very short segment to work from).

Do a close observation of this artifact. To gather ideas and observations, use the table below as a guide.

Content	Context	Form and Media
What the image is of	Origin, year made, for what purpose	Line, shape, color, light and dark, texture
What is going on	Maker, artist, his or her life	Space or point of view used
Setting of image	Where image is kept, exhibited, viewed	**Size and scale:** of object within, **or** size relationship between viewer and the work
What objects in the image symbolize or signify	Cultural associations	
Image title or text in the image	Connotations brought by the viewer	**Media:** photo, painting, sculpture, billboard, etc.

> **Exercise: Close Looking at Content, Context, and Form (continued)**
>
> Start by simply looking and writing down your observations. What is going on in the image?
>
> Research the image's maker, origin, and purpose. What was the context when the image was created? What might the purpose have been? What is the new context that you bring as a viewer? Look at the visual artifact's form. What is its color, shape, size, texture, point of view, etc.? Very few visuals use *every* formal element; which seem to be most important to the visual artifact you chose? What effect does the form have on the viewer? Does this effect reframe the content in any special way?

VISUAL ARRANGEMENT

Writers take great care to put their words and ideas in orders that make sense, or create the best effect. A story or argument can be told in organized parts: a beginning, middle, and end; a situation, a problem, a solution. We need unity to have a sense of order, a sense that all the things being talked about are tied together for a reason.

However, there can be such a thing as too much unity. For one thing, too much repetition and order can have a choking, stagnating effect. Perhaps our story or argument is about a conflict or a problem, and unified harmony just doesn't fit the bill; or, maybe we want to spotlight a person, place, or idea and make it more visible. In these cases, we can put the techniques used to create unity in reverse gear and create emphasis instead.

In forming ideas and communicating them to others, we slide back and forth on a spectrum from unity to emphasis: from *"this is very much like that, we are all one people, we can learn from these similar situations"* to *"this is different from that, a new situation has changed this person's life, this situation is urgent because of x, y, and z."*

Visuals also communicate by using unity and emphasis. With repetition and orderly arrangement of visual parts, we get a sense of harmony and unity. In an image where unity prevails, we see the whole before the parts, and our eyes travel the surface of the image as we look. By contrast, when one visual part is brighter, bigger, or shoved off to the side of a group, it is emphasized and we fixate on it. In an image where emphasis prevails, we see one focal point first. Our eyes will travel to other parts of the image, but they are always drawn back to that attention-grabbing focal point.

Chapter 13   Visual Rhetoric and Design

Figure 5. Andrei Rublev's "Trinity" is an image in which unity prevails.[6] (Andrei Rublev [Public domain] https://commons.wikimedia.org/wiki/File:Angelsatmamre-trinity-rublev-1410.jpg.)

Unity and emphasis can be used within one artifact of communication, or used to arrange and curate massive collections of communications: salon walls, web galleries, magazine spreads, and poster displays. Unity gives balance and order to a menagerie of different works, and emphasis draws us in to notice one work before the others. In this section, we will spend extra time on using unity and emphasis to arrange collections of text and images on the page or screen. This practice is known as **page layout** or **document design.**

UNITY

Within any narrative or argument, we need unity to have a sense of order, a sense that all the things being talked about are tied together for a reason, that they have something in common with each other.

You've probably already worked with unity in your writing. Placing words in close **proximity** to each other in a sentence, as in *"I thought of age, loneliness, and change,"* prods the reader to consider those things as a unified group, even though they don't necessarily always appear hand in hand. Themes, images, and sounds can unify writing through their **repetition:** echoing phrases such as "I have a dream," a story bookended with similar scenes, or sounds that rhyme or have alliteration. Characters or ideas can be neatly connected and **aligned** with each other by simply sitting on the same line of text, in a well-crafted transition sentence or line of poetry. Events that take place at the same time are collected into **containers:** sections, chapters, or between pauses of a speech.

There are techniques of visual unity that relate to these: **proximity, repetition, alignment, and containment.** These techniques arrange visual bits into families or groups, and create a sense of visual harmony. **Read the tutorials** *(https://ukwrite.files.wordpress.com/2012/01/vislit-unity.pdf)* to learn about proximity, alignment, repetition, and containment and how they work as visual cues.

Exercise: Website or Printed-Page Markup

Check out the **tutorial on unity in document design** *(https://ukwrite.files.wordpress.com/2012/01/vislit-unity.pdf).* Here, proximity, repetition, alignment, and containment are used to order a webpage that holds many different kinds of information. Take a look at a website or print publication that holds dense amounts of information in one page or screen. Mainstream newspapers, magazines, and their companion websites are great examples. Draw a sketch of the page or screen layout, with wiggly lines for text and cartoon squares for images. Note and include any bold type, dividing lines, gutters (empty space), or containment boxes.

After you've sketched the layout, now, mark where proximity, repetition, alignment, and containment are used to let the reader know:

- What text goes with what images?
- What stories or images are related?
- What parts perform similar functions?

It all looks and sounds so simple, doesn't it? However, editors do make tragic mistakes in document design. Check out some of these layout mistakes. How did unity work against the editors' intentions?

Chapter 13   Visual Rhetoric and Design

EMPHASIS

Emphasis can be thought of as the antithesis of unity. Unity groups visual bits into a unified whole. With emphasis, one part sticks out boldly and becomes a focal point. Our attention is transfixed to that point; everything else takes on a secondary role.

Perhaps you've noticed how emphasis works in written texts. If repetition and similarity create harmony and unity, then a striking **contrast** against that harmonious backdrop will draw our attention: an event of violence in a peaceful setting, a short chapter in a novel full of long chapters, a drop in volume in an otherwise rowdy and loud speech. The **placement** of different parts of writing can also draw the reader's attention. Opening and closing paragraphs are great places to put those scenes or ideas that will stick in the reader's memory. (In visual design, the placement with the most emphasis is near the center, or in a spot that is "pointed to" by other lines and edges.) If proximity encourages us to see things as a group, then moving a word away from others draws attention to it. In this example, the ellipses are very intentional, they **isolate** the word:

> "Alone" … The word is life endured and known.

Isolation, placement, and **contrast** are also ways that we can create visual emphasis, or "focal points." **Read the following tutorial** *(https://ukwrite.word press.com/tutorials/visual-literacy/)* to learn more about these techniques, and how they work in visual narratives and arguments.

Figure 6. Leonardo da Vinci's *Last Supper* employs emphasis: Christ is in the center, isolated from other figures, shapes point towards him, and a bright window creates value contrast. (Leonardo da Vinci [Public domain] https://commons.wikimedia.org/wiki/File:Leonardo_da_Vinci_-_The_Last_Supper_high_res.jpg.)

Exercise: Poster Scavenger Hunt

Check out **the tutorial on emphasis in document design** *(https://ukwrite.files.wordpress.com/2012/01/vislit-emphasis-1.pdf)*, then take a break from the classroom and stretch your legs! The tutorial illustrates how print advertisements of the 50s and 60s used emphasis to draw the reader's attention away from other content. Your campus has several places that are hot spots for posters and flyers, and these crowded poster walls function in a similar way.

Divide into teams, with each team heading to a different poster-populated area. When you arrive at your destination, step far back from the poster wall, or walk casually through the hallway. What poster are your eyes first drawn to? What flyer would grab your attention even if your mind was busy looking for an open study carrel? Which technique(s) of emphasis does the poster use to make it stand out from the other posters? Take a picture, make a photocopy, or take the poster itself (just put it back where you found it when the activity is over) and bring it back to class and share.

MORE ARRANGEMENT TECHNIQUES

While talking about unity and emphasis in writing and visual communication, we also have focused on unity and emphasis in document design. Here are a few more strategies that will help you arrange text and images in a way that best suits your purpose.

Juxtaposition

Juxtaposition is the act or instance of placing two things near each other, side by side, or one after the other. When two things are juxtaposed, our senses pick up on more differences and similarities. Juxtaposing characters in TV and movies emphasizes the personality and characteristics of both: Penny and Sheldon in *The Big Bang Theory,* Liz Lemon and Jack Donaghy in *30 Rock,* or Leslie Knope and Ron Swanson in *Parks and Recreation.* The characters aren't pitted against each other, but each character's traits become more vivid in the other's presence.

Figure 7. These side-by-side images from Mark Laita's photographic work "Created Equal" juxtapose two similarly sized photos of people in similar poses. We can't help but compare and contrast the two. (Photo by Mark Laita courtesy of Fahey/Klein Gallery.)

Figure 8. These images from Nicolai Howalt's photographic work "141 boxers" juxtapose two similar photos of a boxer before and after a fight.

In visual art and design, juxtaposition happens when two things of similar size and type are placed near each other, usually one on the right and one on the left. When the two images are aligned and of the same size and shape, we can't help but see the frames as reflecting mirrors. We scour the image and see differences and similarities we may not have noticed otherwise. Juxtaposition is the driving force behind before-and-after photos, and humorous side-by-side images of celebrities who were "separated at birth."

If you're working on a document that closely examines the similarities and differences of two people, places, events, or ideas, consider juxtaposing two images by cropping them to the same size and placing them side-by-side. Giant multi-sided mirrors of juxtaposition can be created using grids.

Figure 9. Unlike Laita's work, which is shown in side-by-side pairs, Howalt's photographs are displayed in a massive grid, juxtaposing not just before-and-after boxers, but boxers young and old, victorious and defeated.

Figure 10. The grid of Roger Shimomura's "24 People for Whom I Have Been Mistaken" juxtaposes images of different Asian Americans. The viewer is left wondering what the artist looks like, and how he could be mistaken for any of these very different looking people.

Grids

Grids with units of equal sizes create super multi-sided mirrors of juxtaposition, prompting the viewer to compare and contrast among a multitude of items. But the grid is also flexible. Images and blocks of text can vary greatly in size and in importance, and the grid will still organize them into a unified piece.

This works because the grid uses all the key ingredients of unity—proximity, alignment, repetition, and containment—to create ordered arrangements. If you need to arrange a large number of very different visual items, like many fabrics in a quilt or many images in a document, the grid is your go-to resource.

For this reason, grids are the backbone of two (and sometimes three!) dimensional multimedia compositions. **Check out these tutorials** *(https://ukwrite.wordpress.com/tutorials/document-design/* and *http:/ukwrite.files.wordpress.com/2012/01/docdes-fvh.pdf),* to see how grids (and riffs off the grid) are used to order information in multiple media, and how you can use grids to design a multimedia document. Whether your project is text heavy or image heavy, serious and informational, or humorous and opinionated, the grid is an arrangement tool flexible enough to fit any need.

Two Kinds of Balance

Symmetrical balance occurs when the visual elements on two sides of a central axis mirror each other. For example, if you draw a vertical line down the middle of a perfect five-pointed star, each side is a mirror reflection of the other. It is symmetrical. "Perfect" is exactly what visual symmetry is: a geometric ideal.

Figure 11. The perfect symmetry of the Grand Trianon at Versailles in Paris, France.[7]

Asymmetrical balance creates a feeling of dynamic movement, or of natural wildness. But a wild appearance does not mean "unplanned"; both the symmetrical and asymmetrical gardens seen here were skillfully planned by the designer.

Figure 12. Just as the symmetry of the Grand Trianon is perfectly crafted, so is the asymmetry of Prospect Park in Brooklyn, New York.[8]

Asymmetrical balance works by balancing one visually interesting form with another. These two visual bits do not have to be mirror images, or even similarly shaped. *They just need to draw the same amount of visual interest.*

Here's an example: In the top image of Marilyn Monroe, her hair has been parted to create sultry blond bangs on the left, asymmetrically balancing her famous mole on the right. Both of these features were visually arresting—they are in every iconic image of the actress—but they are of opposite sides of her face. The bottom two images approximate what Marilyn would look like with truly symmetrical features.

Figure 13. This image shows Marilyn Monroe's carefully-crafted, signature asymmetrical look (top), as well as her face PhotoShopped in perfect symmetry (bottom).[9]

Check out more examples of balance in the following tutorials, including the use of symmetrical and asymmetrical balance in document design. Your page layout grid can be filled in ways that are symmetrical or asymmetrical. If you are working on a document that strives for balance and order, try a two-column or four-column grid: it will lead to symmetrical balance. If you are working on a document that cries out for a feeling of movement or drama, try a three-column grid: it will lead to asymmetrical balance.

Visual Hierarchy

Westerners like to think we read left to right, top to bottom, but we learned from the tutorials on emphasis that we are more inclined to look at what is most different from the rest: what is unusually large, brightly colored, in motion, or being pointed at. If you are still in doubt, turn your web browser's ad blocker off and see how much time passes before your eyes are thrown off course by a pink hula-hooping bear touting low prices for pharmaceuticals. That web ad took over the high ground in the screen's **visual hierarchy,** its set of focal points that vary in amounts of emphasis.

Visual hierarchy can be very useful. Imagine you are looking for a specific quote that you *know* is in a 600-page printed textbook, but you can't find it in the index. You scan pages by reading the largest text first, and when we've found the right section, we can bother with the small text.

In the 1800s, large broadsides played games with visual hierarchy to create intentional miscommunications. Large fonts, when seen from a distance, would tell a different story from the real text.

Figure 14. This Civil-War era broadside attracted viewers by posing as a news headline. When the smaller text is read, one realizes it is an ad for quack medicine. This broadside advertises the opening of Indian Territory to homesteaders. Is the odd use of visual hierarchy an intentional part of its rhetoric?

Any visual medium can have a sequence of visual hierarchy, guiding a viewer from the most attention-getting focal point to more and more subtle focal points, leading the viewer along a nonlinear path, picking out bits of a narrative or communication along the way.

Figure 15. "Harlem" (1946) by Jacob Lawrence shows a city block. The viewer's eyes move from building to building, seeing both comic and tragic events. However, the large white building of the upper class pulls for our attention more than the events in the lives of the less-visible residents.[10] (© 2015 The Jacob and Gwendolyn Knight Lawrence Foundation, Seattle / Artists Rights Society (ARS), New York.)

You can use visual hierarchy in your own document by using different degrees of emphasis throughout the pages. **Check out this tutorial to see more** *(https://ukwrite.files.wordpress.com/2012/01/vislit-emphasis-1.pdf).*

Exercise: Analyzing Page Layouts (starring Bill Cunningham)

Bill Cunningham photographs fashion in New York City from the runways and high society parties to the sidewalks of Brooklyn and the Bronx. He himself doesn't dress fashionably (he rides a bicycle and wears a blue plastic poncho repaired with duct tape), but his fashion insights and photography are world-renowned.

Every Sunday in the *New York Times,* Bill Cunningham creates a carefully laid out page of photographs with a central theme. Just as we arrange our clothes for the day to suit our personalities, Bill Cunningham arranges his layouts to suit the topic of his photo essay.

Each of these examples uses a different type of layout. Choose one, and analyze how the layout works. Is it symmetrical or asymmetrical? (One of these uses a type of symmetry we have not included in this text!) How do your eyes move along the page? Which directions do the people walk, face, or look? What are the main focal points? The secondary focal points? What is repeated? What comparisons and contrasts are made?

Read the text in the page. What is the photo essay about? How does the layout suit this topic?

If you'd like to get to know Cunningham better, you can **watch the documentary** *Bill Cunningham New York* *(https://vimeo.com/ondemand/billcunninghamny),* check out **his YouTube channel** *(https://www.youtube.com/playlist?list=PL074352F6ACE39E76),* or look at his slideshows at the *New York Times* website. But to find these page layouts, do a Google search.

Exercise: Your Own Curation

A great way to practice organization of your own multimedia compositions is to play with organizing the writings and photographs of others.

If you've been working on a writing project, you no doubt have a "shoebox full" (or bookmark folder, or Pinterest board) of artifacts relating to your topic. If not, pick something you're a bit obsessed with, or pick something from the list of random topics below. Collect articles, quotes, interviews, photographs, posters, charts, maps, and other materials relating to your topic.

Now, curate and arrange your materials into an orderly layout. You can cut and paste into a word processing document, or if your eyes are burning from screen fatigue, go old school—print it out and use scissors and tape. This is just for practice, so there's no need for polished finished products.

What will be the main focal point of your collection? What will be the secondary focal points? What images and text go together? You can make the reader associate them by aligning them into columns of equal width, pushing them closer together, or putting them in a box. Does a symmetrically balanced layout suit this topic or does asymmetrical balance suit it better? Do you want blank space to give the layout a buoyant feel, or should you fill it with dense amounts of text and information? What about a grid layout that is tilted at an angle? When you are finished, share your curation with the class.

Random Topics to Choose from if You Cannot Think of One Yourself

- Penguins
- Conan O'Brien
- Beyoncé
- Tap dancing
- NASCAR
- Tasmanian devils
- Pool (swimming or billiards)
- Wind power
- Palm oil
- Australia
- Migraines
- Soccer
- Bricks
- All-terrain vehicles
- Honey bees
- Dinosaurs
- NASA
- Astigmatisms
- Mountain biking
- The Westminster Dog Show

> ### Exercise: Photo Scavenger Hunt
>
> Get some photography practice by going on a photo scavenger hunt. Choose a category of subjects that you can find in your community, such as images of horses, things that are blue, drawings of faces, things that make annoying noises (or you may choose a more serious and academic topic, such as product labels that use demeaning stereotypes). Hit the town and grab as many images as you can. Write about 400 words of text about your scavenger hunt results. Arrange your images into a page layout. You can consider the same questions above as you arrange your layout.

MEDIA LITERACY AND VISUAL RHETORIC

Media literacy entails many of the elements you have already learned about so far. **Media literacy** is a form of **visual literacy** that requires us to engage in **close looking** to not only interpret what we see, but to discern **the ethos and rhetorical intent of how** *and* **where information is packaged, circulated and consumed by us.** In other words, media literacy draws on our critical thinking skills, our rhetorical analysis skills, and our visual literacy skills, in order to understand how media messages influence our reception of information *and* evaluation of that information. This may seem like a tall order, but you already utilize media literacy skills to some degree every day. When you drive by a billboard, listen to a podcast, check the news, or when you scroll through TikTok videos, Instagram stories and YouTube comments, you make judgments about the information you see. Furthermore, the media messages you encounter everyday also influence you. The two umbrella questions we need to address when it comes to media literacy are the following:

1. What factors influence our judgements about media messages?
2. How do these messages influence our thoughts, feelings and behaviors?

What distinguishes media literacy from typical rhetorical analysis is the emphasis on the stakes involved. Media literacy calls on us to recognize the extent to which media shapes our thoughts, feelings and behaviors. In addition, media literacy requires us to pay particular attention to where and how a message is framed, how that message circulates, and the consequences of that framing and circulation. Performing media literacy means *slowing down* and looking closely so that we may critically and responsibly consume and share information.

Goals of Media Literacy

- To critically evaluate media messages and the contexts in which they appear
- To understand how media messages can be constructed to influence our thoughts, feelings and behaviors
- To understand how and why various media platforms and mediums frame content differently, and to recognize how that framing influences our engagement with the content
- To conscientiously create and share media messages

How to Practice Media Literacy—Ask Questions

- Who constructed or shared this message? What kind of stakeholder is the creator or sharer?
- What design elements (e.g., order, juxtaposition, emphasis, etc.) or creative choices are used to attract and manage my attention?
- How might other audiences understand this message differently than me?
- What values or points of view are represented in the message? Which are omitted from the message?
- Where is the message located (e.g., social media platform, newspaper, website, etc.)? What are the constraints and affordances of the message's medium? What values or points of view are expressed by the location in which the message is presented to the audience?
- Why was the message created or shared? In other words, what is the message trying to accomplish? What thoughts, feelings and behaviors is the message trying to influence?

Note: These questions have been added to and adapted from https://medialiteracynow.org/what-is-media-literacy/.

You've probably noticed that these questions share much in common with those that guide visual rhetorical analysis. That's because visual rhetorical analysis is the primary toolkit you can utilize to develop your media literacy.

Exercise: Media Literacy and Multimedia Comparison of Online News

Multimedia comparison is a key aspect of media literacy. Digital media environments, such as news sites, are designed strategically to influence your interaction with that source and the information they want you to consume. Therefore, it is important to look at multiple sources to understand the impact of the context in which information is presented in order to discern the rhetorical aims and legitimacy of the information you encounter. A good way to practice visual rhetorical analysis and media literacy is to compare the home page of different media sites that identify themselves as news sources.

- Visit the home page of the following website—nytimes.com, foxnews.com, thegatewaypundit.com, and mcsweeneys.net.
- The first step for visual rhetorical analysis is to simply pause and notice what you're looking at. What do you see on each site's home page? Make a list (colors, photos, types of headlines, graphics, text, links, ads, etc.…).
- The second step is to examine how the site is managing your attention. How are you visually being guided through this content? What do you notice first, or more, and why? (line, emphasis, scale, color, unity, etc.)
- The third step is to consider how these design and content choices correspond to the rhetorical aims of the source. How are those choices trying to influence your thoughts, feelings or behavior? How are they trying to influence your assessment of the information presented?
- Finally, ask why the information source is trying to influence you in these ways. Does the explicit intent align with the implicit intent? How would you describe the site's ethos? What about its credibility or the legitimacy of the information on the site?

For an example of multimedia comparison, see the brief video [video link/file link].

Put simply, media messages and platforms are powerful tools of influence and we are so inundated with their presence that we must learn how to responsibly obtain and share information. In fact, because our society is so media—saturated and media literacy is so essential to responsibly engaged citizenship that 38 states thus far have either proposed or passed legislation to add media literacy to their state's public school curriculum in the last five years (Kentucky is not one of the 38 states. To see an interactive map of each state's legislative efforts regarding media literacy, visit *https://medialiteracynow.org/your-state-legislation-2/)*. In the next section, we'll take a closer look at the dangers of media manipulation and disinformation.

Media Manipulation and Disinformation

Media literacy especially matters because media can very easily be manipulated and the nature of online media lends itself very readily to the amplification of **misinformation** and **disinformation.** The slender difference between misinformation and disinformation is the degree of intent. **Misinformation** is simply the spreading of any false information; intent to mislead may factor into misinformation, but is not necessary to the spread of misinformation. In contrast, **disinformation** refers to deliberately false or misleading information that is intentionally spread in order to achieve particular and harmful rhetorical goals. **Disinformation campaigns** seek to create and amplify narratives and information in order to falsely discredit individuals, groups, and movements such as Black Lives Matter. The malintent behind disinformation campaigns is sometimes further complicated by a strategy known as **astroturfing,** which entails "concealing the operators and origins of a campaign in order to create the false perception of a grassroots movement or organic support for a specific cause" *(mediamanipulation.org)*. Disinformation is very similar to **fake news.** What distinguishes **fake news** from disinformation is the narrative framing of the content. **Fake news** platforms and content are intentionally designed to mirror the form and design of legitimate news sources in order to present themselves as legitimate sources of verified and researched information. Fake news is often also dictated more by pathos than logos.

Unfortunately, it is very difficult to contain misinformation and disinformation online, and the reality is that even if such illegitimate information is countered, corrected, or even taken down, the original spread of false or misleading information has already made an impact. It has already influenced people's feelings, thoughts and behaviors. A prime example of such an impact is the rise in misconceptions about a link between vaccines and autism, which has also led to declining vaccination rates and an evolving public health problem. Despite a complete lack of evidence to support the notion of any kind of link between vaccines and autism, the anti-vaccination movement has not dissipated. Instead, misconceptions continue to influence people's behaviors. Concerns about the growth of anti-vaccer sentiment prompted the U.S. Committee on Health, Education, Labor, and Pensions to hold a hearing addressing this issue February 10, 2015, which led to the report, "The reemergence of vaccine-preventable diseases: exploring the public health successes and challenges." Clearly, there is a lot at stake with misinformation and disinformation.

While the spread of false and misleading information can be strategically amplified by calling on large networks of people to continuously post and share problematic or banned content (e.g., **distributed amplification**), it is not unusual for the spread of mis- or disinformation to be rooted in just one ill-conceived media message. For example, let's take a closer look at the story behind Figures 16 and 17[11].

Chapter 13   Visual Rhetoric and Design

On the evening of November 5, 2019, Democrat Andy Beshear narrowly won the governorship by a projected margin of .04 percent, or 5,333 votes more than his Republican opponent Matt Bevin. That same evening, as you see in Figure 16, posted on X (the social media outlet known as Twitter at the time of the post), writing "Just shredded a box of Republican mail in ballots. Bye bye Bevin." This post promptly circulated throughout the platform, as you can see in Figure 17. However, the post in Figure 16 was meant as a joke by a college student. The post was tagged and removed by X within one hour, but by then the post had already been screen captured, reposted and quoted by several other users with many more followers. As a result, the false post led to additional unfounded questioning of the election results, including news conferences and the creation of robocalls to Kentucky residents requesting they report "suspected voter fraud." Bevin refused to concede the election until November 14, 2019. By then, doubts about Kentucky's election integrity had already been sown as the conversation quickly amplified from an ill-conceived joke to unfounded accusations of a rigged election. A loss of faith in election integrity continues to be a pressing topic for the American public. This is where we can return to our media literacy questions to help us navigate and critically analyze this series of events. Who constructed or shared this message? What kind of stakeholder is the creator or sharer? Why was the message created or shared? What thoughts, feelings and behaviors is the message trying to influence? How is the media platform impacting the spread and influence of this message?

Figure 16. This tweet was quoted and amplified by other Twitter users.

Figure 17. The post about the election was quoted and amplified by other X users.

Media can also be easily manipulated with affordable and accessible technology, such as photoshop, to swap faces, or any number of video editing applications to alter the audio of a video. These types of media manipulation are known as **cheap fakes** because they do not stem from machine learning (e.g., artificial intelligence). **Deep fakes** require advanced technology and stem from machine learning. For example, the generation of fake user profiles and accounts on social media is an example of the use of machine learning to create deep fakes. Computer generated people can also be used in videos, in which they look like real people made to say and do whatever the creator chooses. Fortunately, deep fakes are not as prevalent as cheap fakes, but that is primarily because cheap fakes are so successful and thus more cost effective. It is important to note that media does not have to be altered though to be manipulated. One of the most prevalent and impactful forms of media manipulation is **recontextualization.** Recontextualized media simply takes any form of media—an image, video or audio clip—out of its original context and places it into a new and false narrative context. For a critical analysis of what happens when a range of media manipulation tactics—cheap fakes, recontextualization, amplification, and disinformation efforts—come together, check out the following case study "Misidentification: How the #Antificat Rumor Caught on Like Wildfire" *(https://mediamanipulation.org/case-studies/misidentification-how-antifafires-rumor-caught-wildfire)*. As you can see, in a media—driven society it is increasingly important to develop strategies to help us navigate and critically evaluate the constant influx of information we encounter.

To read more about the spread of voter misinformation in Kentucky's 2019 governor election, read the following:

- *https://www.nytimes.com/2020/10/26/technology/5-lessons-on-voter-misinformation-from-kentuckys-election-in-2019.html*
- *https://www.kentuckylawjournal.org/blog/recount-a-tale-of-kentuckys-gubernatorial-election*

Additional materials on the spread of voter misinformation and disinformation:

- https://www.nytimes.com/2020/11/23/technology/election-misinformation-facebook-twitter.html
- https://misinforeview.hks.harvard.edu/article/research-note-examining-false-beliefs-about-voter-fraud-in-the-wake-of-the-2020-presidential-election/
- **Washington Post Live Podcast:** *https://www.washingtonpost.com/podcasts/post-live/voting-matters-disinformation/*

Additional materials on vaccine misconceptions:

- https://www.govinfo.gov/content/pkg/CHRG-114shrg93357/pdf/CHRG-114shrg93357.pdf
- https://www.ncbi.nlm.nih.gov/pmc/articles/PMC6122668/
- https://www.nature.com/articles/d41586-020-02989-9
- https://autismsciencefoundation.org/what-is-autism/autism-and-vaccines/

Additional materials on media literacy and media manipulation:

- *https://mediamanipulation.org/*
- *https://medialiteracynow.org/what-is-media-literacy/*
- *https://datasociety.net/library/deepfakes-and-cheap-fakes/*
- *https://knightfoundation.org/features/misinfo/*
- *https://www.pewresearch.org/topic/news-habits-media/media-society/misinformation/*
- *https://www.npr.org/2020/06/16/878169027/study-exposes-russia-disinformation-campaign-that-operated-in-the-shadows-for-6*
- *https://www.newyorker.com/magazine/2017/02/27/why-facts-dont-change-our-minds*
- *https://www.courier-journal.com/story/entertainment/music/2021/05/11/kentucky-venues-report-uptick-in-ticket-scams/4962857001/*

NOTES

[1] Donald Norman. From "Epilogue: We Are All Designers." *Emotional Design,* last modified March 20, 2003, http://www.jnd.org/dn.mss/CH-Epilog.pdf.

[2] "Fountain (Duchamp)." *Wikipedia,* last modified June 9, 2014, http://en.wikipedia.org/wiki/Fountain_(Duchamp).

[3] "An Interview with Marcel Duchamp." *Art Newspaper,* last modified March 29, 2013, http://www.theartnewspaper.com/articles/An-interview-with-Marcel-Duchamp/29278.

[4] Kenneth L. Smith, Sandra Moriarty, Keith Kenney, and Gretchen Barbatsis, eds. *Handbook of Visual Communication: Theory, Methods, and Media.* Routledge, 2004.

[5] Neil Hirschfield. "Teaching Cops to See." *Smithsonian,* October 2009, http://www.catalystranchmeetings.com/art-work/downloads/Smithsonian_magazine_Oct_2009-Teaching_Cops_to_See.pdf.

[6] "Trinity (Andrei Rublev)." *Wikipedia,* June 30, 2014, http://en.wikipedia.org/wiki/Trinity_(Andrei_Rublev).

[7] "Grand Trianon." *Wikipedia,* last modified June 11, 2014, http://en.wikipedia.org/wiki/Grand_Trianon.

[8] "Prospect Park (Brooklyn)." *Wikipedia,* last modified June 27, 2014, http://en.wikipedia.org/wiki/Prospect_Park_(Brooklyn).

[9] David M. Harrison. "A Study of Asymmetry of Faces." *Upscale,* accessed June 29, 2014, http://www.upscale.utoronto.ca/GeneralInterest/Harrison/Parity/FaceStudy/FaceStudy.html.

[10] Jacob Lawrence. "Harlem." *The Jacob and Gwen Knight Lawrence Virtual Resource Center,* accessed June 27, 2014, http://www.jacobandgwenlawrence.org/artandlife04.html.

[11] The tweet in Figure 16 is no longer available on the X platform, since it was flagged and taken down by X per their policies regarding election misinformation. In fact, many posts related to the original post were removed. The post in Figure 17 was still available as of spring 2021, however.

Understanding Genres

Recommended as needed
for WRD 110/111/112

Chapter 14

Chapter 14   Understanding Genres

GENRES AS FORM, FUNCTION, AND ACTION

When you hear or read the word "genre," what springs immediately to mind?

If you're like many people, there's a good chance that you'll think of music, movies, or literature. For example, you might think of the different genres of music that you love or the genres of movies that you always avoid. If I asked you, "What genre of music is Lady Gaga?" There's a strong chance you'll quickly reply that her music is "pop." And if I followed up with a similar question about Jay-Z, you might immediately say "rap." We could do the same with popular movies and books, and you likely wouldn't miss a beat. In addition, there are often genres within genres—subgenres, if you will.

For example, take a quick look at the answers on a Reddit post to the simple question: **"What genre [of music] would you consider Coldplay?"**[1] (https://www.reddit.com/r/Coldplay/comments/18ws4ki/what_genre_would_you_considered_coldplay/). Extrapolating from the answers, we can determine a few patterns:

- The genre mentioned the most is "rock" in different forms.
- Many respondents argue that Coldplay's music is some sub-genre of "pop" or "alt" as separate from the "rock" genre.
- Some responses fuse these genres together, offering "pop rock" and "alt rock" as choices.
- In response to the original poster's combining of "alt rock band that mixes pop and electronic sounds," one response authoritatively writes "There's an exact term for that: permanent wave."

So what can we take away from this simple discussion of one band's music? Does this get us any closer to an understanding of genre? Indeed, the example illustrates at least **four aspects of genre** that will help guide us through the remainder of this chapter.

Genres Are about Categorizing

At the most basic level, genres are about *categorizing* phenomena in the world. This can include music, hairstyles, forms of photography, games, software, academic writing—you name it. Even if you didn't have a ready definition of the term "genre" (and to be fair, few people do!), you likely understood that genre has something to do with *kinds of things*—kinds of music, kinds of movies, kinds of writing, etc. The *Wikipedia* definition of a music genre, for example, suggests that it is "a conventional category that identifies pieces of music as belonging to a shared tradition or set of conventions."[2] This focus on *shared traditions* and *conventions* is crucial, and leads directly into three more nuanced aspects of genre.

Genres Are about Negotiation

Even though they often seem authoritative and set in stone, genres are a bit fuzzy in actual practice, and they take shape (as we can see in the brief example above) through the *negotiation of people* who care about a given genre.

For example, one of my favorite bands is My Bloody Valentine, whose work is often seen as part of the "shoegaze" genre. The *Wikipedia* entry for "shoegazing" ("a subgenre of alternative rock") tells us that the genre is related to a heady list of other subgenres—dream pop, neo-psychedelia, noise pop, post-punk, and space rock[3]. ("Shoegazing"). Ultimately, who really cares that My Bloody Valentine is categorized as shoegaze rather than dream pop? Well, the point here is that *somebody* does care. In this case, it's typically fan communities and music journalists (both amateur and professional) who have deep and continuing interests in accurately naming and classifying a band's work. The folks who care thus negotiate the parameters of a genre. Why do they care so much? Because how a band you love is classified says something meaningful about you as a person (shared traditions, remember?). The negotiation of genres through argument is thus as much about the formation of *stable identities* as it is simply classifying someone's music.

Genres Are Malleable

Since genres are negotiated by people with competing and even contradictory views, genres are *malleable*—they change over time because humans and technologies and knowledges change over time. Writing researcher Clay Spinuzzi argues that genres are both woven and spliced: genres may evolve slowly over time as new knowledge, ideas, and arguments are accepted and woven into our understanding of a given genre; but genres may also adapt to major disruptions, as new ideas are spliced onto old ways of doing things.[4] For example, new technologies are often spliced directly into existing genres: The combination of sophisticated cameras in mobile phones with widespread social media has greatly impacted the genre of "documentary photography." Today, rather than a news crew being the first to provide photos and video of breaking events, it is often accomplished by ordinary citizens with mobile phones. The genre of documentary photography has thus become more expansive, even as it retains some core shared traditions.

Genres Are Tied to Social Actions

Finally, the combination of points 1, 2, and 3 lead to the most important aspect of genre that we can take away from this simple example: genres are intimately tied to social actions in the world (Miller).[5] Genres *shape* social life and social groups (what does it mean to be "punk"? what does it mean to be a documentary photographer in the age of social media? what does it mean for a band you enjoy to be "alternative" rather than "pop"?) while they are simultaneously *shaped by* the constant work of interested people who negotiate and develop them. Spinuzzi argues that genres are where the social and the material meet[6]—we work with genres through physical and digital artifacts and tools (songs, images, essays), and our work with these material forms is always rooted in social expectations (traditions, conventions, norms) and social actions (getting things done in the world).

Most people never get much beyond the first aspect of genre, which we'll call the **iTunes™ model:** genres classify phenomena, and that's about the only reason we should pay attention to them. But as we can see through aspects 2, 3, and 4, there is much more to genre than the iTunes™ model. We'll call this more complex and nuanced understanding of genre the **rhetorical model:**

> Genres classify phenomena through the continual, complex negotiation of interested people, and as such, they change over time—often through the developmental weaving of new ideas and perspectives, and sometimes through the splicing and adaptation of disruptive innovations; above all, these negotiations and evolving understandings of a given genre are rooted in meaningful social actions.

Finally, the rhetorical model of genre involves both past, present, and future social actions. In other words, when you use a genre in school or in your profession, you are working with something that has taken shape through complex historical negotiations, something that has likely changed over time (often substantially), something that is sanctioned and approved for use by a given community or organization at the present time, and something which adds to future understandings of the phenomena. Here's a very quick example:

Figure 1. A Tweet composed by Dr. Jenny Rice on the platform formerly known as Twitter.[7]

This is a Tweet, a form of social media posting unique to the platform formerly known as Twitter. Twitter has since changed names and is now known as X. Twitter referred to its mode of communication as 'tweets' and were introduced as a broad genre of brief online and mobile communication. Tweets are a broad genre of brief online and mobile communication. As you might imagine, there were even subgenres of tweets (e.g., direct @replies, public @replies, retweets, #lazytweets, etc.) that followed the early social media trends of tagging posts. The conventions of this genre developed rapidly between 2006, when the service began, and 2008, when the norms, shared expectations, and shared traditions of the service solidified after lots of negotiation between passionate users and software developers. Did you know, for example, that in the early days of Twitter and other social media platforms usernames were not hyperlinked? These conventions developed as the new genre developed—as people argued for and negotiated what would be useful and conventional, thus shaping the genre and what it means to be a user of that genre. When my colleague Dr. Rice posted this on Twitter, she included my username which notified my mobile phone of the post. Through this post, we're calling upon years of negotiation and literally billions of previous instances of the genre; we're using something that is now a stable and accepted genre to accomplish socially meaningful tasks in the world—in this case, a quick pointer to a work email (another genre!) that needs my attention. Finally, we're signaling to each other (and the public community of Twitter and then X users who follow each of us) that emerging forms of social media are an acceptable part of our work interactions, and we're establishing possible future expectations about how we'll use this genre in similar ways.

If you can keenly develop your understanding of the rhetorical model of genre and apply it in your everyday life, you'll develop an academic and professional superpower. This is because, as human beings, we're constantly using genres, even if we don't realize that we're doing so, and even if we don't recognize a given genre while we're using it. But make no mistake: our ability to use genres effectively—to show that we know what a genre does and how it relates to other work in the world—marks us as a **member** of a given community (or as an **outsider,** if we use genres poorly, or if we use the wrong genres). Indeed, learning how to use the genres of a community (ways of talking, writing, dressing—think about all the things that made "grunge" grunge, "punk" punk, or "rap" rap) is tantamount to being a member of the community. It is to display, at one and the same time, an understanding of how that community *knows* and shares knowledge, and who they *are* and will be.

In the remainder of this chapter, we'll explore these four aspects of genre—and the rhetorical model of genre—in more detail. Our goal is threefold: a) to better understand genres and why they're important; b) to better understand the work that genres do in academic and professional environments of all kinds; and c) to develop strategies for understanding and using genres in practice, in order to become more effective writers and communicators.

NAMING, CATEGORIES, KNOWLEDGE, AND EXISTENCE

Let's begin by refashioning the iTunes model of genre, applying some know-how from the rhetorical model. The very act of naming or categorizing phenomena has real power. Categories are rarely simple (as we have already seen), and in many scenarios, the stakes and implications for assigning phenomena (or people) to a given category are very high. Genres, of course, are more than just names or categories; but for now, let's explore some of the implications of naming and categorization before moving on to the work of genres in more detail.

The sociologist Kathy Charmaz has argued that "categorization spawns expectations."[8] To name something—to categorize something—is to establish expectations about future interactions with and understandings of that phenomenon. Names and categories that become stable and achieve some measure of staying power can have real and tangible impacts on all manner of phenomena, and more important, individuals and groups of people. Think for a moment about the differences between these categories and what it might mean to be labeled by them:

- Immigrant
- Native
- Alien
- Naturalized citizen

On the surface, this is the iTunes model of political categorization applied to groups of people in a given country. But these categories are anything but simple and clear, and they are fraught with real-world implications that impact everything from physical movement to job prospects to health care. Being deemed an "immigrant" or "alien" rather than a "native" or "naturalized citizen" has immediate and lasting (sometimes life-long) effects. According to Charmaz, "names construct and reify human bonds and social divisions."[9] Categories can grant power to phenomena and individuals, but categories can also take power away, allowing one group of people to dismiss phenomena or others that don't fit within the categories they've developed.

Names, categories, and genres thus draw lines around phenomena; in the rhetorical model, we ask questions about those lines, about who draws them, and about what drawing them means for the people and phenomena affected by them (again, everything leads to how we understand social actions in the world). As Charmaz argues, names and categories "provide ways of knowing—and being"[10] and they are "rooted in actions and give rise to specific practices."[11] Names, categories, and genres matter in both subtle and profound ways, shaping what kinds of phenomena count as knowledge, and what the use of that knowledge says about who a given group of people *are* and what they *will* be.

While the political categories above are not genres, we can see from the example that naming and categorization carry real and lasting effects. And yet we also know that genres are themselves, at the most basic level, about categorizing phenomena. In the rhetorical model of genre, therefore, the categorization of a given type of music or writing or software (etc.) has several important implications:

- The very act of naming establishes expectations about phenomena (calling something a "tweet," rather than a "message," impacts how people view the interaction).
- Categories (and the things assigned to them) come with indicators of the power relationships, standards, and norms valued by a given community.
- Names and categories help people organize and circulate standardized knowledge, and they also stabilize specific forms of being (existence).

In the rhetorical model, exploring how a given instance of writing or music or art came to be assigned to a particular category or genre is crucial, for doing so can reveal much about who has power, who doesn't, what counts as knowledge, how that knowledge is presented to the world and shared among others, and what that knowledge says about the existence of a given group (and the identities of its individual members).

ARGUMENT, NEGOTIATION, AND THE MALLEABILITY OF GENRES

By digging a bit deeper and exploring how categories and genres come to be historically established—through the argument and **negotiation** of deeply interested individuals and groups—we can learn even more about a given genre and what the use of that genre says about the people who use it.

Let's have a look at an example: **this unique image** *(https://www.flickr.com/photos/blprnt/6281853518/in/photostream/)* displays historical pages from the magazine *Popular Science,* a sample that is arranged chronologically and that represents work from 1882 to 2007.[12] We shouldn't draw too many conclusions from this single image, but we can make a few safe and well-grounded assumptions:

- Early issues of *Popular Science* used few images and illustrations.
    - There are many reasons for this early lack of images, but two are key:
        - Technologically, it was difficult to include high quality illustrations and visuals in the early years of the magazine.
        - Historically, many visual forms of evidence and knowledge (particularly photography) were seen as suspect in the sciences and social sciences.

- Over time, the magazine incorporated more and more visuals into its articles; contemporary issues could fairly be described as *image-intensive,* a major change.
- What we're seeing in this visual representation is the evolution of years and years of debate, argument, and negotiation among passionate scientists, editors, science writers, academics, and lay audiences about how scientific knowledge will be produced and consumed (and thus, who these scientists, editors, science writers, academics and lay audiences *are* and *will* be).

Another way of thinking about the evolution of articles in *Popular Science* is to focus on the development of shared traditions and conventions. In the late 1880s, articles published in the magazine all looked very similar visually. There were clear and generally agreed upon norms for publishing work in *Popular Science;* one such convention was the overwhelming preference (and technological necessity) for words rather than images in articles. Stated yet another way, the *genre of Popular Science articles* in the 1880s included a set of expectations based in the shared traditions and conventions of scientists, editors, science writers, and lay audiences.

Figure 2. *Popular Science Monthly* (Feb. 1941)" by Katherine of Chicago.[13]

If you were a scientist or science journalist publishing in *Popular Science* at the time, this all would have seemed relatively stable and well established from your perspective. For example, if you were preparing an article in 1902 that you hoped to have published later that year, you might say to yourself, *"I'm only going to include a single drawing*—Popular Science *never publishes articles with more than one!"* And you would not be wrong to do so.

But how do these shared traditions, conventions, and norms come to be established and shared (that is, *normative*) in the first place? Typically, they form through rigorous and often prolonged argumentation and negotiation.

Let's jump forward in time a bit and consider a different example. Now it's 1935, and you're preparing an article that you hope to have published later that year, an article that includes seven detailed and essential figures and images. You know that unlike the old days, over the last 20 or 30 years *Popular Science* has increasingly published articles that have impressive figures; however, the majority of articles in the genre remain dominated (visually) by words. Your article about a recent scientific breakthrough relies heavily on visual evidence and explanation, but you remain nervous because *Popular Science* has never published an article with more than three figures …

What happened when you submitted your well-researched but visually intensive article for publication? Very likely a vigorous debate occurred among editors and scientists about possible changes to the shared expectations and norms that have guided the genre of *Popular Science* articles over the last fifty years. There were heated arguments *("should we/can we publish all these figures?!")*, appeals to both old ways and new ways of doing things (*"we've never published so many figures!"; "we'll be the first to publish so many figures!"*), discussions of precedent (and the possibility of establishing new precedents), and probably a few shouting matches and some hurt feelings.

The point is simple: from inside a given genre at a particular moment in time, things seem perfectly stable, even monolithic—it looks like we've *always* done things a certain way. But when we get up into a hot air balloon and survey the development of a genre over a long period of time, we can see evidence of widespread change. And we can be assured that many of these changes occurred gradually through small instances of argumentation and negotiation. The accumulation and stabilization of all of these smaller arguments and negotiations are what form shared traditions, conventions, and norms over time. They are what make certain kinds of writing, music, or photographs *normative* and generally expected for a particular group of people using a particular genre of communication. This is why Spinuzzi argues that genres carry a "galaxy of assumptions, strategies, and ideological orientations" along with them.[14] Genres, he adds, are a form of *social memory* for a given group or organization—they are ways of making and sharing knowledge, and ways of seeing the world and being in the world.[15]

Again, why does any of this matter? First and foremost, when you produce work in a given genre, you're implicitly wrestling with all of this previous negotiation and change. By working in a particular genre, you are responding to complex histories of negotiation and social memory, and you are implicitly positioning yourself as a member of a given group or community (an academic major, for example). In doing so, you are sharing in the history of that group or community—what it means to be "one of them"—and as such, you are engaging the shared traditions and conventions that they have come to value and accept. When you use the wrong genre, or when you use the right genre poorly, you are essentially turning your back on all of this complex history, these shared values and expectations, this complicated social memory, and the normative view of knowledge and reality prevalent within a particular group.

In the rhetorical model, therefore, genres are where knowledge is negotiated and made, and it is through genres that knowledge is distributed and circulated. And those genres, which carry past, present, and future expectations about the community's knowledge and norms, substantially shape what it means to be a part of the community.

Finally, one very tricky characteristic about genres is that they do adapt and change over time—they seem incredibly stable and yet, as we have seen, they are also flexible and malleable. This is because, as Spinuzzi argues, genres develop over time through the weaving of new ideas (a more subtle and slow moving kind of change) and the splicing of innovations and technologies (typically a more disruptive and immediate kind of change). In our example from *Popular Science,* we can think of the article from 1935 with seven figures as a kind of weaving. When that article was published, it represented an incremental change in the tradition: Yes, *Popular Science* published an article with seven figures, but the magazine continued to prefer articles that were visually dominated by words. In any given year, a few more articles with several images might be published, the editors and scientists would have ongoing debates and negotiations, and the result of these small changes would be *woven* into the fabric of the genre, creating a new normal. But at some point in the latter half of the twentieth century, technological innovations and philosophical transformations toward visual representations of scientific evidence created a series of *spliced* changes to the genre, resulting in an explosion of visually-intensive articles. These historical trends thus shape the genre, how knowledge is shared within the community, and what it means to be a member of that community.

GENRES AND SOCIAL ACTION

The politics and power of naming and categorization, the establishment of shared traditions and conventions through argument and negotiation, and the adaptability of genres to new knowledge and technologies all point toward this most crucial aspect of the rhetorical model: People constantly use genres to get things done in the world. Genres are complex and historically rich means for accomplishing work that matters within a given group, community, academic discipline, or professional organization. This is why a strong understanding of how a particular group uses genres is a potential superpower—genres are the regular and expected ways that people make and circulate knowledge and show others that they understand what it means to be a member of a given community. Writing and communication theorist Carolyn Miller persuasively argues that genres are ways of *acting* in the world;[16] a genre embodies typified (that is, characteristic or expected) responses to recurring social situations that display an understanding about how to participate in a given community.

Take, for instance, the genre of the hashtag. The hashtag (#) as a genre has many uses. It can be used to group together conversations, get more characters into a post on X (formerly Twitter), give a wedding party a unique name and photo album, or even for activism. Social activism on X is a direct result of the hashtag. When people use a hashtag to enter into a conversation to raise awareness or protest, I like to call this "Hashtag Activism." Groups such as Black Lives Matter create hashtags to join people together (#BLM, #Handsupdontshoot, #ICantBreathe). More organic movements, such as "Me Too" or "Water is Life," gain popularity not from a governing organization, but from the repeated use of their hashtags (#MeToo, #TimesUP, #WaterisLife, #NODAPL). When writers re-tweet or reuse these hashtags, they are spreading awareness and participating in a larger conversation. Hashtags are a genre with many conventions and constraints, but they are a genre that engages in social media like none other.

Similarly, genre theorists Anis Bawarshi and Mary Jo Reiff argue that "genres reflect and coordinate social ways of knowing and acting in the world."[17] Learning and effectively using the genres of a given academic discipline or professional organization, therefore, are about *enculturation* within a particular social and historical context—about learning how social relationships govern everyday practices, and about how "to think and act and recognize situations in a particular way, and to orient oneself to particular goals, values, and assumptions."[18] Bawarshi and Reiff demonstrate how important genres are to the knowledge and ongoing work of a community:

> *Because genres are how we mutually construe or define situations as calling for certain actions, they help supply what Miller calls social motives: "[A]t the level of genre, motive becomes a conventionalized social purpose, or exigence, within the recurrent situation" (35–36). By associating social purposes with recurrent situations, genres enable their users both to define and to perform meaningful actions within recurrent situations.*[19]

Using a genre is about accomplishing *meaningful* actions within a given community. Using a genre poorly, misunderstanding a genre, or simply using the wrong genre may be seen as an affront to the "goals, values, and assumptions" of a given community.

Because of the importance of genres in meaningful social actions, some scholars of writing and communication actually advocate the teaching of genres from the earliest stages of education, alongside grammar and writing processes. For example, scholars of Systemic

Functional Linguistics and English for Specific Purposes see the teaching of genres as a way to "'demystify the kinds of writing that will enhance learners' career opportunities and provide access to a greater range of life choices'"[20] (Hyland, quoted in Bawarshi and Reiff 43). Bawarshi and Reiff note that "genres not only help members of a discourse community to achieve and further their goals; genres also help new members acquire and become initiated into a discourse community's shared goals."[21] Again, using a particular genre effectively has important implications for knowing and being within a given community.

Genres are realized in everyday life through *specific* instances of *use*. One post to TikTok is not a genre, but an instance of communication within the broader genre of TikTok posts. One rhetorical analysis essay exploring representations of gender in a popular advertisement is not a genre, but an instance of knowledge making within the broader genre of academic rhetorical criticism. However, in order for these instances to be effective and do the social work in the world that is intended in each scenario (a response to an email, a demonstration of learning and analytic acumen), the person posting the TikTok or writing the essay must meet the shared expectations, traditions, and goals of the community. Effective academic and professional writing and oral communication depends not simply upon sharing specific instances of knowledge, but on demonstrating an understanding of the broader traditions and expectations that have shaped a given genre.

Your academic major and discipline have their own rich history of intellectual, philosophical, and technological development. Indeed, an academic discipline is itself a kind of social memory. To be a member of this discipline—and to affect the social actions related to it—you will need to learn particular ways of doing things, many of which are undertaken through genres. Your eventual profession will also have a particular history, social memory, and set of core values. And the organization in which you work will in turn have its own, even more specific and locally situated, histories, social memories, and values. Communicating effectively within your discipline, within your profession, and within your particular organization will be predicated upon a sophisticated understanding of the common genres that each uses, an understanding that can be developed by applying the rhetorical model we've explored in this chapter.

STRATEGIES FOR UNDERSTANDING GENRES

In this final section, we'll consider some strategies for applying the rhetorical model of genre to everyday practice. In particular, we'll apply the model to common scenarios in academic and professional writing and communication. The focus here will be tilted toward academia, but many of the strategies may be adapted to workplaces as well.

Names, Categories, and Forms

You've got to start somewhere, so why not begin with the obvious? What are the *names* of the common genres used in your field? Ask a professor, graduate student, or an advanced undergraduate how people in the field communicate, and what they call the various modes of communication they use.

Let's say that your major is computer science. How do computer scientists make and distribute knowledge? What are the names for the material artifacts through which they do so? And what kinds of writing will undergraduate computer science students do in their course work? Here are a few potential answers:

- Books
- Blog posts
- Explanatory essays
- Requirements lists
- Tutorials
- Proceedings papers
- Academic journal articles
- Reflective essays
- Instructions
- User profiles
- Prototypes

We might be tempted to just assume that the dominant genre for learning things in just about any field is the book. But in many disciplines, especially those where developments are rapidly moving, proceedings papers are the most important ways to make knowledge (and my guess is that this a genre you've never encountered!).

After learning some of the basic categories and category names (that is, genres), you should move next to an exploration of form. You should literally look at a dozen examples of these different genres to see what makes them different from one another. Ask yourself: *What does an important book in computer science* look like? *What do proceedings papers look like, and how is their form different from tutorials or journal articles? What does a requirements list look like? What does a user profile look like?*

Develop a basic understanding of the norms for each category; doing so will allow you to recognize the genres that are important in the field, and more importantly, to understand what kinds of knowledge each genre is designed to produce. Of proceedings papers we might ask the following basic questions:

- How long are proceedings papers, typically?
- Which venues and conferences are the most influential and widely attended?
- How long are introductions, methods sections, conclusions?
- How many other works are typically cited or referenced?
- Which citation style is valued by the field?

Will you be writing in the same way as a published computer scientist? Of course not! But you can adapt what you learn from an examination of names, categories, and forms to your own instances of writing within these genres.

Histories of Negotiation

The next strategy involves learning about the most important debates and the most important players within a given field. It's easier to learn about these histories than you might imagine ….

While you're examining the form of the most important genres in your field, play close attention to the references lists and to key problems. Whose names appear again and again? What kinds of historical problems are continually discussed?

Ask your professors, some graduate students, or advanced undergraduate students about those recurring names and problems. This will generally lead you into an exploration of those key debates that have shaped the norms, expectations, and knowledge of your field (and, by extension, the genres used in these debates).

How can this help you write more effectively? Well, if the professional computer scientists keep referencing the work of a handful of influential professionals, there's a good bet that it will be very good for you to reference them as well. Shared traditions, remember? By learning about the key figures, the key debates, the major events in the history of your field, you show, through your own writing and communication, that you are becoming a member of the discipline or profession.

Development and Change

And as you're exploring these key figures and debates, you'll likely learn more about the way genres have developed through the weaving and splicing of new ideas and innovations.

As a computer science student, you might explore the development of LaTeX, a powerful markup language developed in the 1980s that dramatically changed the way many professional computer scientists write about their work and distribute knowledge.[22] And learning LaTeX may help you better adapt to the genres in which you'll write during college, making it easier for you to include formulas and code snippets in your work.

Actions and Impact

Finally, continually ask questions about the audiences and purposes involved with every instance of writing and communication in which you are engaged. For example, consider asking the following questions:

- What is this tutorial supposed to *do*, and for whom should it be designed?
- What is the purpose of a requirements list, and how can it help me create better programs?
- How have other computer scientists addressed major problems in the field, and how has their work shaped social actions today?
- What is the purpose of this reflective essay? How have such essays been used by this professor in the past? What are her expectations about the genre?
- What is the purpose of clear code commentary? How can it help other programmers understand my code? Where are the best, most visible places to include comments?

While our example involves a computer science student, these four aspects of the rhetorical model of genre may be adapted to any major, to any profession, and to any organization in which you may eventually work. Continually ask these questions and develop your superpower!

GENRE AND AUDIENCE

We know that texts have target audiences, but they also need to be aware of secondary audiences. Even though the impulse is to just say "a general audience," as has been pointed out in Chapter 3, that does not exist. Genres exist for creators and audiences. Writers need to be aware of their target audience, and specialized forms of communication emerge to help with that. Let's think of the examples below, identifying audiences and the ways each example communicates.

Let's start with this: let's say you find a piece of paper on which is written:

        D   A   B   F#   G   D(low)   G   A

What are your thoughts? What does this mean? Is it a code? Why is there a hashtag after the F? Don't those go before something? What is a D(low)? How could this mean anything to anyone? If it means something, what could it mean, and to whom?

Many of you probably figured out that this is some sort of musical notation, denoting chords or notes. But how do we know what to do with that, even if we are a musician? Let's look at another way this could be presented:

Figure 3. Musical notation.

This version has the benefit of letting us know the cleft, so we can probably figure out which instrument (or narrow the pool of potential instruments) for this, and know the note duration—assuming, of course, that we know how to read standard Western notation, which not all musicians do. So we can't just say this is for musicians; what is the specific target audience of musicians this is for?

Now let's look at that yet another way:

How about this? It's got the same number of lines as the previous example, but is it the same thing? Again, this can be useful to some musicians, but meaningless to others. Who is the audience for this? How does it differ from the specific audiences for the previous two examples? How can we determine the specific audience for each of these?

For extra credit: Have you figured out what famous composition these examples come from?[23]

WIKIPEDIA AS A GENRE

I'm sure you are all familiar with *Wikipedia,* and you probably haven't given a second thought to the structure and format of *Wikipedia* pages (unless, of course, something changes and you have trouble navigating the new page or finding information we know we saw there once). For most of your lives, *Wikipedia* has had more or less the same form with which we are now familiar, and which seems to be what a *Wikipedia* page just naturally is. But, like all genres, that format, and the expectations for what pages will contain, has grown and changed with *Wikipedia.*

When *Wikipedia* started, most pages were essentially short encyclopedia entries, befitting the name *"Wikipedia,"* submitted and edited by users, ideally (although rarely actually) with an extensive list of references at the end for those who wanted to dive deeper. However, as *Wikipedia's* popularity has grown, users have demanded more from the pages, such that *Wikipedia* pages, in general, have grown far longer and the coverage on each page more extensive. Now, pages that are more like *Wikipedia* ones are typically flagged as "stubs" and have a notice at the top asking for users to contribute more information to expand the page. Furthermore, community standards on the types of sources has changed, and is continuing to change; although scholarly, peer-reviewed sources are not the norm for *Wikipedia* pages, many have started to at least incorporate these, even if they are not heavily relied upon (yet). Despite the questionable quality of many sources upon which pages still rely, the community has at least demanded sources—pages that have few sources are often flagged and bear a disclaimer which also asks visitors to contribute by providing more sources and citations.

The *Wikipedia* page we all know (and love—or hate), then, is the product of ongoing negotiation. But what is it that makes the *Wikipedia* page a recognizable genre (it's more than the name *"Wikipedia"* at the top of the page). It's even more than the template form we're used to seeing—after all, *Wikipedia* pages look different on laptops vs. mobile phones, but we can still recognize a *Wikipedia* page when we see and read it. What is it that makes a *Wikipedia* page so recognizable? Moreover, how can so many *Wikipedia* pages, created by so many different and varied contributors, have a relatively uniform look and feel? This activity is designed to get you thinking about the traits of the *Wikipedia* page as a genre and understand the negotiation and development that *Wikipedia* and its contributors have engaged in to create the genre we know today.

In thinking about genre, we need to think about audience. It is tempting to say that *Wikipedia* pages are written for the general public audience; after all, anyone on the internet can read a *Wikipedia* page. However, as we will see, the authors of *Wikipedia* pages know that there is no such thing as a general public audience. Information must be delivered in ways that appeal to a specific target audience, while providing information that also helps secondary audiences get up to speed or know what they need to look into more in order to more fully understand the subject.

Look at the *Wikipedia* pages for several things you are interested in. (If you don't know where to start, here are a few suggestions that can get you thinking of the types of things to start looking into: Shred Guitar, Curling (Sport), Hedgehogs, Sergio Leone (film director), bucket hats. Find a few that have substantial pages. Now, let's think about several observable features that can help us start to figure out the genre traits. Ask the following questions about these different features and figure out the answers based on what you are observing about these pages (as representatives of the *Wikipedia* genre):

- Structure:
    - What about a page's structure lets us know it is a *Wikipedia* page?
    - What is it about the layout and presentation of information that denotes a *Wikipedia* page?
        - Are there different sections? If so, how are they differentiated?
    - How are paragraphs and information ordered? Are there any specific patterns the presentations of information seem to follow?
- Organization:
    - How is the information on a *Wikipedia* page organized?
    - If there are sections, how are they organized?
        - Is there a specific order in which the sections seem to appear across pages?
    - How do the pages keep from repeating information in different sections?
- Images:
    - Do the pages feature images?
    - How are the images used?
        - Is it strategic, or are they just there for the sake of being there? If it's strategic, what is the logic of including images when and where they are?
- Citations:
    - Are there citations? If so, why?
        - How are the citations provided?

- What types of sources are cited?
- How are sources cited in the body of the text?
    - How about "Works Cited" (or an equivalent)?
- Audience:
    - Who is the target audience (or audiences) for this page?
        - What helps you determine that as the target audience?
        - What are the things the page(s) assume the reader already knows?
    - Who are the secondary audiences for the page?
        - What are the features that let us know this is included for the benefit of secondary audiences?
- Argument:
    - What is the point of a *Wikipedia* page?
        - That is, what is unique about what it presents and how it presents it?
            - Don't just say "to tell us about *x*." There are lots of things that do that, and lots of ways to do that that aren't like a *Wikipedia* page. How is it presented here, and why is it presented in this manner, as opposed to the many other possible ways?
    - What types of arguments do *Wikipedia* pages advance?
        - Is it a one-sided debate?
        - How is bias managed?
- Style/Voice:
    - What is the style of a *Wikipedia* page?
    - What is the voice of a *Wikipedia* page?
        - How does the genre let many different authors speak with one unified voice?

NOTES

1. What Genre Would You Considered Coldplay?, *Reddit*. www.reddit.com/r/Coldplay/comments/18ws4ki/what_genre_would_you_considered_coldplay/. Accessed 24 Apr. 2024.

2. "Music Genre." *Wikipedia,* last modified June 17, 2014, http://en.wikipedia.org/wiki/Music_genre.

3. "Shoegazing." *Wikipedia,* last modified June 29, 2014, http://en.wikipedia.org/wiki/Shoegazing.

4. Clay Spinuzzi. *Network: Theorizing Knowledge Work in Telecommunications.* Cambridge University Press, 2008.

5. Carolyn R. Miller. "Genre as Social Action." *Quarterly Journal of Speech,* 70, 1984.

6. Brian McNely. "'That Light-Bulb Feeling': An Interview with Clay Spinuzzi." *Present Tense: A Journal of Rhetoric in Society* 3, no. 1, 2013.

7. Jenny Rice. X post, August 13, 2013, 8:54 a.m., https://x.com/jennyrice.

8. Kathy Charmaz. "The Power of Names." *Journal of Contemporary Ethnography* 35, no. 4, 2006: 396.

9. Ibid.

10. Ibid.

11. Ibid.

12. "*Popular Science* 1882—2007." *Flickr,* last modified April 29, 2010, https://secure.flickr.com/photos/culturevis/4564315478/.

13. Katherine of Chicago. "Popular Science Monthly (Feb. 1941)," *Flickr,* uploaded January 3, 2010, https://www.flickr.com/photos/modashell/4242117792/in/photolist-7sRXPW-m5SX8L-m2fZH4-8dm3zX-dU5gze-gM7Ekk-9sTFjW-7xrU8R-6Z84hE-6J2yQg-71rhtP-fi8qFU-e3f8WZ-97AWca-fySpT1-6XVRS5-buRpSc-97icwv-8VA1bs-dCvrD8-hXfQzd-bUTSX4-85BiSh-6YNPiz-6Z84ch-9hjSnf-8dpjyy-axbvd3-8h1Xt6-9w3uVe-8EkhC8-6ZJmb2-9kDvfq-fJVbpK-7xNxZa-6cdnhn-9KDcm4-9evK2s-7upxk3-mDEcEQ-9wna7q-7fZpiJ-fyC7fX-anASJi- 6TfQQF-9F2KTs-m2fYBM-e7Zmfr-e861Hb-97AVZz.

14. Clay Spinuzzi, *Tracing Genres through Organizations.* The MIT Press, 2003, p. 43.

15. Ibid., 41.

16. Miller, "Genre as Social Action."

17. Anis Bawarshi and Mary Jo Reiff. *Genre: An Introduction to History, Theory, Research, and Pedagogy.* Parlor Press, 2010, p. 5.

18. Ibid., 61.

19. Ibid., 72.

[20] Ken Hyland. *Genre and Second Language Writing.* University of Michigan Press, 2004, p. 11, quoted in Anis Bawarshi and Mary Jo Reiff. *Genre: An Introduction to History, Theory, Research, and Pedagogy.* Parlor Press, 2010, p. 43.

[21] Bawarshi and Reiff. *Genre.* p. 45.

[22] "LaTeX." *Wikipedia,* last modified June 5, 2014, https://en.wikipedia.org/wiki/LaTeX.

[23] If you answered Pachelbel's "Canon in D," congratulations!

How to Make Your Own Documentary

Recommended as needed
for WRD 110/111/112

Chapter 15

Every narrative film is in the process of turning into a documentary, just as every documentary is struggling to become a piece of fiction.

—Jean-Luc Godard

Let's say you've been tasked with making a short documentary, perhaps as an assignment for your WRD class. (If so, your instructor will determine the specifics of the assignment, and this chapter should be regarded less as template for those exact needs and more of a general overview.)

Congratulations. You're about to learn a little about a time-honored and more effective than ever way to forge an argument—and maybe a lot about yourself. Don't be daunted by the technology. Your equipment can be as simple as your iPad or your telephone. The real raw materials are your imagination, your reasoning, and the unlimited narrative potential of the real world around you.

You're also lucky to be living in a time when the documentary form is thriving and justly celebrated. Films like *Man on Wire* and *Searching for Sugarman* are finding large enthusiastic audiences who appreciate the particular power of the actual stories they tell. And the do-it-yourself aesthetic which has always driven this form is now enhanced by the availability of inexpensive and relatively impressive ways of filming and editing.

ONE: PRE-PRODUCTION

So, what kind of a documentary do you want to make? Will it present a political argument, or attempt to expose a particular social or economic issue? Will it be an autobiography of sorts, an expression of the motivations and tensions which helped make you who you are? You might try to document a particular process, showing us not only how it happens but in what sequence, with what sense of cause and effect, and what the outcomes and consequences are. A cinéma vérité approach calls for as little intrusion as possible—no incidental music, voiceover, graphics, the closest you can get to a fly on the wall. Or would you rather intrude, insert yourself in the center of the story?

Maybe you'd like to use photographs, film, and other archival footage out of context to make ironic connections to the material you've filmed yourself. Or maybe the mockumentary form appeals to you—a piece of fiction, sometimes carefully crafted, sometimes largely improvised, which purports to document a phenomenon which never actually happened.

These are just a few of the almost infinite possibilities. One thing I've learned, after years of teaching narrative film history and now immersion in the alternate universe of documentaries, is that there are if anything even more possibilities with the documentary form than the fictional one. Each subject finds its own form.

Perhaps it is easier at this juncture to think about what a documentary *isn't*. It isn't a news report, for instance, which insists, in its "fair and balanced" way, to present just the facts and only the facts. Unlike traditional notions of journalism, a documentary ought to have a point of view. On the other hand, this doesn't call for reckless bias either. The challenge of balancing logos and ethos here is the delicate art of acknowledging contrary claims and counter-arguments while not falling into the kind of bland, chit for chit argument of "one for you, and one for me" which refuses to take any position and ends up convincing no one of anything.

You don't want to preach to the already converted, but it is futile to worry too much about die-hard partisans on the other side. These issues are much more obvious in political arguments, but even something as tangibly subjective as your autobiography needs to consider such audience concerns as tone, rhythm, and emphasis.

But a documentary is not an advertisement either—a glittering and manipulative attempt to overwhelm and seduce the viewer, a momentarily distracting shiny object to make her crave something she never even knew she needed.

Nor is a documentary a simple report, a summary of facts and figures.

So, thinking about what your subject is and how you are going to present it is step one. Brainstorm this problem the same way you would any writing project. Here's a good way to get your feet wet, get to know your colleagues a little better, and make yourself a little more comfortable with the process on a very micro-level.

Chapter 15   How to Make Your Own Documentary

Exercise: The Proust Questionaire

Break into pairs. (This exercise will work best if you choose to work with a classmate you don't know very well.) Now locate a famous set of thought provoking questions called the Proust Questionnaire at the following web link: *http://www.vanityfair.com/magazine/2000/01/proust-questionnaire*. Note that these questions, unlike the usual bland getting-to-know-you formulas, are actually quite probing, resist generic responses, and call for maturity, reflection, and self-awareness.

Your responses are not framed, in other words, to impress each other, your teacher, or most importantly yourself, but to dig down deep, just as most of you are undergoing a huge transition in the coming of age experience. Take plenty of time—think of this as the pre-interview—just talking over your reactions and getting comfortable with your "subjects." Some of the questions may be beyond you—you probably don't know at your age when you were "most happy"—and some of them may just not click. Not to worry. All we really need for this exercise are a good seven or eight answers.

Now you are ready to film the interviews. Set up two chairs so that the subject is looking at the interviewer, with the camera at somewhat of an angle. Let your subject take her time, and try not to accept short, glib, or superficial answers. Give yourself some dense and passionate material to work with. In terms of ratio, it would be nice to get ten or fifteen minutes of material which you will then edit down to around a minute. Once you have a rough cut of the content (all of these steps of the process will be explored in more detail later in this chapter, so read the whole piece first so you can try to apply these ideas from the get-go), go back and drop in some appropriate images, music, etc. to augment the portrait.

Instructors, this process could take a day or two in the opening weeks of the course, but you should set aside another day for the students to screen their work together and begin the assembling of a creative community which can effectively but diplomatically workshop the process.

So now that you've given it a try on a small scale, let's start thinking again about pre-production on your larger project, which you might envision as running five to eight minutes or so. If that doesn't sound like much time to you, consider the issues of editing, compression of material, and even aural density—a minute of well made film is usually the product of hours of careful work.

Think of it this way: Your problem here is almost exactly the opposite of the college student's traditional dilemma of "padding out" a paper. There, the unfortunate result is running on and on for pages to reach some minimum. Here, the easiest thing in the world to do is turn a camera on a blank wall for half an hour, but that doesn't make you Andy Warhol. You want the maximum of engagement, intensity, and edification for each moment of your film without resorting to hyper-caffeinated editing or otherwise bombarding the viewer with too much information at once.

As with a chapter, though, try to narrow your thesis as much as possible. Some of the same rules apply: Don't take on too large and unmanageable a topic, find one aspect of a larger idea which interests you most, see what's been done in a similar vein, etc. The more you can focus your topic, the more you can exclude from the net you're casting, the better off you'll be.

Once you've chosen your subject, pre-production can begin in earnest.

Casting is as important here as in any fictional film. You want not just your primary subject but witnesses who will be supporting/refuting/contextualizing that subject to be as vivid, pointed, and intriguing as possible. Although the word "casting" sounds antithetical to what you're doing, just going out on the street and interviewing random observers is more likely to produce a mess than a masterpiece.

Bear in mind that some people just want to be on camera so much that they will be impossible to pull into any kind of serious conversation. Such "naturals" should probably be avoided. On the converse, some very thoughtful and incisive people who could be of great value to your project are going to be shy and intimidated by the filming process, and you should be willing to devote some energy into putting them at ease. (One suggestion here is to simply audiotape the most extremely camera-shy and loop their voices over other images. Voices over other images, in general, are to be encouraged at all costs.)

Sometimes the **setting** is as much important as the characters. Don't forget that this is a visual medium, and no matter how much your subject may have to say, the physical details of his environment will have a lot to do with the finished story. This might be a good place to think about **B roll**—footage of the environment which is not dominated by verbal content.

Even though it's great to get an interview right in the middle of the process you're dealing with (because it might bring out the best in the witness), the sheer level of noise associated with a lot of the most interesting environments suggests that just getting plenty of visual coverage of that environment, documenting the processes involved as vividly as possible, might be preferable. Then you can get the people in a better sound situation (don't forget that we have soundproof rooms and even a green screen room in the Media Depot of the Young Library) and overlay good sound and good images. But, with maybe a few exceptions, the images are vital to the form you are working with.

A **crew** in this case might be just a partner to watch the camera and sound while you are interviewing, but it helps a lot, no matter how small or short the production, to have another set of eyes on the recording of the event while you attend to the event itself. You don't want to mess up full concentration on either the interview or the equipment by doubling up on both. On the other hand, too many people around the edges can be a real distraction to cast and crew both, so keep things to a minimum.

You are asking people for valuable slices of their personal time, so it's important to pay attention to **scheduling.** Probably your project will not require an inordinate amount of synchronization, but always allow more time than you think you will need for interviews, which might prove much more fruitful than you expected, or which might be interrupted by unforeseen factors like weather or equipment problems.

Also, be careful about backing up interviews too close to each other, or not allowing enough breakdown and travel time between them. Even the most cheerful and cooperative witness is going to become disgruntled and even hostile if put on hold for too long.

Now you will need to do some **research.** How much? This varies according to your subject matter and how much you already know about it (which, believe me, is never half as much as you think you do). But you can basically never be over-prepared. And herein lies a paradox: on the one hand, you'll want to have as much information available as possible, and you'll need to be armed with more thoughtful, nuanced, open-ended questions than you'll probably ever be able to use.

On the other hand, you want to be able to abandon all of this on a second's notice when a new vein of information/opinion/anecdotal evidence opens up which you had never considered—and many times, it will. But you can't expect to fly by the seat of your pants—if you don't feel confident with the preparation you have already done, you won't be able to knowledgeably and competently improvise when new revelations turn up.

Another way to look at this: You want to be over-prepared, but you don't want the interview to feel like it. If you are fumbling with your notes or reading off prefabricated questions in a rote manner, you will be responded to in kind—off the cuff, glib answers, or robotic boilerplate rhetoric.

Either of these is a death sentence to your documentary. In terms of the interview, there are two extremes to avoid. One is trying so hard to look like an expert that you either alienate or intimidate the witness, either way obviously undercutting not only the interview but probably the whole vibe of the witness when your intended audience encounters them.

The other is looking—as opposed to coming across as well prepared, open-minded, and professional—so bent upon a particular thesis that the witness (and later, the audience) decides you are so convinced of your own conclusions before the investigation has even begun that there is no room left in such an airless argument for any other way to look at it. Even the scent of de facto reasoning like this will contaminate the entire argument.

The best scenario of all is to have a sequence of prepared questions which you never have to refer to. As we will discuss in the next section, the goal—for the interviewer, for the witness, and ultimately for the audience—is to feel like you're in the middle of the liveliest and smartest *conversation* anybody has ever had about this topic.

TWO: THE SHOOT

Don't be late. On the other hand, particularly if you're setting up in someone's home or business, don't get there too early either. You want to allow time to do some pre-interview warm-up while your crew gets the scene set, but it helps to have at least a pretty good idea of how tight time is and how you can make the best of it.

If you have a chance to do a pre-interview, talk about anything *except the subject of the interview.* The idea here is to develop a relationship with the witness, establish a comfort zone, and get them situated for the camera. You do not want him/her to wear out his/her mojo before you're ready for it. However, at least the impression of a pleasant relationship is worth the world, especially if the witness is not experienced in this situation. (If he/she is experienced, you may have the opposite problem, which is not so much teasing it out of him/her, but trying to steer him/her at all.)

On the technical side, choose a quiet and reasonably uncluttered area to stage the interview. Sound is more crucial than anything in this case: if we can't hear what the witness is saying, no amount of ingenious visuals will save it. Make that your first priority, and be sure to check and double check it before you start, both position and audibility. Check one last time with the actual witness and his/her individual tone. (At the end of the interview, ask for a moment of silence which you can record for ambient sound if you need it.)

Frame the shot in terms of the **rule of threes.** If you think of the space you have to work with inside the frame as a tic-tac-toe board broken into nine squares, consider placing your subject—not to the absolute extremes—but not exactly in the middle either, just a bit aslant one way or the other. Too much symmetry can be fearful. Then you might fill in some of the negative space opposite the witness with a flower, books, something to balance it out. But if it looks absolutely centered and symmetrical this subconsciously bores the viewer.

Again, put the camera where it enhances this composition, but not where the witness is looking right at it. You want him/her to forget about the camera if at all possible. Also, if you maintain constant eye contact throughout the interview, this will keep him/her where you want him/her, while—crucially—maintaining the intensity of everyone's engagement in the conversation. (This means, first and foremost, being well prepared enough to not have to break away to fumble with notes.)

Regarding the placement of the camera: I highly recommend placing whatever you are using—camera, iPhone, tablet, whatever—in a stable, stationary position for the duration of the interview. Many first time documentary makers have romantic illusions of "going hand held," and this approach simply causes many more problems than it solves in interviews. The time for camera movement is during the B roll shooting, when you're not concerned with sound. Even there a little bit of shaky goes a long way. You want the interview to be as stable and smooth as possible, and that means keeping the camera still.

If your subject does not seem exceptionally nervous, discuss this next issue before you start. Even though you want the interview to be a conversation, people tend to drop their antecedents a lot when they speak informally, and this can play hell with you in the editing room. So, for instance if the question is "What color were Warren Oates' eyes?" you might get a beautiful poetic response like "Blue. The color of the blue-grass, the color of the sky. The bluest blue you ever saw." Great stuff, except nobody will know that *Warren Oates'* particular eyes were the subject of that sentence. So if he/she can just back up and say "Warren Oates' eyes were blue. The color of bluegrass, etc." it will be much easier to weave in smoothly to the final edit.

(If he/she seems overly anxious anyway, though, this advice will just make him/her more so.) If you don't have that establishing context, the alternatives are to leave in the question (which I am totally against; the only time you should show yourself or leave in your question is in special instances when it has an unusually heightened emotional impact) or use a graphic, which can work sometimes but often just looks amateurish.

Digressions can be tough to call. If the witness gets way off your original subject, think quick and ask yourself: Is he/she so nervous that I need to let him/her get a little of this out of his/her system? Is he/she so off track that I need to step on them immediately to get back to topic? Or, sometimes: Yes, this isn't what I asked but it's great stuff and I need to think about how to follow up this new development instead of trying to drag it back to my next preconceived question. Digressions can ruin an interview, or make it truly great. And you will need to make the call on the spot.

Be sure to thank the witness at the end. I always make a point of asking if there was something he/she really wanted to say which didn't come up in the questions. After that moment of ambient sound, be sure to ask him/her if he/she is aware of any resources—be it other people, photos, video, etc.—which might be useful to your project. You would be amazed what this will generate sometimes.

Now get all the B roll you can. What is the environment like? What kinds of processes are going on? Are there paintings or posters on the walls you might want to use for a close-up or a cutaway? If there is a natural environment involved at all—woods, plants, trees, animals—be sure to capture both the sights *and* the sounds of it as much as possible.

You're ready for the most challenging part of the process of all.

THREE: POST PRODUCTION

Now the wild, wild work begins. Prior to this, you have established the parameters and focus of your subject and shot (most of, probably) the raw footage. Now it's time to arrange those pieces of the puzzle into a compelling sequence. Before the actual edit begins, however, there are at least a couple more details to consider.

You do *not* want the film to be an unvarying succession of mid-range interview shots, an uninterrupted parade of what are rightly derided as "talking heads." We have all grown accustomed to such a wide range of visual stimuli that the talking heads will be a lot more compelling if we've got a variety of images to look at while they are *doing* at least some of that talking—photos, selfies, headlines, graphics, B roll footage and such moving images footage as home movies, film clips, and even stock footage.

So collect as much of this as you can. It will be a crucial layer to the finished product. Ideally, a lot of it will come from research and your interview subjects. But there are plenty of links to archival sites which you are freely encouraged to use.

This goes double for music and leads us to the question of copyright. Follow your instructor's lead on this one. Personally, after dealing with intellectual property problems for more than twenty years, swimming against the vast and murky tide of unions and agents and lawyers who protect (and exploit) the increasingly arcane details of ownership and ancillaries, it seems like such a soul-killing process that I encourage you , as students and under the legal exemption for student work (which must be unpaid for and unpublished), to grab it when and where and while you can get it. While you are protected, my argument goes, why not benefit from working with the very best and most particular materials available?

But ... you can't profit from it, (don't worry too much there; the profit margin on documentary work is pretty much a sad punchline anyway). And your instructor might insist you generate your own material, partially on the argument that facing these inevitable realpolitik practicalities makes for a better learning experience.

Either way, you'll need to think about how to handle narration, i.e., the process of giving the viewer an overview and a context for what she is seeing/hearing. Cinéma vérité has proven that it can be done with nothing more than sensitive and nuanced editing—and even though I write a lot of voice-over, I absolutely agree that on some platonic level that is often the ideal—but it's a mighty hard thing to execute.

Excise, at all costs, anything which even momentarily snags up your viewer. She needs to know where she stands because in five minutes it's going to be over. And—especially when the rough draft edit is done—you're going to spot holes where context or clarification or just a single telling detail are needed.

Subtle use of **voice-over** is one solution, but consider what voice-over *shouldn't* try to do: point out the obvious, berate the viewer before she can begin to develop her own reactions, transparently try to manipulate her reaction. Too much pathos and a killing blow to ethos, a laundry list of facts and statistics which no one will remember minutes later.

A note on logos: Logic, and a logic you develop for yourself, will be crucial to your documentary argument, but sheer numbers, in particular, what Mark Twain calls "lies, damned lies, and statistics" are almost impossible to make stick in a short film. Better—almost always—to let the particular and the local speak for the abstract and the universal.

Instead, good VO should provide a context, subtly cue us for what we should be anticipating to see and hear, and—most importantly—set the tone for the documentary, supplying a lens through which we can at least believe we are drawing our own conclusions.

Another option: text or graphics. A little bit of either goes a long way. Just as you want to exclude your own questions from the video, repeating every question in text gets old fast. Better to employ a few "chapter headings"—a la Tarantino—maybe just a work or two which establishes the context without over-explaining it. Less is more. I am almost always against large blocks of text on film because I hate trying to read too many words on a screen. That's what books are for.

As for graphics, there are all kinds of groovy little gizmos on most editing software that reverse the shot, or polarize it, or frame in in a cute geometric pattern, etc. *Eschew* these at all costs. They are the mark of an amateur who has just found a new toy. A straight cut or—if you need a pause for dramatic emphasis—a standard dissolve is usually plenty. Having a "hand drawn" or cartoonish look, or even brief bursts of animation—especially in credits or visualization of a complex idea—can add a lot, but only if it looks like You Did It Yourself and weren't just randomly clicking apps.

Now let's think about the rough cut. At every level, WRD is all about the idea that any and all forms of discourse constitute writing, whether it be a chapter or a blog or a text or … a film. Visual rhetoric is rhetoric just the same. But again, there are useful distinctions, comparisons and contrasts underneath this larger notion of *composition*.

Think of it this way: you are *building up* a chapter, generating words and moving outwards. Whereas, if you've done your homework on the pre-production and the actual shoot, you should have such a wealth of resources, an embarrassment of riches, that it's much more a matter of a process of *elimination* of honing down, of finding the central ideas and sculpting out the most effective components.

Try to think of a rudimentary beginning, middle, and end, while leaving open, only temporarily, the idea that any of these could be swapped out if necessary. (And if the middle is a bit of a muddle, fear not. It's almost always that way, and if you've got some bookends on either side you can always return to it.) Here's the thing: Assemble the interview "beats" by content (it might even help to work off a written transcript or just close your eyes and listen to it like the radio).

Then cut each of these elements longer than you expect them to end up, knowing that the second run through will be plenty of time to start trimming. For now, leave plenty of room on either side of the edit, and make an initial assemblage of these first chunks which will serve not so much as building blocks, but, in some instances, as scaffolding which can be removed after the building is completed. Odds are good it will run two or three times longer than your final cut.

Now start whittling it down from there. Subtract what is not essential.

Think of this first edit as the bottom layer of a cake you are building upward, into more and more narrow slices. Weave your characters (because that's what they are, and it behooves you not to use so many that they only appear once or there is no sense of personality developed) in and out so that they can tell their part of your story.

Eventually each witness will need, at the very least, what is called a **lower third,** text (usually but not always at the bottom of the frame) which spells out their name, title (if needed) and their particular ethos in terms of this rhetorical situation: i.e., "Tom Marksbury, film historian." You may just need the one tagline/ID for a short film, but if it's been a while since we've heard from this person, repeat.

The next layer of the cake—after you've *tightened*, every time through, the longer cut to your increasing satisfaction—is dropping in the archival material. Look for two primary opportunities here: 1) any time you want to break away from the talking head—usually best to let somebody either start their comment and cut away so that he finishes it as a disembodied voice over another image, or 2) vice versa, where we are looking at the illustration of the comment and then return to the witness for the dramatic finish.

Some documentaries are stark, relentless, almost fixated on certain images. Others are dense (sometimes too dense) with constantly fluctuating patterns of images which almost dare you to look away. Both your content and your own temperament will dictate which approach you take—and there is certainly room, within reason, for a mixture of both. Always remember that these suggestions are all only *alternatives,* and that you should never try to please everybody by throwing every possible alternative in. *Construction* means building it up; *editing,* in the end, means scaling it back and cooking it down.

The other issue to consider—let's call it "covering over"—involves jump cuts. Nobody speaks in perfect paragraphs—and you probably don't want verbiage that textbook like in your film anyway. So you want to preserve their conversational style, but all of us have little tics and tricks—"umm," "like," etc.—we habitually use to buy time to put our next piece of thought together.

Some of that is fine, but a lot of it can be a real distraction. So you may want to make a tiny cut for better continuity and flow. *Oral* continuity, however, is inevitably going to interrupt visual continuity, so sometimes where that little slice is missing you might want to paper over the cut with a visual—photos, cartoons, etc. Sometimes jump cuts are not "accidents" at all, but are used deliberately to provide an edgy, exciting style (see Godard or way too many music videos). A little of this goes a long way; don't overuse them.

Along these same lines, consider the impact of the long unbroken take versus lots of very quick, even frenzied, sometimes nearly subliminal editing. Both have their place, but too much of either can be really tedious and/or headache-inducing. If a subject builds to an especially extended emotional or impactful moment, you don't want to interrupt it. Keep in mind, too—not only when you're editing but in the initial interview itself—to allow a moment *after* a particular high point (in other words, don't step on it at the time or cut it too short later). Sometimes the subject will sigh, or smile, and add some little bit of body language which greatly expand the impact of what he "just said."

On the other hand, probably for better *and* worse, we've all come to expect hyper-editing which forces a number of images (and remember the first rule of montage sometimes dictates not just a series of similar images but a collision of violently contradictory ones) to wash over us. Again, this is excellent in short spurts, but only to a point, and certainly not unabated. Too much of it, just like too much of any of these other tactics, and the mind simply shuts down.

The last layer is the voice-over, if you decide to use it, and the music. Again, if you want to use *any* music you find particularly appropriate, fine with me. But your instructor may want you to consult one of the many websites where you can find uncopyrighted generic music for free. Or better yet, for you musicians out there, why not compose and perform your own soundtrack music? It worked for John Carpenter in *Halloween.*

Again and again, though, *less is more.* You don't want overly emphatic, even melodramatic music stepping on every lovely point you've already made perfectly well, and you don't want a nonstop wallpaper of back to back music through every second of the film. It is *not* a music video. No need to include that entire guitar solo because it's always been your favorite—and the last thing you want to do is drown out the speaker. Unless a short burst of lyrics is unusually relevant to the proceedings, instrumental music in general is less distracting and will cause you fewer sound mixing problems.

Speaking of—once you're close to a final cut, try to adjust the soundtrack audio so that all sounds are reasonably consistent. Nobody is expecting Academy Award quality technical work on any of these issues, but it's very important that the sound—the audible end of the story you are telling visually—be reliably audible and more or less consistent.

That about does it. Don't get too fancy with the credits, but include some, and don't forget to document everything you've borrowed, the same as you would on the "Works Cited" page of a chapter.

Give it a good title, and put the title up early. The credits should come at the end of such a short film; otherwise, it seems like a very pretentious instance of the cart before the horse. But in terms of cuing an audience (who are only going to be spending a very small amount of time with your film) what to expect (and what not to expect, and what to continue to think about after the film is over and beginning to resonate), a bold, provocative, and short title can go a long way.

All right, then. You've got it. Hard work but more fun than you expected, right?

Now: Repeat. Do it again.

BIBLIOGRAPHY

As with screenwriting, there are way more books and software on the market than you will ever find useful. The best way to learn is just to grab a camera and get out there. I did want to mention a few solid nuts-and-bolts approaches, and a couple slightly more philosophical overviews. Many of the technical problems which may arise can be investigated on YouTube.

NUTS AND BOLTS

The Shut Up and Shoot Documentary Guide, Anthony Artis, Focal Press, 2008.

- Every bit as basic as it sounds. Covers a lot of territory in very direct and succinct terms. Absolutely jargon free, but with a useful glossary and lots of visual illustration. Almost a total focus on technical problems, not much on process.

Writing, Directing, and Producing Documentary Films and Videos, 4th edition., Alan Rosenthal, Southern Illinois University Press, 2007.

- Much more info on process here—Rosenthal is very good at leading you through the questions you need to be asking both way before you shoot and way after you have all the raw footage you need. There's a little too much focus on feature length films, thus you will find sections on working with film stock, budgets, and grant proposals, more than you will probably need. But for navigating through the steps and underlining what you need to be concentrating on, even for a very short film, a very useful text.

Documentary Storytelling: Creative Non-Fiction on Screen. Sheila Curran Bernard, Focal Press, 2011.

- Very helpful emphasis on narrative as the backbone for any kind of film, non-fiction or not. She can help you structure your material, think about pacing and exposition, what to emphasize and what to exclude, etc. Again, this veers a little more to the conceptual, but her storytelling instincts are very sound, and she can help you get in better touch with yours.

SLIGHTLY MORE AESTHETIC/PHILOSOPHICAL (FOR STUDENTS WHO WANT TO DIG A LITTLE DEEPER)

Introduction to Documentary, Bill Nichols, 2nd edition, University of Indiana Press, 2006.

- Probably the most incisive and comprehensive thinking about the form in terms of both theory and application. Nichols devotes a chapter each to nine essential questions, from "what makes documentaries engaging and persuasive?" to "how have documentaries addressed social and political issues?" which he proceeds to answer to both very practical and extremely philosophical terms.

Documentary: A Routledge Film Guidebook, Dave Saunders, Routledge Press, 2010.

- Tends to concentrate on more recent work, which might be more useful to first year students who might be otherwise overwhelmed by the vast history of the documentary form. Special attention to experimental work and marginalized voices.

Documenting the Documentary: Close Readings of Documentary Films and Videos, edited by Barry Keith Grant and Jeanette Sloniowski, Wayne State University Press, 1998.

- Excellent critical analysis of canonical films from *Nanook of the North, Man With the Movie Camera,* and *Triumph of the Will* to more recent classics like *Grizzly Man* and *Four Little Girls.* Particularly useful for more advanced students who might want to write *about* documentaries.

EVEN MORE PHILOSOPHICAL (BUT ESSENTIAL IF YOU REALLY WANT TO KEEP DOING THIS)

Ways of Seeing, John Berger, Penguin

On Photography, Susan Sontag, Picador

Both these books are both extremely philosophical—almost metaphysical—but very practical at the same time, the best of all possible combinations. Berger is of great use to anyone trying to figure out any kind of visual image in any kind of frame, and his discussions of such issues as perspective and point of view will benefit not only the casual art fan but, crucially in our case, anyone trying to compose and frame up the images he is trying to compile for a documentary.

In a similar vein, Sontag is really talking about the moral implications of the choices we make when we photograph (violate? validate? Impose our own unconscious set of values upon?) Anything up to and including ourselves. You don't want to be a cultural tourist, and you want to take responsibility for your own agenda—which first and foremost means realizing that you have one) and Sontag can straighten you out on that right away.

A FISTFUL OF DOCUMENTARIES

My two documentary production classes (WRD 312: Introduction to Documentary and WRD 412: Intermediate Documentary) both feature a wide variety of works which stress an even wider range of structural, expositional, and narrative techniques. I also teach a History of Documentary course (WRD 311) which traces the evolution of the form from the Lumiére Brothers at the turn of the twentieth century to … well, yesterday. What follows, though, is a very short and selective list of films which might inspire students at the first year Composition and Communications level.

Somewhat Experimental

Grizzly Man (Werner Herzog, 2005) 103 m

Not only a compelling portrait of Tim Treadwell, who dedicated his life to grizzly bears and was eventually mauled to death by one, but a fascinating subtext as Herzog, well known for his own completely antithetical obsessions with nature, wrestles with his own subjective point of view while trying to assemble Treadwell's footage in ways the activist could never have predicted or intended.

Exit Through the Gift Shop (Banksy, 2010) 87 m

Again, a dance of focus between the ostensible "director" (Terry, who may or may not be real) and "subject" (Banksy, ditto). To call this a "mockumentary" would be to sell it short by half. It's almost like crawling through a hall of distorting mirrors, while learning a lot about commercial and outsider art along the way.

This Is Spinal Tap (Rob Reiner, 1984) 82 m

The mockumentary actually goes all the way back to *Haxan: Witchcraft through the Ages*, from silent film days, but this evisceration of "Behind the Music" clichés, following the pathetic and vainglorious reunion of a third rate hair metal band, not only illuminates the connection of insecure teenage boys to preening cockrockers, but explodes most of our most naïve assumptions about what documentaries can and can't do along the way.

Cinéma Vérité

Salesman (Albert and David Maysles and Charlotte Zwerin, 1968) 84 m

As close to pure vérité as you can get. Seemingly without any directorial mediation, we travel with four itinerant Bible salesmen as they ply their wares across the country. What seems to start out as a fairly conventional morality play (the men are preying upon and profiting from the guilt and naïveté of their lower working class Catholic customers) becomes a multi-faceted study in what Thoreau called "lives of quiet desperation" and the cracks in the American dream.

Hoop Dreams (Steve James, 1994) 171 m

An epic masterpiece of socioeconomic reportage, as we follow two aspiring basketball players from inner-city Chicago as they move from their hopeless neighborhoods to scholarships in the white suburbs, trying for the big prize of a professional career. Again, the ostensible subject keeps splitting into more and more layers as we watch the sad and glorious trajectory of their efforts to get out and make it.

Engaged History and Activism

When the Levees Broke: A Requiem in Four Acts (Spike Lee, 2006) 226 m

The Hurricane Katrina story, told through a rich vein of resources including news footage, interviews with regular citizens and pundits alike, vivid graphics, and a haunting sense of growing quiet outrage you might not expect from Spike Lee. More even-handed than you'd think, and infinitely more effective because of it. (In marked contrast to Michael Moore.)

The House I Live In (Eugene Jareck, 2012) 108 m

A history and critique of the failure of the so-called Drug War, at once personal, even intimate, and, for once, a sweeping and persuasive use of statistics and numbers. Jareck manages to find the common line where disenchanted police who don't have time and supplies to do their real jobs and activists like David Simon (creator of *The Wire*) agree about this failure in terms of wasted money, wasted lives, and sheer human futility.

The Thin Blue Line (Errol Morris, 1988) 101 m

Created by America's greatest documentary maker (in my opinion) and both a life-changing experience and an argument that both the true crime genre and the artful use of re-creations don't have to be the kind of law and justice porno we watch on reality television shows like *Cops*, etc. Randall Adams, the subject of the film, was wrongly convicted of murdering a police officer. Based on the impact of the documentary, Adams was released; he subsequently sued Morris for the rights to his story.

AUTOBIOGRAPHY

Stories We Tell (Sarah Polley, 2013) 108 m

A young actress becomes obsessed with re- (and de-)constructing what she thought she understood about her childhood after the death of her mother. Almost painfully intimate, and a disarming mix of family photos, home movies, interviews that might as well be called interrogations, and re-creations that you may not even be able to spot.

Tarnation (Jonathan Caouette, 2004) 88 m

Supposedly made for $200 on a laptop computer, this is one of the most harrowing and confessional films I've ever seen—the director's difficult and abusive childhood is examined in excruciating detail—and yet there is not an ounce of self-pity to be seen. Far from it, after basically spending ninety minutes inside this guy's head and history, you feel an affirmation of the human spirit. Very instructive in its innovative use of found footage, archival, and homemade graphics.

KENTUCKY

Harlan County USA (Barbara Kopple, 1980) 103 m

Near-Vérité but skillfully manipulated depictions of the coal strikes of the late nineteen seventies. The sheer will and endurance of the miners—and especially the women who support and often guide their efforts—show how little rhetoric means compared to flawed human scrappiness. A blow against the empire in general, and Duke Power in particular.

Stranger with a Camera (Elizabeth Barrett, 2000) 61 m

The flip side of *Harlan County USA*. Like Kopple, the subject of this film came to Appalachia with the best of intentions, but unlike Kopple, she was unable to convince the local citizenry that she wasn't an intrusive outsider. A meditation on both the tremendous moral responsibilities and the inherent dangers of documentary film making.

Buy the Ticket, Take the Ride: Hunter S. Thompson on Film (Tom Thurman, 2007) 77 m

All right, I wrote it—but it's still pretty good. I like to point out two opposing directions the subgenre of films we might as well call "portrait of the artist" can go wrong—either it's a hagiography, where all the warts are surgically removed and nothing exists except the positive and adulatory, or the patho-biography, which goes beyond warts-and-all to reveal mostly all warts. Hunter had a lot of warts, yet he changed American writing. This is our attempt to explain these contradictions.

Making an Informative Podcast

Recommended for WRD 111/112
or as needed for WRD 110

Chapter 16

We've read about incorporating sources in our writing, ways to incorporate materials into presentations, identifying and understanding genres, and making a documentary. The multi-media focus of the documentary is important for us in thinking about how the skills we are learning in our WRD classes transfer beyond the WRD classroom—it can be tempting to think of our WRD classes as boxes we need to check, but these classes give us the skills we need to succeed in college and in our careers. Some of you may go on to create video materials akin to what is asked of you in making a documentary. Others of us may be called upon, either in our careers or because of our personal interests, to participate in one of the most prominent popular genres today, the podcast.

Podcasts are a relatively new genre, but they take much from the past. The power of audio has long been known, from the oral storytelling tradition that birthed now classic epic poems, such as *Beowulf* and Homer's *The Iliad* and *The Odyssey*, into the twentieth century with the enormous popularity of the radio—it used to be far more than talk radio and the same 300 songs on every station.

Even with the genre's predecessors, it is still surprising that podcasts have become as popular as they have. Part of the popularity is likely due to the fact that podcasts are relatively easy and affordable to produce, and they are typically free and easy to access for listeners. But that can't be the only reason for such popularity.

Exercise: Thinking about Podcasts and their Popularity

- How many of you listen to podcasts?
- What podcasts do you listen to?
- Why do you listen to those podcasts?
- What do you like about them?
- How did you find out about them?
  - What drew you to them in the first place?
- Why do you think podcasts have gotten so popular in the last few years?

Chances are you and your classmates listen to a range of different types of podcasts. Maybe you like comedy podcasts, like *I Don't Know About that with Jim Jefferies* or *Nobody Listens to Paula Poundstone;* maybe you like scripted fiction podcasts, like *Faerie* or *Mind's Eye;* maybe you like people reading stories, like *LeVar Burton Reads* or *The Ellery Queen Mystery Magazine Podcast;* maybe you like stories from real life, like *Dog Tales* or *Beautiful Anonymous;* maybe you like interview and conversation shows, like *The Joe Rogan Experience* or *Armchair Expert;* maybe you like true crime, like *My Favorite Murder* and *Unsolved Murders* … and the list of genres goes on.

If you are asked to make a podcast for your WRD class, chances are you need to make an informative podcast. That is, you will be making a podcast with the primary intention of informing listeners about something. You will be talking about the research you have done, and possibly making an argument (that depends on what the instructor wants from the assignment, so make sure you listen to the instructor and read any descriptions of the assignment in the syllabus, on Canvas, and in class handouts). To be able to do that, though, we need to have an idea of what makes the informative podcast, as a genre, work. That is, we need to figure out what "conversation" we are entering into and what are the conventions listeners have come to expect from the genre.

Exercise

Many of you may already have some experience with the informative podcast genre, so you can already start thinking about the things that let you recognize an informative podcast from other types of podcasts. But we probably haven't yet delineated the genre.

Let's start by listening to an episode of an informative podcast together. Listen to this episode of the *NPR* podcast *The Indicator:* (https://www.npr.org/2020/11/03/930923756/what-elvis-can-teach-us-about-vaccine-marketing) While listening, think about several things to start figuring out how the genre works:

- What are the identifiable traits of the genre?
- How is information presented?
  - How do the speakers keep the information both educational and engaging?
- How do the speakers keep respectful, informative tones while still keeping your interest?
- How do the podcasters establish their credentials?
  - How do they maintain those credentials (or ethos) throughout the podcast?
- How is narrative used to help listeners keep track of information and understand new information?
- How is information contextualized?
- How are sources cited, and how is the reliability of those sources established?

Now that we've started to identify what we think may be some conventions of the genre, we need to put that to the test by listening to other informative podcasts to make sure we have identified some of the defining traits and characteristics of the genre.

Exercise (Continued)

As you work on your own podcast, you'll want to make sure you continue listening to informative podcasts to help you better understand the genre and refine your work. But for now, let's look at one more example. This time, you choose. Find an informative podcast. It could be another episode of *The Indicator,* but it will prove helpful to listen to a range of different shows to best understand how different people have approached the genre. Below is a list of shows to consider—but if you already have a good one you know and like, feel free to use that, so long as it is an informative, researched podcast:

- *Science vs.* (looks at the science of our everyday lives)
- *Short Wave* (another science podcast, giving short science lessons with real world questions and applications)
- *Astonishing Legends* (a well-researched show on the paranormal, in which the hosts are very good about citing their sources, but the episodes tend to be long)
- *Hardcore History* (an incredibly well-researched show on subjects in history, but the episodes are **very** long)
- *You Must Remember This* (about Hollywood history)
- *Hidden Brain* (on psychology and science)
- *Planet Money* (economics)
- *99% Invisible* (architecture and design)
- *TedTalks/TED Radio Hour* (range of mostly science-related topics)
- *RadioLab* (range of mostly science-related topics)
- *History Chicks* (women in history)
- *Bowery Boys* (New York City's history, focused on specific locations and people)

As you listen, continue to think about the above questions, as well as what you can use for your own podcast:

- How is the information woven together to present a coherent overview instead of just a 'wall of facts'?
- How is information contextualized?
- How does the presenter keep things informative while also being engaging?

SCRIPT

The podcast will likely come near the end of the semester, so you should have already done a lot of research, found a lot of good, reliable, unbiased sources, and have a lot to say about your topics. But now how do we keep from just sounding like we're reading what other people have said, even though we are relying a lot on the work of others? Additionally, how do we get something that sounds as natural as the podcasts we've listened to?

If you've ever read one of your own papers aloud, you've likely noticed that it sounds weird when you actually hear it. That is because almost all of us write differently than we speak. We learned in school about the standards of academic writing, and so we write papers for our classes in the style we have learned is appropriate for an academic setting. Unfortunately, that same style does not translate well to the spoken word of a podcast. That means that when we write the script, we need to think about it as something we will need to read. We also need to take time to read what we have written out loud so that we can note things that don't sound right and fix them before we record.

Exercise: Essay vs. Speech

To help us think about the different ways we need to approach something for oral presentation vs. an essay, let's look at an example. Below are two passages, one from an article published in the peer-reviewed journal *Metal Music Studies,* the other taken from a conference presentation the author gave while he was preparing that article. As you read each of these, make note of the differences between the two versions. Why do you think the author changed things for the article vs. the presentation?

Article:
- Almost from heavy metal's start, the genre looked at the dark side of rock and roll. Heavy metal looked outside the standard topics of rock lyrics, which typically revolved around lived or desired experience, and instead gathered lyrical inspiration from literature, particularly that of horror and/or the supernatural. Although literary adaptation and appropriation is prevalent in heavy metal, one band, Iron Maiden, has almost made it into a unique art. The song "Rime of the Ancient Mariner" exemplifies the band's approach, not just alluding to but fully adapting Samuel Taylor Coleridge's Romantic narrative poem of the same name. In adapting the poem to song form, lyricist Steve Harris utilized both the poem and the glossing Coleridge added in 1817. Harris conflates the text of Coleridge's poem with that of the glossing, treating the two parts as one and the same text, providing a new,

Exercise: Essay vs. Speech (Continued)

hybrid version of the tale; additionally, Harris and his band mates use their unique medium to add original twists and to adapt the tale's complexities in their own way.[1]

Presentation:

- As rock and roll grew, it also fractured, with one of its subgenres, Heavy Metal, becoming a rival to the rock mainstream. Defined by Black Sabbath, heavy metal looked beyond the standard topics of rock, gathering lyrical inspiration from a more "academic" source: literature, particularly that of horror and the supernatural, served as a continual fount of inspiration for metal songwriters. This literary inspiration is on full display in Iron Maiden's "Rime of the Ancient Mariner," a heavy metal adaptation of Samuel Taylor Coleridge's poem of the same name. For the adaptation, lyricist Steve Harris utilized both Coleridge's poem and his 1817 glossing, treating them as one and the same text, creating a new version of the tale, supplemented by the additional possibilities of a new medium.[2]

One important thing for us to keep in mind as we write, and as we may have noted in the previous exercise, is that we need to say—and hear—what we write, and we need it to sound natural. An important thing here, as it is in preparing a speech, is to remember that you need to breath. If you have long sentences with no natural places to stop, you may run out of breath, and if you sound exasperated because you're running out of air, the listener is going to start to feel exasperated—and you don't want to lose the listener!

It's also important to think about how you are going to use your sources. You need to cite your sources, but oral citations are not the same as written citations, and you must be aware of this as you write your script. We can't hear the MLA and APA style parenthetical citations, nor the footnotes of Harvard or Chicago style, in a podcast. That means you need to figure out how you are going to "introduce" your source, establish their credentials, and weave their material, be it quotation, summary, or paraphrase (you'll likely end up using a combination of all three). (If you are unsure of the difference between these and how to work them in, see the first half of the chapter on Citation.)

PRACTICE

I know it can be tempting to just want to write the script and then press record, but that is a bad approach for several reasons. The first is that you will likely have some nerves about the recording process, which means that when you start to speak, you will speak quickly and likely speed up, just like you do when you give a speech in front of a class. You need to practice so you can carefully control the speed at which you give the information so your listener can understand everything you say.

Second, you need to make sure you have your enunciation down. When reading a script, it can be very easy to slip into a sort of mumble-speak, but your listener likely will not be able to understand it. Thus, you need to practice, making sure you are clearly enunciating all your words so your listener can understand all your valuable information.

Third, you may have some words or names in your script which you always seem to be able to pronounce when you read them in your head, but when the time comes to say them out loud, suddenly you realize that you either don't know how to pronounce them or are unknowingly pronouncing them incorrectly (a great local example of this is Versailles Road—natives of Lexington know how it is pronounced here, but those of us from other places are likely to pronounce it like that place in France). Make sure you have confirmed and practiced all your pronunciations.

Fourth, as noted above, you need to know where to put in pauses so you can breathe. You don't really know your limit until you've practiced, so read the script aloud several times. Any time you hit a tough spot, make note, and after that run, try to correct it.

Fifth and finally, your podcast likely has a minimum, and possibly a maximum, time in which it must run, and there is no way of knowing how long what you have actually is if you don't practice it and time your practice. Your instructor will likely give you page/word count that approximate the time, but everyone has a natural speaking rhythm which creates variation. (I was once in a graduate class in which we had final presentations, and my presentation was as long as all the other students, but my "script" was more than a page shorter than any of the others because I naturally speak at a slower pace—but no one thought I was deliberately speaking slowly or trying to draw things out to compensate for having less material.)

RECORDING

Once you have written, revised, and practiced your script and think you're ready to record, think again, because you still have some preliminary work to do.

First, figure out how you want to break up the script so you can record it in chunks. I know it's tempting to think "I'll just pound this out in five minutes then get on with my life," but that is not a good approach. I have seen many great presentations in my years of teaching, but I have never seen a perfect presentation: students always mispronounce something, or verbally stumble a bit, or need to go back to clarify something, etc. It happens. It's only natural. It's not a big deal in an in-person presentation. But in a podcast, there is no reason for such errors: we have the opportunity to take it again, so we should.

Think about it another way: this podcast is likely a huge part of your grade. Do you want your grade to suffer just because your dog started barking four and a half minutes into your six minute record? If you have your script broken up into one to two minute chunks, instead of trying to get a great six minutes, you can have several amazing short sections that you then edit together. That way, if you make a mistake or there are uncontrollable noises, you can just record again without feeling like you've now lost five minutes of work.

Some of you may have recording and editing software that you've used before and you love. Great. For those of you who are inexperienced with audio recording and editing, there are several resources for you. First, if you feel completely overwhelmed, make an appointment at the Media Depot in the Hub in the basement of Young Library. There are knowledgeable folks there who can help you. You can also reserve a room to record it, so if your five roommates always seem to be home and noisy, you can go there for a quiet place to record.

If you have your own quiet place to record, you still need software for recording and editing. If you are completely inexperienced, I recommend you start with Audacity. It is a free, open-access program, which means you can download it for free just by searching for it. It takes a little getting used to, but it is relatively user-friendly for recording your podcast chunks and editing the pieces together—and it is also pretty easy to Export different file types, so you should be able to get a file in the format required by your instructor (I ask for mp3 files, which you can get from the "Export" option under "File" in Audacity; check your course information for the type of file your instructor wants). Below are some other options:

- Sound cloud (web-based recording and editing)
- Garage Band (for those who have Mac computers)
- Adobe Audition (This can be daunting for a beginner, but is very close to professional level recording and editing software. The Adobe Creative Cloud Suite, of which this is a part, is available to you, free of additional charge, through UK's tech hub.)

Be aware that each program takes some getting used to, so make sure that, before you start recording your podcast, you experiment within the program, making sure you know how to record, how to edit what you have recorded, how to put together different pieces you have recorded, and how to get the correct file type from the program. Now, you are finally ready to record. Remember to record in short chunks, and don't be afraid to re-record a chunk if you need to.

Many podcasts are audio only, and if that's what your instructor wants, you've got the basic tools here you need. If your instructor wants video, as some podcasts are, (or if you're feeling ambitious and want video to be more like Rogan), the tools here are still useful, but you'll want to also look to information in Chapter 16: "How to Make Your Own Documentary" to learn more about video recording and editing—because your instructor almost certainly doesn't want the raw footage rolling that a celebrity like Rogan commands (even Alex Jones, the most unprofessional of all recording professionals, often edits the raw footage of his live show to make the videos and feeds he posts for viewing and listening online).

Good luck, and welcome to the exciting world of podcasting!

NOTES

[1] Roberts, Justin J. "Rime of a Metal Mariner." *Metal Music Studies,* vol. 3, no. 1, 2017, p. 63.

[2] Roberts, Justin J. "Rime of a Metal Mariner." Presentation given at the Annual National Joint Popular Culture Association/American Culture Association Conference, April 2015.

Considering Accessibility and Disability

Recommended for WRD 111/112
or as needed for WRD 110

Chapter 17

INTRODUCTION TO ACCESSIBILITY AND DISABILITY

The rights of any marginalized group are heavily dependent not only on activism, but on technical writing. How the legislature is written and the wording used have lasting impact on communities, so it is important to understand how necessary understanding rhetoric is. In other words, understanding rhetoric and its place within activism, in this case disability rights, is pivotal to navigating the world—particularly as disability diagnoses become increasingly common between long Covid sufferers and improved diagnostic methods (StatsRRTC).

The **Americans with Disabilities Act (ADA),** which requires certain levels of accessibility and equitable treatment in the United States, was passed not only due to the activism and lobbying of disabled people, but also their ability to articulate the needs and goals of the very legislation that they were lobbying for. The ADA depended on an understanding of technical writing and rhetoric by its sponsors, and without these skills the movement may not have found as much comprehensive coverage in the legislature written by and passed by others.

A Short History of ADA and the Disability Rights Movement

Disabled people struggle for accessibility rights across the globe. In the U.S. there are a few legal protections that have been put into place thanks to the disability rights movement. In the 1970s The Rehabilitation Act of 1973 (Section 504) and the Education for All Handicapped Children Act of 1975 were passed. Section 504 "provided equal opportunity for employment within the federal government and in federally funded programs, prohibiting discrimination on the basis of either physical or mental disability" (ADL). This act's equitable language and legal protections were the result of disability activists lobbying and marching to have civil rights language that represented and included disabled people. The 1975 act ensured access to education for disabled children. These acts were precursors to the eventual passing of the ADA (Section 508) in 1990.

Disabled people continued to lobby for legal protections to their civil rights and a draft ADA bill was prepared by the National Council on Disability in 1988 (DREDF). The ADA would be passed in 1990 and ensures equal opportunity to employment and accomodations. The ADA mandates the provision of reasonable accommodations by businesses and prevents the refusal of service by businesses to people on the basis of disability. These legal protections are not always realized and people and accommodations are still ignored for a variety of reasons, but disability justice advocates remain vocal and involved.

Exercise: Shruti Rajkumar

Disabled activist Shruti Rajkumar believes that the ADA was a necessary victory for the disabled community, but that more can be done to serve disabled people in the U.S. Rajkumar writes:

> *The burden shouldn't fall on us to constantly fight against violations of our civil rights. In an ideal world, the ADA would be enforced more, and owners of bars and restaurants would prioritize access to all. I wish I was able to access every place in society with ease. But that isn't the reality for myself and so many others.*
>
> *I'm immensely grateful to be a part of the ADA generation and will never take for granted how hard disability activists fought for the civil rights protections that I benefit from every day. But at the same time, I want more for myself and my community, whether it be through expanding or modernizing existing laws, or bringing forward new policies to advance our rights and access. (Rajkumar)*

Either in small groups or as a large group with your instructor, discuss the quote. What problem is Rajkumar identifying? What are the solutions to her problem? Are there ways this quote reflects problems in the scholastic or classroom space? If so, what are those problems and what are the potential solutions? What rhetorical techniques (see *Analyzing Arguments* in Chapter 6: Rhetorical Analysis) does Rajkumar use?

PERSON-FIRST VS. IDENTITY-FIRST LANGUAGE: LISTENING TO DISABLED ACTIVISTS AND USING THEIR LANGUAGE

In recent years there has been a debate within the disabled activist community, which focuses on the rhetorical stakes of identifying language. This debate is about the use of **person first language (PFL)** that places the person's identity before their disability (i.e., person with disability, person with blindness, person with autism, etc.) and the use of **identity first language (IFL)** that places the person's disabled identity first (i.e., disabled person, blind person, autistic person). This debate exemplifies how important it is to research the communities and people you are discussing:

1. Not everyone is in agreement on terminology and that requires researchers to acknowledge and use the language that is preferred by their chosen subject
2. Words *do* mean different things and the rhetoric we choose to use has implications beyond the page.

The following section will break down this debate and also give you tools for identifying preferred language amongst research subjects for future use.

As a disclaimer: No group is monolithic or homogenous and making assumptions on how a group operates or identifies based on a single encounter can not only reflect poorly in your final work but can also hurt and misrepresent your research subjects, an outcome that can be avoided through compassionate rhetorical choices. This type of rhetorical debate is also prominent in houseless activism, for example, as activists believe that not having a house does not equate to not having a home. Activists will also say someone is experiencing houselessness because unlike disability, houselessness is not a state that permanently impacts personhood.

Ultimately, many historically misrepresented communities and activists within those communities *do* care about the labels they are given. Attention to identifying language acknowledges the damage that negative rhetoric can, and has, done to communities who have been flattened into just a label. Positive rhetoric also helps communities that have been mislabeled and misrepresented in ways that prevent them from accessing the care and help they need.

The Difference of Opinions Between PFL and IFL

PFL grew in popularity after the passing of the ADA, and as disability rights came into the spotlight, government officials as well as educators and doctors "adopted [it] as a general linguistic rule" (Ferrigon). The use of PFL has faced criticism by the disabled community, however, due to the rhetorical concerns PFL creates. Activists like Cara Liebowitz, Nancy Mairs, and Imani Barbarin reject the use of PFL and instead use IFL and other terminology that they feel better encapsulates their experiences as disabled people. In other words, PFL rejects how much disability impacts and forms disabled people's lives and experiences, whereas activists feel that identity-first language better encapsulates how deeply ingrained disability is into disabled lives.

Disability's stigma in social life is part of daily life for many people, and the treatment of disability as something that is demeaning or makes someone worth less than others is part of **ableism.** Ableism is the discrimination of disabled people by focusing on able-bodied (or abled) people and ignoring the needs of disabled people. Ableism can appear in unknown biases against people who are different, who fear medical diagnoses, and who disregard needs of disabled people on a global scale. Ableism also views disability as something requiring a cure or a fix, when the reality is many people experience disabilities that cannot or will not go away (Dunn).

There are different forms of ableism, from social ableism, to internal ableism, or even global ableism. Ableism has made disabled people wary of the labels they use as many labels have become stigmatized and unappealing. However, disabled activists are reclaiming their power through the term "disabled" in an attempt to counter the social ableism they have experienced and pave the way toward a more inclusive future.

Brut. Media profiled Imani Barbarin after she began a social media campaign #WhenICall-MyselfDisabled. While profiling Barbarin and the social media movement she started, *Brut. Media* found that many disabled people claimed the title disabled because it is a part of who they are and to claim another title invokes self hatred, misery, and is just untrue (Brut.). Barbarin goes on to say that choosing her title, saying disabled, is revolutionary and an attempt to help other disabled people take their power back (Brut.). This movement shows how alienating PFL can feel to disabled people, as if the way they navigate the world and are impacted by disability is not integral to their lives. This is important because disability is made disability—is so strongly felt by disabled people—due to inequitable access and denial of needs in society at large.

Cara Liebowitz, a disabled writer, understands the attraction to PFL because she "[doesn't] want to be identified solely on the basis of [her] disabilities" (Liebowitz). However, disabled people cannot be separated from their disabilities, which are integrated into who they are (Liebowitz). While the intentions of PFL may be good and meant to show respect to disabled people, treating disability as a linguistic add-on also implies that it can be easily removed when it, in fact, is part of a person's experience and navigation of the world. Liebowitz succinctly explains why IFL is often preferred within the disabled community:

> *Identity-first language is founded upon the idea of the social model of disability. In a nutshell, the social model says that though our impairments (our diagnostic, medical conditions) may limit us in some ways, it is the inaccessibility of society that actually disables us and renders us unable to function. The most basic example is wheelchair accessibility. If I am using my wheelchair and I can't go to a restaurant because it doesn't have a ramp, am I disabled by my cerebral palsy or am I disabled by the inaccessibility of the restaurant? (Liebowitz).*

Liebowitz's example, which questions whether society disables her or her disability, is one often discussed within the disabled community and disabled theorists reiterate that the creation of an accessible world would change the way disability exists and is largely viewed by non-disabled people. In other words, beginning with accessibility would change what disability means as the world becomes more inclusive, and inaccessibility (which is disabling) decreases.

Though the ADA ensures many legal protections, the world has been developed around the assumption that disability is abnormal while ability is normal and, therefore, the world has been focused on abled people. Disability, then, becomes an experience of inequity and difference which is centered in identity-first language whereas person-first language tries to instead separate the person from their disability, both metaphorically and linguistically as the word "with" literally separates the person from their disability (i.e. person *with* disability).

Crip Theory

Nancy Mairs wrote "I am a cripple. I choose this word to name me" (37). Mairs was an author whose ideas on personal identity and chosen titles fit into a larger movement around crip theory and crip activism. Crip theory developed from an intersection of queer and disability studies and is an attempt to reclaim a word that has been used both derogatorily and to incite pity (McRuer and Cassabaum). Crip theory, though recent, already has a rich history and a lot of theoretical engagement, which you can read more about and find sources for on Oxford Bibliographies "Crip Theory" page (McRuer and Cassabaum). Mairs also exemplifies how people within the community choose their own terms and it is their lead, and the terms they are comfortable with, that you should use to describe your research and research subjects.

This term is in the process of reclamation and the community is split on the use of cripple and crip. You can find some guidelines for use in the "Terms to Avoid" section that appears later in this chapter. It is worth noting that this term is also dependent on socio-geographic factors as it is not recommended for use in describing disabled people within areas that use crip not as a disability term, but to identify a violent group or gang-related activity.

Identifying Support Groups Versus Hate Groups

When researching disabled people and disabled groups, it is important to practice due diligence when vetting your sources. For example, the Autistic Self Advocacy Network labels Autism Speaks as a hate group (ASAN). While Autism Speaks (AS) and its signature puzzle pieces are probably the most well-known autism group, autistic people believe AS's mission is counter to their own. To elaborate, AS's goal is to cure autism, whereas many autistic people, including those in ASAN, do not want to be cured; they simply want society to be more accepting and inclusive of their support needs (ASAN). ASAN circulated a flier on AS, explaining that "Autism Speaks uses its platform and advertising budget to portray autism and autistic people as mysterious and frightening" (ASAN). ASAN instead asks that people rely on ASAN, Autistic Women & Non-binary Network (AWN), and Self Advocates Becoming Empowered (SABE).

Autism Speaks' successful marketing campaign means that it appears to be a trusted source. The reality is that autistic people largely do not trust this network and it, therefore, should be a source used with caution. AS exemplifies that just because a purported disability service is well-known and popular does not mean it serves the community it is named for. This is another case where you should let the community that you are researching identify the terms and sources they are comfortable with and in the meantime look up how the community feels about the source you are using.

Exercise: Imani Barbarin

Activist Imani Barbarin wrote about her experience as a Black disabled woman during the pandemic in the *Cosmopolitan* article "The Pandemic Tried to Break Me, but I Know My Black Disabled Life is Worthy." Barbarin is an accomplished public speaker with a masters in Global Communication and is often engaged in speaking commitments and trainings due to her expertise in the field.

> *If I learned anything about myself during these unprecedented times, it's that self-love is an ongoing, nonlinear practice. I'm never going to reach a point at which self-love simply exists, especially when my personhood is held up against racial, mental, bodily, and desirability standards I will scarcely ever be able to meet. But I no longer feel guilt about what I am not. Instead, I choose to accept and celebrate what I am, however fragile that acceptance might be. For Black disabled people, self-love is not simply an aesthetic or a trend but a fundamental lifeline we tap into through unapologetic advocacy work and collective support and remembering. As our ancestors have taught us, we are all we have.* (Barbarin).

With your class, or in smaller groups, evaluate the closing of her *Cosmopolitan* piece. What are some key terms she identifies with? Why are her chosen terms important, according to Barbarin? What type of rhetorical appeal is she using (referring to the appeals in Chapter 6: "Rhetorical Analysis"—ethos, pathos, and logos). Does Barbarin's chosen rhetorical appeal have the desired effect—in other words, is her argument successfully articulated?

> ### Exercise: Imani Barbarin (continued)
>
> For the extended version of this assignment, you will rhetorically analyze Barbarin's entire essay as a class or in smaller groups. What is the exigence? What is Barbarin's evidence? What rhetorical appeals does Barbarin use throughout the essay? How does Barbarin's essay identify the importance of language in relation to disability activism? How much importance does Barbarin place on rhetoric and chosen nouns for identity as a disabled activist?
>
> Another option is to explore Barbarin's website, Instagram, X, or TikTok. Barbarin uses her platform to identify public communications that fail to protect or care for disabled people. She also, often, identifies the rhetorical choices that are flawed and instructs people on bettering their communication skills. Barbarin, as a communications expert and disability activist, often speaks on the importance of communication experiences for achieving her goals; these experiences are great sources for not only bettering your knowledge about disability and disability activism, but also learning how and why activists make the rhetorical choices they do.

TERMS TO AVOID

Over the years many terms have been used to negatively describe disability and are, therefore, no longer appropriate when discussing disabled people due to the traumatic pasts they reference. These terms are not only used to discriminate against disabled people but also to make non-disabled people feel worse about themselves by suggesting they are disabled. The use of disability as a slur is rooted in many problems, including one of social inequality in disability and the consideration of disabled people as less than. Disabled people exist with disability, but that does not make them anything other than disabled—certainly not a source for ridicule or ignorance.

The following are two lists of terms. The first list is full of terms that should be avoided when discussing disabled people, or people in general, due to their histories and their use as slurs. The second list is full of terms that should be used with caution, requiring you to research and confirm that the terms are the ones that are correct for communicating your meaning and not simply popularized misrepresentations of your topic. These are not exhaustive lists, but they cover many of the more commonly heard terms. You should always prioritize the terms someone uses to describe themselves.

The best rule of thumb is to let your research subjects lead the language you use to refer to them, instead of relying on language you are familiar with which could be out of date or may no longer apply to the group you are talking about. If you are new to a term, do some research before you use it. Generally a quick search will tell you what you need to know.

Terms to Avoid

- **The R-Slur:** This term has recently come back into vogue and is overwhelmingly used to negatively describe people. Though the term was originally introduced to describe mental disabilities, it has long been used as an insult that reduces people to their disability.
- **Spaz:** Having spastic muscles (or spasming) is a very real, and painful, condition that many disabled people experience. Calling someone a spaz or saying someone is spazzing out not only has become a derogatory identifier for someone who does not fit into social norms, but also socially excludes people with turrets and tics, people who have a loss of bodily control and function, as well as those who cannot regulate their emotions (among others). Spaz should never be used to describe someone who is or is not disabled due to its negative history, its negative connotations, and its general ignorance of disabilities associated with spasms.
- **Insane, Crazy, Deranged, Lunatic, Maniac:** These are terms that have been used to describe behavior viewed as different or aberrant; however, these terms have ultimately been reduced to insults over someone's mental state but do not exist within the DSM IV and are not descriptors or actual disabilities or disorders.
- **Differently-Abled and Handicapable:** These terms minimize and mitigate many of the support and accessibility needs of disabled people.
- **Special Needs:** Special needs has not only been used negatively, directed toward people who operate differently, but also implies that it is special to need support, instead of the reality that everyone, disabled or not, has different support needs that change and fluctuate over time.
- **Dumb:** Used in the past to describe deaf people and currently often used interchangeably with "stupid" meaning of lesser intelligence, this term implied deaf people were of lesser intelligence or lacked understanding due to their disability.
- **Stupid, Imbecile:** Used to describe people who seem to have lesser intelligence when so-called intelligence is not only subjective but also based on access and support.
- **Confined to a Wheelchair or Wheelchair Bound:** These terms make wheelchairs, important mobility tools, sound like a prison when the reality is that wheelchairs provide freedom and access for people who need them. Wheelchairs do not confine their users but instead provide the support needed for their freedom and mobility.

- **Crack-Head:** Not only minimizes the very real struggle that is addiction, but also identifies any behavior that is viewed as socially different as associated with drug use, masking the behavior in relation to drug use and addiction and villainizing difference as unethical and potentially dangerous.
- **Gimp:** This term originated as an offensive term for people who walk with a limp. This term has never been used other than as an insult or a term meant to solicit offense.
- **Inspirational:** When disabled people are called inspirational, a few things happen: first, disabled people are measured only through their ability to be inspirational; second, a disabled person is reduced to their inspiration story and their very real struggles and hardships are overlooked; third, calling disabled people inspirational and highlighting an ability to overcome only serves abled people as it reframes the current system of limited access and support as survivable via a few success stories.
- **Mental:** Using the terms mental illness or neuro divergent are acceptable ways of framing non normative mental processes. To be "mental," however, implies craziness, difference, and a lack of control which are not positive associations for people actually dealing with mental illness and neuro divergence.
- **Midget, Munchkin:** Dwarfism is associated with many other disabilities and is, itself, a broad categorization of several genetic differences and disabilities that little people experience. The cited terms have been used to negatively describe little people and demean them for their different bodies and statures. These terms have also made little people into caricatures of themselves and have been subject to stereotypes and ridicule.
- **Psycho(tic):** Psycho has been associated with killers, most famously in Alfred Hitchcock's *Psycho,* neuro divergence, and people who experience psychosis. While people can experience psychosis, the associated disorders are no longer called psychotic disorders and the caricature of a psycho can be explained by any number of mental health stigmas and misrepresented neuro divergence. This is a moment where a symptom of a broader disability will use person-first language, as it is a symptom and not the disability itself. For example, one would say "a person experiencing psychosis" as opposed to "psychotic person" due to both its lack of description of specific dysfunction as well as its use as an insult. Even when using psychosis, one should tread carefully and make sure that is the medical term assigned to what you are speaking about and that the person you are representing is comfortable with that term.

- **Schizo:** Schizo, much like psycho, uses what once was a medical term that was turned into a pejorative term aimed toward neuro divergent people. Schizophrenia is a very specific mental disorder that makes it difficult for sufferers to interpret reality. Schizo should not be used towards people experiencing psychosis, people experiencing a different mental disorder, or even schizophrenics as it is exclusively an insult that minimizes (both figuratively and literally through the shortening of the word) the reality of schizophrenia and other mental health disorders.
- **Victim:** Calling disabled people victims interprets disability as something that is tragic and full of suffering. While disability can involve suffering and it is important for those realities to be out in the open, disabled people are not victims or inspirations: disabled people are disabled people who have a variety of experiences and realities which can all be acknowledged and not minimized to an ableist interpretation of disability.

Terms to Use With Caution

- **Hysterical:** Hysteria is an ailment rooted in sexism that was used as a catch-all term for women experiencing any number of undiagnosed physical or mental ailments. The word is derived from the Greek word for "uterus" and the disease was originally thought to be caused by "roaming uteri" which were impacting a person's health (McVean). Women were called hysterical when they experienced symptoms which included physical pain, depression, and anxiety, among many others. To call someone hysterical is to use a term that, in reality, prevented people with uteruses from receiving treatment for decades and also minimizes the very real physical or emotional conditions that person is living with. Many suffered due to this pseudo scientific diagnosis that was essentially made up to label seemingly difficult women.
- **Crip:** As previously mentioned, there has been a reclamation movement for crip in disability studies and disability activism. This word, however, is not accepted by all disabled people for a variety of reasons including sensitivity to its past misuse, trauma, as well as not correctly describing the disability. This is a word that should be used only when it has been claimed by your chosen research group or subject.
- **Dwarf:** Some little people self identify with this term as a label for their condition; however, this is not a term you should use without deep consideration and research as it is a term that is also used to discriminate against people in diverse bodies. Little person and person with short stature are more broadly accepted labels within the community.

- **Narcissist:** Narcissistic Personality Disorder is a real disorder, but has very specific requirements for diagnosis. People can be selfish without necessarily being a narcissist. NPD is a serious disorder and labeling all selfish behavior as narcissism takes away some of the meaning behind the word. Descriptions of behavior should be specific and factual. Identifying behavior with proper terms helps us discuss mental health, abuse, and toxic behavior appropriately and productively.
- **Schizophrenic:** This term should only be used to label actual diagnosed schizophrenics. There are other disorders that have symptoms like delusions and problems determining reality that are not schizophrenia, so this term should be used only in diagnostic discussion of schizophrenia or when a subject has used the term to identify themselves after diagnosis (i.e., *not* in the case of someone saying "sometimes I feel a little schizophrenic," but only in a situation where they have been diagnosed as schizophrenic).
- **OCD (Obsessive Compulsive Disorder):** OCD is a real disorder but it does not mean being clean or organized. A person cannot be "kind of" OCD: OCD is a very serious disorder that deals with intrusive thoughts, compulsions, and disordered behavior. This could include feeling compelled to count things or becoming convinced someone they love will be hurt if they do not perform a specific ritual. This disorder is taxing and can be dangerous for its sufferers. OCD should only be used to identify someone who has been diagnosed and not to, again, minimize the seriousness of this condition by comparing it to liking a clean space.
- **Intrusive Thoughts:** The use of this term has increased in popularity recently. Intrusive thoughts are not sudden thoughts, but instead thoughts that feel violating, violent, or dangerous. They are, by definition, disturbing or troubling unwanted thoughts that are often recurring and greatly trouble the person experiencing them causing great anxiety and worry (Bilodeau). Intrusive thoughts should only be used to identify actual intrusive thoughts.

Exercise: Case Study

1. Choose a word associated with a disability that you are familiar with or from the lists provided. Do a deep dive into the word's history (origin, original meaning, colloquial meaning, evolution, etc.) and the word's contemporary meaning and usage. Describe why the word is or is not harmful to the communities it is meant to represent and whether it should or should not be used to identify disabled people.
2. Write a narrative that describes your findings on your chosen word.

ACTIVITY

Think about some aspect of your day today, such as getting coffee, leaving your dorm room, walking to class, taking a test, etc. Write down all the steps you had to take to complete that activity or assignment. Now imagine that you were hearing impaired, visually impaired, or physically impaired. How would that single aspect of your day have been impacted by some sort of disability? For example, does the route you walk to class have stairs? How would you navigate that if you could not take stairs? How would your normal morning routine be different if you were unable to hear? You may not have to imagine and, for the purpose of this assignment, do not need to disclose if you are imagining or not. Now, refer back to the original steps you wrote down to complete that activity, and write down whether or not you would be able to complete that activity—what different steps would you have to take? What support would you need? What could be done differently by the people and world around you to support someone trying to complete that task with a disability?

Another way of thinking about this is using Catharine Savini's method from "Looking for Trouble: Finding your Way into a Writing Assignment." The Savini method follows four steps:

1. Noticing;
2. Articulating a problem and its details;
3. Posing fruitful questions; and
4. Identifying what is at stake (Savini 56).

For this assignment imagine this method using these words:

1. Noticing what activities that should be easy are not for disabled people on campus.
2. Articulating what is creating barriers for disabled people to complete these activities or assignments including, but not limited to, physical barriers, lack of support, lack of accessibility, and lack of respect toward disabilities by others.
3. Ask yourself, what could be done to help break down the specific barriers you noticed for disabled people? What solutions are possible here? What more do you need to know/question in order to articulate an answer?
4. What does the lack of accessibility you noticed mean for not just disabled students, but the community as a whole? How would fixing this problem benefit both disabled students and non-disabled students? How would the University ignoring barriers such as the ones you noticed affect students?

These questions will help you identify what is at stake.

You can also think through this by using skills from Chapter 2: "Rhetorical Situation," by finding the exigence for the barriers you have discovered, thinking about the audience (who the target is as well as who a solution would primarily benefit), and the constraints that might apply to what can be done to address the problem. This exercise also uses skills from Chapter 6: "Rhetorical Analysis," specifically the section on the *Rhetorical Analysis of Spaces* on page 145. Refer to these sections for additional support if needed.

Now, write a letter or phone call script addressing any problems of accessibility you observed during this activity. In this letter or script, you should identify what the problem was, what specific barriers to access it created, what possible solutions are, as well as why this is a problem (what is at stake). You can bolster this work with any ADA compliances that are being violated, but just because the problem is not violating ADA law, does not mean it should be ignored. There is an example form letter and phone call script at the end of this activity. You should address it to whom you think is best situated to solve the problem.

- Is this a city property issue? You should look at the Access Lexington Commission and its current council members, which can be found at this link: *https://www.lexingtonky.gov/boards/commission-people-disabilities*.
- If it's a local business, you should contact the business owner.
- If there's a systemic accessibility issue on campus, you could contact one of the ADA Coordinators in the ADA Compliance office at UK. Information for coordinators and the office can be found here: *https://ieeo.uky.edu/key-priorities/ada-compliance*.

In order to choose who is best situated to receive your letter or phone call, you should do your own research into the people, their positions, and what a reasonable solution is. In other words, now that you have identified the problem, you must identify whose problem it is and, hopefully, figure out in your research who is best situated to help, whether that's an ADA office that must enforce compliance, or a community member that has stated their investment in improving the experience of the student body. If you have trouble detecting who is best situated for this letter, ask for help! Reach out to the Office of Institutional Equity and Equal Opportunity, or ask your librarian and professor for research advice.

In completing this assignment, you will not only have completed a piece of technical writing, but also learned to navigate a system that is not centralized. In other words, whenever people encounter barriers, they must navigate a complicated system that *is* confusing in order to figure out who to address the problem to and what to say. While this assignment does not require you to research the body of the letter or script, it will require you to search for who is best aligned to take your complaint and solve the problem. Creation of accessibility for all requires advocacy and as you've learned, this advocacy is incredibly important for the continued creation of accessibility for all.

Your professor may or may not require you to send this letter off. It will be dictated in their assignment outline and the goals of their class, so think carefully about what you are trying to accomplish, how to articulate your goals, and who you want to articulate those goals to.

FORM LETTER

Your Name
Date

Full Name of Recipient
Recipient's Address

Dear [Recipient's name],

Any greetings you wish to write. Introduce yourself and your relationship to the University/Lexington community/recipient. Identify your purpose for this letter.

Identify the problem you noticed, the questions you have, and what is at stake should the barrier to accessibility continue to exist.

Identify any solutions, what the benefit of implementing the solutions are, and how the campus/city/business would benefit as a whole.

Sincerely,
Sign Your Name
Type Your Name
Restate Who You Are (i.e. student, employee, etc.)

PHONE SCRIPT

Hello, my name is [your name].

I am calling about [problem you noticed, explaining why it is important, questions you have, and the stakes].

I have called you because [state why you are contacting this person as opposed to someone else—why they are best suited for your call].

I believe that solving this problem will benefit [beneficiaries] because [how it will benefit both disabled people, the community at large, and the person you're contacting].

Thank you so much for your time.

CREATING INCLUSIVE DIGITAL TEXTS

Refocusing on how to include accessibility in your life as a student requires you to pay attention to the content you create and put out into the world. Rhetoric requires the rhetorician to make intentional choices that effectively communicate a specific point. Rhetorical choices can either include or exclude particular audiences. This section focuses on accessibility and the importance of designing content that provides for otherwise marginalized people, such as disabled people.

While it may not seem important to always create accessible content, particularly in a classroom setting, the reality is that 1 in 4 adults are disabled in the United States (CDC). Whether you are aware of it or not, you will encounter classmates, colleagues, teachers, bosses, and others throughout your life who are disabled. Consequently, creating accessible content allows a quarter of the population to engage with content they would otherwise be unable to. Every target audience includes people who require your content to be accessible. As a result, best practice is to make all of your work accessible.

In addition to the practical and immediate reasons to make your documents accessible (i.e., the existence of people who require accommodations), the government also requires accommodations under Section 508 of the United States Workforce Rehabilitation Act of 1973. According to Section 508, governmental agencies must uphold a certain level of accessibility within their information and communication technologies (Section 508). Accessibility is, therefore, something encountered throughout life.

Taking measures to make your digital content accessible can seem like an intimidating task at times, particularly if you are unfamiliar with how to create accessible content. This section will walk you through essential steps you can take to make digital texts accessible.

Photographs, Charts, and Illustrations

One step toward accessibility you have probably already encountered hundreds of times throughout your life: adding alt-text to images. Simply put, alt-text describes an image, which may be a photograph, an illustration, a chart, or a graph. Blind people use screen readers or tools like OrCam to read documents. Without alt-text vital information can be lost, making the document fundamentally inaccessible to people who require these tools. You can add alt-text in most word processors and website builders (think Wix, Weebly, WordPress, Adobe Spark) by right-clicking on an image and choosing "edit alt-text." If you are creating a physical document, putting a description before or after an image is a simple way to generate alt-text and it also benefits any readers who need clarification or additional support in understanding the included picture. Accessible measures, such as the inclusion of alt-text, help everyone, from those with vision loss to those who are encountering something new for the first time and need additional support.

Like regular images, embedded images, such as watermarks, can disrupt screenreaders. Creating watermarks that are not images prevents disruptions such as this from occurring. Blank cells in a table or graph or large empty spaces in a document can cause problems for accommodating technologies and should be avoided.

Hyperlinks

Hyperlinks can also pose problems for those using different technologies to navigate a webpage. Including a description of the hyperlink alongside the hyperlink prevents accessibility issues that may otherwise occur. When embedding a hyperlink within a specific section of the text, it is crucial to connect the hyperlink to the words that describe it instead of an entire block of text, which could confuse, or text that does not represent the hyperlink appropriately, as that would be misleading. Including a description of a hyperlink allows those in need of accommodations, as well as those without, to navigate web pages and digital texts more efficiently. Once again, making something accessible benefits everyone engaging with the content.

Making PDFs and Digital Files Accessible

As with alt-text, many document processors have already created shortcuts to help check documents for accessibility. The documents students most frequently encounter are PDFs and digital word documents. If your document has a "tools" bar (usually at the top of the screen like in Microsoft Word and Google Docs or to the side like adobe PDF), your document likely has a tool for checking accessibility. In these cases clicking on "tools" and then navigating to "accessibility" will probably flag any barriers to accessibility within your document while also instructing you how to correct these issues. Flagged items generally include images, tables, and text colors that may challenge specific visual impairments.

Video and Audio Files

You are likely familiar with subtitles and transcripts already. Closed Captioning and subtitles describe speech in a video and any additional audio information a viewer may want or need. Subtitles are generally in sync with a video, with the action on-screen aligning with the subtitles' descriptions. A transcript is a written record of a video or audio file which is not necessarily synced to a video or audio file. Transcripts, like subtitles, make what would generally be an auditory experience accessible to those who are deaf, hard of hearing, or who have trouble processing information auditorily.

Subtitles and transcripts can be one of the more time-consuming and challenging accommodations, but there are a few tools you (as a university student) have available.

If you have access to Zoom (which you should as a student), you are likely able to go to your Zoom settings and turn on live closed captioning and downloadable transcripts. You can set your Zoom to use one or both of these features, leaving you with either a downloadable transcript of your recording or synced captions. This tool is helpful if you need to record a video or interview. Though these are both beneficial tools, it is also vital to proofread computer-generated captions and transcripts as they struggle with certain accents and can also misidentify words.

YuJa is another tool that you have access to through your institution. YuJa will run an uploaded video through a program that creates closed captions and transcripts. Like Zoom, the program will sometimes misunderstand language or have difficulty interpreting accents; proofreading is necessary before sending out a digital text to larger audiences. Each of your professors can turn on access to YuJa through each of your Canvas course pages. If you do not see YuJa in a Canvas shell on the navigation menu to the right of the screen, you might request your professor to turn YuJa access on to make the course more accessible.

There are some free online transcription tools that you can easily google, but both Zoom and YuJa are generally more reliable. If you use YouTube, you can also access their automatic captioning service. You can visit Google's instructions on adding captions to a YouTube video here: *https://support.google.com/youtube/answer/6373554?hl=en#zippy=%2Cautomatic-captions-on-long-form-videos-and-shorts*. TikTok also has a caption setting for videos, and in both YouTube and TikTok's case, any content published for a broader audience using captions will benefit and provide access to a wider range of individuals.

If you are recording a scripted video, the script can also function as a transcription, so long as there were no necessary digressions or additions beyond the script's use.

Organizing Accessible Content

Accessible documents, websites, and other digital texts have clear headers that describe their content. Subheaders should be organized in descending importance and numerical order. If a document has columns, charts, or tables, they need a header or label in addition to being fully described with alt-text. Marked sections, subsections, illustrations, and more not only provide a reader with clear guidance but also make digital texts accessible.

Additional Notes on Accessibility

As illustrated in each of these examples, accessibility benefits readers who need accommodations and those who do not. Similarly, it is not only disabled people who need accommodations but also those who need additional guidance through new and unfamiliar content. When content is accessible, everyone wins: from the creator, whose content can reach a larger audience if accessible, to audiences. Creation with inclusion as the goal is creation that succeeds for the creator and audience alike.

Works Cited

ADL. "A Brief History of the Disability Rights Movement." *ADL,* https://www.adl.org/resources/backgrounder/brief-history-disability-rights-movement.

ASAN (Autism Self Advocacy Network). "Think Before You Donate to Autism Speaks, Consider the Facts." *ASAN,* https://autisticadvocacy.org/wp-content/uploads/2017/04/AutismSpeaksFlyer2020.pdf.

Barbarin, Imani. "The Pandemic Tried to Break Me, But I Know My Black Disabled Life is Worthy." *Cosmopolitan,* 2022, https://www.cosmopolitan.com/entertainment/a39355245/imani-barbarin-black-disabled-activistself-love/.

Bilodeau, Kelly. "Managing Intrusive Thoughts." *Harvard Health,* 2021, https://www.health.harvard.edu/mind-and-mood/managing-intrusive-thoughts.

Brut. "#WhenICallMyselfDisabled: The Power of Language and identity." *Brut. Media,* https://www.brut.media/us/entertainment/-whenicallmyselfdisabled-the-power-of-language-and-identity-5e6f1141-3ffc-45d3-8fb4-eb4320d1c4e3.

Centers for Disease Control and Prevention. "Disability Impacts All of Us." *CDC,* https://www.cdc.gov/ncbddd/disabilityandhealth/infographic-disability-impacts-all.html.

Disability Rights Education and Defense Fund (DREDF). "The History of the Americans with Disabilities Act." *Disability Rights Education and Defense Fund,* 1992, https://dredf.org/about-us/publications/the-history-of-the-ada/#:~:text=Spurred%20by%20a%20draft%20bill,1988%20in%20the%20100th%20Congress.

Dunn, Dana. "Understanding Ableism and Negative Reactions to Disability." *American Psychological Association,* https://www.apa.org/ed/precollege/psychology-teacher-network/introductory-psychology/ableism-negative-reactions-disability.

Ferrigon, Phillip. "Person-First Language vs. Identity-First Language: An Examination of the Gains and Drawback of Disability Language in Society." *Journal of Teaching Disability Studies,* 2019.

Liebowitz, Cara. "I am Disabled: On Identity-First Versus People-First Language," *The Body is Not an Apology,* 2015, https://thebodyisnotanapology.com/magazine/i-am-disabled-on-identity-first-versus-people-first-language/.

Mairs, Nancy. "On Being a Cripple." *The Social Medicine Reader,* Volume II, Third Edition: Differences and Inequalities, Volume 2, edited by Jonathan Oberlander, Mara Buchbinder, Larry R. Churchill, Sue E. Estroff, Nancy M. P. King, Barry F. Saunders, Ronald P. Strauss and Rebecca L. Walker, Duke University Press, 2019, pp. 37–47.

McRuer, Robert, and Emma Cassabaum. "Crip Theory." *Oxford Bibliographies,* 2021, https://www.oxfordbibliographies.com/display/document/obo-9780190221911/obo-9780190221911-0109.xml.

McVean, Ada. "The History of Hysteria." *McGill Office for Science and Society,* 2017, https://www.mcgill.ca/oss/article/history-quackery/history-hysteria.

Rajkumar, Shruti. "The ADA was a Victory for the Disabled Community, But we Need More. My Life Shows Why." *NPR,* 2022, https://www.npr.org/2022/07/29/1113535976/ada-disabilities-act-activists-more-protections.

Savini, Catharine. "Looking for Trouble: Finding Your Way into a Writing Assignment." *Writing Spaces: Readings on Writing,* Volume 2, 2011.

"Section 508." *US General Services Administration,* https://www.gsa.gov/policy-regulations/policy/information-integrity-and-access/it-accessibility-section-508.

The Rehabilitation Research and Training Center on Disability Statistics and Demographics (StatsRRTC). "Annual Report on People Disabilities in America: 2023." *Institute on Disability/UCED, The University of New Hampshire,* 2023.

ChatGPT and LLMs and Their Place in Writing Classes

Recommended for WRD 111/112
or as needed for WRD 110

Chapter 18

Generative Artificial Intelligence (GenAI) and Large Language Models (LLMs) use is on the rise, especially in writing-intensive classes. This growing trend is no surprise considering these systems' abilities to speedily produce human-like responses. AI technologies that make use of LLMs to create text documents can save instructor and student users a lot of time—input a prompt and it can generate lesson plans, writing exercise prompts, exam questions, essays, scripts, and even discussion responses (though the quality of the output may vary). Its use, however, comes at a cost. Academic dishonesty concerns, privacy breaches, data exploitation, idea theft, and spread of misinformation are just a few of the risks of OpenAI use. Considering the risks associated with these systems and the increasing likelihood of their integration into different fields and careers, students and teachers need to familiarize themselves with GPT's potential dangers and advantages. So, what do you need to know about GenAI systems so you can use them responsibly?

ACADEMIC INTEGRITY

One of the concerns surrounding GPT and LLM-generated content is how students may use it in their course assignments, and how this can lead to academic dishonesty issues. The following are some example scenarios of AI-use that constitute academic dishonesty:

- A student submits an AI-generated essay as their own work.
- A student writes an essay and incorporates direct quotes and citations from an AI-generated product.
- A student submits a prompt, revises the product a bit, and submits it.
- A student uses ChatGPT to write a discussion post in response to a class assignment prompt and takes out a sentence here and there.

Regardless of whether it's an accident or if a student only incorporates some AI-generated content without citation, this is still considered academic dishonesty. And, the consequences of academic dishonesty for the student varies depending on the instructor's and university's policies. Per UK's policy, consequences can range from a 0 for the assignment to a 0 for the overall course and a required meeting with Academic Ombud Services.[1] If you are interested in incorporating AI-generated content, you should first consult your instructor about their policy about AI use in their class and assignments. Additionally, if you use generated content in an assignment, you need to be transparent about it and appropriately cite the information. For more information about citations for AI-generated content, check out the MLA Style Center (https://style.mla.org/citing-generative-ai/).

PRIVACY CONCERNS

Before you use any kind of AI system, it's likely you'll need to provide some degree of personal information and accept its terms and conditions. Depending on the site, the personal information you'll provide may include your name, e-mail, and even payment information. The collected personal data doesn't stop there. For example, OpenAI tracks your browsing history on the site and retains all information submitted into the chat function. This means that any information you put into the chat, which may include personal details, is logged and vulnerable to potential misuse. As writer Kate Veale notes, "It's easy to fall into the trap of accidentally giving ChatGPT your private details without realizing it until it's too late, especially if you use it to proofread personal or professional documents."[2] Take, for example, how some people use ChatGPT to generate resumés, CVs, personal statements, and cover letters, all of which likely contain addresses, phone numbers, names and contact information of references, etc. Veale continues to say that "OpenAI gives very vague information about who it shares your data with, and for what reason. It says it may provide your personal information to vendors and service providers to assist in meeting business needs and performing certain functions. These providers include web hosting services, cloud services, other IT providers, event managers, email services, and analytics services." What can you do to mitigate the issue of your personal information being collected and distributed? Veale says that one of the ways users can combat this issue is by removing private information from your prompts before you input them into OpenAI systems.

Unfortunately, however, removing personal information from your prompts alone does not guarantee your privacy. Writer Matt Burgess says that "Millions of pages scraped from the web, Reddit posts, books, and more are used to create the generative text system" and that "[s]cooped up in this data is some of the personal information you share about yourself online."[3] Regardless of whether you now privatize your accounts, it's possible that any information you had already posted online has been stored by an OpenAI system. But, some measures you can take to minimize the amount of additional personal information of yours being made available for OpenAI systems to share are not tagging your location in posts, not sharing personal addresses or contact information online, or using specially designated e-mails when you need to share your email to a profile. Overall, a good rule of thumb is to be careful of what you post on the internet.

ADDITIONAL GPT AND LLM CONCERNS

Although AI systems pull from a variety of digitized content, this does not necessarily mean that the information and citations they output are accurate or even real. Writer Anna Mills says that "Large language models (LLMs) can mimic language patterns, but they cannot understand them." In fact, she found that "[s]ince [the LLM] had no ability to check the accuracy of the word sequences it generated, it made up sources, facts and figures."[4] As such, even if students use just a single quote from a segment generated by AI, it's not guaranteed that the quote and/or source referenced even exists or is being accurately credited. Though a ChatGPT user could technically fact-check the information produced, there is still the risk of unnoticed/unfixed misinformation. Another risk associated with AI-generated misinformation is the possibility that incorrect information about someone is widely shared, which can have serious consequences for the person in question. Due to these risks, users need to be cautious of what information they use from AI and how they use that information, and what they input into these systems.

Responsibly using GPT and LLM systems is also tricky because of the systems' problematic principles. Citing ideas and research and giving credit where credit is due are priorities in the writing class. As such, ChatGPT and LLM systems' tendency to fabricate sources, research, and quotations, not give appropriate credit to researchers and writers, and perpetuate bias go against the writing class's objectives. An especially troubling issue is the human costs of OpenAI. Professors Chris Gilliard and Pete Rorabaugh document this in their article "You're Not Going to Like How Colleges Respond to ChatGPT":

> [I]t's imperative to understand what this tool is—or more explicitly, what is required for it to exist. OpenAI paid outsourcing partner Sama $200,000 to teach ChatGPT how not to be violent, racist, or sexist. Sama's workers were compensated between $1.50 and $2 an hour to keep ChatGPT from mimicking the worst kinds of human behavior. Kenya-based workers interviewed by Time reported being "mentally scarred" by performing the job (https://time.com/6247678/openai-chatgpt-kenya-workers/).[5]

In addition to the issue of worker exploitation, there is also the issue of biased information and whose voices are not included in the data that AI systems pull from. Professor Sidney Dobrin notes that marginalized people's data has been historically excluded from digital databanks, and this leads to biased results in "favor of data that is widely and digitally available."[6] Mills also notes that bias is also the result of these systems reproducing the stereotypes and data pulled from sources that are not guaranteed to be credible or reliable. Dobrin says that consequently, "[c]urrent AIs are not able to discern value or accuracy or bias in the data they scrub. They are only able to identify patterns within the data, and thus they often incorporate inaccurate, false, or biased information." There are clearly a lot of issues and concerns surrounding the ethics of AI technology and its increasing prevalence in classroom and career settings. So, what can you do to prepare yourself to be a responsible user of these systems?

RESPONSIBLE USE

It looks like GPT and LLMs are here to stay; therefore, it's important that students and instructors understand how technologies like ChatGPT can be responsibly used inside and out of the classroom. Over-relying on tools such as ChatGPT can be an obstacle in students' development of research, critical thinking, and problem solving skills. But, using ChatGPT responsibly can yield some productive results. Below are examples of how ChatGPT can be incorporated into the writing class to help students strengthen their writing and communication skills:

- As suggested by Mills, students can prompt a response and critique the output. This exercise can help students identify AI-generated response shortcomings. Additionally, students could practice improving rhetorical choices by revising an AI response to better suit a specific genre. Consequently, this exercise can help strengthen students' workshopping, argumentation, and revising skills.
- As suggested by Dobrin, "Students can use GenAI's basic response as jumping-off points for follow-up questions" and class discussions.
- ChatGPT can be used in the beginning stages of brainstorming ideas for an assignment. Then, the student can intervene and develop, think through, research, and test out their ideas and arguments.
- Using ChatGPT can also help students improve their critical skills of assessing accuracy and relevance. For example, students can go through an AI response and critique how the research is integrated, identify what information is inaccurate, and find relevant research to replace the AI-generated research.

NOTES

[1] "Academic Offenses Rules for Undergraduate and Graduate Students." *UKY.EDU,* www.uky.edu/universitysenate/ao#:~:text=Senate%20Rules%206.3.,-2%20(%22Cheating%22&text=It%20includes%2C%20but%20is%20not,determination%20of%20the%20final%20grade.

[2] Veale, Kate. "Does CHATGPT Have Privacy Issues?" *Make Use Of,* 13 Apr. 2023, www.makeuseof.com/chatgpt-privacy-issues/#:~:text=Its%20privacy%20policy%20states%20that,ChatGPT%20a%20cybersecurity%20risk%20too.

[3] Burgess, Matt. "ChatGPT Has a Big Privacy Problem." *Wired,* 4 Apr. 2023, www.wired.com/story/italy-ban-chatgpt-privacy-gdpr/.

[4] Mills, Anna. "Seeing Past the Dazzle of ChatGPT." *Inside Higher Ed,* 18 Jan. 2023, www.insidehighered.com/advice/2023/01/19/academics-must-collaborate-develop-guidelines-chatgpt-opinion.

[5] Gilliard, Chris, and Pete Rorabaugh. "You're Not Going to Like How Colleges Respond to ChatGPT." *Slate Magazine,* 3 Feb. 2023, slate.com/technology/2023/02/chat-gpt-cheating-college-ai-detection.html.

[6] Dobrin, Sidney. *Talking About Generative AI: A Guide for Educators.* Broadview Press, Summer 2023.

Navigating Team Dynamics in the Writing Classroom

Recommended for WRD 111/112
or as needed for WRD 110

Chapter 19

Chapter 19   Navigating Team Dynamics in the Writing Classroom

TEAMWORK IN WRD 110 AND WRD 111

Regardless of your major, many of the classes you'll take in college will incorporate teamwork—whether it be in pairs or small groups—in their in-class exercises and/or formal assignments. In biology labs, students are routinely tasked with working with a lab partner to prepare the materials for an experiment, divvy up who will conduct what step and record outcomes, and collaboratively write the final lab report. In a marketing class, students may be tasked with a hypothetical client project and must work with a small group to plan and pitch a marketing campaign that meets the client's specific requirements. A majority of jobs will require some degree of teamwork, and successful teamwork takes practice. Therefore, it's important that we practice good teamwork dynamics, even in the writing class.

In your WRD 110 class, you'll likely work in pairs or small groups for in-class activities and discussions. Otherwise, the major assignments for your WRD 110 class will be independently produced. In contrast, WRD 111 is deeply rooted in group work. In WRD 111, you'll work on written assignments as well as a digital project with a group of peers. As you may know from personal experience, although group work has its advantages, it also has its many challenges. These challenges largely derive from the mistaken assumption that students innately know how to navigate working in teams. Or, it's assumed that students will just 'figure it out.' A lot of team dynamic success comes down to organization and time management skills as well as the ability to set clear expectations and implement structures to help support the team as they progress toward their project deadlines. All these things take time to learn. As such, the goal of this chapter is to demystify the teamwork process and introduce students to strategies that may help improve your teamwork experience in the college-level writing class and prepare you for teamwork in future jobs.

Team Contracts

Before people or organizations work together on a project, they often sign a contract. Contracts generally detail the expectations of all parties involved, payment and product deadlines, repercussions for missing deadlines or poor product quality, etc. Ultimately, they are in place as "safety nets." Also, implementing a contract is not only helpful for business arrangements—it's also practical for class team projects.

The purpose of team contracts in the writing class is to help team members hold each other and themselves accountable during the project process. Ideally, the team contract should be a collaborative effort and should, ideally, outline the following:

- Team member expectations (i.e., how team members are expected to treat one another, how team members will communicate their concerns, etc.), back-up plans,
- Modes of communication
- Tentative schedules for meetings and deadlines
- Policies that hold members responsible for their contributions, and a "process for dealing with unmet expectations or other problems that may arise" ("Making Group Contracts")[1]
- "Method[s] for peer feedback during the project so that problems can be addressed before the project ends" ("Making Group Contracts")

In some cases, students may need to create a team contract from scratch, or the instructor may give students a customizable template with starter prompts and space for teams to add to it. If you're hitting a roadblock while trying to brainstorm what to include in your team contract, reflect on the following prompts and consider how you may implement your responses into your contract:

- Think back to your previous experiences with teamwork.
  - What went well?
  - What challenges came up?
  - What do you wish you and your team had done differently to mitigate some of the issues that arose?
  - What conditions/rules/etc. could you implement in this contract to help prevent or minimize these issues?

Coordinating Time to Meet Outside the Classroom

One of the challenges with teamwork projects is coordinating multiple schedules to find common days and times that work for everyone to discuss project progress or work on the project together. Even if your instructor schedules in-class workdays for teams to work together, you'll still need to work with your group outside of those designated class times.

First, you'll need to identify how frequently your team will meet outside of class. Some groups may choose to have weekly meetings regardless of whether they are all actually coworking on their project at every meeting. Even if it's not the same time/day every week, planning ahead and arranging routine meetings can relieve the pressure and stress of last-minute scrambling to find time to meet with the team. Alternatively, some groups may choose to only meet when they need to record, film, etc. together, and they'll otherwise regularly check-in with each other via text or email.

Using a polling service like **When2meet** helps teams easily identify the times/days they're available, and provides a visual to indicate which times/days work best for everyone. You'll also want to consider whether you and your team will meet in person or via Zoom (or a similar video chat platform). This will depend on your team's needs at the time, and it's important to also consider which meeting modality will help you and your team work most productively and effectively at that time.

Communication and Communication Modalities

How will the team communicate outside of class? Will you use text, email, Canvas messages, *GroupMe, WhatsApp, Slack?* The list of possible communication modes goes on. In recent years, we've noticed more and more students communicating through apps like *Snapchat* for team projects. However, using apps like these provide their own challenges. For example, there's the chance a *Snapchat* message with important information could possibly go unsaved. *Snapchat* messages don't preview the content of the chat (and you won't see the content unless you do the half-swipe-preview trick) so it's more likely for messages to go unseen for a longer period of time than a text. You also can't search through *Snapchat* messages like you can with text or email where you can insert keywords into a search bar and quickly find the message(s) you're looking for.

Regardless of whether your instructor allows or disallows social media as a mode of communication for a team project, we highly recommend choosing a modality that you and your team members have easy access to and that you check regularly. At the same time, do not feel like you have to give your personal phone number to peers if you're not comfortable with this. An easy workaround is using your university email or a chat app like *GroupMe* and coming to an agreement with your peers that everyone will check the chosen platform daily.

What's important is that whatever modality the team chooses, the team sets clear communication expectations. For example, when can your peers expect to hear from you? Are there some days where you'll be busier and consequently slower to respond to messages? Will the team work with a 'business hours' model (i.e. team members will respond within reasonable time during regular business hours, and late night messages are understood to likely go without response till the next day)? If the team decides to communicate via email, how often will the team agree to check their email to ensure timely responses?

Strategies for Smooth(er) Sailing

There's no fool-proof plan to ensure a perfect, obstacle-free teamwork experience. However, there are strategies that can help make teamwork easier to navigate and manage.

Back Scheduling

Look at the project deadlines provided by your instructor, determine all that needs to be done to achieve the assignments, then collectively decide when each smaller task needs to be done (Rehling 238).[2] It's recommended that you create a collaborative calendar document that details these smaller deadlines so it can be easily referred to by all team members and revised as needed.

Delegating Tasks

Not every component of an assignment will need to be done together as a team. While some things may require synchronous work, other work can be done remotely and independently. After you determine which components of the project can be done independently, you'll need to decide who will be responsible for what. As you work with your team to delegate tasks, consider each team member's strengths and which tasks may best suit them. For example, which team member is especially organized and can put together an outline for the project's written content? Which team member enjoys creative outlets and can mock up website or video design concepts? Which team member feels confident in their research inquiry skills and can write interview questions? It could be helpful to have an initial assessment at the beginning of teamwork in which team members identify their strengths and the things they know they need to work on. That way, team members can make more informed decisions regarding who will take on what tasks, and they will have a better understanding of where other members may need help down the line. Overall, it's important that the team discuss and agree upon what everyone will work on, instead of just one or two members assigning tasks to the entire team.

Some additional questions to consider as you delegate tasks are as follows:

- How can research be divided up amongst members?
- How will the writing be split amongst team members?
- Who will be in charge of submitting which assignment?
- Who will be in charge of editing?
- Who will check that the final product meets assignment description expectations?

Suggestion: Create a shared checklist identifying all team assignments and breaking down the various steps that need to be completed to achieve the final project and by when. Then, as the team works on the project, check tasks off. This visual cue can be helpful for folks who need to see the details and to-do's all in one place, instead of spread out over a planner.

Notetaking During Team Meetings

Designate a "notetaker" for each meeting (this can be a different person each meeting to share the work responsibility). This person will be responsible for taking notes about what was discussed during the meeting as well as sending out a brief summary of team decisions, next steps, etc. to have for reference at a later time. Your team designated notetaker at the time can also be the member responsible for sending out a reminder message for the next meeting. While it's assumed that everyone should put meeting times/dates in their calendars or phones, it can be helpful to have someone respond to the last meeting notes message with a meeting reminder. That way, team members are also reminded to review what was discussed at the previous meeting and what they are expected to prepare for the next meeting.

Using Collaborative Applications

Use *Google Drive* to house all team materials, drafts, etc. in one place. *Google Drive, Google Docs,* etc. are helpful because they give everyone access to the necessary documents at any given time, and you don't have to wait for team members to send you their most recent version of the document they're working on. Furthermore, using *Google Docs* allows teams and/or the instructor to access the editing history to see who contributed what and when, if necessary.

Setting Meeting Agendas and Goals

A couple of the challenges of teamwork are making sure you're setting realistic goals for each team meeting and that the team stays on task during the meeting time. As a team, you'll need to decide: What are two or three things the team wants to accomplish during this designated meeting time? This is the time to assess your team's progress and set project priorities ("Use Student Teams Effectively").[3] Deciding on the meeting's objectives before the start of the meeting helps teams use the time productively and minimizes the likelihood of the meeting having to go over time or having to schedule an additional meeting to finish the discussion.

Routine Check-Ins

Depending on how often you and your team meet during the project process, you may also want to implement regular check-ins with your team. For example, if you meet outside of class, in person or via *Zoom* every two weeks, you may want to schedule weekly (or *more* frequently, if needed) brief check-ins via whichever communication modality you and your team agreed on. In these check-ins, team members can give mini "status reports" and respond to the following prompts:

- What are you working on for the project?
- What challenges are you currently experiencing?
- What support from team members would be helpful at this time?

It can be hard to ask for help when you need it but the hope is that by establishing routine check-ins, you'll have these built-in opportunities dedicated to team members sharing what they need.

Additional Teamwork Challenges and How to Work Through Them

Below are some additional, common teamwork challenges that you may encounter in and out of your writing class. For each team challenge identified, we've identified some strategies for how you and your team can mitigate their effects.

Procrastination

Commonly cited reasons for team and individual procrastination are team miscommunications, feeling overwhelmed, time management challenges, distractions, busy schedules, etc. Procrastination in teamwork can also occur when a team member feels isolated from the other team members and they do not feel like they are listened to or included in the team project (Sorkin).[4]

- If team members are struggling with procrastination, "the best thing teams can do is to try to help them and look for solutions together" (Sorkin). And, in order for people to feel comfortable sharing their struggles with their team members, the team must "create an environment where everyone feels ... they can be honest and open about their thoughts and opinions" (Sorkin), without having to worry that they will be shamed or ignored.

◎ If you or a team member find yourselves procrastinating assignments and rushing to get things done and submitted on time, this is a good time to meet with your team and talk about what might have caused the procrastination and collectively brainstorm solutions. Did the workload feel overwhelming? Did the tasks take longer than expected? Would it be helpful to schedule mini tasks into a planner so you can see exactly what steps you need to take to get to the final product? Referring back to the *Routine Check-ins* section, ask what support from team members would be helpful at this time, as well as going forward?

Unproductive Feedback

When team members share feedback with each other, some people may be inclined to jump right into the "problems" they've noticed. This is likely not ill-intentioned; however, this "can be overwhelming and put your colleagues on the defensive" ("Group Writing").[5] As a consequence, team members can feel isolated from the rest of the team and this can subsequently affect team communication and productivity. On the opposite end of the peer feedback spectrum, don't feel like you need to counteract this issue with the feedback "sandwich method" (i.e. saying something positive, giving critique, saying something positive). This method can actually lead members to "distrust praise" and distract from the purpose of giving constructive feedback ("Feedback Strategies: The Pros and Cons of the Sandwich Approach").[6]

◎ The goal of giving peer feedback should be to address the things that are going well as well as the things that need improvement (without trying to flank the 'bad' with compliments). Constructive feedback should be as follows:

- **Timely:** The sooner the feedback is given, the sooner your peer can implement the feedback.[7]
- **Specific:** Give clear examples of what you are referring to when you're discussing what your peer does well and what could use improvement.
- **Actionable:** Give your peer clear, realistic ideas of what they can do to improve their contributions.

◎ As you prepare to give peers feedback, consider implementing Emily Wray's RISE[8] model for giving feedback:

- Reflect: "Share what stood out to you and why."
- Inquire: "Analyze and ask questions to gain clarity."
- Suggest: "Introduce ideas for improvement." "Offer suggestions."
- Elevate: "Share any insight or encouragement you how to approach or optimize similar situations in the future."

Team members repeatedly not meeting teamwork expectations: This challenge can take a multitude of forms. Commonly cited examples of this are 1) a member has to "[wait] for other group members to do all of the work" ("Group Writing"), 2) a majority of the work falls onto one person ("Group Writing"), and 3) there are "dominating or reluctant" team members ("Group Work").[9]

- Ideally, when these issues arise, you'll have a team contract in place that details the consequences if a team member does not fairly/productively contribute to the team project. After multiple attempts to address the identified concerns, if a team member (or members) continues to not contribute to the project as expected and they are not receptive to peer feedback, this is the time to ask your instructor to intervene.
- It can be hard to decide when is the right time to ask for your instructor's help to resolve team dynamic issues. A good rule of thumb is: if a team member's contributions and/or participation does not improve after the third time it's addressed, you should reach out to your instructor. From there, your instructor may decide to have a meeting with the individual(s) first before they talk with the team as a whole or they may decide to meet with the team altogether to discuss the expressed concerns.
- Your instructor's approach to instructor-intervention for team projects may vary. But what's likely to happen is that either a) there will be a plan made for workarounds for how the team can continue working on the project together while also minimizing the issue, or b) in more extreme cases, they may decide that the best way to proceed is to separate the group into smaller groups or make it an individual project.

Exercise

As a class, brainstorm a list of possible challenges/scenarios that can occur during teamwork. Then, brainstorm possible strategies for mitigating said challenges. For example, how would you address the issue of a team member not doing their work and instead leaving it to other members to do? How would you bring this up to them and what would you say? What would you do if they felt defensive? (Note: During the brainstorming process, pulling from past experiences can be helpful so that students can think about how they handled challenges then and what are some other strategies that could be applied to that situation if it were to happen again.)

Team and Self Evaluations

Your instructor will likely have you complete a team and self evaluation/assessment at some point during the project process. Some instructors assign one at the midway point of the project and at the end to track how teamwork dynamics changed between those times. This also gives instructors the opportunity to identify any patterns of challenges amongst team evaluations that need to be addressed as a class. Alternatively, your instructor may assign just one team and self evaluation at the end of the project in which you will reflect on the overall experience of working together on this project.

The evaluations themselves may come as a worksheet that you fill out or your instructor may give you a series of prompts to respond to in paragraph-format. Regardless of the format, you'll ultimately be tasked with honestly and critically reflecting on prompts similar to the following:

- How did the team delegate project tasks?
- How did the team resolve conflicts? What strategies did the team implement to resolve disagreements?
- What did your peers do well?
- What could your peers improve on for future team projects?
- How would you describe and evaluate their communication and participation?

It's important that you review these prompts periodically during your teamwork project process so the team can provide timely feedback. Furthermore, although the aforementioned questions are addressing specific team members, you can also apply these questions to yourself. What did you do well as a team member? What could you have done better as a team member? What strategies/lessons will you take from this teamwork experience and implement into future team projects? Remember, these assessments are not in place for "dragging" team members for what they did or did not do. Rather, these assessments are opportunities for you to critically reflect on what challenges arose, why they arose, and how the team worked through them (or, should have worked through them). And finally, your instructor may have you directly share your written team assessments with your peers or they may collect them, anonymize the assessments, then share them with your peers. Regardless of how the peer assessments are distributed, remember to make your feedback fair, constructive, specific, and actionable.

NOTES

1. "Making Group Contracts." *University of Waterloo Centre for Teaching Excellence,* https://uwaterloo.ca/centre-for-teaching-excellence/catalogs/tip-sheets/making-group-contracts.

2. Rehling, Lu. "Foregrounding Positive Problem-Solving Teamwork: Awareness and Assessment Exercises for the First Class and Beyond." *Journal of Business and Technical Communication,* vol. 24, no. 2, 2010, pp. 234–244. Web.

3. "Use Student Teams Effectively." *Duke Learning Innovation & Lifetime Education,* https://learninginnovation.duke.edu/resources/art-and-science-of-teaching/use-student-teams-effectively/. Accessed 8 Apr 2024.

4. Sorkin, Lee. "Procrastination and How to Overcome It With Your Team." *Invite Japan,* https://www.invitejapan.com/en/procrastination-how-to-overcome-with-team/. Accessed 8 Apr 2024.

5. "Group Writing." *University of North Carolina at Chapel Hill Writing Center,* https://writingcenter.unc.edu/tips-and-tools/group-writing/. Accessed 30 Mar 2024.

6. "Feedback Strategies: The Pros and Cons of the Sandwich Approach." *Findlay Online,* https://online.findlay.edu/2579-2/#:~:text=Many%20business%20professionals%20tout%20the,the%20blow%20of%20the%20critique. Accessed 11 Apr 2024.

7. "Effective Feedback in Clinical Education." *Columbia University Center for Teaching and Learning,* https://ctl.columbia.edu/resources-and-technology/resources/effective-feedback-clinical/. Accessed 11 Apr 2024.

8. "Students: Did your teacher ask you to use the RISE Model to provide peer feedback?" *RISE MODEL,* https://www.risemodel.com/students. Accessed 15 Apr 2024.

9. "Group Work." *Harvard University: The Derek Bok Center for Teaching and Learning,* https://bokcenter.harvard.edu/group-work#:~:text=giving%20students%20a%20chance%20to,chance%20to%20teach%20each%20other. Accessed 30 Mar 2024.

INDEX

A

Ableism 404
Accessibility and disability 402–419
    Hyperlinks 417
    Inclusive Digital Text 416
    Making PDFs and files accessible 417
    Organizing Content 419
    Photographs, Charts, and Illustrations 416–417
    Terms to avoid 408–412
    Video and Audio Files 418
Active reading 120
Allusions 55
Americans with Disabilities Act (ADA) 402
    Disability rights movement 402–403
    History 402–403
Appeal to clarity 70–79
Appeal to interests 50–52
Appeal to knowledge 54–59
Appeal to language 64
Appeal to provocation 60–63
Appeal to stickiness 52–54
Argumentative conclusion 160
Attention catchers 286
Audience 34–39, 46, 137, 291–292
    Target audience 291
Author 137

B

Balance 334–336
Believing Game, The 126
Brainstorming 87–89

C

ChatGPT and LLMs 421–425
    Academic Integrity 422
    Additional GPT and LLM Concerns 424–425
    Privacy Concerns 423
    Responsible Use 425
Citation 230–231
    Captioning images 301
    Citation styles 239–242
    For documentaries 386–388
    Verbal citations 300–302
Claims 139, 153
Composition
    Arrangement 93–94
    Following a classical template 94–115
        Pomodoro technique 100
    Invention 85–92
    Recursive composition process 116–117
Constraints 39–42
Content 319
Context 319

D

Deductive arguments 162
Deductive reasoning 13–16
Descriptive language 258
Designing presentation aids 294–296
    Charts and graphs 297
    Parallelism and counterpoint 297–298
Diction 257
Disinformation 343
Documentaries 372–377
    B roll 375
    Casting 375
    Mockumentary 372
    Rule of threes 378
    Setting 375
    Voice-over 380

Index

E
Enthymemes 13, 56
Evidence 154–157, 178
    Ethos 7–8, 140, 254
    Evaluating sources 179–182, 226
    Integrating sources 189–190
    Introducing sources 194
    Logos 11–16, 140, 254, 380
    Pathos 8–11, 140, 254
    Quoting, paraphrasing, and summarizing 193
    Rhetorical Appeals 7–16
    Scanning 186
    Skimming 186
    Understanding sources 184–187
Exigence 31–34, 136

F
Fake news 343
Fallacies 163–166
Figurative language 258
Form 321–327

G
Gender neutral pronouns 67–71
Genre 47, 350–370
    Categories 354–355
    Genre and audience 363–364
    Social actions 352–353
    Wikipedia as a genre 364–367

I
Identity first language (IFL) 403
Inductive arguments 162
Inductive reasoning 11–13
Informal sources 171
Informative podcast 391–400
    Practice 397
    Recording 398–399
    Script 395–396
Inventing arguments 20–21

L
Logical argumentation 159–163
    Conclusions 160–161
    Premises 160–161

M
Media literacy 340–347
    Goals 341
    How to practice 341
    Media manipulation and disinformation 343–347
Misinformation 343

N
Nominalizations 269–270

O
Organization 96–97
    In spoken communication 285–290

P
Passive voice 268–269
Peer review
    Checklist 131–133
    For public speaking 307–309
    Preparing questions 129–133
Perorations 288
Person first language (PFL) 403
Person-First vs. Identity-First Language 403–408
    Crip theory 406
    Support groups vs hate groups 406–408
Progymnasmata 140–144
    Characterization 143
    Chreia 142
    Common Topic 142
    Comparison 143
    Confirmation 143
    Description 144
    Encomium 143
    Fable 141
    Invective 143
    Law 144–148
    Maxim 142
    Narrative 141

Index

    Refutation 142
    Thesis 144
Pronoun
    Personal pronouns 67
    Possessive pronouns 67
    Preferred pronoun 68
Pronouns 67–71
Proofs 139
Public speaking 284–310
    Constraints 293
    Delivery 302–303
    Group presentations 289–290
    Moderators 290
    Monroe's Motivated Sequence 289
    Power Poses 306
    Practice 304–306
    Vocal projection 303
Punctuation 277–279

R

Recontextualization 345
Research 205
    Interviews 210–213, 376–377
    Primary research 206, 207–216
    Secondary research 206, 217–224
Revision 109–115, 198–199
Rhetoric
    Artistic and non-artistic arguments 6, 178
    Definitions of 2, 284
    Kinds of 5
    Rhetorical deliberation 3–4
    Sophistic appeals 22–26
Rhetorical analysis 136–139
    Chart 146–147
    Example of 138–139
    Exercises 140–144
        Characterization 143
        Chreia 142
        Common Topic 142
        Comparison 143
        Confirmation 143
        Description 144
        Encomium 143
        Fable 141
        Invective 143

        Law 144–148
        Maxim 142
        Narrative 141
        Refutation 142
        Thesis 144
    Of spaces 145
Rhetorical argumentation 150–176
Rhetorical situation 30

S

"So what?" question 125–127
Stakeholders 167–168
    Stakeholder analysis 169
Stasis claims 17–19
Stasis theory 16–21, 150
Style 254–255
Syllogism 13
Syntax 264–275

T

Team dynamics 427–438
    Teamwork in the classroom 428–436
Text 137–138
Tone 257
Transitions 287

U

Unity and emphasis 328–330
Universal Design 292

V

Visual design 312
Visual hierarchy 336–340
Visual literacy 340
Visual literary 312
Visual rhetoric 312, 340–347
Voice 255–264

W

Warrants 157–159